Tax and Estate Planning Series

PLANNING AN ESTATE
Second Edition

A GUIDEBOOK OF PRINCIPLES AND TECHNIQUES

Harold Weinstock
Member of the California Bar

SHEPARD'S/McGRAW-HILL
P.O. Box 1235
Colorado Springs, Colorado 80901

McGRAW-HILL BOOK COMPANY

New York ● St. Louis ● San Francisco ● Colorado Springs
Auckland ● Bogota ● Hamburg ● Johannesburg ● London
Madrid ● Mexico ● Montreal ● New Delhi ● Panama
Paris ● São Paulo ● Singapore ● Sydney ● Tokyo ● Toronto

Revised edition of *Planning An Estate A Guidebook of Principles and Techniques* by Harold Weinstock (Shepard's/McGraw-Hill, 1977).

12345678910SHCU8921098765432

Library of Congress Cataloging in Publication Data

Weinstock, Harold, 1925-
    Planning an estate.

    (Tax and estate planning series)
    Bibliography: p.
    Includes index.
    1. Estate planning—United States. 2. Inheritance and transfer tax—Law and legislation—United States.
I. Title. II. Series.
KF750.W43 1982   343.7305'3   82-5883
                      347.30353   AACR2

Hardbound Edition ISBN 0-07-069010-3
Student Edition ISBN 0-07-069011-1

TO MY FAMILY

BARB, NEIL, MIKE AND PHIL

WITH LOVE

Preface

This book is intended for all those who have a serious interest in estate planning. It is written primarily for estate planners, that is, those persons whose work requires them to have a detailed knowledge of estate planning, such as attorneys, accountants, life insurance underwriters, trust officers and financial planners. The sophisticated estate owner may also find it useful.

In the preface to the first edition, I expressed the hope that the book would also be of use to students who are studying estate planning. I am particularly pleased that the book has found acceptance as a textbook in many estate planning courses.

My objective is to describe the planning tools and techniques which are necessary to solve specific estate planning problems frequently encountered by the estate planner. The book is not concerned with drafting, but only with planning. The attorney, once he understands which tools should be used in a given matter, should be able to find the appropriate form in a form book to help him draft the necessary documents.

The text is designed so that it can be read from start to finish and thereby give the reader an overview of the entire subject. It can also be used as a reference book if the reader wishes to look up a particular point. Sufficient theory is presented so that the reader can evaluate alternate solutions. My aim, however, is to have the book serve as a practical planning guide.

This second edition brings up to date the earlier text written in 1977. The first edition followed a significant change in estate planning law resulting from the enactment of the Tax Reform Act of 1976. The passage five years later of the Economic Recovery Tax Act of 1981, Pub. L. No. 97-34, brought even more drastic changes in estate planning theory and practice. This edition was written after the enactment of the 1981 Act and is therefore up to date as of the present time.

A somewhat greater than usual emphasis, but, in my opinion, not an undue one, is placed on community property. A significant portion of the potential readers live in community property states, and for them this subject is extremely important. In this age of mobility, the subject is also important for readers in noncommunity property states, because many of them have clients who are moving either to or from community property jurisdictions.

Chapters 6, 7, 10 and 11 are based in part on materials which I wrote for a book, *Estate Planning for the General Practitioner,* published by the California Continuing Education of the Bar. I am most grateful for its permission to use these materials here. In addition, I have borrowed portions from the following articles which I authored: "How to Avoid Probate—A Tax Analysis" 26 *Journal of Taxation* 38; "Buy-Sell Agreements" 105 *Trusts and Estates* 338; "Considerations in Designating the Beneficiaries Under a Life Insurance Policy" 105 *Trusts and Estates* 679; "The Marital Deduction—Problems and Answers Under Rev. Proc. 64-19" 43 *Taxes* 340; "The Short-Term Trust" 50 *Taxes* 153; "The A-B-C's of Generation Skipping Trusts" 52 *Taxes* 68; "Accumulation Trusts and Charitable Remainder Trusts" (co-authored with others) 23 *Univ of So Cal Tax Inst* 501 and "What if the Wife Dies First" 28 *Univ of So Cal Tax Inst* 55. I acknowledge with appreciation the permission of the publishers allowing me the use of these articles.

I am indebted to many persons who helped and encouraged me with this book. To three persons in my law firm I owe special thanks. My partner, Louis A. Reisman, gave of his vast knowledge of employee benefits and helped me with Chapter 13. My associate, Martin Neumann, painstakingly analyzed the text of the first edition in order to pinpoint the areas requiring revision. He then reviewed the entire manuscript of this edition, making valuable suggestions, and almost singlehandedly prepared the index. Invaluable assistance was given to me by my legal assistant, Roslyn Perlmutter. Utilizing her expertise with words, style and grammer and knowledge of estate planning and probate practice, she spent countless hours reworking the text helping to make the ambiguous, clear and the complex, readable. Any errors or deficiencies which remain are entirely my responsibility.

I would also like to include my thanks to my most capable secretary, Sharon Sanderson, not only for typing the original and revisions of the manuscript, but for keeping up my spirits during the entire process.

Los Angeles, California
June, 1982   Harold Weinstock

Contents

Detailed Analysis

Preface
1 **Introduction to Estate Planning**

§1.1   I.   What is Estate Planning?

4 Obtaining the Marital Deduction and the Community Property Exclusion to Save Death Taxes

6   Avoiding Probate

11 Annuities

13 Employee Benefits

14   Making Gifts to Charity

Tables

Index

Introduction to Estate Planning

1

§1.1   I.   What is Estate Planning?

An estate plan is an arrangement for the use, conservation and transfer of one's wealth. The process by which an estate plan is created is called estate planning. This process involves much more than merely preparing the estate owner's will. A well thought out estate plan concerns itself with the creation of an estate where none would otherwise exist, the increase of an existing estate to meet the needs of the owner and his family, and the preservation and protection of the estate from unnecessary taxes and costs.

II.   Objectives of Good Estate Planning

§1.2   A.   Lifetime Objectives

A good estate plan should provide for the best utilization of the owner's assets during his lifetime. With this in mind, the estate plan should anticipate and, after the owner's objectives are ascertained (see §1.15), provide for such lifetime needs as funds for children's education, income for retirement, re- placement of income in the event of disability and management of the estate in the event of incapacity. These and similar objectives may be accomplished by the use of certain tools examined in this book, as for example, utilizing a funded revocable living trust (Chapter 7), making gifts (Chapter 8), setting up a short-term trust (Chapter 9), utilizing life insurance for retirement (Chapter 10), acquiring annuities (Chapter 11), rearranging business interests during life (Chapter 12), arranging for employee benefits (Chapter 13) and making charitable gifts (Chapter 14).

§1.3   B.   Death Transfer Objectives

A good estate plan should provide for the disposition of assets on death in such a way that the estate being passed on is maximized and is left in accord- ance with the wishes of the decedent and the needs of his family. In carrying out this goal of estate planning the planner should realize that he cannot accomplish his task unless in a very careful manner he first ascertains the estate owner's objectives. (See §1.15.) Only after this is done, can he suggest and tailor for the owner certain tools detailed in this book which may help to carry out these objectives. Examples of such tools are obtaining the marital deduc- tion and the community property exclusion (Chapter 4), bypassing the second tax (Chapter 5), avoiding probate (Chapter 6), using a revocable living trust (Chapter 7), purchasing life insurance (Chapter 10), handling a business inter- est (Chapter 12), and making charitable gifts (Chapter 14).

§1.4   C.   Tax Planning

Tax saving methods can frequently be employed to achieve many estate planning objectives. By minimizing taxes, the estate owner will have not only a larger estate to enjoy during his lifetime but also a larger one to satisfy the needs of his family after his death.

The fact that a good estate plan will frequently save taxes is also useful in itself because it awakens the estate owner to the need for planning. An estate owner may have a natural reluctance to plan his estate. Planning forces him to come to grips with matters that he dislikes thinking about. How will he provide for himself in the event of retirement or illness? Who will receive his estate after his death? How will his children be cared for? (For an interesting study of the psychological aspects of testamentary disposition, see Shaffer, *Death, Property and Lawyers* (Dunellen Publishing Co, Inc (1970)). Planning also requires the owner to divulge financial and other private facts about himself and his family, which may make him uncomfortable. Discussing with the owner methods of saving taxes causes no psychological distress and easily opens the way for a franker discussion of the other elements of planning.

It is important to emphasize, however, that tax saving is only one aspect of estate planning. It should always remain secondary to the carrying out of the underlying objectives of the estate owner. A tax plan should never be used if it conflicts with what the owner really wants to do. For example, income producing assets should not be gifted to family members to save income taxes when the owner does not really want the recipients to have the income. A plan which does not conform to the way the estate owner wishes to leave his assets, despite the fact that it saves taxes, is a poor one.

III.   Occupations Involved in Estate Planning

§1.5   A.   The Estate Planning Team

There are at least four occupations involved in estate planning, the attorney, the accountant, the life insurance underwriter and the trust officer. In addition a financial planner, an investment advisor and an appraiser may from time to time become involved in the estate planning process. While each of these occupations has different duties and responsibilities they should be encouraged to work as a team. In this way the estate owner will benefit from the expertise of each occupation, and each will use its knowledge and skills to the best advantage of the public. See §§1.6 to 1.9 for a brief discussion of the role of the life insurance underwriter, the accountant, the trust officer and the attorney.

Each occupation should be aware of the fact that certain aspects of estate planning may only be engaged in by a licensed practitioner in a specific field. For example, to the extent estate planning involves the practice of law, such as the drafting of a will or trust, it may only be accomplished by an attorney;

to the extent it involves the selling of life insurance, only by a life insurance underwriter; and to the extent it involves the preparation of financial statements, only by an accountant.

Despite the fact that each occupation is prevented from practicing all aspects of estate planning, each individual member of the team should attempt to become as knowledgeable as possible in the entire subject. Just as any specialist must understand the entire body of knowledge of which his specialty is a part in order to properly practice his specialty, so must each team member understand the entire estate planning process to make a worthwhile contribution in his own area.

Various organizations have sprung up in recent years to foster cooperation and the interchange of knowledge among the various occupations engaged in estate planning. In the main they are called "Estate Planning Councils." It is estimated that 169 of these councils, with almost 16,000 members, belong to the National Association of Estate Planning Councils. See 4 *Estate Planning* 127 (1977).

§1.6   B.   The Life Insurance Underwriter

Life insurance is, or should be, an integral part of most estate plans. Particularly in an estate where the assets are insufficient to support the estate owner's family in the event of his death is insurance a necessity. Moreover, where the estate is nonliquid, insurance is often the only way to assure adequate liquidity to pay estate and inheritance taxes and other cash demands, thereby avoiding a forced sale of estate assets. Insurance can also be used for various business-related purposes such as funding buy-sell agreements and providing for one's retirement through the use of retirement income policies or the funding of pension and profit sharing plans.

The life insurance underwriter's role is to measure the estate owner's need for life insurance, to determine the amount and type needed, to develop a life insurance program in coordination with the client's objectives, and to sell such insurance.

§1.7   C.   Trust Officer

The trust officer's experience in administering estates and trusts is of great value in the estate planning process. He also has considerable knowledge about investments and how they are to be dealt with in an estate plan. The trust officer's role is to analyze the estates of his institution's customers and discuss with them the problems of use and disposition involved in such estates. He should assist the customer in using the institution's trust services and facilities as a means of solving the customer's estate planning problems. While the trust officer should not give specific legal advice, he may make general suggestions regarding the nature and objectives of a will and a trust and the consequences of estate, gift and income taxes.

§1.8   D.   Accountant

The accountant is frequently the person most familiar with the estate owner's financial affairs. By virtue of this familiarity, he is frequently in the best position to call the client's attention to and to advise on the necessity of an estate plan, as well as on subsequent revisions warranted by changes in the owner's financial situation. It is his role to develop, classify and summarize the information concerning the estate owner's assets, liabilities and income which is needed in developing an estate and tax plan. He is also in a unique position to pinpoint the business problems which will arise on the estate owner's death.

§1.9   E.   Attorney

It is the attorney's responsibility to collate the information and suggestions provided by the other members of the estate planning team and to synthesize it into a cohesive legal plan which will meet the client's needs and objectives. In evaluating the tools to be employed in effectuating the plan, he will do legal and tax research, give legal advice and draft the necessary legal documents. It is the attorney's duty to interpret the law and apply it to the client's specific financial situation for he is ultimately responsible for all legal aspects of the plan.

Another occupation which has emerged in estate planning in recent years is that of the legal assistant. An experienced legal assistant performs tasks in predeath estate planning as well as in the administration of an estate following the estate owner's death. Such a person, working under the supervision of an attorney, will obtain information needed in order to prepare the estate plan, make computations of taxes and expenses and draft legal documents.

IV.   Information Needed to Prepare an Estate Plan

§1.10   A.   Collecting Facts—The Checklist

An estate plan is only as sound as the facts upon which it is based. It is the estate planner's responsibility to elicit all of the relevant facts and circumstances concerning the estate owner and his family, as well as the financial details of the estate. For the type of information which should be obtained, see §§1.11 to 1.14.

Many estate planners develop a checklist or questionnaire as a guide to obtaining the necessary data and ensuring that details will not be overlooked. Although there are published checklists available, and a few are presented here, see §§ 1.11 and 1.12, the reader may wish to develop his own. For an extremely detailed and comprehensive questionnaire, see Bush, "Estate Planning — The Client Interview" 33 *NYU Inst on Fed Tax* 3 (1975). There is much to be said for the reader's developing his own checklist because it will be best adapted to his individual thinking process and use.

The checklist or questionnaire may be given to the estate owner to fill out or may be used primarily as a guide for the estate planner during his interview with the owner. While it may save time initially if the estate owner attempts to fill out the questionnaire, there are several drawbacks to this approach. To be useful to the planner, the list must be all-inclusive, but typically very little will apply to any one owner. Therefore, the owner may be confused by irrelevant inquiries, embarrassed by his lack of understanding, or disturbed by the extent of the invasion into his personal affairs. As a result he may put off answering the questions and indefinitely delay the planning of his estate. On the other hand, if the checklist is not given to the owner, the estate planner, in his discussion with the owner, will be able to determine which specific subjects should or should not be pursued without requiring the client to make this determination. Additionally, the estate planner has the opportunity to answer the owner's questions, convince him of the need for detailed information, and establish the rapport which will be crucial to the entire planning process.

§1.11   B.   Family Facts

The first category of information which is needed in order to prepare the estate plan is what may be called family facts. The following information should be obtained in this regard with respect to the estate owner, his spouse, and where relevant, with respect to each child and other intended beneficiaries of his estate:

1.   Name,
2.   Address,
3.   Birthday,
4.   Marital status,
5.   Prior marriages,
6.   Occupation,
7.   Health,
8.   General financial status, including needs and prospects,
9.   Degree of financial management, experience and ability,
10.   Present will (obtain copy),
11.   Location of Safe deposit boxes.

§1.12   C.   Assets and Liabilities

Once the family facts are ascertained, the estate planner should obtain a complete listing of the estate owner's assets and liabilities. If the spouse's estate is being planned at the same time, such a listing of the spouse's assets and liabilities is also necessary. The following is a suggested checklist of assets and liabilities about which the estate planner should inquire:

1. Cash, bank and savings accounts
   a. Location of account
   b. Amount
   c. How title is held
2. Securities
   a. Name
   b. Quantity
   c. Adjusted income tax basis
   d. Date acquired
   e. Present value
   f. How title held
3. Real estate
   a. Location
   b. Nature
   c. Adjusted income tax basis
   d. Date acquired
   e. Present value
   f. Encumbrances
   g. How title held
4. Business interests
   a. Name
   b. Location
   c. Per cent owned
   d. Names and relationship of co-owners
   e. Form of organization
   f. Description of business
   g. Buy-sell agreement (obtain copy)
   h. Present value
      i. Owner's estimate
      ii. Last five years financial statements (obtain copies)
      iii. Other information regarding value
   i. Adjusted income tax basis
   j. Date acquired
   k. How title held
5. Accounts and notes receivable
   a. Name of debtor
   b. Face amount

    c. Interest rate

    d. Security for indebtedness

    e. Payment terms

    f. Present value

    g. How title held

6. Major tangible personal property

    a. Description

    b. Adjusted income tax basis

    c. Date acquired

    d. Present value

    e. How title held

7. Retirement benefits

    a. Type of plan

    b. Projected retirement benefit

    c. Amount of vested death benefit

    d. Death beneficiary

8. Life insurance

    a. Company

    b. Policy number

    c. Insured

    d. Kind of policy

    e. Age at issue

    f. Owner

    g. Beneficiary

    h. Face amount

    i. Cash value

    j. Policy loan

    k. Dividends on deposit

    l. Annual premium

    m. Special provisions

    n. Projected cash value at retirement

9. Beneficial interest in estates of others (actual or potential)

    a. Actual or potential?

    b. Nature of interest

    c. Estimated value

10. Assets over which the owner has a power of appointment

    a. Instrument creating the power (obtain copy)

      b. Description of the power

      c. General or special?

      d. Value of assets subject to the power

11. Miscellaneous assets

      a. Description

      b. Adjusted income tax basis

      c. Date acquired

      d. Present value

      e. How title held

12. Liabilities

      a. Nature

      b. To whom owed

      c. Payment terms

In inquiring about each asset and liability, the estate planner should, in many instances, obtain documents from the owner that contain pertinent information. Often the owner's memory may be faulty. Helpful documents include stock certificates, real estate deeds, notes, mortgages, buy-sell agreements, retirement plans, life insurance policies, premarital agreements, and property settlement agreements.

Where assets are owned in common by husband and wife, as in joint tenancy, tenancy-in-the-entirety, or tenancy-in-common, the estate planner should obtain information regarding the contribution made by each spouse to the acquisition of the asset and whether or not a gift tax return was filed. If the spouses are, or were, domiciled in a community property state, the planner should obtain information necessary to determine which assets are, or were, community property. (See §4.34.) Inquiry should be made as to the estate of each spouse at the time of the marriage, the place of marriage, assets acquired during the marriage, the spouses' domicile at the time of the acquisitions, the source of funds used for such acquisitions and the amount of any gifts or inheritances received during the marriage.

§1.13 D. Income of Estate Owner, Spouse and Other Family Members

In addition to a listing of assets and liabilities, information regarding the income of the estate owner and the various members of the family should be obtained. This information is important in many aspects of estate planning, such as ascertaining the need for income replacement in the event of death, and the feasibility of gift or trust planning. Copies of recent income tax returns should be obtained as an aid in securing this information.

§1.14   E.   Prior Taxable Transfers

The estate planner should obtain information regarding any prior taxable gifts made by the estate owner and his spouse. This information, which may be secured from prior gift tax returns, if any were filed, is needed in computing the gift tax cost of future gifts as well as the estimated estate taxes which will be due on the estate owner's death. (See §§2.3 and 2.36.)

Additionally, if the estate owner within the past ten years inherited any assets from an estate which paid an estate tax, the value of the transferor's estate, the value of the inherited assets, and the amount of the estate tax paid in the transferor's estate is needed. This information will enable the estate planner to compute the credit for the federal estate tax paid on prior transfers. (See §2.28.) The amount of this credit, if material, is required in estimating the estate taxes which will be due on the estate owner's death.

§1.15   V.   Ascertaining the Estate Owner's Objectives

Ascertaining the estate owner's objectives is the most important step in the estate planning process. In order to formulate a sound estate plan, the plan must be constructed on the foundation of the owner's objectives. There are many tax and other estate planning tools. To select the appropriate ones for the individual whose estate is being planned requires a knowledge of his specific objectives, apart from tax considerations, regarding the disposition of his estate, his retirement and his business, if he owns one. Frequently the estate owner has not given sufficient thought to his own desires and objectives. His thinking should be stimulated by the planner. For some suggested questions to pose to the estate owner, see §§1.16 to 1.21.

A.   Beneficiary Objectives

§1.16   1.   Planning for the spouse

In planning for one's spouse, the estate owner must decide how much of the estate is to be left to the spouse and the manner in which it should pass to such spouse. The following questions will help the estate owner make these decisions:

a.   What portion of the estate should go to the spouse in preference to other beneficiaries? If the estate owner has difficulty in arriving at a conclusion, the following subsidiary questions will be helpful.

    i.   What are the financial needs of the spouse compared to the needs of other beneficiaries?

    ii.   What is the degree of love and affection for the spouse?

iii. What are the feelings of the estate owner regarding the possibility of the spouse remarrying?

iv. What is the likelihood that the spouse will care for the children and other relatives out of the share left to such spouse?

b. Of the portion of the estate going to the spouse should it, apart from any tax considerations, go outright or in trust? Subsidiary factors to consider are:

i. What is the financial ability and experience of the spouse?

ii. Does the spouse want the burden of outright ownership?

iii. Does the estate owner want to control the eventual disposition of the principal not used by the spouse during such spouse's lifetime?

c. If there is to be a trust for the spouse, then

i. Who is to be the trustee?

ii. Should the spouse receive all the income currently or should income distributions be discretionary with the trustee?

iii. Should principal be available for the spouse?

iv. If principal is to be available for the spouse, is the amount of the distributions to be in the sole control of the trustee or should the spouse have a power of withdrawal, perhaps up to a specified maximum?

v. Should the trust continue on the same terms for the spouse in the event of such spouse's remarriage?

vi. Upon the surviving spouse's death is the balance of the trust to go to named beneficiaries or to the surviving spouse's appointees?

d. Should gifts of life insurance or other assets be made to the spouse during the estate owner's lifetime or should the entire estate pass only on the owner's death?

§1.17   2.   Planning for the Children

The estate owner must consider questions such as the following in order to formulate his planning objectives with regard to his children:

a. What portion of the estate should go to the children in preference to other beneficiaries?

b. Of the portion of the estate going to the children, should an equal share go to each child or do any of the children have special needs?

c. Should the children receive at least some benefit from the estate while the surviving spouse is still living or should they wait until both parents die?

d. Should the children's shares be placed in trust or distributed outright?

e. If there is to be a trust for the children, then

    i.   Who is to be the trustee?

    ii.   Should the children receive the income currently or should income distributions be discretionary with the trustee?

    iii. At what ages should principal be distributed to the children?

f.   If a child does not survive until the age of distribution, who is to receive his share, the child's children, the child's spouse, the estate owner's other children or other beneficiaries?

g.   If any of the children are minors, who should be nominated as the guardian of the child's person?

h.   Should gifts be made to the children during the owner's lifetime or should the estate pass to them only on the owner's death?

§1.18   3.   Other Individual Beneficiaries

Other individuals whom the estate owner may wish to provide for may be his grandchildren, parents, brothers, sisters, and sons- and daughters-in-law. Also, he may wish to include more distant relatives such as nieces, nephews, and cousins or a good friend or loyal employee. The following are a few questions which will stimulate the estate owner's thinking in this regard:

a.   Should a portion of the estate be left directly to the grandchildren even if the children survive the estate owner?

b.   Are there any persons whom the estate owner is supporting during his lifetime and who will need funds after his death?

c.   Are there any persons whom the estate owner wishes to "remember" in his estate plan, even in a token way, to repay a kindness or perhaps to spare a person from feeling slighted if left out?

d.   To whom does the estate owner wish to leave his estate, if his primary beneficiaries, such as his spouse and issue, do not survive him?

§1.19   4.   Charitable Beneficiaries

Where the estate owner has a strong desire to leave some of his estate to charity, he will usually make his wishes known. In many instances, however, his desires are latent. A few questions should be asked to ascertain the owner's real objectives in this regard:

a.   Should a portion of the estate be left on the estate owner's death to charity in preference to other beneficiaries?

b.   If a part of the estate is to be left to charity, to which charities should it be left?

c.   Should the charitable bequests be outright or restricted to specific purposes?

d.   Should a charity be designated as a contingent beneficiary in the event the primary beneficiaries do not survive?

e.   Should charitable gifts be made during the owner's lifetime?

§1.20   B.   Retirement Objectives

The estate planner must uncover the estate owner's objectives regarding his retirement to help him plan for that period of his life. The following questions are useful in this regard:

a.   Does the estate owner have a strong desire to retire?

b.   What is his anticipated lifestyle during retirement?

c.   At what age would he like to retire?

d.   To what extent is the estate owner willing to save now in order to create an adequate estate for his retirement, either voluntary or forced by age or disability.

§1.21   C.   Business Objectives

Where the estate owner is the owner of, or has an interest in, a business, his intentions concerning selling or continuing the business after his disability, retirement or death will play an important part in planning his estate. Questions such as the following will help in framing the owner's objectives:

a.   Are the estate owner's services crucial to the continuation of the business or are there other key personnel who can continue it?

b.   Are there one or more family members or loyal employees for whom the owner wishes the business to continue or is it acceptable for the business to be sold on the estate owner's disability, retirement or death?

c.   If the business is to be sold, can arrangements be made beforehand or will it have to be sold or liquidated at the best price obtainable at the time of death, disability or retirement?

d.   If the business is to be continued, can a way be found to insure that those family members who do not participate in the business can receive an adequate income?

§1.22   VI.   Steps to Follow in Analyzing and Formulating the Estate Plan

Once the basic information discussed in §§1.11 to 1.14 and the estate owner's objectives, apart from tax considerations (see §§1.15 to 1.21), are obtained by the estate planner, he must have a methodology for using these data to construct the estate plan. There is no one method which is best in all situations. The method used depends on the thought processes of the planner and also on the peculiar characteristics and problems of the particular estate being planned. By way of illustration, however, the following steps will serve as a guide:

1. Segregate the assets of the estate into three categories:
   a. Cash
   b. Readily convertible to cash
   c. Nonliquid assets and those desired to be retained.
2. Add up the present values of the assets in each category and then total the three categories.
3. Subtract the present liabilities of the estate owner.
4. Estimate the amount of expenses and claims arising on the estate owner's death. These will include income tax liabilities, last illness and funeral expenses and costs of administration.
5. Compute the federal estate and any state inheritance taxes arising on the death of the owner.
6. Decide which assets, if any, will have to be used, and if necessary, sold or liquidated, to provide funds to pay the expenses, death claims and death taxes on the estate owner's death.
7. Assign the remaining assets to the beneficiaries according to the estate owner's objectives.
8. Determine whether the estimated distribution to each beneficiary will be sufficient to meet that beneficiary's needs.
9. Tabulate the assets and income which will be available to the estate owner on his retirement or disability.
10. Develop a plan to increase the estate (and, if necessary, to make it more liquid) for the estate owner's possible retirement or disability and for his beneficiaries on his death by
    a. Suggesting a savings program which will enable him to purchase life insurance, disability insurance and other investments;
    b. Decreasing his income tax burden during his lifetime; and
    c. Reducing the expenses, claims and taxes arising from his death.
11. If the estate owner is married, repeat steps (1) through (11) for the spouse's estate on the assumption that the spouse survives him.

This list is merely an outline of the basic steps the planner should follow in analyzing and planning the estate. The planner should project various contingencies into the analysis so that the estate will be properly planned if one of them should occur. For example, he should consider that the spouse may predecease the estate owner, or both may die simultaneously, or they may outlive their intended beneficiaries. Every effort should be made to think of as many contingencies as possible because they may have a significant impact on the feasibility of the plan ultimately selected. Since an estate plan is based on the owner's situation and desires at the time it is created, periodic reviews will assure its continued effectiveness in the light of changing circumstances.

VII. Recommended Reading

Astrachan, "Why People Don't Make Wills" 118 No 4 *Trusts and Estates* 45 (1979)

Bush, "Estate Planning — The Client Interview" 33 *NYU Inst on Fed Tax* 3 (1975)

Casner, *Estate Planning* (Little, Brown and Co 1961, currently supplemented)

Coster, " 'Whole Person' Estate Planning" 117 *Trusts and Estates* 376 (1978)

Crumbley and Milam, "Personalizing the Estate Planning Process" 116 *Trusts and Estates* 8 (1977)

Eber, "The Personal Audit: The First Step in Life-Time Finances and Estate Planning" 1 *Estate Planning* 30 (1973)

Eierman and McGarry, "Insurance Man vs. Trust Man: A Myth?" 98 *Trusts and Estates* 830 (1959)

Harris, "Code of Ethics for Trust Men" 103 *Trusts and Estates* 1186 (1964)

Lunton, "Accountant's Role in Estate Planning" 5 *Estate Planning* 40 (1978)

Melfe, "The Trust Industry in the Decade Ahead" 10 *Univ of Miami Inst on Estate Planning* 900 (1976)

Milam, "What is the Scope of the CPA's Estate Planning Responsibility to his Client?" 3 *Estate Planning* 174 (1976)

Pedrick "When Does the Estate Planning Team Huddle" 5 *Univ of Miami Inst on Estate Planning* 1900 (1971)

Schlesinger, *Immediate Pre-Mortem Checklist* (The Lawyers Cooperative Publishing Co 1972)

Shaffer, *Death, Property and Lawyers* (Dunellen Publishing Co, Inc 1970)

Shaffer, "Some Thoughts on the Psychology of Estate Planning" 113 *Tursts and Estates* 568 (1974)

Wormser, "Reflections on Half Century of Estate Planning" 115 *Trusts and Estates* 458 (1976)

Comment, "The Unauthorized Practice of Law by Layman and Lay Associations", 54 *Calif L Rev* 1331, 1353—1356 (1966)

Overview of Tax Principles

2

VIII.   Recommended Reading

§2.1   I.   Introduction

The purpose of this chapter is to introduce the general principles of estate and gift taxation and, also, those portions of the income tax which deal with the basis of assets received by gift or inheritance. This brief overview will enable the reader to better understand the in depth treatment of tax considerations discussed in many of the following chapters of the book. The discussion includes the changes made in the federal tax law by the Economic Recovery Tax Act of 1981. Although in many instances the taxes imposed by the various states are similar to the federal taxes, brief reference is made to state taxation.

Two important tax subjects which are involved in estate planning are not discussed in this chapter but are covered later in the book. The first is the income taxation of trusts and trust beneficiaries. For a discussion of this subject, see §§8.44 and 8.45. The second is the tax on generation-skipping transfers, introduced by the Tax Reform Act of 1976. This tax is discussed in §§5.34 to 5.39.

§2.2   II.   Unified Federal Estate and Gift Transfer Tax System

In 1976, with the enactment of the Tax Reform Act of 1976, the previously separate gift and estate tax systems were combined into a unified transfer tax system. Prior to 1977, it was possible for an estate owner to dispose of his wealth partly by lifetime gifts and partly through dispositions on death. Each set of transfers had its own exemptions and separate progressive rate schedule. Hence, by dividing his transfers between lifetime gifts and testamentary dispositions, he could utilize the exemptions available for both taxes and pay at the lowest rate of each tax. For example, a single person with a $1,000,000 estate, by giving away $300,000 in taxable lifetime gifts, paid $54,075 in gift taxes and $175,774 in estate taxes, or total taxes of $229,849. However, if he retained his $1,000,000 until death, the estate taxes were $303,500.

Since January 1, 1977, there has been a unified estate and gift tax imposed on the value of the property transferred. The same rates ultimately apply whether the property is transferred as an inter vivos gift or whether the value thereof at the time of the gift is included in the decedent's gross estate. Therefore, many of the tax savings provided by the previous law, under which gift tax rates were lower than estate tax rates and there were two sets of exemptions, are no longer available. The tax incentive to make gifts during life in order to remove the value of the gifted property from the gross estate has been greatly reduced. Nevertheless, several estate planning advantages in making gifts still exist (see §§8.3 to 8.5, 8.9 and 8.10).

III. The Federal Estate Tax

§2.3 A. Steps to Follow in Making Computation

The federal estate tax is in general computed in the following manner:

1. List and value the property included in the gross estate (see §§2.4 to 2.16).

2. Subtract from the gross estate the allowable deductions (see §§2.17 to 2.23) to arrive at the taxable estate.

3. Add to the taxable estate any taxable gifts (see §§2.37 to 2.44) made after December 31, 1976, (except for gifts which are already included in the gross estate, see §§2.12 to 2.15), to arrive at the tax base.

4. Compute the tentative tax on the tax base by using the unified rate schedule (see Appendix, Table II).

5. Subtract the gift tax on post-1976 gifts included in items (1) and (3) which would have been payable, if the estate tax rate schedule in effect at the decedent's death had been applicable at the time of such gifts.

6. Subtract from the amount of the tentative tax the unified estate tax credit (see §2.25).

7. Subtract from the net tax arrived at in item (6) the following available credits:

   a. Credit for state death taxes (§2.26);

   b. Credit for gift tax on pre-1977 gifts which are included in the gross estate (see §2.27);

   c. Credit for federal estate tax previously paid (see §2.28);

   d. Credit for foreign death taxes (see §2.29).

The effect of adding the taxable post-1976 gifts to the tax base and subtracting the gift taxes paid on such gifts is to tax such gifts at the marginal estate tax bracket.

The computation of the federal estate tax may be illustrated by a simple example. Assume the decedent, a single person, dies after 1986 leaving an estate of $1,000,000. His debts, funeral expenses and costs of administration total $100,000. During his lifetime he made post-1976 taxable gifts of $200,-000 on which he paid $7,800 of gift tax.

Gross estate	$1,000,000
Less deductions	100,000
Taxable estate	$ 900,000
Add post-1976 gifts	200,000
Tax base	$1,100,000

Tentative estate tax	$ 386,800
Less gift taxes payable on post-1976 gifts	7,800
	$ 379,000
Less unified credit	192,800
Estate tax payable (subject to credits described in step (7))	$ 186,200

§2.4   B.   Property Includable in Gross Estate

Assets are included in the gross estate because they are owned by the decedent at the time of his death (§§2.5 to 2.10) or because the decedent either transferred them too closely to the date of his death or in such a manner that he retained certain prohibited benefits or rights in the property (§§2.12 to 2.15).

§2.5   1.   Property Owned at Time of Death

I.R.C. §2031 provides that a decedent's gross estate includes the value, at the time of his death, of "all property, real or personal, tangible or intangible, wherever situated." However, this definition is subject to the limitation of I.R.C. §2033, which states that the gross estate includes such property only to the extent of the decedent's interest therein at the time of his death.

§2.6   a.   Treatment of Community Property

Community property is most commonly all property acquired during marriage by either spouse while domiciled in a community property jurisdiction, except property received by inheritance or gift. (For a full discussion of community property, see §§4.34 to 4.36). Where each spouse has a vested interest in one-half of the community property, on the death of a spouse, only one-half of the community property will be includable in that spouse's gross estate.

§2.7   b.   Treatment of Joint Tenancy Property

Property held in joint tenancy is generally included in the decedent's gross estate, except to the extent the surviving joint tenant can show original contribution to its cost. I.R.C. §2040. Where such contribution can be shown, the percentage of the acquisition cost which the survivor contributed is the percentage of the value of the joint tenancy asset which is excludable on the decedent joint tenant's death. The survivor's contribution does not include funds originally given to the survivor by the decedent. However, under the Economic Recovery Tax Act of 1981, where the joint tenants are husband and wife, on the death of the first spouse to die only one-half of the value of the asset is included in such spouse's gross estate regardless of which spouse furnished the consideration. For a more detailed discussion of the estate tax treatment of joint tenancies, see §§6.18 and 6.19.

§2.8 c. Property Subject to a General Power of Appointment

A power of appointment is a power given by one person to another (i.e., the holder) to designate who is to receive an asset. For example, if A creates a trust and gives to B the power to determine who is to receive the trust principal, B is the holder of a power of appointment. A general power of appointment allows the holder to appoint to himself, his estate, or his creditors. A special power of appointment is only exercisable in favor of someone other than the holder, his estate or creditors. However, a power to invade for oneself under an ascertainable standard relating to health, support and education is considered, for tax purposes, to be a special power. See §§5.3 to 5.6, for a full discussion of powers of appointment.

Under I.R.C. §2041, property subject to a general power of appointment at the time of death is included in the decedent's estate. Property subject to a special power of appointment is not included. For the treatment of a power to consume 5 per cent of the principal or $5,000 per year, whichever amount is greater, see §5.5.

§2.9 d. Life Insurance

As a general rule, proceeds of an insurance policy on the life of the decedent are included in his gross estate. However, if the policy proceeds are not payable to his estate, and the decedent retained none of the incidents of ownership, the proceeds are not included in his estate. I.R.C. §2042. The decedent is deemed to have an incident of ownership in the policy if he has the right to borrow on the policy, the right to cash the policy, the right to change a beneficiary, or if he retains a reversionary interest in the policy which is valued at more than 5 per cent immediately before his death. See §§10.11 and 10.12.

§2.10 e. Annuities

An annuity is an agreement to pay a person a fixed sum at periodic intervals usually for as long as the person lives. (See §11.1.) A straight life annuity is one which ceases on the annuitant's death (see §11.3). It is not included in the annuitant's estate. A refund annuity (see §11.4), a life annuity with a term certain (see §11.5), and a joint life and survivor annuity (see §11.6) may have value after the annuitant's death. Such value will be included in the decedent's estate, at least to the extent that the decedent contributed to the value of the annuity still to be paid after his death. I.R.C. §2039. (See §11.10.)

§2.11   f.   Assets for Which Qualified Terminable Interest Property Marital Deduction Was Previously Allowed

Normally where a person is only an income beneficiary of a trust created by another, the assets of the trust are not included in such income beneficiary's estate. See §5.3. Where, however, the surviving spouse is the income beneficiary of a qualified terminable interest property marital deduction trust (see §2.22 and Chapter 4) created by the previously deceased spouse, the trust assets may be includable in the survivor's gross estate. Such inclusion is required where the executor of the spouse who died first makes an election to take the marital deduction with respect to this trust. I.R.C. §2044. The purpose of this treatment is to permit the assets to escape estate tax on the death of one spouse, but not on the death of both.

2.   Property Transferred By Decedent During His Lifetime

§2.12   a.   Gifts Made Within Three Years of Death

Prior to 1982, all gifts made within three years of the donor's death, except those qualifying for and not exceeding the annual gift tax exclusion, were includable in the gross estate. I.R.C. §2035. The Economic Recovery Tax Act of 1981 substantially modified this rule. Under present law, only gifts of life insurance and other transfers made within three years of death where the gifted property would otherwise be included in the gross estate (see §§2.8, 2.13, 2.14 and 2.15) are includable. I.R.C. §2035(d)(2). Gifts of life insurance are includable even if they do not exceed the $10,000 annual gift tax exclusion. I.R.C. §2035(b)(2). However, the transfers discussed in §§2.8, 2.13, 2.14 and 2.15 are not includable if they qualify for and do not exceed the $10,000 annual gift tax exclusion.

The effect of including the gift in the gross estate is in many instances more disadvantageous than causing the amount of the gift to be taxed at the estate tax rate through the operation of the unified estate and gift tax system. See §2.2. Including the gift in the gross estate subjects its value to the estate tax rate at the time of death rather than at the time of the gift. Hence, where the asset appreciates in value between the date of the gift and the date of death, it will be subject to a larger estate tax.

The amount of gift tax payable on any gift made within three years of death is also includable in the gross estate. I.R.C. §2035(c). This rule applies to all gifts, not merely those involving life insurance or those which are otherwise includable in the gross estate. For example, the estate owner makes an outright gift of $1,000,000 in cash to a child, and the donor pays $200,000 of gift tax. If the donor dies within three years of the gift, the $200,000 is includable in the gross estate. The purpose of this "gross up" provision is to prevent an individual who expects to die shortly from making a taxable gift of property in order to keep the amount of the gift tax out of his estate and thus pay a lower estate tax. See §8.5.

§2.13   b.   Transfers Taking Effect at Death

The gross estate includes the value of property gifted by decedent during his lifetime which takes effect on his death. Such a transfer is one where the donee must survive the donor in order to obtain the property, and the donor retains a reversionary interest which, immediately before his death, exceeds 5 per cent of the value of the property. I.R.C. §2037. For example, assume A (the donor) creates a trust where the income is payable to B, and on B's death the principal is payable to C, if A is not then living; otherwise, the principal reverts to A. If A's retained interest, valued actuarially at the time of his death, exceeds the 5 per cent limit, the value of the trust assets will be taxable in full. If the actuarial value is less than 5 per cent, then only the actual percentage of the value of the property is includable in the decedent's estate.

§2.14   c.   Gifts with Possession or Enjoyment Retained

The entire value of gifted property is includable in the donor's gross estate if he retained the right to income for his life or for any period which does not terminate prior to his death. I.R.C. §2036. For example, A creates a trust where the income is payable to A for life and remainder to B. The trust assets are included in A's estate. If A creates a trust where the income is to be paid to A for 15 years and then remainder to B, but A dies at the end of 12 years, the trust assets are similarly included in A's estate. On the same basis, if the income, instead of being payable to A, were to be used by the trustee for the support of A's minor children, the trust assets would be includable in A's estate. *Estate of Joseph G Gokey* 72 TC 721 (1979).

§2.15   d.   Transfers with Retained Power to Alter, Amend, Revoke or Terminate

The value of gifted property is includable in the donor's gross estate to the extent he retained the right to alter, amend, revoke or terminate the transfer. I.R.C. §2038. It is immaterial that the donor's power is not exercisable in favor of himself. For example, A creates a trust where B is the designated beneficiary, but he reserves the right to substitute C. The assets will be included in A's estate. However, if the exercise of the retained power is governed by an ascertainable standard, the transferor has not retained sufficient ownership rights to trigger inclusion under §2038. *Jennings v Smith* 161 F2d 74 (2d Cir

1947). Hence, if in the previous example, A's right to substitute is dependent upon the needs of C, the trust assets will not be included in A's estate.

§2.16   3.   Valuation of Includable Assets

Generally, the value of property included in the gross estate will be the fair market value at the date of death, that is, the price at which a willing seller will sell and a willing buyer who has knowledge of the facts will purchase. Reg. §20.2031-1(b). Under I.R.C. §2032, the estate representative may elect to value all of the property included in the gross estate as of six months after the decedent's death for estate tax purposes. If the election is made, the six-month valuation date applies to all property included in the gross estate, with the exception of property sold, distributed, exchanged, or otherwise disposed of during the six months following the estate owner's death. Such property is valued as of the date of its disposition. For a full discussion of the alternate valuation election, see §15.27.

There are special rules applicable to valuation of real property devoted to farming or used by a closely held business. I.R.C. §2032A. See §15.28.

C.   Deductions from Gross Estate

1.   Charges Against the Estate

§2.17   a.   Funeral Expense

A deduction is allowed for funeral expenses in those amounts actually expended and payable out of the decedent's estate under local law. Thus, in those community property jurisdictions which deem funeral expenses to be an obligation of the entire community property, only one-half of the amount expended will be allowed as a deduction from the decedent spouse's gross estate. However, where the funeral expenses are chargeable only to the decedent's interest in the community property, the entire amount will be deductible. Also included as deductible funeral expenses are reasonable expenditures for a tombstone, monument or mausoleum, a burial plot and its future care, and the transportation expenses of the person bringing the body to the place of burial, to the extent such expenses are allowed under local law. Reg. §20.2053-2.

§2.18   b.   Administration Expenses

Administration expenses are deductible from the gross estate to the extent they are not claimed as deductions on the estate income tax return. See §§15.15 to 15.25. Administration expenses include executor's commissions, attorneys' fees, court costs, accountants' and appraisers' fees, and other expenses incurred in preserving and distributing the estate. The deduction is limited to those expenses actually and necessarily incurred in the administration of the estate and does not include expenditures incurred for the individual benefit of the heirs, legatees, or devisees. Reg. §20.2053-3.

§2.19 c. Debts of the Decedent

Amounts representing personal obligations of the decedent existing at the time of his death and enforceable against his estate may be deducted from his gross estate. Interest accrued on the obligation at the time of death is also deductible. Reg. §20.2053-4. Examples of such debts of a decedent are income taxes on earnings in the year of death and expenses of his last illness.

§2.20 d. Mortgages and Liens

A deduction is allowed for the unpaid amount of a mortgage or other indebtedness, including interest accrued to the date of death, on any property in the gross estate. If only the specific property is chargeable with the indebtedness, then the net value of such property is included in the gross estate. On the other hand, if the estate is liable, the full value of the property is includable, and a deduction is allowed in the amount of the mortgage or lien. Reg. §20.2053-7.

§2.21 2. Losses During Administration

Losses arising from casualty or theft during administration of the estate are deductible from the gross estate to the extent they are not compensated for by insurance or otherwise. I.R.C. §2054. Such losses are only deductible from the gross estate if they are not claimed as income tax deductions. See §15.15.

§2.22 3. Marital Deduction

An estate is generally allowed an unlimited marital deduction for property passing to the decedent's spouse. I.R.C. §2056(a). However, see §4.4 for a discussion of the computation of the marital deduction for the estates of decedents whose wills were executed prior to September 12, 1981, and were not subsequently amended to specifically refer to the unlimited marital deduction allowable by the Economic Recovery Tax Act of 1981.

The marital deduction is generally not allowable where the interest passing to the surviving spouse is a life estate or other terminable interest, except in the case of a qualifying terminable interest election under I.R.C. §2056(b)(7). A qualifying income interest requires that the surviving spouse be entitled to receive all the income from the property at least annually and that no person be able to appoint the property during the spouse's lifetime to anyone other than the spouse. For a full discussion of the marital deduction, see Chapter 4.

§2.23   4.   Charitable Contributions

A deduction without limitation is allowed for the value of property included in the decedent's gross estate which is transferred on his death to qualifying governmental, charitable or religious organizations. I.R.C. §2055. Where a remainder interest is contributed, the value of such interest, determined actuarially, is deductible if the charitable remainder trust qualifies as an annuity trust, a unitrust or a pooled income fund. See §§14.23 to 14.33.

§2.24   5.   Orphan's Exclusion

For persons dying prior to 1982, a deduction was allowed for an amount which passed to a child of the decedent where the decedent had no surviving spouse and the child had no living parent and was under 21 years old. I.R.C. §2057. The deduction was limited to $5,000 multiplied by the number of years that the child was under age 21. The Economic Recovery Tax Act of 1981 repealed this deduction with respect to decedents dying after 1981.

§2.25   D.   Unified Credit Against Estate Tax

I.R.C. §2010 ultimately allows a credit of $192,800 against the estate tax of every decedent, a significant increase over the $47,000 credit in effect during 1981. The new unified estate tax credit is to be phased in over five years, according to the following schedule set forth in I.R.C. §2010:

For decedents dying in	Credit allowed
1982	$ 62,800
1983	$ 79,300
1984	$ 96,300
1985	$121,800
1986	$155,800
1987 and thereafter	$192,800

The above credits are, in effect, equivalent to exemptions as follows:

For decedents dying in	"Equivalent" Exemption
1982	$225,000
1983	$275,000
1984	$325,000
1985	$400,000
1986	$500,000
1987 and thereafter	$600,000

Hence, when the tax base (see §2.3) in an estate does not exceed the "equivalent" exemption, there will be no federal estate tax. It is important to remember, however, that, where the estate exceeds the "equivalent" exemption, such "equivalent" exemption is to be disregarded in computing the tax. The tentative tax is computed in the usual manner (see §2.3), and from such tax is deducted the unified credit. For the reduction of the unified credit as a result of certain gifts made during the period September 9, 1976 to December 31, 1976, see §2.45.

E.   Credits Against Tax

§2.26   1.   Credit for State Death Tax

In computing the federal estate tax, a credit is allowed for state death taxes actually paid in respect of any property included in the decedent's gross estate. I.R.C. §2011. The amount of the credit allowed is the lesser of the state death taxes actually paid or the amount stated in the table appearing in I.R.C. §2011(b). (See Appendix, Table III.) It is important to note that the amount of the taxable estate for purposes of the table is the taxable estate less $60,000. Hence, if the taxable estate is $1,000,000, the maximum credit is based on a taxable estate of $940,000.

§2.27   2.   Credit for Gift Taxes

A credit against the estate tax is available for gift taxes paid with respect to gifts made prior to January 1, 1977, if any portion of such gifts must be included in the decedent's gross estate. I.R.C. §2012. For example, assume the decedent prior to 1977 transferred assets to a trust and retained the income. He paid a gift tax on the remainder interest. Upon his death, the trust assets are included in his estate (see §2.14). The amount of the gift tax will be credited against the estate tax. For limitations on the amount of the credit, see I.R.C. §§2012(a) and (b). This credit is to prevent a double tax liability on gifts made prior to the unification of the estate and gift taxes. The credit is not allowed for gifts made after 1976 because all gift taxes paid, whether or not on taxable gifts included in the gross estate, are subtracted from the tentative estate tax. See §2.3.

§2.28   3.   Credit for Federal Estate Tax Paid on Prior Transfers

In order to prevent double taxing of the same property to two decedents where one inherited from the other within a short period of time, I.R.C. §2013 allows a limited credit for the estate tax previously paid with designated maximum amounts. If the transferor–decedent died within two years before or after the transferee–decedent, the gross estate of the transferee–decedent is allowed 100 per cent of the maximum amount as a credit since estate taxes were recently paid by the transferor's estate. If the transferor predeceased the transferee-decedent by more than two years, the maximum credit is reduced by 20 per cent, with an additional 20 per cent for each additional two-year period, as shown in the following table:

Period of Time by Which the Transferee's Death Follows the Transferor's Death	Per Cent Allowable
2 to 4 years	80
4 to 6 years	60
6 to 8 years	40
8 to 10 years	20
10 years and thereafter	none

The credit otherwise allowable may not generally exceed the lesser of (1) the amount of the estate tax in the transferor's estate attributable to the property inherited by the transferee, or (2) the amount by which the estate tax in the transferee's estate, without regard to this credit, exceeds the estate tax in the transferee's estate computed by excluding from his gross estate the value of the inherited property.

§2.29   4.   Credit for Foreign Death Taxes

If a foreign country imposes death taxes on property situated in that country and such property is also included in the gross estate of the decedent because he is a United States citizen or resident, his estate is allowed a credit for the foreign death taxes paid with respect to property taxed by both countries. I.R.C. §2014. The credit cannot, however, exceed the portion of the United States tax attributable to such property. See I.R.C. §2014(b).

§2.30   F.   Filing of the Return and Payment of the Tax

The federal estate tax return (Form 706) must be filed for every estate where the gross estate exceeds the following amounts:

Year of Death	Amount of Gross Estate
1982	$225,000
1983	$275,000
1984	$325,000
1985	$400,000
1986	$500,000
1987 and thereafter	$600,000

The return is due within nine months of the estate owner's death. The estate tax is also due and payable at that time, but an extension of time for payment is available for reasonable cause. I.R.C. §6161(a). This extension may not be for a period in excess of 10 years. If the time for payment is extended, interest is charged on the unpaid tax liability. The interest rate is adjusted annually by the Internal Revenue Service to reflect the then current prime interest rate. The adjusted rate for the year commencing February 1, 1982, is 20 per cent.

There are also provisions for an alternate extension of time in which to pay a portion of the estate tax where a significant portion of the estate consists of an interest in a closely held business. I.R.C. §6166. For full discussion of these provisions, see §§12.51 to 12.57.

§2.31 IV. State Death Taxes

In general, there are three types of state death taxes; namely, an estate tax, an inheritance tax and a "pickup" estate tax. A majority of states impose an inheritance tax rather than an estate tax, and most states employ a "pickup" estate tax in addition to their inheritance or estate tax in order to take advantage of the maximum state death tax credit allowable for federal estate tax purposes.

§2.32 A. Estate Tax

As with the federal estate tax, state estate tax is imposed on the right to transfer property. Therefore, the tax is against the decedent's net estate as a whole, and the value of the net estate determines the estate's tax bracket and the tax liability. Exemptions, deductions and credits similar to the federal system are generally allowed by states using the estate tax method. See Appendix, Table VI, for the New York state estate tax rates.

§2.33 B. Inheritance Tax

An inheritance tax, on the other hand, is imposed on the right to receive, and the tax liability is based on each beneficiary's distributive share. Each beneficiary is liable for the tax on his share although the tax may be payable by the executor or administrator of the estate. Generally, the beneficiaries are divided into different classes depending on the degree of relationship to the decedent, with lower tax rates and larger exemptions for closer relatives. See Appendix, Table V, for California inheritance tax rates and exemptions.

§2.34   C.   "Pickup" Estate Tax

A supplemental tax is generally employed to absorb any difference between the state inheritance or estate tax payable and the maximum state death tax credit allowed under I.R.C. §2011. Through such a "pickup" tax, the state may collect the maximum state tax allowable under the credit at no additional expense to the taxpayer. For example, assume that State A imposes an inheritance tax of $25,000 in a given estate. Assume also that the maximum credit for state death taxes allowable by the federal government in the assumed estate is $30,000, provided this amount is actually paid to the state (see §2.26). State A imposes a "pickup" tax of $5,000. Hence, the total cost to the estate will not be increased, because without the "pickup" tax the federal government would have collected $5,000 more. By reason of the "pickup" tax, State A, rather than the federal government, receives this $5,000.

V.   The Federal Gift Tax

§2.35   A.   Effect of Unification on Gifts Made After 1976

The introduction of the unified estate and gift tax transfer system by the Tax Reform Act of 1976 (see §2.2) did not eliminate the imposition of a gift tax on lifetime transfers. The gift tax is paid when the lifetime transfer is made, but on the donor's death the amount of the gift is subjected to the full estate tax, against which the gift tax is credited. The gift tax is, in effect, a "prepayment" of a portion of the estate tax.

§2.36   B.   Steps to Follow in Computing the Gift Tax

The federal gift tax is computed in the following manner:

1. List and total all gifts made by the donor during his lifetime through the current calendar year, making the following adjustments:

    a. Exclude the portion of any gift which qualifies for the annual exclusion (see §§2.39 and 2.40).

    b. Subtract all the gift tax deductions (see §§2.42 to 2.44).

    c. Subtract from the total gifts made before 1977 the amount of the lifetime exemption applicable to such gifts which the donor elected to use.

2. Compute the tentative gift tax on the aggregate total adjusted gifts for all years, through the current calendar year, arrived at in Item (1), by using the current gift tax rate schedule (see Appendix, Table II).

3. Compute the tentative gift tax on the aggregate total adjusted gifts for all prior years, by using the current gift tax schedule.

4. Subtract Item (3) from Item (2), arriving at the tentative tax on the gifts made during the current year.

5. Subtract from Item (4) the unused portion of the unified credit against the gift tax (see §2.45), arriving at the net gift tax payable.

From an examination of the above steps, the reader can see that the gift tax is cumulative. The prior gifts push the current gifts into higher brackets. The following is an example of the gift tax computation for gifts made in 1987, where the donor had made gifts prior to 1977, as well as during 1979 and 1981:

Pre-1977 gifts (after annual exclusions and deductions)		$ 530,000
Less: lifetime exemption used by donor		30,000
Net taxable pre-1977 gifts		$ 500,000
1979 gifts (after annual exclusions and deductions)		100,000
1981 gifts (after annual exclusions and deductions)		900,000
1987 gifts (after annual exclusions and deductions)		500,000
Total gifts		$2,000,000
Tentative gift tax on total gifts		780,800
Less tentative gift tax on pre-1987 gifts		555,800
Tentative tax on 1987 gifts		225,000
Less unified credit	$192,800	
Less unified credit allowed on gifts in 1979 and 1981	47,000	$ 145,800
Gift tax payable		$ 79,200

§2.37   C.   Transfer Subject to the Gift Tax

The gift tax is imposed on irrevocable gifts. The donor is primarily responsible for the tax. I.R.C. §2501. A transfer, even if not cast in the form of a gift, is subject to gift tax to the extent that property is transferred for less than adequate and full consideration. I.R.C. §2512(b). For example, A sells to B, his son, an asset worth $100,000 for $60,000. A has made a gift to B in the amount of $40,000.

Where the gift or transfer is not complete, it is not taxable at the time of the transfer. For example, if the donor reserves the power to reacquire the asset or change the beneficiary, the gift is deemed to be incomplete. See Reg. §25.2511-2.

The gift tax is measured by the fair market value of the transfer on the date of the gift. For the definition of fair market value, see §2.16.

§2.38 D. Split Gifts

A gift made by one spouse to a third person may be treated as a gift made one-half by each spouse. Both spouses must, however, consent to treat all gifts made to third parties during the calendar year as split gifts. I.R.C. §2513(a). Split gifts are generally advantageous because the tax bracket on the gift is lowered and the annual exclusion and unified credit are doubled. For example, if the husband makes an outright gift of $750,000 to A, the gift tax (assuming no prior gifts and the availability of a unified credit of $192,800) will be $55,500. If the gift were treated as a split gift, each spouse would be deemed to have made a gift of $375,000 and there would be no gift tax.

Where husband and wife make a gift of community property to a third person, each spouse automatically makes a gift of only one-half of the asset. Hence, the split gift consent is not required.

E. Exclusions

§2.39 1. Annual Exclusion

The first $10,000 per year of gifts which a donor gives to each of any number of beneficiaries is excludable in computing the gift tax. I.R.C. §2503(b). For example, a donor could even give away $1,000,000 in one year with no gift tax consequences as long as he does not give any one donee more than $10,000. If they so desire, a husband and wife may elect to treat all gifts made by either as having been made one-half by each of them. (See §2.38.) In this way, they may give up to $20,000 per year to each donee without paying gift tax. I.R.C. §2513. The amount of the annual exclusion prior to 1982 was only $3,000. Hence, gifts have now become a more significant planning tool.

The annual exclusion is allowable, however, only for gifts of a present, and not a future, interest. For an interest to be a present one the unrestricted right to the immediate use, possession or enjoyment of the asset must be given. See Reg. §25.2503-3(b). The best example of a gift of a present interest is an outright gift. However, if a gift is made in trust and the trust provides that the income is to be paid currently to the income beneficiary, the income interest is a present interest, but the gift of principal is a future interest. The value of the income interest is calculated by using the tables set forth in Reg. §25.2512-9(f). See Appendix, Table VIII. Where the trustee is given discretionary powers over the payment of income, or the trust requires that the income be accumulated, there is no gift of a present interest, unless the trust qualifies as a minor's trust. See §2.40.

§2.40   a.   Transfers for the Benefit of Persons Under 21 Years of Age

Gifts to persons under age 21 are often desirable. They can also provide income tax advantages when income-producing property is given to such a person who is in a lower income tax bracket than is the donor. However, since minors (usually persons under age 18) are under a legal disability which restricts their use of property, and since many persons between age 18 and age 20 may not be mature enough to manage their assets, special rules apply to gifts to persons under age 21, which would otherwise be future interest gifts. I.R.C. §2503(c) provides that no part of a gift made to a person under age 21 will be considered a gift of a future interest if the principal and income may be expended for the benefit of such person, and if any amounts not so expended will be distributed to the donee upon reaching the age of 21.

§2.41   2.   Exclusions for Educational or Medical Expenses

Ordinarily where one pays for the support, medical care or education of a person whom he is not obligated to support, such payments will constitute taxable gifts. For instance, a parent has the duty to support his minor children, but not his adult children. The Economic Recovery Tax Act of 1981 provides for an unlimited exclusion for amounts paid on behalf of any individual for medical payments or tuition, but not for any other educational or support expenses. Moreover, the payments to be excluded must be paid by the donor directly to the medical care provider or educational institution. I.R.C. §2503(e).

F.   Deductions

§2.42   1.   Marital Deduction

Subsequent to 1981, a donor is allowed an unlimited marital deduction for lifetime gifts of separate or community property made to his or her spouse. I.R.C. §2523(a). The deduction is not, however, allowable for a gift of a life estate or other terminable interest, except in the case of a qualifying terminable interest election under I.R.C. §2523(f).

In order to have a qualifying terminable interest, the donee spouse must be entitled to receive all the income from the property at least annually and no person may be able to appoint the property during the spouse's lifetime to anyone other than the spouse. If the election is made by the donor, there will be no gift tax at the time of the gift, but if the donee spouse during lifetime disposes of his or her qualifying interest in the terminable interest property, or when the donee spouse dies, such property will then be subject to gift or estate tax.

§2.43   a.   Application to Interspousal Gifts of Community Property

When a gift is made of community property by one spouse to the other as the recipient's separate property, there is a gift of only one-half because the donee spouse already owns the other one-half. The taxable one-half is subject to the marital deduction, if the gift is made in a qualifying manner.

Similarly, where a gift of one spouse's separate property is made to the community property, there is only a gift of one-half because the donor spouse is a recipient of one-half. The taxable one-half is likewise subject to the marital deduction, if the gift is made in a qualifying manner.

§2.44   2.   Charitable Contributions

In computing taxable gifts, I.R.C. §2522 allows an unlimited deduction for the amount of gifts made to qualifying charitable, religious or governmental organizations. Where a remainder interest is contributed, the value of such interest, determined actuarially, is, with a few exceptions, deductible only if the charitable remainder trust is an annuity trust, a unitrust or a pooled income fund. See §§14.23 to 14.33.

§2.45   G.   Unified Gift Tax Credit

A unified credit against the gift tax is allowed pursuant to I.R.C. §2505. As of January 1, 1987, an individual is entitled to a credit of $192,800 against the gift tax. Until that time, the allowable credit is as follows:

When gift made	Credit allowed
Jan. 1, 1977 through June 30, 1977	$ 6,000
July 1, 1977 through Dec. 31, 1977	$ 30,000
Jan. 1, 1978 through Dec. 31, 1978	$ 34,000
Jan. 1, 1979 through Dec. 31, 1979	$ 38,000
Jan. 1, 1980 through Dec. 31, 1980	$ 42,500
Jan. 1, 1981 through Dec. 31, 1981	$ 47,000
Jan. 1, 1982 through Dec. 31, 1982	$ 62,800
Jan. 1, 1983 through Dec. 31, 1983	$ 79,300
Jan. 1, 1984 through Dec. 31, 1984	$ 96,300
Jan. 1, 1985 through Dec. 31, 1985	$121,800
Jan. 1, 1986 through Dec. 31, 1986	$155,800

The credit is reduced by any amount of the credit allowed for previous gifts. For example, if $100,000 of the credit was used up in 1986, the credit available in 1987 is only $92,800.

The unified gift tax credit takes the place of the $30,000 lifetime exemption of I.R.C. §2521, which was repealed by the Tax Reform Act of 1976. However, the unified credit (for both estate and gift taxes) is reduced for gifts made during the period September 9, 1976 to December 31, 1976, where all or part of the former lifetime exemption was used. The reduction is for an amount equal to 20 per cent of the portion of the lifetime exemption used during that period. Hence, if the entire lifetime exemption of $30,000 was used during that period, the unified credit for post-1976 gifts must be reduced by $6,000.

§2.46 H. Gift Tax Return

The gift tax return, Form 709, is due annually on or before April 15 following the year the taxable gift is made. However, for the calendar year in which the donor dies, the gift tax return is required to be filed no later than the due date for filing the donor's estate tax return (including extensions). See §2.30.

§2.47 VI. State Gift Taxes

Sixteen states impose a gift tax.[1] In general there are two types of state gift taxes. The first is a tax similar to the federal gift tax, a tax imposed on the total taxable gifts as a whole. See Appendix, Table VII, for New York state gift tax rates. The other, which is imposed by a majority of the sixteen jurisdictions, is a tax imposed separately on the transfers to each beneficiary. Generally the beneficiaries are divided into different classes depending on the degree of relationship to the donor, with lower tax rates and larger exemptions for close relatives. See Appendix, Table V, for the California gift tax rates and exemptions.

VII. Basis of Property for Federal Income Tax Purposes

§2.48 A. Property Acquired from a Decedent

For the purpose of determining gain, loss, and depreciation, an asset acquired from a decedent receives an income tax basis equal to the fair market value of the asset on the date of the decedent's death or, if the alternate valuation date was used in computing the federal estate tax (see §2.16), then its value on the latter date. I.R.C. §1014(a). To illustrate, assume an estate owner dies on November 1, 1985. The decedent owned an asset which has an adjusted basis of $10,000 and is valued for estate tax purposes at $25,000. The new basis of this asset will be $25,000.

---

[1] California, Colorado, Delaware, Louisiana, Minnesota, New York, North Carolina, Oklahoma, Oregon, Rhode Island, South Carolina, Tennessee, Vermont, Virginia, Washington and Wisconsin

Assets "acquired from a decedent" generally include all assets which are subject to estate tax in the decedent's estate, not merely those inherited in a legal sense. Those assets transferred by the decedent during his lifetime, but includable in his estate for estate tax purposes (see §§2.12 through 2.15), also receive a new basis. I.R.C. §1014(b). Although only one-half of the community property is included in the gross estate, both halves of a community property asset receive a new basis. I.R.C. §1014(b)(6). However, only that portion of a joint tenancy asset includable in the gross estate receives a new basis. The excludable portion retains the survivor's basis. The includable portion of a joint tenancy asset is discussed in §§2.7, 6.19 and 6.21. For the basis of an income in respect of a decedent item, see §2.50.

It is important to note that assets which are included in a marital deduction bequest (see Chapter 4) receive a new basis, even though such bequest is, in effect, not subject to estate tax. It is therefore possible for an estate owner, by utilizing the unlimited marital deduction, to pay no estate tax but still receive a new income tax basis for his assets on death.

§2.49   1.   Assets Acquired by the Decedent Within One Year of Death

Certain assets, however, do not receive a new income tax basis on death, but retain the adjusted basis which they had immediately prior to the decedent's death. These assets include items of income in respect of a decedent (see §2.50) and assets gifted by the decedent during lifetime, which are not included in the gross estate but which are added back to the estate tax base (see §2.3). The Economic Recovery Tax Act of 1981 also provides that the new basis rules will not apply to appreciated assets acquired by the decedent by gift within one year of his death, if such assets pass from the decedent either to the donor or to the donor's spouse. For example, assume that A transfers an asset with a basis of $16,000 to B, who dies within one year. Assume the basis of the asset is $15,000 just prior to B's death and the estate tax value of such asset was $50,000. If A receives the asset from the decedent, A's basis in the asset will be $15,000. If A subsequently sells the asset for its fair market value of $50,-000, he will recognize gain of $35,000. I.R.C. §1014(e).

§2.50   2.   Income in Respect of a Decedent

Income in respect of a decedent is a term describing the items of income earned by a decedent during his life, but not yet reportable by him before his death. For example, the decedent's salary is paid monthly. He dies a few days prior to the receipt of his paycheck. When received, such salary is reportable as income by the recipient, i.e., his estate or other beneficiary. I.R.C. §691. The recipient is, however, allowed an income tax deduction for the portion of the estate tax attributable to the income item which is included in the gross estate. I.R.C. §691(c).

As is indicated in §2.49, income in respect of a decedent does not receive a new basis on the decedent's death. Such income is taxed to the recipient in the same manner that it would have been taxed to the decedent if he had lived to receive the item. If the item is ordinary income, such as a salary payment, no offsetting basis of any kind is allowed; the entire amount would be taxable. On the other hand, if the income in respect of a decedent item results from a sale made prior to the decedent's death, the decedent's basis in the asset is subtracted from the proceeds of the sale in computing gain or loss. For example, the estate owner sells an asset with an income tax basis of $20,000 for $50,000 several months before his death. The payment is received by his estate after his death. The basis of the asset to the estate would be $20,000 and the gain to the estate, $30,000. This gain would, however, be reduced by any estate tax attributable to the $30,000 includable in the gross estate. See I.R.C. §691(c)(4).

§2.51 B. Property Acquired by Gift

Where the property is acquired by gift, the basis of the property for determining gain, depreciation or depletion is the same as it would be in the hands of the donor or the last preceding owner who did not acquire it by gift. I.R.C. §1015. The same rule applies for the purpose of determining loss, except that where such basis is greater than the fair market value at the time of the gift, the fair market value will be the basis for determining any loss.

I.R.C. §1015 allows an increase in basis for the federal gift tax paid on the transfer. For gifts made after December 31, 1976, the increase is limited to the portion of the gift tax paid on the amount by which the fair market value exceeds the donor's adjusted basis immediately before the gift. Hence, if A gives an asset to B with a basis of $50,000 and a fair market value of $70,000 and pays a gift tax of $10,000, B's basis will be $52,857 ($50,000 plus [2/7 times $10,000]).

In applying the rules for determining gain or loss in the case of property acquired by gift, it is possible that there will be neither gain nor loss. For example, an individual is gifted an asset which at the time of the gift has an adjusted basis of $100,000 and a fair market value of $90,000. He later sells the asset for $95,000. Since the basis for determining gain is the donor's adjusted basis, or $100,000, there is no gain. Since the basis for determining loss in this example is the fair market value, or $90,000, there is also no loss. Reg. §1.1015-1(a)(2).

§2.52 C. Holding Period

Where a capital asset is held for more than one year before it is sold, the gain or loss will be long-term. Long-term capital gains are taxed at more favorable rates than short-term gains.

The holding period of a gifted asset includes the holding period of the decedent or the donor. I.R.C. §1223(2). Hence, if A purchases an asset six months before gifting it to B, the six-month period during which A held the asset is added to B's holding period.

The holding period of an inherited asset commences with the date of death. However, all inherited assets are automatically entitled to long-term capital gain treatment regardless of the actual length of the holding period. I.R.C. §1223(11)(A).

VIII.   Recommended Reading

Hastings, "Income in Respect of a Decedent: A New Look Under the Tax Reform Act of 1976 and the Revenue Act of 1978" 37 *NYU Inst on Fed Tax* 43-1 (1979)

Conf. Comm. Report on the Tax Reform Act of 1976, H.R. No 94-1515, 94th Cong. 2d Sess (1976)

House Comm on Ways and Means, Estate and Gift Tax Reform Act of 1976, H.R. Rep. No 94-1380, 94th Cong. 2d Sess (1976)

Conf. Comm. Report on the Economic Recovery Tax Act of 1981, H.R. 4242, 97th Cong. 1st Sess (1981)

Standard Federal Tax Reporter (Commerce Clearing House)

Estate and Gift Tax Reporter (Commerce Clearing House)

Mertens Law of Federal Gift and Estate Taxation (Callaghan & Co)

Federal Tax Estate and Gift Taxes (Prentice Hall)

Rabkin and Johnson, *Federal Income, Gift and Estate Taxation* (Matthew Bender)

Planning a Small Family Estate

3

§3.1   I.   Introduction

This chapter will emphasize planning a small estate, particularly one where the estate owner has young children. If the estate is small and the beneficiaries are capable of handling and managing assets, outright dispositions are generally sufficient. However, other factors must be considered and further provisions made when the estate owner has minor children or there are older children or other beneficiaries who are in need of financial management.

II.   Planning for the Surviving Spouse

§3.2   A.   The Surviving Spouse as the Primary Beneficiary

Where there is an estate of not over $600,000 and each spouse wishes to leave the estate to the other, the surviving spouse should in most instances be made the outright beneficiary. Where the survivor has at least a minimum of financial capability, the use of a trust to provide management for the surviving spouse is ordinarily not feasible. A professional trustee's fees may be uneconomical in relation to the size of the trust. Moreover, there are no important tax considerations which require the use of a trust for the purpose of saving taxes upon the subsequent death of the survivor. Where the decedent dies after 1986, there will be no federal estate tax unless the estate is in excess of $600,000. (See §2.25.) If the estate is larger than the one discussed here, tax considerations may dictate the use of a trust. See Chapter 5 for a discussion of bypass trusts.

Even if the surviving spouse is to inherit the entire estate in an outright manner, where there are young children, the estate plan should provide for a trust into which the estate will pass on the survivor's death. See §§3.17 to 3.19 for a discussion of the trust for the children.

§3.3   1.   Are Wills Necessary?

The first question which arises in a small estate is whether each spouse needs a will to pass his estate in an outright manner to the survivor. If either spouse dies without a will, that portion of such spouse's estate which is not held in joint tenancy or is not payable by contract, such as a life insurance policy, will be disposed of under the laws of intestacy. In most states, a portion of the estate, under the laws of intestacy, will go to the children, even if one spouse survives. In some community property states as, for example, California, community property, under the laws of intestacy goes entirely to the surviving spouse. However, even in these community property states, at least a portion of the decedent spouse's separate property will go to the children. Hence, in many instances, unless there is a will, the entire estate will not go to the survivor and the couple's objective of having the entire estate go to the survivor will not be carried out.

§3.4   a.   Advantages of Having a Will

Even if the entire estate under the laws of intestacy goes as intended to the surviving spouse, there are important advantages in leaving a will. First, under a will the estate owner may name the persons or entities of his choice to act in a fiduciary capacity after his death, such as the executor of his estate. Second, the will may waive a bond for the fiduciary if the estate owner so wishes. In the absence of a will, an administrator will be appointed by the court and a bond may be required even if the administrator is a close relative or a major beneficiary of the estate. The bond premium, which is borne by the estate, is expensive in relation to the size of a small estate.

§3.5   2.   Alternatives to Having a Will

In a small estate, it may be theoretically possible for the couple to leave the estate to the surviving spouse without the necessity of each having a will. By holding title to their various assets in joint tenancy with right of survivorship, the assets will pass to the survivor by such right of survivorship upon the death of either of them rather than under the laws of intestacy or the provisions of a will. In a small estate, most assets can be placed in joint tenancy without serious tax consequences. See §§6.12 to 6.25 for a full discussion of joint tenancy. Moreover, if there is an insurance policy, naming the spouse as the beneficiary, the proceeds will be paid to such spouse under the insurance contract, again without reference to a will.

Despite the fact that a will may not be required in order to leave the estate to the surviving spouse, the estate plan would be incomplete without one. If both spouses should die together, or in any event, upon the death of the survivor, provision should be made for the children. To make such provisions, a will or other dispositive instrument is required.

§3.6   III.   Planning for the Minor Children on the Death of the Surviving Spouse

Presumably, as long as one parent is living, he or she will provide love, personal care and financial support for the children. Upon the death of the remaining parent, or if both parents should die simultaneously, arrangements should have been made to continue meeting the minor children's personal and financial needs. In most states minors are persons under the age of 18, although there are exceptions when those who would otherwise be minors are married or emancipated.

A. Providing Personal Care and Supervision for the Children

§3.7   1.   Appointment of a Guardian of the Person

The court will appoint a guardian of the person for the minor children. The parents' testamentary choice of a guardian, while generally not absolutely binding upon the court, is highly persuasive. However, the preferences of a minor 14 years of age or older for a particular guardian may be determinative, even over the choice of the parents. In no instance will a person who is unwilling to serve and accept the attendant responsibility be appointed.

Since the guardian of the person will be largely responsible for the upbringing of the children, the parents should give careful thought to this decision, preferably, while both are alive and can discuss their preferences and concerns together. Upon the death of one parent, the surviving parent will normally be entitled to the custody of the children. However, each spouse's will should reflect his or her choice of guardian in the event the other spouse does not survive.

§3.8   a.   Factors to Consider in Selecting a Guardian of the Person

The guardian of the person acts as a surrogate parent to the children for their custody and care, but is not responsible for any property they may own. In addition to providing such tangibles as food, shelter, clothing, health care, and education, for the cost of which the guardian will be reimbursed (see §3.12), the guardian of the person will be the person to whom the children will look for love and emotional support.

§3.9   i.   Continuity of Love and Affection

Due to the personal nature of the guardianship relationship, it is highly desirable for the guardian and the decedent's children to feel a close emotional attachment to each other. The parents should first consult with the person they intend to name as guardian of their children to ascertain the potential guardian's ability to accept so great a responsibility and his or her willingness to do so. If the children are mature enough, the parents should also determine the children's feelings about prospective appointees in order to select someone in whom the children have confidence and trust. A relative or friend of the family who has already established a close, affectionate relationship with the children and has a deep concern for their well-being is a positive choice.

If possible, the children should remain together rather than be separated into more than one new home. Therefore, the guardian selected should have the ability to take care of all of the decedent's children.

§3.10 ii. Age and Health of the Potential Guardian

Despite a prospective guardian's willingness to serve and an already established relationship with the children, practical considerations of age and health cannot be ignored. While grandparents, for example, may have the desired relationship with the children, they are usually a poor choice because of their advanced age and often poor health. The guardian must have the stamina, as well as the maturity, to undertake the responsibilities inherent in assuming the role of guardian.

§3.11 iii. The Family Situation of the Potential Guardian

In addition to the relationship between the decedent's children and their guardian, the manner in which the children and the other members of the guardian's family interact will be crucial in determining the success of the guardianship. If jealousy or animosity exists between the guardian's children and the decedent's children, or if the guardian's spouse is uncooperative, then it is best to make a different choice.

§3.12 b. The Financial Impact on the Potential Guardian

The financial impact of the decedent's children on the guardian and the other members of the guardian's family must be anticipated and provisions made to alleviate this added burden. The guardian of the person is not legally obligated to support the decedent's children out of his own personal funds. The fiduciary who is appointed to manage the children's property, whether it be a guardian of the estate or a trustee, will distribute the funds required for their support. However, care must be taken by the testator-parents to provide a sufficiently large estate to cover the costs of maintaining the children at least throughout the period of the guardianship. If the size of the estate is insufficient, the guardian will probably resort to his own resources, which could strain his family's budget and in turn create resentment toward the decedent's children.

To protect their children from this stressful situation, the parents should consider ways in which they can increase the size of their estate. Detailed investment planning is beyond the scope of this book, but insurance is one method of increasing the size of a small estate.

§3.13 c. Providing Financial Benefits to the Guardian

In addition to providing adequately for the personal needs of their children throughout the guardianship of the person, the parents may be wise, if their estate is sufficiently large, to authorize that some portion of the estate be used for the benefit of such guardian and his family. This will ensure that the guardian and his family do not suffer, even indirectly, from the presence of the decedent's children in their home.

Provision may be made in the estate owner's will to cover expenses arising out of the increased size of the guardian's family, but not incurred solely for the benefit of the decedent's children. For example, this could include the cost of moving to a larger house or enlarging the guardian's present house, and increased housekeeping and child care expenses. In addition, consideration may be given to providing some funds for the direct benefit of the guardian and his family, particularly if their financial resources are limited.

In fact, there are several reasons for the estate owner to authorize the use of funds for the direct benefit of the guardian and his family. The parents will probably wish to express their gratitude to the guardian for his or her willingness to assume the role of parent for their children. Also, if the funds available to support the testator's children will provide them with advantages which the guardian is unable to afford for his own family, the apparent discrepancy in lifestyles may very well cause the decedent's children to become objects of resentment more than if the estate were insufficient and they were dependent, in part, on the guardian for financial support. Thus, for altruistic and selfish motives alike, it is best if the arrival of the testator's children can improve the quality of life which the guardian and his family enjoy and be one in which all may share equally.

§3.14 B. Providing Management and Conservation of the Children's Property

Minors are restricted by law in their ability to deal with property. As a practical matter, children, even young adults, frequently do not have the necessary knowledge and sophistication to handle their financial affairs. Therefore, arrangements should be made for a fiduciary to manage the children's estates upon the death of their parents. Such a fiduciary may, in the case of minor children, be either a guardian of the estate (see §§3.15 and 3.16) or a trustee (see §3.17), and in the case of adult children will be a trustee.

§3.15 1. Appointment of a Guardian of the Estate

If the parents leave assets outright to their minor children either by intestacy, in their wills, or as named beneficiaries of an insurance policy, a guardian of the estate will have to be appointed to collect and manage such assets. Such a guardian may be designated in the testator's will, but the appointment will usually be made by the court.

§3.16   a.   Disadvantages of the Guardianship of the Estate

In almost all cases, the guardianship method of holding assets for minor children results in a poor estate plan, compared to the trust method. A guardianship of the estate has the following disadvantages:

1. A guardianship bond may be repaired and its cost must be borne by the guardianship estate.

2. The guardian often must obtain permission and approval of the court for sales, investments and distributions. This results in delay and added expense.

3. The guardian must file periodic accountings with the court. This results in the expenditure of accounting and legal fees which could have been avoided.

4. The assets must be divided between the guardianship estates of each of the children at the time of distribution to the guardian. They may not be distributed to a common fund and held for the benefit of all of the children. The required division may well become disadvantageous should it develop that one child has greater needs than the others. For the use of a common fund, see §3.18.

5. The guardianship terminates and the funds must be distributed outright when the minor reaches the age of majority. Particularly since the age of majority is now almost universally age 18, rather than 21, this termination constitutes a major disadvantage. It is unrealistic to expect an 18-year-old to have attained sufficient maturity to handle important financial matters. Too great a burden will be placed on the young person and he may misuse or dissipate his inheritance.

6. The income from the assets of the guardianship estate is taxable to the child, regardless of whether it is actually distributed to him. Reg. §1.641(b)-2(b). This may place the child in an unnecessarily high income tax bracket.

§3.17   2.   Use of a Trust

A much more acceptable alternative than the distribution of assets to a guardian of the estate is the payment thereof to a trust for the benefit of the minor children. Moreover, in the case of adult children who are not yet financially mature, a trust is preferable to an outright distribution, because the assets will be managed for them.

A trust is an excellent estate planning tool. It will eliminate the disadvantages of a guardianship. (See §3.18.) Moreover, it can be structured to provide flexible management for the beneficiaries who are too young or who, for other reasons, are incapable of management. Moreover, by giving the trustee broad discretion, the needs, as well as the financial maturity of the beneficiaries, can be taken into account in making distributions of trust income and principal. For suggested trust provisions for children, see §3.18.

A trust is also a most worthwhile receptacle for life insurance and employment benefits. By making the proceeds of this type of asset payable to a trust, rather than to the decedent's estate, probate can be avoided. See §§6.29 to 6.31 for a discussion of avoiding probate with respect to these benefits. In addition, by having these proceeds paid to a trust into which will flow the decedent's remaining assets, there will be unified management and distribution with regard to the entire estate.

The trust for the children may be either a living trust or a testamentary trust. For a full discussion of the type of trust to use, see §§7.34 to 7.37.

§3.18   a.   Advantages of a Trust

In addition to the beneficial uses of a trust discussed in §3.17, a trust will specifically eliminate the problems of a guardianship (see §3.16) in the following ways:

1.   Fiduciary bonds may be avoided.

2.   Court control, and its attendant expense and delay over sales, investments and accountings may be lessened or even eliminated.

3.   Much greater flexibility may be achieved where distribution is made to a trust rather than to a guardian. The management of the property may be continued after the minors have reached the age of majority. Moreover, a common trust fund out of which all of the children are supported, based on their needs rather than a predetermined manner, may be provided.

4.   Tax savings are possible in that income will be taxable to the trust rather than to the beneficiaries, except to the extent that it is actually distributed to them. I.R.C. §§641, 651, 652, 661 and 662. Where the trustee has discretion in making distributions, he may distribute or retain income in a manner which takes advantage of the possible lower tax brackets of the trust or the beneficiaries and the additional $100 exemption available to the trust (see I.R.C. §642). For a discussion of trust income taxation and the effect of the throwback rule, see §§8.44 and 8.45.

§3.19   b.   Provisions of the Trust

The major purpose of a trust for the benefit of children is to provide for their care until they are mature enough to manage their own finances. This purpose can frequently be achieved by certain commonly used provisions, such as the following:

1.   Typically, the trust instrument in a small estate will instruct the trustee to use the net income and principal for the support and education of the

estate owner's children. In determining the amount ot be used for the support and education of a child, it is in many instances desirable to give the trustee discretion to take into consideration any other income or resources of a child, including a child's ability to earn income if the child has already completed his education. In this way, the children can be encouraged to get their own start in life rather than becoming too dependent upon the support received from the trust during their formative years.

2.   The trust instrument may also provide that the estate be divided, usually equally, into a separate trust for each of the children, or it may provide for a common trust fund out of which all of the children are supported and educated in accordance with their needs. If the estate owner is concerned that one child may need greater support than the others, perhaps because such child is the youngest, the trust can provide that the entire trust estate remain intact for all the children, as a common fund, until the youngest reaches, say, age 21, at which time the then remaining trust estate is divided into equal shares, one for each child. The instrument may then provide that these equal shares be distributed or, alternatively, that they continue in trust for the benefit of each child as a separate trust. Each separate trust will then set forth the ages at which distributions are to be made free of trust, for example, one-third at age 25, one-half of the balance at age 30, and the entire balance at age 35.

3.   Spendthrift provisions may be included that will restrict the sale or transfer of a beneficiary's interest and protect the beneficiary's interest from the claim of creditors. If not for this provision, a beneficiary could defeat the purpose of the trust by borrowing money or otherwise incurring debts, conditioned upon assigning his trust interest to secure such obligations.

4.   The trust instrument should designate a trustee and provide for one or more successor trustees in the event that the appointed trustee is unwilling or unable to serve. Consideration should be given to which person or institution should be selected. If professional management of the assets is desired, it may be advisable to designate a capable corporate trustee to act either as a sole trustee or as a co-trustee. In small estates, however, it should be recognized that many institutions will not act where the asset value is less than a specified amount. In such cases, it is possible that a knowledgeable family member or close friend will be willing to act as trustee. Where an individual is designated, the trust instrument should specify whether or not a bond is to be required.

IV.   Recommended Reading

Seligmann, "Distributions to Children in the Sprinkling Trust" 114 *Trusts and Estates* 78 (1975)

Stiler, "Estate Planning Changes Necessitated by Statutory Reduction of the Age of Majority" 1 *Estate Planning* 2 (1973)

Whipple, "Who Should Be Property Guardian for a Minor?" 96 *Trusts and Estates* 1125 (1957)

Wicker, "Spendthrift Trusts are an Excellent Way to Leave Money to Someone Who Can't Handle It" 2 *Estate Planning* 202 (1975)

Williams, "Factors to Consider in Creating Trusts for Groups of Children or Grandchildren" 114 *Trusts and Estates* 140 (1975)

Wormser, "Pity the Poor Guardian" 8 *Univ of Miami Inst on Estate Planning* 1600 (1974)

Obtaining the Marital Deduction and the Community Property Exclusion to Save Death Taxes

4

49

§4.1 I. Introduction

The marital deduction and the community property exclusion are extremely useful estate tax tools. They enable married couples to leave all or a portion of the total estate to the surviving spouse, free of death tax. The community property exclusion pertains only to community property assets. (See §§4.34 to 4.36.) It excludes the surviving spouse's one-half of the community property from the decedent's gross estate. The marital deduction applies to the decedent spouse's separate property and such spouse's one-half interest in the community property. It permits such property to be deducted from the gross estate, if certain requirements are met. (See §§4.10 to 4.25.) The community property exclusion is available because, in general, under state law only one-half of the community property is considered to belong to the decedent spouse. (See §4.36.) In contrast, the marital deduction is entirely a matter of legislative grace and, therefore, a more complicated tool.

II. Marital Deduction

§4.2 A. General Description and Background

The marital deduction was first allowed by the Revenue Act of 1948. Its purpose was to equate, insofar as possible, the federal estate tax treatment of separate property with the treatment of community property. If it were not for the marital deduction, a spouse who built up a $1,000,000 community estate would only be taxed on $500,000 on his death, while one who created a $1,000,000 separate property estate would be taxed on the entire amount. Accordingly, from 1948 to 1976, the law provided that the maximum marital deduction was limited to one-half of the adjusted gross estate, which in essence meant one-half of the net separate property of the decedent. For the definition of the adjusted gross estate, see §4.5.

The Tax Reform Act of 1976 brought about the first major change in the amount of the maximum marital deduction. That Act amended §2056 of the Internal Revenue Code to increase the maximum marital deduction to the greater of $250,000 or one-half of the decedent's adjusted gross estate. Accordingly, in estates of under $500,000, it was possible to deduct not only the decedent's separate property, but also the decedent's one-half of the community property, if that were necessary to bring the total deduction up to $250,000.

The Economic Recovery Tax Act of 1981 completely eliminated any limitation on the amount of the marital deduction. For married persons dying after 1981, with the exception described in §4.4, the deduction is unlimited. Hence, a married person, regardless of whether his estate consists of separate property or community property, can now formulate his estate plan so as to completely eliminate any federal estate tax on his death.

B. Computing the Maximum Marital Deduction

§4.3 1. General Rule

The unlimited marital deduction, for persons dying after 1981, is computed by simply subtracting from the gross estate the value of the property passing to the surviving spouse. See I.R.C. §2056(a). For an exception to this rule, see §4.4.

§4.4 2. Computation Under Pre-September 12, 1981 Formula Maximum Marital Deduction Clause

The unlimited marital deduction will not apply automatically to a decedent's will or trust, dated before September 12, 1981, if it contains a formula clause expressly providing for a marital deduction bequest to the spouse. Congress felt that many testators may not intend to give more than the greater of $250,000 or one-half of the decedent's adjusted gross estate to the surviving spouse. For this reason, the Economic Recovery Tax Act of 1981 provides that the unlimited marital deduction does not apply to wills or trusts unless (1) the formula clause is amended to refer specifically to an unlimited marital deduction, or (2) a state law is enacted, applicable to the estate, which construes the formula clause as referring to the unlimited marital deduction. Economic Recovery Tax Act of 1981, §403(e)(3). No state has yet adopted such a law. For a description of how to compute the maximum marital deduction in those estates where the estate owner, deliberately or otherwise, has failed to amend his pre-September 12, 1981 will or trust which contains a formula marital deduction clause, see §§4.5 to 4.7.

§4.5   a.   Adjusted Gross Estate

For estates of $500,000 or more it is important to compute the adjusted gross estate in order to determine the 50 per cent maximum limit. I.R.C. §2056(c)(1). See §4.4. The adjusted gross estate, in an estate which does not contain community property, is the gross estate less the total deductions allowed under I.R.C. §§2053 and 2054 for such items as expenses, indebtedness and losses.

The computation of the adjusted gross estate may be illustrated by an example. Assume that the decedent spouse has a gross estate of $800,000. The expenses, indebtedness and losses total $200,000. The adjusted gross estate is $600,000 ($800,000 minus $200,000). The maximum marital deduction is therefore $300,000 (50 per cent times $600,000). If the adjusted gross estate were less than $500,000, the maximum marital deduction would be $250,000.

§4.6   b.   Reduction of Marital Deduction for Lifetime Gifts to Surviving Spouse

The "limited" estate tax marital deduction applicable to pre-September 12, 1981 instruments may have to be reduced by certain lifetime interspousal gifts. If the gifts made by one spouse to the other after 1976 and before 1982 totaled less than $200,000, the estate tax marital deduction will be decreased by the amount by which $100,000 exceeds 50 per cent of such gifts. For example, if the husband made total gifts to the wife during the period of 1977 to 1981 of $120,000, the estate tax marital deduction otherwise available on the husband's death will be decreased by $40,000 ($100,000 minus 50 per cent of $120,000).

§4.7 c. Community Property and the Maximum Marital Deduction

The adjusted gross estate, in an estate containing community property (see §4.34), where the decedent does not amend a pre-September 12, 1981 instrument containing a marital deduction formula clause, is the gross estate less the sum of the following deductions:

1. The decedent's portion of any community property which is included in the gross estate: For this purpose, community property includes not only assets which are legally community property at the time of the decedent's death, but also separate property which resulted from an equal division of the community property. I.R.C. §2056(c)(2)(C).

2. The total deductions allowed under I.R.C. §§2053 and 2054 for such items as expenses, indebtedness and losses, but only to the extent such items are attributable to the decedent's separate property.

The computation of the adjusted gross estate, where community property is involved, may be illustrated as follows: Assume the decedent spouse has a gross estate of $800,000, consisting of $600,000 of his separate property and $200,000 representing his one-half interest in the community property. The expenses, indebtedness and losses total $200,000, which are attributable to the decedent's separate property and his one-half of the community property. The adjusted gross estate is computed as follows:

Gross Estate		$800,000
Less Community Property Included in Gross Estate		200,000
		$600,000
Less:		
Expenses, indebtedness and losses	$200,000	
Less portion attributable to community property ($200,000/$800,000 times $200,000)	50,000	
Portion Attributable to Separate Property		150,000
Adjusted Gross Estate		$450,000

The maximum marital deduction in this example is, therefore, $225,000 (50 per cent times $450,000). The basic reason the maximum marital deduction is less in this example than in the one contained in §4.5, even though the size of the gross estate is the same, is because in this example the estate contains community property which is excluded from the computation of the adjusted gross estate. If the law did not require this treatment of the community property, the result would be unfair because the surviving spouse's one-half of the community property is already not taxed and one-half of the decedent's would be deductible, resulting in a tax on only one-fourth of the community property.

Although community property does not enter into the computation of the adjusted gross estate, the marital deduction bequest may be satisfied with a community property bequest. For example, if an estate consists of two assets, a separate property asset of $600,000 and a community property asset, of which the decedent's one-half is worth $300,000, the maximum marital deduction (assuming no expenses, debts or losses) will be $300,000 ($600,000 times 50 per cent). This $300,000 amount may be satisfied, if the decedent wishes, by leaving his interest in the community property asset to his spouse and the separate property asset to other beneficiaries.

As previously indicated, where the estate is less than $500,000, the maximum marital deduction is not computed on the amount of the adjusted gross estate, but a deduction of up to $250,000 is permitted. (See §4.2). Since this alternative permits more than one-half of the estate to be deductible, a spouse holding only separate property would have greater tax advantages than one holding community property, unless the $250,000 alternative limitation was made available to community property estates. Hence, in those estates where the $250,000 limitation is used, the community property will not eliminate the entire marital deduction. However, the $250,000 limitation will be reduced by the community property included in the gross estate reduced by its share of expenses, debts and losses. I.R.C. §2056(c)(1)(C). Hence, if the estate consists of community property, the decedent's one-half is $200,000, and the expenses, debts and losses chargeable to the decedent's one-half are $20,000, the marital deduction is computed as follows:

Maximum Marital Deduction		$250,000
Less:		
Community property	$200,000	
Less expenses, debts and losses	20,000	
		180,000
Marital Deduction		$ 70,000

§4.8 C. To What Extent Should the Marital Deduction be Used?

In determining the extent to which the marital deduction should be used in planning a particular estate, an analysis should be made of the estates of both spouses. Although the use of an unlimited marital deduction will avoid federal estate taxation in the estate of the first spouse to die, it is important to consider the fact that such a bequest will increase the taxable estate of the surviving spouse. Where the total estate of the surviving spouse is not likely to exceed the amount of the equivalent exemption, which will be $600,000 in 1987 and thereafter (see §2.25), it is usually advisable, from a tax point of view, to take full advantage of the unlimited marital deduction. However, where the estate is larger so that the amount passing to the survivor will be taxed in the survivor's estate at a higher marginal rate than it would have been in the estate of the decedent, a closer examination is needed to determine whether it is worthwhile to have some of the assets taxed in the first estate. (See §15.39 on the use of disclaimers in conjunction with a formula marital deduction bequest.)

For example, take the case of a married couple, where the husband has an estate and the wife has no estate at all. The couple desires to minimize the estate tax on each of their deaths by the use of an "A-B" trust plan. See §5.2. Under this plan, on the husband's death (assume he dies first), the marital deduction portion of his estate will go into the "A" trust and the residue of his estate will go into the "B" trust. The "A" trust is designed to qualify for the marital deduction (see §§4.14 to 4.24); the "B" trust, to give the wife, and, perhaps other persons, benefits during her lifetime, but to keep the principal out of her estate (see Chapter 5).

If the husband's estate is $1,350,000, and he leaves an unlimited marital deduction (i.e., $1,350,000, see §4.3) to the "A" trust, the entire estate will go into the "A" trust and none into the "B" trust. There will be no tax on the husband's death, but the assets remaining in the "A" trust will be taxable on the wife's subsequent death, resulting in an estate tax of $298,500.[1] It is not necessary, however, for the husband to leave the entire estate to the wife in order to avoid the imposition of any federal estate tax on the husband's death. As an alternative, he could use an optimum marital deduction bequest. Such a bequest may be defined as one where only the amount necessary to eliminate the estate tax would pass under the marital deduction bequest to the "A" trust. The balance of the estate would be distributed to the "B" trust. If an optimum marital deduction clause is used, and assuming no other deductions or credits, the "equivalent exemption" of $600,000 (assuming the husband dies after 1986, see §2.25) will be allocated to the "B" trust and the balance of $750,000 ($1,350,000 minus $600,000) will be allocated to the "A" trust. Under this estate plan, there will be no estate tax on the husband's death and a tax of only $55,500 on the wife's subsequent death.

In an estate of this size, it is usually advisable to use at least an optimum marital deduction bequest and thereby avoid paying any estate tax on the husband's death. The reason is that the top marginal bracket in the wife's estate (i.e., 37 per cent) is no higher than the bottom bracket in the husband's

---

[1] The federal estate tax computations in this example are based on the assumptions that the asset values do not change; the decedent dies after 1986, when the unified credit is $192,800; and the wife outlives the husband for a least 10 years so there is no credit for the tax, if any, on the prior transfer (see I.R.C. §2013).

estate. To illustrate, if the husband divided his estate so that $650,000 went to the "A" trust and $650,000 to the "B" trust, there would be a tax of $27,750 on his death and a tax of $27,750 on the wife's subsequent death, or a total of $55,500 on both deaths, which is no less than the amount which would have been paid if there had been a total deferral of the tax on the first death. On the other hand, if the husband's estate is $2,000,000, and an optimum marital deduction bequest is left to the "A" trust, $1,400,000 will thereby be allocated to the "A" trust, and $600,000 to the "B" trust. This will result in no tax on the husband's death, but a tax of $320,000 (with a marginal rate of 43 per cent) on the wife's subsequent death. If, however, the estate were divided equally, $1,000,000 to the "A" trust and $1,000,000 to the "B" trust, there would be a tax of $153,000 (with a marginal rate of 39 per cent) on each death, or a total of $306,000, or a tax savings of $14,000.

Where it is projected that the marginal tax rate will be higher on the death of the second spouse to die, the choice to be made is whether to defer the entire estate tax on the death of the first spouse to die or to pay some estate tax on the first death so as to reduce the marginal rate, and in turn to pay less tax, on the second death.

The following factors tend to favor the use of complete deferral:

1. The surviving spouse will have the use and benefit of the deferred tax money during such spouse's lifetime. In the above $2,000,000 estate example, the wife during her lifetime, will have the use and benefit of $153,000 more than she would have had if the estates had been equalized.

2. The income earned on the deferred tax money may more than offset the cost of deferral. Unless the wife, in the above example, dies very soon after the husband, the income on the $153,000 would more than likely exceed $14,000, the amount which would have been saved if the estates had been equalized.

3. The surviving spouse may reduce her estate during lifetime by consumption or a program of making annual exclusion gifts (see §8.3).

4. Any liquidity problem existing on the first death is eliminated. There may be a liquidity problem on the second death; but it is at least psychologically preferable to solve the most immediate problem first.

5. When the surviving spouse dies her assets will receive a new income tax basis (see §2.48). As a result, any appreciated assets will receive a higher basis than they would have if the estates had been equalized.

The following factors tend to favor the use of equalizing the estates:

1. Any growth, after the decedent's death, arising from the portion of the estate passing to the "B" trust is kept out of the survivor's estate. In the above $2,000,000 estate example, if an optimum marital deduction bequest is made and if 100 per cent growth occurs after the husband's death, there would be $2,800,000 in the "A" trust on the wife's subse-

quent death, resulting in an estate tax of $983,000. On the other hand, if the estates had been equalized, only $2,000,000 would be taxed in the wife's estate, resulting in a tax of $588,000. The benefit of equalization in this situation is a tax saving of $395,000 ($983,000 minus $588,000), which substantially exceeds the additional tax of $153,000 on the first death.

2.   The surviving spouse may be in a high income tax bracket and therefore would not need the income from all of the decedent's estate. Under these circumstances, the income from the marital deduction bequest will only increase the survivor's taxable income as well as his or her estate. By equalizing the estates, more income will be earned by the "B" trust, which can be structured as a discretionary trust so that the income is distributed and taxable to persons other than the surviving spouse (see §5.10).

3.   The owner of a large estate may wish to leave more than the amount of the equivalent exemption to persons other than the spouse, such as, for example, the children.

The choice of whether to defer the estate tax or to equalize the estates and pay some tax on the death of the first spouse is often a difficult one. The decision depends upon various factors which are difficult to evaluate when the estate is being planned. Fortunately, the tax law provides a mechanism whereby the choice can be delayed until after the death of the first spouse to die, at which time the decision may be easier to make. In the above examples, the husband can leave an optimum marital deduction bequest to the wife, but provide that if she disclaims all or any portion of the bequest, the portion disclaimed will pass into the "B" trust. By disclaiming, the wife can reduce the marital deduction bequest and thereby minimize the eventual estate tax payable on her death. For a discussion of the use and requirements of qualified disclaimers, see §§15.38 to 15.41.

§4.9   D.   Planning to Avoid Loss of Marital Deduction When Spouse with Larger Estate is the Survivor

The possibility of the spouse with the smaller estate or with no estate at all dying first should not be overlooked in planning the estate. See Weinstock, "What if the Wife Dies First?" 28 *Univ of So Cal Tax Inst* 55, 74-76 (1976). If no planning measures are taken, the result will be unfavorable from a tax point of view.

For example, if a wife without an estate is the first to die, on the husband's subsequent death the entire estate will be taxed. Consideration should therefore be given to increasing the wife's estate while both husband and wife are still alive, to insure that the wife's estate consists of at least the amount of the equivalent exemption. In that way, upon the wife's prior death, her estate may be left to a bypass trust or to the children and thereby reduce the death taxes which will be paid upon the husband's subsequent death.

The wife's estate can be increased by simply having the husband make lifetime gifts to her, such gifts being totally exempt from gift taxation. For a full discussion of interspousal gifts, see §8.14.

Another way in which the wife's estate may be increased is through the purchase of life insurance on her life. If the wife does not have a sufficient estate to pay the premiums, the husband will have to make gifts of money to her to enable her to defray the cost. Such gifts, however, will typically be eligible for the gift tax annual exclusion and marital deduction. Hence, there will be no gift tax cost for the buildup of the wife's estate by the face amount of the life insurance. The wife should be made the owner of the policy so she can make the proceeds payable to a bypass trust or to the children on her death.

§4.10   E.   How to Qualify for the Marital Deduction

Not all property included in the gross estate and passing from a decedent to the surviving spouse will qualify for the marital deduction. I.R.C. §2056 and the Regulations thereunder set out specific technical requirements which must be met for the property interest passing to the spouse to be a deductible interest.

§4.11   1.   Avoid the Terminable Interest Rule

If the interest passing from the decedent to the surviving spouse will terminate or fail because of a lapse of time or the occurrence of an event or the failure of an event to occur and then pass to some other person, no marital deduction will generally be allowed with respect to such interest. I.R.C. §2056(b). Thus, if the surviving spouse's interest will terminate upon his or her death or remarriage, the interest is terminable and does not qualify for the marital deduction. Similarly, no death taxes or other obligations of the decedent's estate should be made chargeable to, or payable from, the marital deduction bequest. Any such charge or payment will reduce the bequest and accordingly the amount of the marital deduction. I.R.C. §2056(b)(4). The purpose of the terminable interest rule is to ensure that property escaping estate tax on the death of the decedent spouse will be subject to tax on the subsequent death of the surviving spouse.

However, not all terminable interests are nondeductible interests for purposes of the marital deduction. (See §§4.13 to 4.18.) The Economic Recovery Tax Act of 1981 introduces a very significant exception to the terminable interest rule. If the bequest passes to a qualified terminable interest property ("QTIP") trust, and the decedent's executor elects to take the marital deduction, such deduction will be allowed. For a full discussion of "QTIP" trusts, see §§4.20 to 4.24.

§4.12   a.   Outright Bequest

Generally, an outright bequest to the surviving spouse will qualify for the marital deduction. However, it is possible to run afoul of the terminable interest rule inadvertently when spouses execute joint and mutual wills fixing the disposition of the estates. If a surviving spouse is _obligated_ to dispose of the inherited property upon his or her death to specific individuals, this restriction may cause the initial bequest to be one of a terminable interest and therefore nondeductible. But see §§4.20 to 4.24.

Obtaining the marital deduction through an outright bequest should be considered. It is the simplest form of bequest to draft and the easiest to understand. Not only are the costs of administering a trust avoided, but it also gives the surviving spouse full control over the handling of the assets contained in the bequest. On the other hand, an outright bequest to the surviving spouse may have certain estate planning disadvantages. First, if the subject matter of the bequest is still owned by the surviving spouse upon her death, it will be included in her probate estate and incur the disadvantages of probate. (See §§6.6 to 6.10.) Second, the estate owner may wish to place certain restrictions on the bequest, or protect it through professional management, and still retain the tax advantages of the marital deduction.

Either or both of the above disadvantages incident to an outright bequest may be avoided by the use of a marital deduction trust. (See §§4.14 to 4.24.) An estate owner who is confident that the surviving spouse will properly handle the marital bequest, but desires to avoid probate on the surviving spouse's death, can designate the surviving spouse as the trustee with full power to terminate the trust. The expense of an outside trustee's fee, as well as any concern on the part of the surviving spouse that he or she has no control over the management or use of the trust assets, will thus be eliminated.

§4.13   b.   Six-Month Survivorship Condition

Generally, if a bequest is conditioned upon the surviving spouse's outliving the decedent for a period of time, the interest will be a nondeductible terminable interest because it fails by reason of the occurrence of an event. However, I.R.C. §2056(b)(3) provides an exception to the terminable interest rule for bequests conditioned solely on survivorship for a period not exceeding six months after the decedent's death. It is also permissible to provide that the interest of the surviving spouse will fail if both spouses die as a result of a common disaster. However, in order to qualify for the marital deduction as a nonterminable interest, neither of the above-mentioned conditions may in fact occur, since in that case the surviving spouse's interest will have actually terminated.

In some instances, it is better planning for the bequest not to fail even if the recipient spouse does not survive either a common disaster or a longer period up to six months. This would be the case where one spouse has a much larger estate and the overall estate tax liability on both deaths is smaller when the maximum marital deduction is obtained on the wealthier spouse's death. In that situation, the will of the wealthier spouse should provide that in the event of a common disaster the other spouse is deemed to be the survivor.

If the interest of the surviving spouse is conditioned upon surviving for a period which may last more than six months, the interest will be deemed terminable even if such interest actually vests outright in the survivor within the six-month period. The surviving spouse's interest should not be conditioned upon survival to the time of distribution or settlement of the estate since these events may not occur within six months of the decedent's death.

§4.14 c. "Power of Appointment Trust"

Another exception to the terminable interest rule is a bequest to a power of appointment type trust. I.R.C. §2056(b)(5). Such a trust qualifies for the marital deduction where two basic requirements are met. First the surviving spouse must be entitled to receive all of the income for life, payable at least annually. (See §4.16.) Second, the surviving spouse must have a general power of appointment (see §2.8) over the principal, which must be exercisable alone and in all events, whether on death or during life. (See §4.17.) These requirements may be met as to only a specific portion of the trust, in which case the specific portion, but not the balance of the trust, will qualify for the marital deduction. (See §4.15.)

§4.15 i. "Specific Portion"

As is indicated in §4.14, a specific portion of the trust may qualify for the marital deduction. Under §20.2056(b)-5(c) of the Regulations, a partial interest in property does not qualify as a "specific portion" unless it is expressed as a fractional or percentile share of the entire interest as, for example, "one-third thereof." However, the Supreme Court has held that this Regulation is invalid, and that the bequest of the yield from a specific amount, accompanied by a general power to appoint, will qualify for the marital deduction. *Northeastern Pennsylvania Natl Bank & Trust Co v US* 387 US 213, 87 SCt 1573, 18 LE2d 726 (1967). For example, a surviving spouse may be entitled to $2,000 per month for life payable out of principal, to the extent that the trust income may be insufficient, and have a testamentary power to appoint the entire interest to himself or his estate. The marital deduction is allowable in an amount equal to the value of property which, at a rate of return available to a trustee under reasonable investment conditions, would produce the $2,000 per month annuity. Such amount could not, of course, be in excess of the entire value of the trust.

Just as the income share may be from a specific portion, the general power of appointment may also relate to a specific portion, rather than to the entire trust. If the income interest and the general power are not in the same proportion, the marital deduction is limited to the smaller share. Reg. §20.2056(b)-5(b). For example, if the surviving spouse is entitled to one-half of the income, but has a power of appointment as to all of the property, the marital deduction is limited to one-half of the property.

§4.16   ii.   Income Requirement

The requirement of a power of appointment trust that the surviving spouse be entitled to the income, payable at least annually for life, in order to qualify for the marital deduction is met if the effect of the trust is to give the surviving spouse "substantially that degree of beneficial enjoyment of the trust property during her life which the principles of the law of trusts accord to a person who is unqualifiedly designated as the life beneficiary of a trust." Reg. §20.2056(b)-5(f)(1). However, provisions granting administrative powers will not disqualify the trust interest unless the intent is to deprive the surviving spouse of the requisite beneficial enjoyment. Reg. §20.2056(b)-5(f)(4). For example, a power in the trustee to allocate receipts and disbursements between income and principal ordinarily will not cause the disallowance of the marital deduction; nor will a delay in funding a marital deduction trust because of a reasonable delay in settling the decedent's estate disqualify the trust interest. Rev. Rul. 77-346, 1977-2 C.B. 340.

The Regulations warn of potential pitfalls in granting certain administrative powers to the trustee. Two important examples are the power to accumulate income and the power to retain nonincome-producing property. Yet the power to accumulate income will not disqualify the interest passing in trust as long as the surviving spouse has the right exercisable annually (or more frequently) to require income distribution. Reg. §20.2056(b)-5(f)(8). The power to retain nonproductive assets will not disqualify the interest if the trust provisions require, or permit the surviving spouse to require, that the trustee either make the property productive or convert it within a reasonable time. Reg. §§20.2056(b)-5(f)(4) and (5).

§4.17   iii.   General Power of Appointment Requirement

To qualify for the marital deduction, the power of appointment trust must give to the surviving spouse the power to appoint the entire principal of the trust either to himself or his estate, or to both. I.R.C. §2056(b)(5). If the surviving spouse has the power to appoint in favor of his or her estate, such power, if exercisable during life, must be fully exercisable at any time and, if exercisable by will, must be fully exercisable irrespective of the time of such surviving spouse's death. Reg. §20.2056(b)-5(g)(1)(ii).

Where the trust provides that the surviving spouse has an unlimited power to invade principal for himself, this will constitute a power to appoint fully exercisable to himself. Reg. §20.2056(b)-5(g)(1)(i). In order to qualify as an "unlimited power to invade", the exercise of the power may not be restricted by any standard, such as insufficiency of income, or purpose, such as support and comfort. Additionally, if the trustee has any discretionary right to refuse payment following the surviving spouse's request, the power to invade is not unlimited.

To qualify for the marital deduction, the power of appointment must be exercisable by the surviving spouse alone and in all events. Reg. §20.2056(b)-5(a)(4). The power is not "exercisable alone" if it requires the consent of any other person, and it is not "exercisable in all events" if it can be terminated during the surviving spouse's life by any event other than his or her complete release or exercise of it. Reg. §20.2056(b)-5(g)(3).

The transfer to the surviving spouse will be nondeductible to the extent that a power is created in the trustee or any other person to appoint a part of the interest to any person other than the surviving spouse. The decedent spouse may, however, name the beneficiaries to whom the trust assets or power of appointment will ultimately go in the event the surviving spouse fails to exercise the power. For example, the estate owner may provide that, in the event his surviving spouse fails to exercise the power of appointment, the trust shall continue for their children.

Finally, the power of appointment may be either an inter vivos power or a testamentary power. Where the estate owner's objective in making the marital deduction bequest in trust, rather than outright, is primarily to avoid probate on the surviving spouse's death (see §4.12), he will normally appoint her as trustee and give to her both an unlimited right to invade principal during her lifetime and a general testamentary power of appointment on her death. On the other hand, where his motive in making the bequest to the trust is to impose management and control over the assets, he will normally appoint a third person or institution as the trustee and limit the surviving spouse's power to either a power to withdraw or a testamentary power, but not both. In the latter situation, a testamentary power is less likely to interfere with the desired management and control of the trust assets. Also see §4.20, for a discussion of a "QTIP" trust. However, an advantage of giving the surviving spouse the lifetime power to withdraw principal should not be overlooked. She will be able to use this power to make gifts of the trust assets and thereby achieve certain estate planning objectives which are discussed in §§8.3 to 8.5 and 8.9. A combination of a special power to make gifts, limited, for example, to the children and grandchildren, and a general testamentary power to satisfy the marital deduction may be advisable.

§4.18   d.   Legal Life Estate with Power of Appointment

The transfer to the surviving spouse need not be in trust in order to qualify for the marital deduction. A legal life estate with a general power of appointment will also qualify. I.R.C. §2056(b)(5). This type of nontrust marital gift is appropriate where there is no need to provide independent managerial judgment. However, even in cases where the surviving spouse is qualified to manage the property, it may be preferable to create a trust which names the surviving spouse as trustee. The trust arrangement provides an established set of rules which facilitate the management of the property.

§4.19   e.   "Estate" Trust

If a decedent transfers property to a trust under which all beneficial interest is in the surviving spouse, this "estate" trust qualifies for the marital deduction since no interest in the trust property passes to anyone other than the surviving spouse or such spouse's estate. I.R.C. §2056(b)(1). The bequest to the surviving spouse is not a terminable interest, but rather qualifies for the marital deduction as an outright bequest.

The estate trust differs from the power of appointment trust (see §4.14) in two major ways. First, income need not be paid at least annually, but may be accumulated solely for the surviving spouse or her estate. Second, the principal and any accumulated income must be distributed to the surviving spouse's probate estate on her death. Reg. §20.2056(e)-2(b)(iii).

Because income need not be currently distributed, administrative powers are not subject to the limitations imposed on a power of appointment trust in order to protect the income interest. The requirement that trust assets be income-producing, or be made so at the request of the surviving spouse, is also not applicable.

Where the surviving spouse's income from all sources is large and she will therefore be in a high income tax bracket, the estate trust may be advantageous when compared to a power of appointment trust or to a "QTIP" trust. (See §4.20.) The trustee of the estate trust can be given the discretionary right to accumulate or distribute income. In this way, income will be available to meet the needs of the surviving spouse, but, if distributions would increase her income tax liability unnecessarily, the income may be accumulated in the trust and taxed at a lower bracket. On the death of the surviving spouse, the accumulated income will be taxed to her estate under the throwback rule. For a discussion of the throwback rule, see §8.45. Since the estate was not in existence prior to the accumulation distribution, it is unlikely that any additional taxes will be due on the distribution. In addition, since the throwback rule does not apply to estates, the surviving spouse's estate can then distribute the accumulated income tax-free to its beneficiaries. As a result, the net taxes paid on the income will be less than if the income had been currently paid to the high-income widow or widower.

Another advantage of an estate trust is that it can distribute income in the form of appreciated assets. The distributee will receive a new income tax basis for the distributed asset equal to its fair market value at the time of distribution. Reg. §1.661(a)-2(f)(1). Moreover, unless the distribution is made to satisfy a specific sum required to be paid to the distributee under the trust instrument, the appreciation will not be taxable to the trust as a gain. Reg. §1.661(a)-

2(f)(3); Rev. Rul. 67-74, 1967-1 C.B. 194. In the case of an estate trust, a distribution in kind will not be considered to be in satisfaction of a specific sum required to be distributed by the trust because of the trustee's power to accumulate current income. By way of example, assume an estate trust has $10,000 of current income, and instead of distributing this sum in cash, distributes an asset worth $10,000 with an income tax basis of $2,000. The beneficiary will include $10,000 in gross income and will receive a new basis of $10,000 for the asset. The trust will not realize any gain on the distribution.

However, where a power of appointment trust or "QTIP" trust (see §4.20) is used, the income must be distributed currently. (See §4.16.) Here, a distribution of appreciated assets may be deemed to be in satisfaction of a specific sum required to be distributed and thereby give rise to gain, taxable to the trust. Accordingly, using the same example given above in the case of a power of appointment trust, the income tax consequences to the beneficiary will be the same but the trust will realize a taxable gain of $8,000 on the distribution.

There is, however, one major disadvantage in the use of an estate type trust. Upon the death of the surviving spouse, the trust assets must go into the surviving spouse's probate estate. The increased costs and other disadvantages of probate may be avoided by using a power of appointment trust or a "QTIP" trust.

§4.20 f. "QTIP" Trust

For decedents who die after 1981, there is an additional method of avoiding the terminable interest rule. This new tool is a bequest to a qualified terminable interest property ("QTIP") trust. I.R.C. §2056(b)(7). For the marital deduction to be allowed, the conditions specified in §4.21 must be satisfied and the decedent's executor must elect to take the deduction on the decedent's estate tax return.

Because this type of bequest does not require that the surviving spouse have the ultimate power of disposition over the trust assets, many estate owners will prefer it over the outright bequest, or a bequest to a power of appointment trust or an estate trust. For example, by using a "QTIP" trust, the decedent can leave his spouse the income only during her life and the remainder, on her death, to the children.

§4.21 i. Requirements

The most important requirement of a "QTIP" trust is that the surviving spouse be entitled to receive all the income from the trust, payable at least annually, for life. I.R.C. §2056(b)(7)(B)(ii). For a discussion of what constitutes a qualifying income interest, see §4.16. Thus, income interests granted for a term of years or life estates subject to termination upon remarriage or the occurrence of a specified event, other than the surviving spouse's death, will not qualify. To avoid a possible disqualifying technicality, the trust instrument should state that any undistributed income, on the surviving spouse's death, must be paid to such spouse's estate, or be subject to a general power of appointment in such spouse.

The second requirement of a "QTIP" trust is that no person (including the surviving spouse) can have any power to appoint the property to any third person during the surviving spouse's lifetime. I.R.C. §2056(b)(7)(B)(ii). For example, the trustee cannot be given the power to use trust property for the support of the children, but may be given the power to distribute principal for any purpose to, or for the benefit of, the spouse. The spouse may also be given the power to assign her income interest to other persons during her lifetime, without disqualifying the trust. Moreover, the Internal Revenue Code permits anyone to be given a power to dispose of the principal after the spouse's death. I.R.C. §2056(b)(7)(B)(ii). As a result, the trust could provide that the spouse, or even a third person, may designate which of the decedent's children and grandchildren are to receive the trust principal upon the spouse's death.

§4.22   ii.   Executor's Election

The value of the bequest to a "QTIP" trust is not automatically deductible. To obtain the marital deduction, the decedent's executor must elect to take it on the federal estate tax return. Once made, the election is irrevocable. I.R.C. §2056(b)(7)(B)(v). It may not always be beneficial to make the election, because, if it is made, the assets in the "QTIP" trust will be includable in the surviving spouse's estate. See §4.23. For a discussion of the extent to which the marital deduction should be taken, see §4.8. Pending the issuance of Treasury Department regulations, it is not clear whether the executor must elect to deduct the entire amount of the "QTIP" trust or whether he may elect only as to a portion of the amount.

§4.23   iii.   Inclusion in Surviving Spouse's Estate

Where the marital deduction is taken on the death of the first spouse to die, the value of the assets in the "QTIP" trust will be included in the surviving spouse's estate. I.R.C. §2044. Unless the surviving spouse's will directs that such taxes should be paid out of his or her other assets, the spouse's executor has the right to recover the estate tax paid from the "QTIP" trust at the highest marginal estate tax rate. I.R.C. §2207(A). For example, assume the decedent has children of a prior marriage. He leaves a "QTIP" marital deduction bequest to his present wife, with the remainder to the children of his prior marriage. Under I.R.C. §2207(A), the estate tax attributable to the "QTIP" assets on the wife's death will, in effect, be borne by the children and not by the wife's estate.

§4.24   iv.   Other Planning Considerations

In general, the chief advantage of the use of a "QTIP" trust is that an element of conflict between the tax objectives and dispositive wishes of many estate owners is removed. This tool enables the decedent to defer the estate tax until the death of the surviving spouse, without giving such spouse control over the ultimate disposition of the marital deduction bequest.

At least two factors should be considered before deciding on the use of a "QTIP" trust. First, the death tax laws of many states do not conform to the federal estate tax. In such states, a "QTIP" trust bequest may not qualify for the full marital deduction, where an outright bequest or a bequest to a power of appointment trust or an estate trust would qualify. As a result, the "QTIP" bequest would increase the state death tax on the death of the first spouse (but may reduce the death tax on the surviving spouse's death).

The second consideration concerns the income tax basis of the "QTIP" trust assets on the death of the surviving spouse (see §2.48). In order for these assets to receive a new income tax basis (which is advantageous where the assets have appreciated in value), they must be "acquired from the decedent by reason of death, form of ownership, or other conditions". I.R.C. §1014(b)(9). It is probable, but not entirely free of doubt, that this requirement is met by a "QTIP" bequest, even though the remainder interest is not acquired from the surviving spouse, but vests as a result of the first spouse's death. Since there is no policy reason for not having the "QTIP" assets receive a new basis on the surviving spouse's death, it is likely that the statute will soon be amended to so provide.

§4.25   2.   Life Insurance Settlement Options

Where the proceeds of a life insurance policy are paid outright to the surviving spouse or to the trustee of either a power of appointment trust, an estate trust, or a "QTIP" trust, they will be deductible for marital deduction purposes. When the proceeds are not paid outright, but in the form of a settlement option, the payment will also qualify for the marital deduction as long as the requirements of I.R.C. §2056(b) are satisfied. For a discussion of the availability of the marital deduction with respect to life insurance settlement options, see §10.33.

F.   Formula Clause Marital Deduction Bequest

§4.26   1.   Description

A formula marital deduction clause is one which achieves the maximum or optimum marital deduction in an exact manner. A simple example is a clause which leaves to the surviving spouse an amount equal to the maximum marital deductible allowable for federal estate tax purposes, reduced by the federal estate tax value of all other assets which have otherwise passed to the surviving spouse. Hence, if the total net estate is $800,000 and of this amount $100,000 is held in joint tenancy by the husband and wife, and the husband leaves the entire estate to the wife, the maximum marital deduction will be $800,000, of which $700,000 will pass under the clause. To illustrate further, assume the total estate is $2,000,000 and of this amount $300,000 is held in joint tenancy, and the husband leaves the optimum marital deduction under a formula clause, to the "A" trust, and the amount of the equivalent exemption to the "B" trust. (See §4.8.) In this case, the marital deduction will be $1,400,000, of which $1,100,000 will pass to the "A" trust.

The formula clause achieves the desired amount of the marital deduction by taking into account the property passing outside of the dispositive instrument and, also, outside of probate. In other words, it is a built-in stabilizer which, if properly drafted, will automatically result in the maximum or optimum marital deduction being obtained regardless of the size of the decedent's taxable or probate estate at the time of his death.

The maximum estate tax marital deduction was increased by the Economic Recovery Tax Act of 1981 to allow any amounts passing from the decedent to the surviving spouse to escape estate taxation on his death. (See §4.3.) In general, the unlimited marital deduction applies to estates of decedents dying after December 31, 1981. However, where the decedent's will or trust contains a marital deduction formula clause and was executed before September 12, 1981, the unlimited marital deduction will not apply to the decedent's estate. If this formula clause is not amended after September 12, 1981, or a statute is not enacted by the state where the estate owner resides, which construes the formula clause as referring to the unlimited marital deduction, the maximum marital deduction for that estate will be the greater of $250,000 or one-half of the "adjusted gross estate." Former I.R.C. §2056(c). (See §4.4 for the computation of the marital deduction under pre-1982 law.) Hence, absent the enactment of state law, if the estate owner wishes the new maximum to apply, he must amend his clause to *specifically* refer to the "unlimited marital deduction." Economic Recovery Tax Act of 1981, §403(e)(3). It is important to note that amendment of the will or trust to provide for an unlimited marital deduction will not be appropriate where the estate owner does not desire to increase the portion of the estate passing to or for the benefit of the surviving spouse.

§4.27   2. Advantages of Formula Clauses

A formula clause has three main advantages over a nonformula clause which attempts to estimate the amount of the maximum or optimum marital deduction. First, a formula clause ensures the maximum tax advantages of the marital deduction without unnecessarily increasing the taxable estate of the surviving spouse. (See §4.8.) Second, the formula clause eliminates the necessity of revising the will every time the value of the estate changes. Third, its use may be beneficial where there is uncertainty as to the amount or nature of the testator's estate. This could occur where transfers are made by the decedent during his lifetime, such as to a trust where he retains certain powers, and there is doubt as to whether the trust assets are includable in his estate. Unless a formula clause is used, the marital deduction may be less than the amount necessary to eliminate the estate tax.

§4.28   3.   Disadvantages of Formula Clauses

A formula clause, while generally advantageous, may have certain of the following disadvantages:

1.   The language used in a formula clause must by necessity be complicated. The clause may therefore be difficult for the estate owner, his executor or even a court to understand.

2.   Use of a formula clause may delay settlement of the estate until there is a final determination of the computation of the federal estate tax. All problems with the Internal Revenue Service regarding includability and valuation of assets in the gross estate, as well as the amount and extent of deductions, must be resolved before the marital deduction bequest can be determined.

3.   Since a formula marital deduction may vary with the value of the gross estate, many factors which change the gross estate could cause conflict between the surviving spouse and other beneficiaries. For example, if the fiduciary elects to use the alternate valuation date (see §15.27), the gross estate will be affected, and thereby, the amount of the marital deduction bequest as opposed to the size of the bequests to other beneficiaries. Reg. §20.2032-1(g). Also, the manner in which the fiduciary elects to claim administration expenses and losses as estate tax or income tax deductions may affect the size of the bequests to the surviving spouse and the other beneficiaries. (See §15.21.) To avoid possible apportionment of tax savings (see §15.25) and to assist the fiduciary in making these discretionary decisions, it is often advisable to include specific instructions to the fiduciary in the will or trust.

§4.29   4.   Selecting the Appropriate Formula Clause

Basically, there are three types of marital deduction formula clauses which have been in wide use. They are a true or strict pecuniary clause, a fraction or share of the residue clause, and a hybrid pecuniary estate tax value clause.

§4.30   a.   Strict Pecuniary Clause

A pecuniary bequest is one of a fixed dollar amount, such as "$1,000 to John Smith." Even when a pecuniary bequest is used as part of a marital deduction bequest, it is essentially a bequest of a specific sum.

An example of a strict pecuniary marital deduction clause is as follows:

If my spouse survives me, the trustee shall divide my residuary estate into two separate trusts, the marital trust and the residuary trust. The marital trust shall consist of that amount which will equal the maximum marital deduction allowable in my estate for federal estate tax purposes, reduced by the final federal estate tax values of all other property interests which pass or have passed to my spouse, under other provisions of this will or otherwise and which qualify for the marital deduction. In no event shall a greater amount be allocated to the marital trust than is necessary to completely eliminate the federal estate tax in my estate, after considering all other federal estate tax deductions and credits (but only to the extent the use of the state death tax credit does not increase the state death taxes payable) to which my estate may be entitled. The trustee shall satisfy the marital deduction bequest in cash or in kind, or partly in each, with assets eligible for the marital deduction; assets allocated in kind shall be deemed to satisfy this amount on the basis of their values at the date or dates of distribution to the marital trust. The residuary trust shall consist of the balance of my estate.

This clause, as any true pecuniary bequest, has certain characteristics. The bequest is reducible to a fixed dollar amount, namely, the amount of the marital deduction which is payable to the legatee. Hence, if the gross estate is $2,000,000 and the marital deduction is $1,400,000, it is this latter amount, rather than a fraction of the estate, which is owed to the marital trust. The amount owed must ordinarily be paid in cash unless the will provides, as the above clause does, that the executor has authority to pay the bequest in kind. The bequest, being a pecuniary bequest, does not share in the income of the estate earned during the period of administration, but may bear interest if not paid within a reasonable period after the decedent's death.

There may be income tax gain or loss consequences arising from the use of a true pecuniary bequest. If the executor must, or desires to, pay the bequest in cash but the necessary cash is not available, he will have to sell assets to raise the funds. Such a sale will result in taxable gain or loss measured by the difference between the basis of the asset and the amount realized on the sale. Ordinarily, the basis of an inherited asset is its federal estate tax value. (See §2.48.)

Where the executor has authority to distribute assets in kind in satisfaction of the pecuniary bequest, then the estate will also realize a taxable gain or loss by virtue of such distribution. *Suisman v Hartford-Connecticut Trust Co* 83 F2d 1019 (2d Cir 1936) cert den 299 US 573, 57 SCt 37, 81 LE 422 (1936). Where an appreciated asset, instead of being sold, is distributed in kind to satisfy a pecuniary bequest, gain will be recognized by the estate only to the extent that on the date of distribution the fair market value of the asset exceeds its federal estate tax value. I.R.C. §§1014(a) and (b). The basis of the asset to the distributee will be equal to the estate's basis, plus any gain recognized on the distribution. Hence, assume the estate distributes stock with a federal estate tax value of $15,000 and a date of distribution value of $18,000, in satisfaction of a portion of a pecuniary marital deduction bequest. The taxable gain to the estate will be $3,000 ($18,000 minus $15,000), and the basis to the distributee will be $18,000 ($15,000 (the estate's basis) plus $3,000 (gain recognized)). Any loss on the distribution would presumably be allowed despite the general prohibition under I.R.C. §267 disallowing losses incurred in transactions between related taxpayers. See *Estate of Hanna v Commr* 320 F2d 54 (6th Cir 1963); see Rev. Rul. 56-222, 1956-1 C.B. 155.

The following factors should be weighed when considering whether to use a strict pecuniary marital deduction bequest:

1. Where the executor is given authority to select the assets to be used in satisfying the pecuniary marital deduction bequest in kind, a variety of after-death planning possibilities will exist by virtue of the executor's power to allocate certain assets entirely to the marital trust while placing others in the residuary trust. If the surviving spouse, for example, will be in a high income tax bracket, it may be preferable to allocate tax-free municipal bonds to the marital trust, the income of which is distributable to such spouse, and high taxable yield assets to the residuary trust, where the income may be taxable at a lower rate. If a family business is involved, it may be desirable from the viewpoint of retaining control to allocate this asset to the residuary trust where no general power of appointment in favor of the surviving spouse need exist. But see §§4.20 to 4.24 on the use of a "QTIP" trust. Moreover, to the extent that it is possible to predict the future growth of an asset, the executor could allocate the growth assets to the residuary trust and the fixed value assets, such as bonds, to the marital trust. This allocation will accomplish tax savings on the surviving spouse's death in that the marital trust is then subject to federal estate tax while the residuary trust has been set up to bypass the surviving spouse's taxable estate. (See §5.2.)

2. In a strict pecuniary clause, the portion of the estate used to satisfy the marital deduction gift will always equal the amount of the marital deduction which has been computed based on estate tax values. Hence, if the value of the assets in the estate increases subsequent to the estate tax valuation date, the excess value will be allocated to the residuary trust where a second estate tax will normally be avoided. (See §5.2.) For example, assume the estate is valued for estate tax purposes at $800,000 and the marital deduction is $200,000. If after the valuation date the estate increases in value to $900,000, only $200,000 will be allocated to the marital trust, but $700,000 will be allocated to the residuary trust. Conversely, if the value of the assets decreases subsequent to the valuation date, only the residuary trust will suffer the decrease in value, while the value of the marital trust will be greater than it otherwise would have been for estate tax purposes on the surviving spouse's death.

3. As previously mentioned, the distribution of assets in kind in satisfaction of a pecuniary gift will result in gain or loss to the estate. This problem may be more apparent than real if the executor is given authority to select which assets to use in satisfaction of the legacy. Such power should

enable him, if he desires, to select assets with a high basis in order to minimize any gain. Moreover, the realization of a gain may sometimes even be desirable. The marital trust will receive a new basis for the assets equal to the federal estate tax value, plus the gain recognized. If the assets are depreciable or if the distributee will otherwise be in a higher income tax bracket than the estate, the realization of gain in order to achieve a higher basis may be worthwhile.

4. Where assets are distributed in kind, the strict or true pecuniary clause necessitates a second valuation of the assets in the estate being made on the date of distribution. This creates problems and additional work, particularly where the assets are difficult to appraise.

§4.31 b. Fractional Share of the Residue Clause

A fractional share of the residue marital deduction clause is not a monetary bequest, that is, it cannot be reduced to a fixed dollar amount; rather, it is a bequest of a fraction of whatever the residue is. Hence, if the estate is $2,000,-000 and the marital deduction is $1,400,000, no specific amount, but rather a 14/20th interest in the entire estate, is payable to the marital trust.

An example of a fractional share of the residue type clause where the residue of the estate goes into trust is as follows:

The trustee shall divide the entire trust estate into two separate trusts, the marital trust and the residuary trust.
1. There shall be placed in the marital trust that fractional share of the assets of my residuary estate, valued at the final federal estate tax value, up to the whole thereof, which, when added to the final federal estate tax value of all assets or interests which pass or have passed to my spouse other than under the terms of this trust and which are eligible to satisfy the marital deduction, results in the maximum marital deduction allowable for federal estate tax purposes in my estate. Anything in the preceding sentence to the contrary notwithstanding, if the aforesaid maximum marital deduction is more than is necessary to eliminate all federal estate tax with respect to my estate, after considering all other deductions, the unified credit and state death tax credit (but only to the extent the use of the state death tax credit does not increase the state death taxes payable in any event without reference to the availability of such credit), but no other credits, then the above-described fractional share shall be reduced so that it will result in the federal estate tax marital deduction that is necessary to eliminate such federal estate tax.
2. All of the rest of the assets passing to the trustee under this will shall be allocated to the residuary trust.

The essential characteristic of the fractional share of the residue bequest is that the marital trust will receive an undivided interest in each asset constituting the residue of the estate.

Insofar as the income tax consequences of this type of clause are concerned, it is clear that no gain or loss will arise on the distribution of the bequest. This is true whether or not the assets have increased or decreased in value from their basis to the estate. Reg. §1.1014-4(a)(3). As a corollary, the distributee will not receive a new basis for the assets distributed. The basis will remain the same as the estate's basis.

The following factors should be considered in the use of a fractional share of the residue marital deduction clause:

1. As previously noted, this type of a clause requires the distribution of undivided interests in each asset making up the residue. With certain assets, this may be impractical and unwise. For example, control of the husband's family business might be lost by allocating a fraction of such business to the marital trust where the wife has the ability through her general power of appointment to appoint to someone outside of the husband's family. But see §§4.20 to 4.24 on the use of a "QTIP" trust.

2. There is no opportunity to allocate growth assets to the residuary trust and relatively fixed value assets to the marital trust, as there is under a pecuniary type bequest. (See §§4.30 and 4.32.)

3. The fact that there is no recognizable gain or loss on distribution may be advantageous or disadvantageous. (See §4.30.)

4. The marital trust will automatically share in any increase in value of the assets during the period from the date of valuation to the date of distribution. If the estate increases in value during this period, the marital deduction gift will have a higher value than would have been the case under a strict pecuniary bequest. (See §4.30.) This higher value will increase the surviving spouse's estate. Conversely, if values decline during the above-mentioned period, the marital trust and hence the surviving spouse's share will be smaller than it would have been under a true pecuniary bequest. This will result in lower death taxes on the surviving spouse's death, but may also deprive the survivor of an adequate marital gift for his or her use during lifetime.

§4.32   c.   Estate Tax Value Pecuniary Clause

An estate tax value pecuniary marital deduction clause is similar to the strict pecuniary clause (see §4.30), except that it requires the executor to satisfy the pecuniary bequest with assets to be valued at their estate tax values rather than their values at the date of distribution. Hence, if the estate, based on estate tax values, is $2,000,000, the marital deduction is $1,400,000, and the estate is worth $2,500,000 on the date of distribution, the marital deduction bequest will be satisfied with assets with estate tax values of $1,400,000. For the effect of Revenue Procedure 64-19, see §4.33.

An estate tax value pecuniary clause might read as follows:

If my wife survives me, the trustee shall divide my residuary estate into two separate trusts, the marital trust and the residuary trust. The marital trust shall consist of that amount which will equal the maximum marital deduction allowable in my estate for federal estate tax purposes, reduced by the final federal estate tax values of all other property interests which pass or have passed to my wife, under other provisions of this will or otherwise and which qualify for the marital deduction. In no event shall a greater amount be allocated to the marital trust than is necessary to completely eliminate the federal estate tax in my estate, after considering all other federal estate tax deductions and credits (but only to the extent the use of the state death tax credit does not increase the state death taxes payable) to which my estate may be entitled. The trustee shall satisfy the marital deduction bequest in cash or in kind, or partly in each, with assets eligible for the marital deduction; assets allocated in kind shall be deemed to satisfy this amount on the basis of their values as finally determined for federal estate tax purposes. The residuary trust shall consist of the balance of my residuary estate.

This type of clause has at least three advantages:

1. Since the satisfaction of the marital deduction bequest is made at estate tax values rather than the values on the date of distribution, no income tax gain will result where appreciated assets are used. Unlike the strict pecuniary bequest, any appreciation on the date of distribution in excess of the estate tax values is not taxed. Hence, under an estate tax value marital deduction clause where the estate distributes stock with a federal estate tax value of $15,000 and a date of distribution value of $18,000, there is no taxable gain.

2. The executor is able to allocate certain assets to the marital trust and others to the residuary trust. This avoids one of the disadvantages of a fractional share of the residue clause (see §4.31).

3. A second valuation of assets, as required when using a strict pecuniary clause, is avoided because the distribution is satisfied on the basis of estate tax values.

§4.33   i.   Effect of Revenue Procedure 64-19

In an estate tax value pecuniary bequest clause, the executor has the authority to select the assets to be distributed to the marital trust. Therefore, he can select those assets which have depreciated in value subsequent to their estate tax valuation. In this way, the marital deduction bequest can theoretically be satisfied with assets which have substantially depreciated during the course of administration, thereby achieving a savings of estate tax upon the death of the surviving spouse. For example, assume the marital deduction is $400,000 and one of the estate assets has an estate tax value of $400,000, but a date of distribution value of $100,000. If the executor could use this asset to satisfy the marital deduction bequest and the surviving spouse dies shortly thereafter, such spouse's estate will have increased by only $100,000 rather than $400,-

000. The use of this type of clause to produce this result is, however, restricted by Revenue Procedure 64-19, 1964-1 C.B. 682.

Revenue Procedure 64-19 allows the full marital deduction where the estate tax value pecuniary clause described above is used, but only if one of the two following requirements can be met.

1. The fiduciary under the requirements of state law or the governing instrument must satisfy the pecuniary bequest by distributing assets having an aggregate fair market value on the date of distribution amounting to no less than the dollar amount of the pecuniary bequest; or

2. The fiduciary under the requirements of state law or the governing instrument must satisfy the pecuniary bequest by distributing assets fairly representative of appreciation or depreciation in value of all property available for distribution.

Hence, the estate tax value pecuniary clause, unless modified to include one of these two requirements, should not be used.

III.   Community Property Exclusion

§4.34   A.   The Community Property System

The community property system is in effect in eight states: namely, Arizona, California, Idaho, Louisiana, Nevada, New Mexico, Texas and Washington. The system in most of these states is derived from the Spanish law, rather than from the English common law of marital property. The basic principles of the community property system are common to all community property jurisdictions; however, the statutes of the various community property states are not uniform. The laws of each of the states have to be examined in order to determine the precise attributes.

In all of the community property states, an estate owner may also own separate property which in general has the same attributes as separate property of a spouse in a common law state. Residents of community property jurisdictions may also own assets in joint tenancy or as tenants in common. These forms of ownership have the same attributes as they do in common law states.

Estate planners in community property states will routinely inquire as to the source of a married estate owner's property interests and the date of acquisition so that a distinction can be made between community property and separate property. However, it is equally important for estate planners in common law jurisdictions, when planning the estate of a married person who lived in a community property state, to trace funds used to acquire his assets. Property interests may have vested in a spouse while the couple was domiciled in a community property jurisdiction even though they have since moved to a common law state. An estate plan which ignores these vested interests and the attendant limitations on the disposition of such property may be fatally defective.

§4.35   B.   Characteristics of Community Property

Community property, in general terms, is all property acquired during marriage by either spouse while domiciled in a community property jurisdiction, except property received by inheritance or gift. The earnings and reinvestments of community property are also community property. The essential characteristic of community property is that each spouse is considered to own one-half.

Separate property assets remain the separate property of the owning spouse. In most states the earnings of separate property also remain separate property; however, in some, such earnings become community property. Separate funds commingled with community funds, to the extent that they can no longer be identified, are usually regarded as community property. In some states the spouses may adjust their respective property rights by agreement and transmute separate property into community and vice versa.

In all community property states, each spouse has the right of testamentary disposition over his or her one-half of the community property. However, some states place the management and control of the community property solely in the husband, while others provide for management and control by either spouse alone or by both husband and wife jointly. In addition, most states place restrictions on a spouse's unilateral inter vivos disposition of community property. Several states require joint consent in order to sell, convey or encumber community real property, and a few require such consent for gifts of community personal property.

§4.36   C.   Tax Exclusion of One-Half of the Community Property

For all tax purposes, community property is treated as owned one-half by each spouse. Hence, for income tax purposes, one-half of the income belongs to each; for gift tax purposes, each spouse is deemed to make a gift of only one-half; and for estate tax purposes, only one-half of the community property is included in the deceased spouse's estate and the surviving spouse's one-half is excluded. The deceased spouse's one-half is subject to the unlimited marital deduction under the Economic Recovery Tax Act of 1981. This Act removed the provisions of prior law which disallowed or restricted the marital deduction for transfers of community property between the spouses.

§4.37   D.   Quasi-Community Property

In most community property states, assets acquired after marriage, but before the couple resided in the community property state, remain separate property. In California, such property is called quasi-community property. For purposes of divorce and inheritance, the nonacquiring spouse has certain rights in the acquiring spouse's quasi-community property. However, for federal tax purposes, such property is treated as the separate property of the acquiring spouse. *Estate of Frank Sbicca v Commr* 35 TC 96 (1960).

IV.   Recommended Reading

Covey, *The Marital Deduction and the Use of Formula Provisions* (Bobbs-Merill Co 2d ed 1978)

Crown, "How to Use Estate Trusts" 116 *Trusts and Estates* 87 (1977)

Friedman, "Choosing the Proper Formula Marital Bequest" 58 *Taxes* 632 (1980)

Kohl and Fisher, "Supreme Court Interprets 'Specific Portion' for Marital Deduction Purposes" 27 *Journal of Taxation* 12 (1967)

Polasky, "Marital Deduction Formula Clauses in Estate Planning Estate and Income Tax Considerations" 63 *Mich L Rev* 809 (1965)

Rosen, "How to Select the Proper Formula Clause to Fit Testator's Desires and Minimize Taxes" 3 *Estate Planning* 20 (1975)

Schaeffer, "Maximum Marital Deduction Clause Not Always the Best Choice" 5 *Estate Planning* 96 (1978)

Wren, "Planning to Avoid Problems Created by Moves Across Borders of Community Property States" 2 *Estate Planning* 216 (1975)

Bypassing the Second Tax

5

§5.1   I.   Introduction

Frequently, an estate owner with a substantial estate will wish to leave all or a major portion of his estate to another person, such as, for example, his spouse or one or more of his children. Leaving the estate outright to the beneficiary will, however, have death tax consequences on the beneficiary's death.

These tax consequences may be illustrated by an example. Assume that A, an unmarried person, leaves B his entire estate of $900,000. The federal estate tax on A's death will be approximately $114,000. B will thereby receive a net inheritance, disregarding state death taxes and other costs, of approximately $786,000. If we assume that B already has an estate of his own of $250,000, B's total estate after the inheritance will then be $1,036,000. If B dies with this size estate, the federal estate tax upon his death will be approximately $167,-760.[1] On the other hand, if B had not inherited A's estate, the federal estate tax on his death would have been zero. Of course, if B had not inherited A's

---

[1] The federal estate tax computations are based on the assumption that the decedent dies after 1986 so that the unified credit is $192,800. Moreover, if B dies less than 10 years after A's death, B's federal estate tax will be reduced by the credit for the tax on the prior transfer. I.R.C. §2013.

estate, he would not have received any benefit from it either. See §4.8 for a full discussion of the tax disadvantage pertaining to a married person, whose estate exceeds $600,000, who leaves the entire estate to the surviving spouse for the purpose of obtaining the unlimited marital deduction.

By the use of a bypass trust the beneficiary may receive the benefit of the inheritance and yet the inherited assets will bypass his estate for death tax purposes. For a bypass trust to achieve this tax result, however, it cannot bypass a person who is of a younger generation than the creator of the trust. If the estate of a person in a younger generation is bypassed, the assets in the trust will be subject to a generation-skipping transfer tax. (See §5.34.) A spouse, regardless of age, is considered to be of the same generation as the creator of the trust. Hence, where the value of the estate is likely to exceed $600,000 by 1987, a bypass trust, used in conjunction with an optimum marital deduction bequest, is the standard estate planning tool to use where one spouse desires the other to receive benefits from a portion of the estate, but wishes to avoid such portion's being taxed again on the death of the survivor. See §4.8.

There are generally three types of trusts for the benefit of a spouse which will be discussed in this chapter. The first type is used where the estate owner desires to give his spouse the maximum benefits from the trust consistent with the bypass of such spouse's estate for death tax purposes. The second type is created where the estate owner desires his spouse to receive only such benefits as the trustee, in its discretion, determines that such spouse should have. The third type is utilized where the estate owner desires that his spouse give up certain rights in assets which belong to such spouse in return for certain benefits out of the owner's estate. While there are variations of each of these types, the three basic types will be discussed in order to illustrate the governing principles.

II. Maximum Benefit Trust

§5.2   A.   Objectives

The first type, which may be called a maximum benefit bypass trust, is frequently a worthwhile tool in many estate planning situations. Let us assume a married couple with children who have an estate of $1,000,000. The couple desire to have the surviving spouse receive the entire estate, but at the same time they desire to reduce death taxes and maximize the amount which, they hope, will eventually go to the children.

To carry out the couple's objectives, what is commonly referred to as the "A-B" trust plan may be utilized. Upon the death of the husband,[2] the portion

---

[2] For the purpose of this chapter, the husband will be deemed to be the first spouse to die and the wife, the survivor. Similar principles apply if the wife has an estate of her own and the order of death is reversed.

of the husband's estate which equals the optimum marital deduction will go into the "A" trust, and the balance of the estate (i.e., the nonmarital deduction portion of the husband's estate) will go into the "B" trust. See §4.8 for the definition of the "optimum" marital deduction. The "A-B" trust may be in the form of a testamentary trust or a revocable living trust which becomes irrevocable upon the death of the first spouse. See §§7.1, 7.2 and 7.34 to 7.37.

In community property states, the plan may also provide that the wife's one-half of the community property will also go into the "A" trust, providing the wife consents to this disposition. In those instances where the wife will permit her one-half of the community property assets to pass into the "A" trust, it may be helpful for the trust to provide that the trustee, with the wife's consent, may allocate her one-half interest in certain community property assets to the "B" trust, provided the husband's one-half interest in other community property assets of equal value is allocated to the "A" trust. In this way, it is possible to prevent the fragmentation of assets and, for example, facilitate the allocation of the entire interest in a residence to one trust and the entire interest in a business holding to the other. Such allocation will not be treated as a sale or exchange for income tax purposes. Letter Rul. 8016050.

As an alternative to the "A-B" trust plan, the marital portion (i.e., the marital deduction bequest and the wife's one-half of the community property) of the estate could pass outright to the wife and the nonmarital portion would pass into the "B" trust. See §4.12 for a discussion of whether the marital portion should pass outright or in trust. In most instances, it is better to have the marital portion of the estate go into the trust (i.e., the "A" trust), if for no other reason than to avoid probate on the surviving spouse's death.

Assuming it is advisable for the marital share of the estate to be held in trust, the "A" trust can be structured in one of several ways. If it is the desire of the couple to leave as much power and control as possible to the surviving spouse (i.e., the wife), the "A" trust could provide that the wife receive all of the net income, have the unlimited right to withdraw principal at any time during her life, and have, upon her death, a general testamentary power of appointment which, if not exercised, will result in the remainder passing to the "B" trust. The part of the total estate going into the "A" trust will not be taxable on the husband's death because this portion of the estate will qualify for the marital deduction and/or the community property exclusion. (See §§4.14 to 4.18.) What remains of these assets on the wife's death will be included in her estate for death tax purposes for at least one of two reasons. First, she will have a general power of appointment over such assets at the time of her death. I.R.C. §2041(a)(2). Second, to the extent that she permitted her one-half of the community property to pass into the "A" trust, she will be deemed to have made a transfer where she retained the income for life. I.R.C. §2036. It should also be noted that where the wife has an unlimited right to withdraw principal from the "A" trust at any time during her life, any capital gains earned by the trust will be taxable to her and not to the trust. See I.R.C. §§676, 677 and 678.

If either spouse is concerned about giving the survivor the unrestricted right to withdraw principal during lifetime and/or a testamentary general power of appointment on death, the "A" trust can be structured as a "QTIP" trust. See §4.20. Such a trust can be limited to an income interest only, or can, in addition to the income, give the surviving spouse or a third party trustee limited rights to invade principal and even the power to dispose of principal on the surviving spouse's death. Where a "QTIP" trust is used and there is community property, the "A" trust should be subdivided into two parts, one of which is the "QTIP" trust and the other of which contains the surviving spouse's one-half of the community property. The part holding the surviving spouse's one-half of the community property, unless a forced widow's election device (see §5.15) is utilized, will provide the surviving spouse with full and unrestricted powers of withdrawal during such spouse's lifetime. Upon the death of the surviving spouse, the remaining assets in the "QTIP" trust (as well as such spouse's one-half of the community property) will be taxable in the survivor's estate. See §4.23.

The portion of the estate going into the "B" trust will be taxable on the husband's death. However, where the "B" trust qualifies as a bypass trust, the assets in that trust will not be taxed again on the wife's death; they will pass free of death taxes to the children or other remainder beneficiaries. For a discussion of the rights and benefits which may be given to the wife in the "B" trust without causing the trust assets to be taxed in her estate, see §§5.3 to 5.6.

Where the couple's underlying desire is for the surviving spouse to receive the entire estate outright and tax saving is the only reason for their use of a trust, more flexibility can be added to the "A-B" trust plan. Each spouse can arrange for his or her estate to go outright to the surviving spouse, but specify that, to the extent the surviving spouse disclaims the estate, the disclaimed portion will go into an "A-B" trust. Thus, when the first spouse dies, the surviving spouse can then decide, with better awareness of the conditions then relevant, whether to take outright ownership of the estate or to allow the estate to go into an "A-B" trust in order to achieve tax and probate savings on such surviving spouse's death. A disclaimer can also be utilized to enable the surviving spouse to later decide the amount of the marital deduction to be taken and the amount of the estate to place in the bypass trust. See §4.8 for a discussion of this topic.

In order for the surviving spouse to avoid being treated, for estate and gift tax purposes, as having transferred the disclaimed property, the disclaimer must be a qualified disclaimer. See I.R.C. §2518. See also §15.38. If the disclaimer is not qualified, the surviving spouse will be deemed to have made a taxable transfer of the disclaimed assets and both portions, that passing to the "B" trust as well as that passing to the "A" trust, will be included in the surviving spouse's estate by reason of the benefits and powers which the surviving spouse has in such trusts. See I.R.C. §§2036 and 2041. Prior to the passage of the Revenue Act of 1978, it was doubtful whether a disclaimer was qualified where it resulted in an asset going into a trust which provided benefits to the disclaiming spouse. The Revenue Act of 1978 makes it clear that such a disclaimer will be qualified, provided the person disclaiming is the surviving spouse of the decedent. See I.R.C. §2518(b)(4).

§5.3   B.   Rights and Benefits to Wife in "B" Trust

In order for the "B" trust to qualify as a bypass trust, the wife may be given substantial rights and benefits, but she may have no power over the principal which constitutes a general power of appointment for death tax purposes. I.R.C. §2041(a)(2). A general power of appointment is defined as a power which can be exercised in favor of the person holding the power, his estate, his creditors or the creditors of his estate, except that a power to invade for the decedent's benefit under an ascertainable standard is not a general power. I.R.C. §2041(b)(1)(A). Accordingly, consistent with the hypothetical couple's objectives of giving the wife the maximum benefits from the estate, she may receive, in addition to all of the net income, the following discussed powers over the principal which will not be considered general powers of appointment.

§5.4   1.   Power to Invade Under An Ascertainable Standard

The wife may have a right to invade principal, limited by an ascertainable standard relating to her support, maintenance, health or education. A power to invade under an ascertainable standard is defined as a special or limited power of appointment which does not cause taxation in the wife's estate. I.R.C. §2041(b)(1)(A). The Regulations under I.R.C. §2041 spell out what is necessary in order for the standard to be considered an ascertainable standard relating to health, education, support or maintenance. Such words as "My wife shall have the right to invade, for the purposes of her health, education, support and maintenance in her accustomed manner of living" are considered as adhering to the standard. Such words as "My wife shall have the right to invade, for her comfort, welfare or happiness" are not considered as conforming to the standard and will make the power a general power of appointment. Reg. §20.2041-1(c)(2). A power to invade characterized simply as for the holder's "accustomed manner of living" failed to meet the ascertainable standard requirement. See Rev. Rul. 77-60, 1977-1 C.B. 282. If this power to invade had been for the holder's "*support* in his accustomed manner of living," there would have been an ascertainable standard. The power to invade "in cases of emergency" also failed the test of an ascertainable standard because the power was not specifically restricted to emergencies involving health, education, or support. *Estate of Sowell v Commr* 74 TC 1001 (1980). Care should be taken to use the correct language suggested in the Regulations in order to avoid the inadvertent drafting of a general power of appointment.

Even though the wife's power to invade principal is limited by an ascertainable standard, it may not be advisable to give her the right to exercise it in favor of persons whom she is legally obligated to support, such as, for example, her minor children. Section 20.2041-1(c)(1) of the Regulations provides that a "power of appointment exercisable for the purpose of discharging a legal obligation of the decedent" is a general power. Despite the wording of the

Regulations, it could be argued that this power should not constitute a general power. It would seem to be unreasonable that a person is considered to have a general power of appointment if he can use property for the support of someone other than himself, while the power will be considered a special power if he may use it to pay bills incurred for his own health, maintenance, support and education. See Moore, "The Tax Importance of Ascertainable Standards in Estate Planning" 111 *Trusts and Estates* 947 (1972). In the interest of caution, however, the power to invade for the support of one's dependents should ordinarily be avoided. See Rev. Rul. 79-154, 1979-1 C.B. 301.

If the wife's power to invade is limited by an ascertainable standard, she may act as the sole trustee of the "B" trust. See Rev. Rul. 78-398, 1978-2 C.B. 237. If the husband desires that the trustee have a power to invade for a purpose which is not limited by such a standard, then an independent trustee should be provided for to hold and exercise this power without the wife's participation. Moreover, if the wife is in need of management assistance, consideration should be given to naming a corporate trustee either as a sole or co-trustee.

Even in a maximum benefit type of trust where the wife's powers of invasion are limited to an ascertainable standard, one should make sure that the administrative powers given to the wife-trustee are not so broad as to constitute a general power of appointment in the wife. See *Estate of Rolin v Commr* 68 TC 919 (1977). For example, it may be dangerous to provide in the trust that allocations of receipts and expenses to income and principal should be made in the sole and absolute discretion of the wife-trustee, or even in every instance under the particular state's Principal and Income Act. For example, under this Act, as adopted in some states, the trustee, where the trust is silent, has broad discretion as to whether or not to establish reserves for depreciation and depletion. See, e.g., California Civil Code §730.14. By investing heavily in depreciable and depletable assets and then by exercising her discretion against the establishment of reserves, the wife-trustee has the power to substantially increase the income at the expense of the principal. This may be considered an unlimited right to invade principal and thereby cause the assets in the bypass trust to be taxed in her estate. See *James L Darling v Commr* 43 TC 520, 533 (1965). It is therefore advisable to provide that, as long as the wife is acting as the trustee, reserves for depreciation and depletion should be maintained. Additionally, the Revised Uniform Principal and Income Act, as enacted in certain of the states, prohibits a premium paid on the purchase of a bond, absent a specific direction in the trust instrument, to be amortized against income. See, e.g., California Civil Code §730.07. To avoid the argument that the wife-trustee can in effect invade principal without the limitation of an ascertainable standard by purchasing bonds at a premium, the trust should require that these premiums be amortized.

§5.5   2. $5,000 or Five Per Cent Power

The wife may also be given the power to invade principal for any purpose (without being limited to an ascertainable standard) as long as the right is limited to the greater of $5,000 or 5 per cent of the principal per calendar year, on a noncumulative basis. Normally, the lapse (i.e., the failure to exercise) of a power of appointment constitutes a release of the power which, because of the other rights which the wife has in the trust, will, in turn, cause the released assets to be taxable in her estate. For example, because the wife is entitled to the income, the release of a portion of the principal will be deemed to be a transfer of such portion of the principal with the income retained by the wife for her life. (See I.R.C. §§2041(a)(2) and 2036(a).) I.R.C. §2041(b)(2), however, provides an exception to this lapse rule. The lapse of the general power is not treated as a release to the extent that the right to appoint is limited to $5,000 or 5 per cent, whichever amount is greater, of the value of the property during any calendar year, on a noncumulative basis.

Under the "five and five" power, the most that will be included in the wife's estate will be the value of the unexercised right which she had in the year of her death, because that would not have lapsed. Hence, there will be included in her estate either $5,000 or 5 per cent of the assets in the "B" trust, whichever amount is greater. All the amounts which had lapsed in the preceding years will not, however, be included in her estate.

§5.6   3. Special Power to Appoint to Third Parties

In addition to her other powers, the wife may be given a special power of appointment allowing her to dispose of the assets in the "B" trust to third parties either during her life or upon her death. The permissible donees may be limited, by the provisions of the trust, to a class such as the couple's children or descendants, or the power may be broad enough literally to permit appointment to anyone to whom the wife may wish to appoint, with the sole exception that she may not be empowered to appoint to herself, her creditors, her estate or the creditors of her estate. So long as the wife may not appoint to herself, her creditors, her estate or the creditors of her estate, the power will be classified as a special power, rather than a general power of appointment, and hence, the assets subject to the power will not be taxed in her estate. I.R.C. §2041(b)(1).

Giving the wife the above-described special power adds flexibility to the estate plan and conforms to the concept of giving the wife the maximum rights over the entire estate. At the time the estate plan is created, the children may be very young. The estate owner cannot know which of the children will turn out to be wealthy, which will turn out to be poor, which will marry well and which will not. The decision of how much to leave to each child, upon the wife's death, can be left for a later day by giving the wife this special power of appointment. The wife, by exercising the power, can not only designate the portion allocable to each child, but also alter the time or manner in which the children receive their shares. For example, she can effect a change in the trust provisions governing the ages when the children receive their shares free of trust. See §3.18 for a discussion of the provisions dealing with distributions to children.

The special power to appoint to third persons may cause adverse tax consequences where the wife, by disclaimer, permits a certain portion of the marital deduction bequest to fall into the "B" trust. See §4.8. It could be argued that the disclaimer is not a qualified one under I.R.C. §2518, because it failed to satisfy the statutory requirement that the disclaimed assets pass without any direction on the part of the disclaiming party. I.R.C. §2518(b)(4). If the disclaimer is not a qualified one, the disclaimed assets will be included in the wife's estate. Until the matter is clarified, caution should be exercised.

§5.7 C. State Inheritance Tax

Under certain state inheritance tax statutes (see §2.33), the gift of either a general or a special power of appointment is considered a taxable transfer from the donor of the power to the donee of the power at the date of the donor's death. See, e.g., California Revenue & Taxation Code §13694. Hence, where either the power to invade principal under an ascertainable standard (see §5.4), which is likely to be used, a $5,000 or 5 per cent power (see §5.5), or a special power to appoint to third persons (see §5.6) is given to the wife, she may be taxable, for inheritance tax purposes, on the portion of the principal of the "B" trust which is subject to the power. If the wife were not given these powers, the remainder interest in the trust would ordinarily be taxed to the children, which, if there is more than one child, will result in taxation at lower rates.

§5.8 D. Gift Tax

Where the wife is given any of the three above-described powers over the principal of the "B" trust, no gift tax problems will normally arise. If the wife has a power to invade principal for support which she is entitled to exercise, but fails to exercise it, the principal will eventually pass to the remaindermen. This release of her power will not cause a taxable gift, however, because a release of a special power is not taxable. (See I.R.C. §§2514(b) and 2514(c)(1).)

Similarly, if the wife has a noncumulative power to invade to the extent of $5,000 or 5 per cent per year, her failure to exercise this power will not be considered a taxable gift to the remaindermen, because the lapse of a $5,000 or 5 per cent power is not treated as a release. (See I.R.C. §2514(e).)

Moreover, where the wife has a special power to appoint to third persons, her exercise of such power during her lifetime will not cause a taxable gift of the principal. The exercise of a special power is ordinarily not subject to gift taxation. (See I.R.C. §§2514(b) and 2514(c)(1).) However, where the wife is entitled to the income from the trust and she exercises her special power to appoint principal to third persons, she will be deemed to have made a taxable gift of a pro rata portion of the income interest. Rev. Rul. 79-327, 1979-2 C.B. 342.

§5.9   III.   Discretionary Trust

The second type of bypass trust for the surviving spouse, which may be called a discretionary trust, is frequently recommended in the following situation. Let us assume that the married couple discussed in §5.2 has an estate of $3,000,000 and that the husband desires to plan the estate in such a way as to have the estate managed for his wife and the trust assets used to support her fully during her lifetime, consistent with saving death taxes on her death and income taxes during her life, as well as ensuring that at least a portion of the total estate will ultimately go for the benefit of their children. These objectives may be achieved for the nonmarital deduction portion of the estate by a discretionary type "B" trust, which is one whereby, during the wife's lifetime, the trustee has discretion to accumulate income and to distribute (i.e., "sprinkle") the income and principal to the wife and the children.

§5.10   A.   Advantages

In general, there are three estate planning advantages which can be obtained, particularly in a larger estate, by using a discretionary bypass trust in preference to a maximum benefit trust. First, a discretionary trust makes possible a flexible pattern of distribution. The income can be distributed to those persons who are in need at the time they are in need. Second, the beneficiaries, by careful planning, may receive more favorable income tax treatment. Income may be distributed currently to persons who are in a low income tax bracket (e.g., the children) or the trust may accumulate all or part of its income. The trust, as a separate tax entity, pays income tax on the accumulated income during the year in which it is earned. I.R.C. §§641 and 661. When accumulated income is later distributed, it is subject to the throwback rule (I.R.C. §§665 through 669), but where the distributee, after making the throwback computation, is in a lower income tax bracket than the wife, the income will effectively have been taxed at a lower rate than if it had been currently distributed to her. (For a discussion of the throwback rule, see §8.45). Third, this type of trust, if the wife is not given powers which for tax purposes are considered general powers of appointment, will not only bypass the wife's estate, but will result in further minimizing the death taxes upon her death. By failing to distribute the income from the "B" trust to the wife, the trustee will, in effect, cause the wife to utilize the principal of the "A" trust to support herself. Reducing the "A" trust will reduce the estate tax upon the wife's death.

§5.11 B. Specific Considerations

Before using a discretionary type bypass trust, certain specific tax considerations should, however, be taken into account.

§5.12 1. Trustee's Right to Sprinkle to a Dependent Person

If the trustee's power to distribute income may be exercised only if needed for the support of a person whom another person is obligated to support, such as, for example, the wife's minor children, the income, to the extent distributed for the support of the minor children, will be taxed to the wife. Reg. §1.662(a)-(4). The trustee's sprinkling power should therefore be carefully drafted so that income may be distributed for nonsupport purposes.

§5.13 2. Substantial Owner Under I.R.C. §678

The wife, even where she is not a trustee, may suffer income tax consequences where she has the power to invade the principal of the discretionary "B" trust despite the fact that her power is a noncumulative power to invade up to $5,000 or 5 per cent, whichever is greater. Arguably, the wife will be taxed on the income earned by the trust up to an amount equal to the principal that she could have invaded, unless her power over the income is limited to an ascertainable standard. I.R.C. §678(a). Hence, these powers should be avoided in a discretionary type bypass trust.

§5.14 3. Trustee with a Sprinkling Power Should Not Also be a Beneficiary

Where the wife-beneficiary in a discretionary type bypass trust is also a trustee, there will be income, estate and gift tax problems. For income tax purposes, the wife will be taxable on the income of the trust where she has the sole power to vest the income in herself. I.R.C. §678(a). Moreover, where the wife, as trustee, has the power to sprinkle to persons whom she must support, any amounts of support actually paid out are taxable to her on the theory that she is vesting the income in herself. I.R.C. §678(c). With this in mind, the wife should not act as the sole trustee.

Insofar as estate taxes are concerned, where the wife-beneficiary is a trustee of a sprinkling trust, even only a co-trustee, and her discretionary powers to distribute income and principal are not limited by an ascertainable standard, she will be deemed to have a general power of appointment with respect to the trust assets. On her death, these assets will be includable in her estate. See I.R.C. §2041(b)(1)(C).

Lastly, the gift tax consequences should be examined. Where the wife-trustee uses her broad discretionary power to distribute the income or principal to third persons whom she is not obligated to support, she will be considered to have made a taxable gift. Taxability results because she will be deemed to have exercised her general power of appointment. I.R.C. §2514(b). All of the above tax consequences will also be present even where the wife-beneficiary is not a trustee, but has the power to remove the trustee and appoint herself as a successor.

Where the couple, for purposes of controlling investments, desires the wife to be a co-trustee, the above-mentioned adverse tax results may be avoided by having the trust instrument state that the discretionary distribution powers shall be exercised solely by the independent co-trustee.

§5.15   IV.   Widow's (or Widower's) Election Trust

The third type of trust for a surviving spouse is a widow's (or widower's) election trust. The widow's election is most commonly used in community property situations. For a discussion of community property, see §§4.34 to 4.36. Many of the same principles are applicable even where the assets are owned as separate property as long as the estate owner is willing to condition the bequest of all or part of his estate upon the recipient's giving up certain rights in the recipient's own assets. Where one spouse does not have an estate, the wealthier spouse may make unlimited tax-free lifetime gifts to the poorer spouse to equalize the estates. (See §2.42.) Accordingly, while the discussion which follows in this section and §§5.16 to 5.31 assumes a married couple owning community property, the reader should bear in mind that the widow's election device may also be used in a non-community property jurisdiction. The reader should also realize that the discussion which follows assumes, for convenience, that the wife is the surviving spouse. Identical principles apply if the husband is the survivor and he is put to an election by the wife.

The widow's election trust is useful in the following situation. Let us assume that the married couple discussed in §5.2 has an estate of $2,000,000 consisting of community property assets. The husband desires to plan the estate in such a way as to provide for independent management of the entire estate, including the wife's one-half, with the income from both halves being paid to her. He also desires that, upon the wife's subsequent death, she have no power of disposition over either half of the estate, but that both halves automatically go to the children. Therefore, the husband leaves his one-half of the community property to a trust whereby the widow will receive the income for her life, with the remainder going to the children on her death, on the condition that she transfer her estate at the time of the husband's death to the same or a similar trust. For a discussion of the "new" type of widow's election, see §5.16.

§5.16   A.   What is the Widow's Election?

The widow's election is a plan whereby the husband attempts to dispose of both halves of the community property. He does this despite the fact that under most community property systems the first spouse to die has no right of testamentary disposition over the other spouse's one-half of the community property. For example, see California Civil Code §§5105 and 5125. He thereby forces the widow to choose between claiming her one-half outright or receiving the benefits given to her out of his one-half. Unless the widow, after the husband's death, affirmatively elects to accept the husband's plan, she will receive her one-half of the community property, but she will forfeit any benefits from the husband's one-half.

There is another kind of device which is frequently called a widow's election, but under which the widow is not forced to choose between receiving her one-half of the community property or the benefits given to her under the husband's will. This plan is sometimes called a "voluntary" widow's election. Here, the husband attempts to dispose of both halves of the community property, but his will or other dispositive instrument permits the widow to receive the benefits given to her out of the husband's one-half, even if she elects to take her one-half outright. This type of plan is used to persuade, but not force, the widow to give up her powers of management and right of disposition over her one-half of the community property. Where the husband's will provides for both halves to go into a trust, the plan is also used to avoid a probate on the widow's subsequent death. The discussion which follows in this chapter is devoted to the "nonvoluntary" widow's election. Where the term "widow's election" is used hereafter, it will mean a "forced" widow's election.

In turn, there are two types of "forced" widow's election plans. The first (sometimes called the "traditional" type) is where the widow is given the income for life from both halves of the community property, but nothing from the principal, which upon her death goes to other beneficiaries, such as, for example, the children. Under the second type (sometimes called the "new" type), the widow is given both the income and principal from the husband's one-half of the community property but from her own one-half, which she is required to place in the "widow's election trust," she is to receive only the income.

The tax objective of each type of forced widow's election is to obtain as large a marital deduction as possible on the husband's death and to exclude all, or as large a portion as possible, of the widow's one-half of the community property contained in the widow's election trust from her estate on her subsequent death. For a detailed discussion of the tax consequences of the widow's election, see §§5.18 to 5.31.

§5.17 B. Nontax Reasons for Using a Widow's Election Plan

There are essentially three reasons, apart from tax considerations, for using a widow's election plan. They are: (1) to provide management for the widow during her lifetime; (2) to prevent the widow from disposing of her one-half of the community property on her subsequent death, so that the ultimate beneficiaries are those named in the husband's will or other dispositive instrument; and (3) by providing that the widow's one-half goes into a trust on the husband's death, to avoid probate of her one-half of the community property on her subsequent death. For the nontax reasons for not using a widow's election plan, see §5.25.

§5.18 C. Tax Consequences of "Traditional" Widow's Election

The tax consequences of the "traditional" widow's election are complicated, but to some extent may be simplified by a basic example which, with variations, will be referred to in the discussion of the various tax consequences. Assume that the husband leaves an estate consisting of $2,000,000 of community property assets, which, after charging his one-half, on his death, with $50,000 of expenses, results in an allocation of $1,000,000 to the widow's one-half of the community property and $950,000 to the decedent husband's one-half of the community property. His will, if the widow elects to take under it, leaves to the widow the income only from both halves of the community property, but none of the principal. If the widow elects against the will, she will receive her one-half of the community property outright, but nothing from the husband's one-half. The widow is 65 years of age at the time of the husband's death.

§5.19 1. Death Taxes on the Husband's Death

On the husband's death the community property exclusion as to the wife's one-half of the community property is available. Consequently, only the husband's one-half of the community property, namely $1,000,000, is includable in his gross estate. Rev. Rul. 67-383, 1967-2 C.B. 325.

The crucial consideration, however, is whether and to what extent the husband's one-half of the community property will qualify for the marital deduction. If the fact that the widow is put to an election is ignored, the husband's disposition could qualify as a "QTIP" trust (see §§4.20 to 4.24) because the wife is to receive the income for life. The husband's estate, under the facts of the basic example, would then be entitled to a marital deduction of $950,000. Where, however, the widow must give up the remainder interest in her one-half of the community property to receive the income from the "QTIP" trust, the marital deduction, at the very least, will be reduced by the value of the remainder interest in her one-half of the community property. *US v Stapf* 375 US 118, 84 SCt 248, 11 LE2d 195 (1963); see Weinstock, "Beyond Freezes: Planning to Reduce the Taxable Estate" 16 *Univ of Miami Inst on Estate Planning* ¶502.2 (1982). At age 65, the value of this remainder interest would be $441,-970 ($1,000,000 times .44197, see Table A, Reg. §20.2031-10). See Appendix, Table VIII. Subtracting her remainder interest of $441,970 from $950,000, the allowable amount of the marital deduction would therefore be $508,030 instead of $950,000.

If the amount of the decrease in the marital deduction does not exceed the amount of the equivalent exemption (see §2.25) in the year of the husband's death, such decrease will ordinarily have no significant consequence. In the above example, if the husband's death occurred after 1985, the amount of the equivalent exemption would exceed the $441,970 reduction in the marital deduction. As a result, there will be no estate tax payable on the husband's death. However, if the wife were older at the time of the husband's death, or the estate were larger in value, the value of the wife's remainder interest and thereby the reduction in the amount of the husband's marital deduction would also be greater. If the wife were 80 at the time of the husband's death, in the above example, the value of the remainder interest in her one-half of the community property would be $698,830.

§5.20   2.   Gift Tax to Widow

Upon the husband's death, the widow will ordinarily be deemed to have made a taxable gift of the value of the remainder interest in her one-half of the community property less the consideration which she receives from the husband's one-half of the community property. *Commr v Siegel* 250 F2d 339 (9th Cir 1957). In the basic example (see §5.18), the consideration which the widow receives is the value of the income interest. By reference to Table A, Reg. §§20.2031-10 and 25.2512-9 (see Appendix, Table VIII), the remainder interest surrendered is worth $441,970 ($1,000,000 times .44197) and the income interest received is worth $530,129 ($950,000 times .55803). Because the widow is receiving more than she is giving up, there is no taxable gift by the widow to the remaindermen. The greater the age of the widow at the time of the husband's death, the more likelihood there is that the value of the remainder interest in her one-half of the community property will exceed the value of the income interest in the husband's one-half of such property. In the basic example, if she were 80 years of age instead of 65, there would be a taxable gift to the remaindermen of $412,718.

The potential gift tax problem illustrated above may be eliminated by the husband's permitting the widow to retain a power of appointment over the remainder interest. Either a general power or a special power will render the transfer "incomplete," and no gift will result. Reg. §25.2511-2(c).

Even if the gift tax problem is eliminated by the use of a power of appointment, the fact that the value of what the widow gives up exceeds the value of what she receives will destroy the widow's election as an effective tax planning device. There will have been an undue reduction in the amount of the marital deduction and, at the same time, the optimum estate tax benefit on her subsequent death (see §5.16) will not have been achieved. Hence, the widow's election, particularly if the widow is elderly, should not be used where the husband's one-half of the community property is left to the widow in the form of a "QTIP" bequest rather than as an outright bequest. (See §5.26.)

§5.21   3.   Income Taxes

There are two important income tax considerations which should be taken into account in connection with the use of a "traditional" widow's election.

One is the income tax consequences to the widow as a result of receiving the income from the entire estate. The other is the potential income tax consequences to the husband's estate as a result of the "transfer" of the income interest to the widow.

§5.22   a.   Income Tax to the Widow

The widow has two separate income tax considerations where she elects to take under the will. First, she may realize taxable gain on the transfer of her remainder interest in her one-half interest in the community property in exchange for the husband's one-half interest. Second, she should realize that she will receive all of the income from both halves of the community property, which may put her in a high income tax bracket.

Insofar as the first consideration is concerned, the widow will be deemed to have made a taxable exchange of a remainder interest in her one-half of the community property in return for the income interest from her husband's one-half. See Freeland, Lind and Stephens, "What Are The Income Tax Effects of An Estate's Sale of a Life Interest?" 34 *Journal of Taxation* 376 (1971). The gain will be measured by subtracting the widow's income tax basis in the remainder interest from the lesser of (1) the value of the income interest, or (2) the value of the remainder interest. The widow's remainder interest, if it is community property, will receive a new basis on the husband's death. I.R.C. §1014(b)(6). Thus, only the appreciation accruing between the date of the husband's death and the time of the exchange will be taxed.

Using the facts of the basic example (see §§5.18 and 5.20) where the value of the widow's remainder interest on the date of the exchange is $441,970 and the value of the income interest in the husband's estate is $530,129, and assuming the basis of the widow's remainder interest is $400,000, the taxable gain to the widow will be $41,970 ($441,970 minus $400,000). The amount by which the value of the income interest exceeds the value of the remainder interest, i.e., $88,159 ($530,129 minus $441,970) constitutes a testamentary gift from the husband to the widow. Conversely, if the value of the income interest in the husband's estate were only $420,000, the taxable gain would be $20,000 ($420,000 minus $400,000). In the latter situation, the amount by which the value of the widow's remainder interest exceeds the value of the income interest in the husband's estate, i.e., $21,970 ($441,970 minus $420,000) will be a taxable gift by the widow (see §5.20). Whatever the amount of the gain, it will be long-term capital gain even if the exchange takes place immediately after the husband's death. I.R.C. §§1223(11) and 1014(b)(6).

The second major income tax consideration is that the widow will have to include the income from both halves of the community property in her taxable income, since all of the income will be currently distributable to her. Hence, if the $1,950,000 of community assets (see §5.18) earns 10 per cent per year, she will have gross income of $195,000 per year. She can, however, amortize her cost of the life estate in the husband's one-half of the community property as an income tax deduction. *Gist v US* 423 F2d 1118 (9th Cir 1970); *Estate of*

Christ v Commr 480 F2d 171 (9th Cir 1973). The amortization deduction, by reference to the facts in the basic example (see §5.18), is computed by dividing the value of the widow's remainder interest ($441,970, see §5.20) by the wife's life expectancy (18.2 years, see Table I, Reg. §1.72-9), or $24,284 per year.

§5.23 b. Income Tax Consequences to Husband's Estate

When the widow elects to take under the husband's will, the transaction will be viewed for income tax purposes as a sale by the husband's estate. Under this theory the husband's estate will be deemed to have sold its income interest in its one-half of the community property in exchange for the widow's remainder interest in her one-half of the community property. The taxable gain would ordinarily be computed by subtracting the seller's basis from the lesser of (1) the value of the widow's remainder interest or (2) the value of the husband's income interest. However, I.R.C. §1001(e) states that where a life estate acquired by inheritance or gift is sold or disposed of, no portion of the basis for such interest shall be allowed. Under the facts of the basic example (see §5.18), the husband's estate will be deemed to have received the value of the widow's remainder interest, namely $441,970 (see §5.20), all of which, if I.R.C. §1001(e) is applicable, will be taxable gain in the year that the widow elects to take under the will. The regulations under I.R.C. §1001(e) do not deal with the question of whether the transfer by the husband's estate by reason of a widow's election will be treated as a sale or disposition for the purpose of disallowing basis. Until the matter is clarified by further interpretation, this potential tax consequence makes it dangerous to use the "traditional" widow's election.

An even more serious possible income tax consequence could come about if the exchange by the husband's estate of its income interest for the remainder interest in the widow's one-half of the community property is treated as an assignment of income by the husband's estate. While it appears unlikely that the widow's election can be treated as an assignment, there is no present authority on point. If it were ever treated as such, the value of the income interest in the husband's estate would be taxable to such estate as ordinary income in the year of election. *Commr v P G Lake Inc* 356 US 260, 78 SCt 691, 2 LE2d 743 (1958).

§5.24 4. Death Taxes at the Widow's Death

The assets in the "QTIP" trust (see §5.19) at the time of the widow's death will be included in her gross estate, if the husband's executor elected to take the marital deduction. See §4.23. However, if the marital deduction was not taken in the husband's estate, the assets will not be included in the widow's estate, unless she had a general power of appointment in the "QTIP" trust (see §5.3).

The portion of the assets in the traditional widow's election trust, which originated in the widow's one-half of the community property, may or may not be includable in her gross estate. If the widow at the time of the husband's death was young enough so that, by reference to the table in the Regulations (see §5.20), the value of the life estate in his one-half of the community property at the time of his death was greater than the value of the remainder interest in her one-half of the community property, she would have received full consideration for the transfer. If that is the case, none of her assets in the widow's election trust, regardless of their value at the time of her death, will be included in her estate. Includability under I.R.C. §2036(a)(1) is required only when the transfer is not for *full* consideration. See §8.48. Under the facts in the basic example (see §§5.18 and 5.20), the value of the income interest in the husband's estate exceeded the value of the wife's remainder interest. Accordingly, her one-half of the community property will not be included in her estate.

On the other hand, where the widow does not receive full consideration, her portion of the community property will be included in her estate at the time of her death. The reason for this is that she retained an income interest in her one-half of the community property, which property she permitted to be transferred on her husband's death. The fair market value of such assets upon her death is thereby includable under I.R.C. §2036(a)(1). The value of the life interest in the husband's estate at the time of the election will ordinarily be allowed as an offset in the widow's gross estate constituting the partial consideration which she received for the transfer which she made. I.R.C. §2043(a); *Estate of Lillian B Gregory v Commr* 39 TC 1012 (1963). However, this offset will not be allowed where the widow retained a general power of appointment over her interest in the community property. See *Estate of Steinman v Commr* 69 TC 804 (1978).

§5.25   5.   Conclusion as to Traditional Widow's Election

Elimination or reduction of the estate tax on the widow's one-half of the community property is the major tax advantage of the traditional widow's election. See §5.24. The significant tax disadvantages are reduction of the marital deduction on the husband's death (see §5.19) and the potentially serious income tax problems at the time the election is effectuated, particularly to the husband's estate (see §5.23). In addition, the device often results in psychological ill effects to the widow, who may feel, with justification, that through a technical device which her husband may not have fully understood, she is being unjustly deprived of a portion of what rightfully belongs to her. For these reasons, it is this author's opinion that the traditional widow's election should be sparingly used.

D.   The "New" Widow's Election

§5.26   1.   Introduction

Another form of widow's election, although new and largely untested, may eliminate the disadvantages of the traditional widow's election. Under this type, the husband leaves all or part of his one-half of the community property to the widow either by an outright bequest or a bequest to a power of appointment marital deduction trust, from which the widow will receive the income and have an unrestricted power of withdrawal of the principal during her lifetime. In either event, the husband's bequest is conditioned upon the widow transferring her one-half of the community property at the time of the husband's death to a trust from which she will receive the income, with the remainder going to the children on her death. This device may be more acceptable than the traditional widow's election, because the widow will feel more adequately compensated for what she surrenders. In addition, the tax consequences may be more favorable.

2.   Tax Consequences of the "New" Widow's Election

§5.27   a.   Death Tax Consequences on the Husband's Death

These tax consequences are generally the same as those applicable to the "traditional" widow's election (see §5.19). Only one-half of the community property is taxable on the husband's death. However, the marital deduction will be reduced by the value of the widow's remainder interest.

§5.28   b.   Gift Taxes to Widow

There will be much less of a chance that the widow will make a taxable gift than there is under a "traditional" widow's election. Since the widow is surrendering only a remainder interest in her estate in exchange for a complete interest in the husband's estate, she will almost always receive more value than she gives up. Taking the facts of the basic example (see §5.18), even if the widow were 108 years old at the time of the husband's death, the value of her remainder interest would be $945,740 (see Appendix, Table VIII, Table A(2)) compared to the $950,000, which she will be receiving from the husband.

§5.29   c.   Income Taxes

Since the "new" widow's election, like the "traditional" one, involves a sale or exchange by each party, there will be taxable gain to the extent of the post-death appreciation. However, since the husband's estate will be selling a complete interest in its one-half of the community property, rather than only a life estate, the disallowance of basis under I.R.C. §1001(e) and the assignment of income problems (see §5.23) will not apply. As a result, the acute income tax problems inherent in the traditional widow's election are eliminated.

One favorable tax consequence of the traditional widow's election is, however, not available when the "new" widow's election is used. The widow will have no amortization deduction since she is not purchasing a life estate (see §5.22).

§5.30   d.   Death Taxes on Widow's Death

Under the "new" widow's election, as with the "traditional" one, the assets remaining from the husband's marital deduction bequest will be includable in the widow's estate on her death. However, as illustrated in §5.28, the widow under the "new" widow's election, unlike under the "traditional" one, will in almost every instance have received full consideration for the surrender of the remainder interest in her one-half of the community property. Her one-half of the community property should thereby be effectively excluded from her estate. (See §5.24.)

§5.31   3.   Conclusion as to the "New" Widow's Election

Although many of the tax consequences described above have not yet been tested by the Internal Revenue Service or by the courts, the "new" widow's election has great potential as an estate planning tool. If successful, it will result in little or no tax on the husband's death, except to the extent that the reduction in his marital deduction exceeds the equivalent exemption. On the wife's subsequent death only the husband's one-half of the estate will be taxed, but none of her own. Estates worth over $1,200,000 will have more favorable tax consequences than would result from the more typical plan where the husband leaves the optimum marital deduction (see §4.8) to his spouse and the balance in a bypass trust. In the latter plan, more than one-half of the estate will be taxed on the wife's subsequent death.

§5.32   V.   Bypass Trust for Beneficiaries other than Spouses

§5.33   A.   Use

Except for the widow's election (see §5.16), which is used most commonly, but not exclusively, in husband-wife community property situations, the other types of bypass trusts, namely the maximum benefit and discretionary "B" trusts, may be used in leaving one's estate to relatives other than a surviving spouse. For example, an estate owner may create either a maximum benefit or discretionary type bypass trust for the benefit of his parents and brothers and sisters, avoiding their estates and directing the remainder to the issue of such beneficiaries. However, if the estate owner creates such a trust for his children, or for other persons of a younger generation than he is, and on their death for their issue, it is necessary to consider the effect of the generation-skipping transfer tax introduced by the Tax Reform Act of 1976. (See §5.34.)

B. Generation-Skipping Transfer Tax

§5.34 1. In General

In general terms, the generation-skipping transfer tax is imposed each time the interest or power of a beneficiary in a generation-skipping trust terminates. I.R.C. §2601. The tax is imposed substantially as though the trust property passed to the next lower generation as a transfer subject to estate or gift taxation. See I.R.C. §2602. For example, assume A creates a trust for B, his nephew, for B's life, and on B's death the trust assets go to B's children. On B's death, the trust assets are taxed by adding them to B's estate and computing the tax at B's marginal estate tax rate. Hence, if B has a $1,000,000 estate and there are $250,000 of assets in the trust, these assets would be taxed at 41 per cent (see Appendix, Table II for the estate tax rates).

Although the estate tax rate is used in computing the tax, the estate is not liable for the payment of the tax. Instead, the tax is payable out of the trust assets. In computing the tax, the trust is entitled to any unused portion of the nephew's unified transfer tax credit, the credit for tax on prior transfers, the charitable deduction (if part of the trust property were left to charity), the credit for state inheritance taxes and a deduction for certain administrative expenses. I.R.C. §2602(c).

§5.35 2. What is a Generation-Skipping Trust?

A generation-skipping trust is a trust with beneficiaries who belong to two or more different generations, all of which generations are younger than the generation of the creator of the trust. I.R.C. §2611(b). For purposes of the tax, certain trust equivalents, such as life estates, estate for years, certain insurance and annuity contracts, and other arrangements where there is a splitting of the beneficial enjoyment of assets between generations, are deemed to be trusts. I.R.C. §2611(d).

Generally, a generation is determined along family lines. For example, the grantor, his wife, and his brothers and sisters are one generation; their children (including adopted children) are the first "younger generation," and the grandchildren constitute the second "younger generation." Husbands and wives of family members are assigned to the same generation as their spouses. I.R.C. §2611(c).

Where generation-skipping transfers are made outside the family, generations are to be measured from the grantor. Individuals not more than 12 1/2 years younger than the grantor are treated as members of the grantor's generation. Individuals more than 12 1/2 years younger than the grantor, but not more than 37 1/2 years younger, are considered members of his children's generation. I.R.C. §2611(c)(5).

A generation-skipping trust may exist in ways not readily apparent because of the way in which a beneficiary is defined. For purposes of the generation-skipping tax, a "beneficiary" includes not only a person who has a beneficial interest in the trust (such as the right to income), but also one who has a power over the trust. I.R.C. §2013(c)(3). In turn, a "power" is defined as the ability to alter or establish the beneficial enjoyment of the income or the principal of the trust. I.R.C. §2613(d)(2). Accordingly, if the trustee has the power to distribute or withhold income or principal, he is considered to be a beneficiary even though he is not a beneficiary in the usual sense of the word. Where the trustee holding such a power is of a younger generation than the trustor, and his power extends to distributing income or principal to persons who are of a younger generation than he is, the trust is a generation-skipping trust. By way of example, the trustor's nephew is the trustee. He has the power to sprinkle income or principal among his own children. The trustee is deemed to be a beneficiary and the trust is a generation-skipping trust.

There are, however, two major exceptions to the above rule under which a trustee with certain powers is treated as a beneficiary for generation-skipping tax purposes. The first exception is where the trustee is an independent trustee, that is, one who has no interest in the trust and is not a related or subordinate trustee. I.R.C. §2613(e)(2). The second exception is where the trustee's power can only be exercised in favor of lineal descendants of the trustor who are of a generation younger than the trustee. I.R.C. §2613(e)(1). For example, the trustor's child is the trustee. He has the power to sprinkle income or principal only among the trustor's grandchildren with the remainder to eventually pass to the surviving grandchildren or their estates. In such a case the trustor's child will not be considered to be a beneficiary of the trust.

§5.36   3.   When is the Tax Imposed?

The detailed rules are complex, but, in summary, the tax is imposed at the time that there is a taxable termination or a taxable distribution from the trust. This means that whenever there is a distribution other than of income from the generation-skipping trust, the tax is imposed. I.R.C. §§2613(a) and (b).

At the time of the taxable termination or distribution, the tax is computed as if the transfer took place from the "deemed" transferor. The "deemed" transferor is not always the life beneficiary of the trust, but is usually the parent of the distributee who is more closely related by blood or marriage to the creator of the trust. I.R.C. §2612. For example, if the trust is for the benefit of the testator's son's wife for her life and, upon her death, the remainder goes to the son's children, the testator's son is the "deemed" transferor. As can be seen, the "deemed" transferor is not always deceased. In the above example, the generation-skipping transfer tax is imposed at the time of the daughter-in-law's death. The tax is computed as if the son made a taxable gift of the trust assets at the time of his wife's death. I.R.C. §2602(a).

§5.37   4. $250,000 Exclusion for Transfers to Grandchildren

In computing the generation-skipping transfer tax, an exclusion is provided for transfers to a grandchild of the creator of the trust to the extent that the total transfers per child of the grantor do not exceed $250,000. I.R.C. §2613(b)(5). This may be illustrated by an example. Assume the grantor has two children each of whom, in turn, has three children. The grantor's will leaves $500,000 in trust for each child (i.e., a total of $1,000,000), with the child to get the income and the remainder to the child's children. When each child of the grantor dies, $250,000 of the assets in that child's trust is excluded from the amount subject to the generation-skipping tax.

§5.38   5.   Effective Dates

The generation-skipping tax is generally applicable to all irrevocable trusts created, or to which there were transfers, after June 11, 1976. Wills or revocable trusts, if in existence on June 11, 1976, and not later amended so as in any way to increase the generation-skipping transfers, are not subject to the tax if the decedent dies prior to January 1, 1983.

The estate owner should, therefore, not make any transfers to irrevocable trusts which were in existence prior to June 11, 1976. Moreover, unless he has a compelling reason, he should not, prior to January 1, 1983, make any amendments to a will or a revocable trust which increase the generation-skipping transfer. Eliminating even a small specific bequest in a will could cause an increase in the amount going to a generation-skipping trust and, thereby, cause the tax to apply on the entire amount in the trust.

§5.39   6.   Planning to Avoid the Tax

The basic mechanism to use in avoiding the generation-skipping tax is to leave assets directly to the lowest generation, without giving an intermediate generation any benefit in the trust. For example, the estate owner can leave a portion of his estate directly to the grandchildren, or in trust for them, without giving an income or other beneficial interest in such portion of the estate to his child. He may, if he wishes, give his child a special power of appointment to dispose of the trust assets to other lineal descendants of the testator who are in a younger generation than the child. I.R.C. §2613(e).

Giving a child this special power adds flexibility to the estate and yet avoids the generation-skipping transfer tax.

VI. Recommended Reading

Abel, "Tax Consequences of Widow's Election: Stapf and Related Cases" 17 *Univ of So Cal Tax Inst* 585 (1965)

Beausang, "Estate and Gift Tax Consequences of Administrative Powers" 115 *Trusts and Estates* 246 (1976)

Berall, Donahue, Oleyer and Tate, "How Powers of Appointment Can Help an Estate Plan Without Causing Tax Problems" 5 *Estate Planning* 210 (1978)

Burch, "Powers to the People: The Use of Discretionary Powers in Estate Planning" 114 *Trusts and Estates* 450 (1975)

Clay, "Planning Generation Skipping Transfers" 116 *Trusts and Estates* 12 (1977)

Freeland, Lind and Stephens, "An Estate's Sale of a Life Interest: Gist and Christ and Beyond" 34 *Journal of Taxation* 376 (1971)

Halbach, "Trusts in Estate Planning" 2 *The Probate Lawyer* 1 (1975)

Kahn and Gallo, "The Widow's Election: A Return to Fundamentals" 24 *Stan L Rev* 531 (1972)

Kassoy, "The Widow's Election: Adverse Tax Consequences Suggest Avoiding Until New Law Sec 1001(e) Clarified" 2 *Estate Planning* 110 (1975)

McCaffrey, "Planning For the Generation-Skipping Transfer" 12 *Univ of Miami Inst on Estate Planning* 2000 (1978)

Miller, "The Measured Voluntary Survivor's Election: A Planning Technique for Both Separate Property and Community Property Estates" 19 *Univ of So Cal Tax Inst* 549 (1967)

Moore, "The Tax Importance of Ascertainable Standards in Estate Planning" 111 *Trusts and Estates* 946 (1972)

Saunders and Jackson, "Use of Disclaimers in Estate Planning Clarified" 6 *Estate Planning* 24 (1979)

Schwartz and Liker, "The Widow's Election" 1 *Univ of Miami Inst on Estate Planning* 67-10 (1967)

Sweeney and Wright, "New Tax on Generation-Skipping Transfers: A New Concept; Planning Implications" 46 *Journal of Taxation* 66 (1977)

Weinstock, "Beyond Freezes: Planning to Reduce The Taxable Estate" 16 *Univ of Miami Inst on Estate Planning* 500 (1982)

Avoiding Probate

6

I. Probate in General

§6.1 A. Purpose of Probate

Probate is a court proceeding which has one major, yet simple, purpose, namely, to clear title to property passing from the decedent to those persons named in his will or entitled to take under the laws of intestacy. Probate ends with a decree of distribution which will serve as the recipient's evidence of title to the property inherited. This title will normally be free of creditor's claims and taxes.

§6.2 B. What is Subject to Probate?

The starting point in determining which assets are subject to probate is to ascertain the ownership interest which the decedent has in each asset. If the decedent is the sole owner of an asset and title is vested completely in his name, this asset is subject to probate. However, where title to the decedent's interest is not solely in his name, or it is owned as community property (see §4.34), further inquiry should be made.

An asset is not subject to probate where the title to the asset on the decedent's death vests by law in another person or where the decedent's death does not cause any shifting in the title to the asset. For example, assets held in joint tenancy with right of survivorship, in a bank account trust or in a funded living trust, even though revocable, and assets disposed of by contract, such as life insurance proceeds, are not subject to probate administration. This chapter will deal with joint tenancy assets, bank account trusts and assets disposed of by contract. The funded revocable living trust is discussed in more detail in Chapter 7.

An asset owned by two or more persons as tenants in common will be subject to probate only as to the decedent's interest. The interests of the survivors already belong to them and are not included in the decedent's probate estate.

If an asset is owned by a husband and wife as community property, the surviving spouse's one-half may or may not be subject to probate depending upon the law of the particular state. In California, for instance, such one-half is not subject to probate. The surviving spouse may, however, elect to subject his or her one-half to probate in order to limit the surviving spouse's personal liability for the debts of the decedent chargeable to the community property. (See Cal Prob Code §§202[b] and 205[a] and [b].) Moreover, at least in California, the decedent's one-half of the community property is also not subject to probate if it goes to the surviving spouse. (Cal Prob Code §202.) The decedent's community property interest passing into a trust, even if the trust is for the benefit of the survivor, must be probated. (Cal Prob Code §204.) Even where the decedent's one-half interest in the community property need not be probated because it goes outright to the surviving spouse, it may be necessary to have a court determination that the assets are, in fact, community property. Otherwise, a title company or stock transfer agent may be unwilling to insure or transfer title without probate because if it should turn out that the asset is separate property and a person other than the surviving spouse has a claim to the separate property, an incorrect transfer will have been made. Accordingly, Cal Prob Code §§650 to 657 provide for court confirmation of the community status of the assets and the procedure to be followed in obtaining such confirmation.

Where the estate is very small, assets which are subject to probate may in many jurisdictions be collected or set aside under a summary type probate procedure which will to a large extent avoid court involvement.

§6.3 C. Distinction Between Assets Subject to Probate and Assets Includable in Taxable Estate

An asset may be included in the decedent's estate for death tax purposes, but not be includable in his probate estate. For example, the decedent's assets held in joint tenancy, in a bank account trust or in a funded revocable living trust will all be included in the decedent's estate for tax purposes but, as indicated in §6.2, are not subject to probate. Moreover, if the decedent retained any of the incidents of ownership in a life insurance policy on his life, or transferred such ownership within three years of his death, the proceeds will be includable in his estate for tax purposes (see I.R.C. §§2035 and 2042), but where payable to a beneficiary other than his estate, the proceeds will not be subject to probate. Lastly, assets which have been gifted by the decedent in such a way that the decedent has retained a prohibited right or power (see I.R.C. §§2036 through 2038), will also be included in the taxable estate, but not in the probate estate. It is, therefore, important to keep in mind that avoiding probate does not necessarily avoid death taxation.

§6.4   D.   Probate Procedure

It is beyond the scope of this book to detail the various probate steps and procedures. In general, however, the probate procedures are intended to carry out the title clearing purpose of probate by seeing to it that three subsidiary functions are performed. These functions are first, collecting and inventorying all assets which are subject to probate administration; second, insuring that creditors and taxes are paid; and, third, causing the estate to be correctly transferred and distributed to the persons who take under the decedent's will or by intestate succession.

Many states are in the process of considering revisions to their probate codes which will simplify probate procedures. A Uniform Probate Code has been approved by the National Conference of Commissioners on Uniform State Laws and has been adopted, in whole or in part, by nine states.[1] In general, the basic concept of the Uniform Code is to eliminate the need for obtaining prior court approval for many of the acts taken by a personal representative between the time of his appointment and the time of final distribution.

II.   Nontax Advantages and Disadvantages of Probate

§6.5   A.   Advantage of Probate

The major nontax benefit in planning an estate so that it will undergo probate administration is that the beneficiaries will be protected by the court's supervision. This ensures that the estate will, in fact, be properly transferred to those who are entitled to receive it. The probate procedure in most jurisdictions provides that the court enter a decree of distribution before final distribution takes place and that the recipients execute, and that the executor files with the court, receipts for the assets before the executor is discharged.

Certain methods of avoiding probate, such as holding assets in joint tenancy, in a bank account trust or by designating a named beneficiary of a life insurance policy, do not cause any great risk that the asset or proceeds will not be distributed correctly. Title companies, transfer agents, banks and insurance companies will, for reasons of their own protection, utilize sufficient procedures to be certain that the transferee is the proper one. However, where assets are held, for example, in a funded revocable living trust (see Chapter 7), an unknowledgeable trustee may misinterpret the dispositive provisions of the trust and make an incorrect distribution upon the decedent's death. Since the court does not supervise a trust distribution through the mechanism of a decree of distribution and the requirement that receipts be filed, an error may

---

[1] Alaska, Arizona, Colorado, Hawaii, Idaho, Montana, Nebraska, New Mexico and Utah.

go uncorrected unless a complaint is made by a beneficiary who should have received more than he did.

§6.6 B. Disadvantages of Probate

There are four major disadvantages of probate when compared to alternate methods of transferring title upon the decedent's death. These are higher costs, more delay, greater psychological ill effects, and more publicity.

§6.7 1. Costs

Probate costs include commissions paid to the executor or administrator, fees paid to the attorney representing the executor or administrator and court-related costs such as filing fees. In addition, appraisal fees, tax return preparation costs, tax planning fees and sales expenses are frequently incurred in connection with a probate. The costs in this latter category, however, may also be incurred even where title is transferred under a method which avoids probate. Notably, certain sale expenses are frequently greater where there is a probate because it is necessary to fulfill statutory requirements and to follow probate procedures in consummating the sale.

From an estate planning point of view, it is usually advisable to assume that at least the amount of the customary probate commissions and fees payable to executors and attorneys, subject to the considerations and adjustments discussed below, will be saved if probate is avoided. In many jurisdictions, the customary probate fees and commissions are set by statute and are called statutory fees. They represent the maximum commissions and fees which may legally be charged by executors and attorneys for ordinary services. In addition, however, the court may award extraordinary commissions and fees for services considered to be beyond the ordinary, such as tax work, litigation and sales of assets.

In many states, the amount of statutory (or otherwise customary) compensation is identical for both the personal representative and his attorney. Such computation is based on the amount of the estate accounted for. The following table is an example of the basis of statutory compensation:

Estate accounted for From (1)	To (2)	Commissions on (1)	Plus % on excess of (1)
$ -0-	15,000	-0-	4%
15,000	100,000	600	3%
100,000	1,000,000	3,150	2%
1,000,000 and over		21,150	1%

Under this table, if the value of the estate is $400,000, statutory compensation of $9,150 ($3,150 plus [$300,000 times 2 per cent]) each would be payable to the executor and the attorney. Once the statutory or customary probate fee and commission are ascertained, it should not be assumed that this is the net amount which will be saved by avoiding probate. Several adjustments must first be made.

The first adjustment is to subtract from the total fee and commission the tax saving attributable to this amount. Probate fees, commissions and expenses are deductible as a cost of administration, at the election of the executor, in computing either the federal estate tax or the income tax of the estate. I.R.C. §§2053, 2054 and 642(g). (See §15.15.) If the estate consists of community property assets, and both halves of the community property are subject to probate (see §6.2), only one-half of these fees are deductible either on the death tax return or on the estate income tax return. The other half may be deductible on the individual income tax return of the surviving spouse as an expense incurred in conserving property held for the production of income. I.R.C. §212. In those estates where an unlimited or optimum marital deduction is taken, there will be no federal estate tax in the decedent's estate. (See §4.8.) In such instances, the executor would normally elect to deduct the probate fees and commissions on the estate income tax return.

The second adjustment to be made in computing the savings of the statutory fees and commissions is to subtract from the after-tax cost of such fees and commissions the estimated cost of certain of the executor's or attorney's services that are normally performed as part of the statutory compensation but that must be performed whether or not the estate is probated. For example, services related to the preparation of tax returns, tax consents to transfer, the obtaining of tax lien releases and other dealings with the tax authorities may not significantly increase the amount of the statutory or other customary compensation paid by the probate estate. If there is no probate, however, the attorney will charge for performing these services. The amount of this charge will vary depending upon the time spent, the complexity of the matter and the amount of responsibility assumed. For estate planning purposes, however, an assumption that these charges will amount to 50 per cent to 70 per cent of the statutory or customary fee appears to be reasonable. To the extent that these charges are tax deductible, only the after-tax cost of these items should be subtracted from the after-tax cost of the statutory fees and commissions. (See discussion in §7.6.)

The next adjustment is to subtract the net additional costs, if any, which have to be expended in planning the estate to avoid probate. For example, in more substantial estates the device most frequently used to avoid probate is a funded revocable living trust. See §§7.3 and 7.4. The additional expenses paid to the attorney for drafting the trust and transferring the title to the owner's assets to it will normally amount to substantially more than the attorney's fee would have been for preparing a will. In addition, the client during his lifetime will have record-keeping and other costs to contend with if his assets are in a funded revocable living trust. These additional fees and costs, less any income tax savings resulting from the deductibility thereof, must be taken into account in computing the net savings to the estate owner by virtue of avoiding probate. (See §7.6.)

Finally, in making a realistic cost comparison, account should also be taken of the fact that the statutory commission and fee rates become smaller on each successively higher increment in the amount of the estate accounted for. Hence, unless probate is avoided with respect to every asset owned by the decedent, only the "lower" portion of the statutory compensation is saved by avoiding probate. For example, by reference to the table set forth above, the statutory compensation (for the attorney and the representative combined) in a $400,000 probate estate totals $18,300, or 4.58 per cent of the estate. If probate were avoided as to an asset worth $50,000, so that the remaining probate estate totaled $350,000, the probate fees and commissions would amount to $16,300, a savings of $2,000, or only one-half of 1 per cent of the probate estate.

§6.8   2.   Delay

Another drawback to probate is that it is time consuming compared to alternate methods of transferring the decedent's estate. Where title is transferred on the decedent's death to a surviving joint tenant, a beneficiary of a bank account trust, or a beneficiary of a funded revocable living trust, or where the proceeds of a life insurance policy are paid to a named beneficiary, these transfers can normally be accomplished as soon as the requisite tax clearances are obtained from the state death tax authorities. Where the assets are subject to probate, however, not only must the tax clearances be obtained, but probate procedures which are often time consuming must be followed. Where there is a probate, it will take a period of time after the decedent's death before the personal representative is appointed and is qualified to act on behalf of the estate. There is then further delay (four to six months in many states) before even a partial distribution may be made and frequently at least one year before final distribution may take place. Aside from the delay in distributing the estate, sales, investments and management of assets during the period of administration may not be accomplished as quickly or easily when there is a probate compared to when there is not. These actions cannot even be undertaken before the representative is appointed, and after he is appointed they may be subject to time consuming court supervision.

On the other hand, the delay factor involved in probate should not be overstated. The widow and minor children are eligible to receive a family allowance during the course of the probate and the representative, in many jurisdictions, may be given the power to invest the assets of the estate in many different ways. Moreover, in those states which have adopted the Uniform Probate Code, in whole or in part, court supervision and delay will be lessened. (See §6.4.)

§6.9   3.   Psychological Aspects

The psychological aspects and effect on the surviving members of the decedent's family should be taken into account in determining whether or not to plan the estate so as to avoid probate. Since probate is generally more time consuming than where probate is avoided, the decedent's family members will be reminded of the traumatic experience of the death for a longer period of time. This, however, may not always be an adverse factor, but may help in releasing their grief in a healthy manner.

§6.10   4.   Publicity

Another frequently cited disadvantage of probate is the publicity attendant thereto. Since probate is a court proceeding, all of the documents filed in the proceeding are a matter of public record. Where probate is avoided, court proceedings are not required. However, transfer agents and title insurance companies frequently require copies of living trusts and other dispositive documents in order to insure titles and make transfers subsequent to the death of the grantor. It is sometimes possible to satisfy these requirements by furnishing abstracts of the documents without disclosing all of the provisions.

§6.11   C.   Creditors' Claims: Probate versus Nonprobate

The situation regarding claims and rights of creditors differs where the estate is subject to probate and where it is not. For example, assets held in joint tenancy, unless transferred in fraud of creditors, are normally not subject to the debts of the joint tenant who dies first, unless, of course, the surviving joint tenant had previously assumed personal liability. Where the estate is probated, creditors must file their claims within a specified period, which varies from state to state, or they are barred forever.

III.   Methods of Avoiding Probate

§6.12   A.   Joint Tenancy

Joint tenancy is probably the simplest way of avoiding probate, but as will be seen this form of titleholding has many estate planning disadvantages. (See §6.22.) A joint tenancy is a joint interest owned by two or more persons in equal shares when expressly declared that the title is held in joint tenancy.

§6.13   1.   Legal Characteristics

The legal characteristics of joint tenancy may vary slightly depending upon the peculiarities of state law. The characteristics set forth in §§6.14 to 6.16 are fairly typical. In some states, a joint tenancy between husband and wife is called a tenancy by the entirety.

§6.14   a.   How Created

A joint tenancy may be created by the owner's conveying to two or more persons, as joint tenants, or by one of the owner's conveying to himself and one or more persons as joint tenants. A joint tenancy in many jurisdictions must, however, be created by a written instrument and not by oral agreement.

§6.15   b.   Legal Effect During Life

During the joint lives of the joint tenants, all of them have an equal interest entitling them to have and hold undivided possession simultaneously. If any one joint tenant conveys his interest, the joint tenancy relationship is severed and the parties become tenants in common as to the conveyed interest.

§6.16   c.   Legal Effect Upon Death

The major characteristic of joint tenancy, distinguishing it from other forms of co-ownership such as tenancy in common or even community property (see §4.34), is that, upon the death of one of the joint tenants, the surviving tenant or tenants become entitled to the sole ownership of the entire property by operation of law. The deceased joint tenant's will does not operate upon the property, and he, therefore, cannot dispose of it upon death to third persons.

2.   Tax Characteristics

§6.17   a.   Gift Taxes

Unless each joint tenant contributes equally to the creation of the joint tenancy, a taxable gift occurs. Where the joint tenancy is created with the separate funds of one of the joint tenants and the other joint tenant contributes none or less than his proportionate share of the consideration, a taxable gift will generally be deemed to have been made by the joint tenant contributing more than his share. For example, if A contributes $100,000 and B $50,000 to the purchase of an asset, and they take title in joint tenancy, A will have made a taxable gift of $25,000 to B. There are, however, three exceptions to this general rule.

First, the most important exception to gift tax liability is where the asset is purchased by husband and wife as joint tenants. For all gifts between husband and wife made after 1981, there is an unlimited marital deduction (see §2.42). Hence, even if the contribution by each spouse is not equal, the gift to the one contributing less than his or her proportionate share is fully deductible and no gift tax is incurred.

Second, where joint tenancy bank accounts are opened, where United States savings bonds are acquired, or where securities which are not registered in the name of the owners, but rather in a "street" name, are acquired in joint tenancy, there is no taxable gift at the time of the transfer. When the noncontributing or lesser contributing tenant makes a withdrawal of more than his portion of the contribution, a taxable gift occurs only at that time.

The third exception to the general gift tax rule is frequently referred to as a joint tenancy "for convenience only." For example, if A purchases securities with his own funds and takes title in the name of A and B as joint tenants with right of survivorship, a taxable gift will not always occur. Even though donative intent is not an essential element of a taxable gift, there must in fact be a transfer of a beneficial interest and a parting of dominion and control on the part of the donor. See Reg. §25.2511-1(g)(1); *Naomi Towle Bucholz v Commr* 13 TC 201 (1949), acquiesced, 1949-2 C.B. 1; *Bouchard v Commr* 285 F2d 556 (1st Cir 1961). Whether or not a transfer of a beneficial interest or a parting of dominion and control takes place must be determined under local law. For example, under California law a joint tenancy title is not conclusive as to the real ownership of the property; it merely creates a rebuttable presumption that it is held in joint tenancy. Such presumption can be overcome by evidence proving a common understanding that the character of the property is to be other than joint tenancy. See *Machado v Machado* 58 Ca2d 501, 375 P2d 55, 25 CaR 87 (1962); *Perkins v West* 122 CaAp2d 585, 265 P2d 538 (1954); *Jones v Kelley* 121 CaAp2d 130, 262 P2d 859 (1953). Hence, where the joint tenancy arrangement is created to avoid probate on death, or perhaps because the stockbroker recommended this form of holding title, and the contributing joint tenant gave no thought to the implications of such holding, it can be argued that there is no intent to transfer beneficial ownership or part with dominion and control and, therefore, there is no taxable gift.

b. Death Taxes

§6.18   i. Rule of Contribution in General

Upon the death of a joint tenant, there is includable in his estate for death tax purposes the entire value of the joint tenancy asset, except to the extent that the surviving joint tenant can prove contribution to its purchase from the survivor's own funds. For this purpose, the survivor's own funds are deemed to exclude funds gifted to him by the decedent. See I.R.C. §2040. If the survivor can prove contribution, then the percentage of the purchase price which he contributed is the percentage of the value of the joint tenancy asset which is excludable on the decedent joint tenant's death. For example, if A contributed $3,000 and B contributed $2,000 to the purchase of a $5,000 joint tenancy asset and on A's death the asset is worth $10,000, 40 per cent or

$4,000 will be excluded from A's estate. If upon the creation of the joint tenancy, a taxable gift resulted and if, because of the rule of contribution, the assets are nevertheless included in the taxable estate of the donor, a gift tax credit will be allowed in computing the estate tax. I.R.C. §2012.

§6.19   ii.   Husband and Wife Joint Tenancy

With regard to an asset owned by husband and wife as tenants by the entirety or as joint tenants with right of survivorship, the above described rule of contribution was changed by the Tax Reform Act of 1976 and then completely revised by the Economic Recovery Tax Act of 1981. If the decedent spouse dies after 1981, only one-half of the value of the property, regardless of which spouse furnished the consideration, will be included in such spouse's estate. I.R.C. §2040(b). For example, assume the husband purchases an asset for $100,000 out of his own funds and makes the wife a joint tenant with him. On the death of the first spouse to die, the asset is worth $150,000. One-half of the value, i.e., $75,000, is includable in such spouse's estate. The one-half which is included will, however, not be taxed because it will be deductible under the unlimited estate tax marital deduction (see §4.3).

Where property is held in joint tenancy by the husband and wife with a third party, the general rule of contribution (see §6.18), and not the husband and wife equality rule, will apply. I.R.C. §2040(b)(2)(B).

§6.20   c.   Income Taxes

Since each joint tenant owns an equal share of a joint tenancy asset, each must report an equal share of the taxable income. Where the joint tenants are husband and wife, this usually presents no problem one way or the other because they will normally file joint income tax returns. It should be noted, however, that if the joint tenancy is "for convenience only" or consists of bank accounts, United States savings bonds, or "street" name securities, the owner, for income tax purposes, as well as for gift tax purposes, will still be considered the contributor. See §6.17.

§6.21   i.   Income Tax Basis

The effect of the joint tenancy holding on the income tax basis of the asset in the hands of the surviving joint tenant should be considered. The general rule is that the surviving joint tenant, to the extent the asset is included in the estate of the deceased joint tenant, will receive a new basis equal to the federal estate tax value of the asset. See I.R.C. §§1014(a) and (b)(9). The portion of the asset which is not included in the decedent's estate will retain the survivor's adjusted basis.

To illustrate the above rules, assume A, an unmarried person, purchases a non-depreciable asset for $100,000 with his own funds, but takes title in the name of himself and B as joint tenants. Upon A's death, the asset is worth $180,000. B's basis will be $180,000. However, if B dies first, A's basis will remain the same as it was prior to B's death, i.e., $100,000. To further illustrate, assume the same facts except that A contributed $75,000, and B, $25,000 toward the purchase of the asset. On A's death, B's basis will be $160,000 ([$180,000 times 75 per cent] plus $25,000). If B dies first, A's basis will be $120,000 ([$180,000 times 25 per cent] plus $75,000).

If the joint tenancy is created by husband and wife, only one-half will be included in the decedent's estate if he dies after 1981. (See §6.19.) As a result, only one-half of the asset will receive a new basis equal to the federal estate tax value on the decedent's death; the other one-half will retain the survivor's adjusted basis. Assume the husband purchased an asset for $100,000 entirely out of his own funds and placed title in joint tenancy with his wife. The acquisition was treated as a gift of one-half from husband to wife (see §6.17). The husband dies first, at which time the asset is worth $250,000. The wife's basis will be $175,000 ([$250,000 times 50 per cent] plus [$100,000 times 50 per cent]). If the wife dies first, the result will be the same.

From a planning point of view, it may be advantageous for the spouse who is the sole owner of an appreciated asset to place it in joint tenancy with the other spouse if it is anticipated that the donee-spouse will die first. Provided the donee-spouse survives for at least one year after the transfer into joint tenancy, one-half of the asset will receive a stepped-up basis when the donee dies. If the transfer had not been made, both halves would have retained the old basis. Where, however, the donee-spouse dies within one year of the transfer, the surviving spouse will not receive a new basis on the donee-spouse's death. I.R.C. §1014(e).

Where an asset owned by husband and wife has its source in community property, a different basis may result if the title is in community property as opposed to joint tenancy. For federal income tax purposes, if the asset is held by husband and wife as community property, upon the death of either spouse, both halves are deemed to be acquired from the decedent and receive a new basis equal to the federal estate value of the asset. I.R.C. §1014(b)(6). However, if the asset purchased out of community property funds is owned by the husband and wife as joint tenants and either dies, only one-half is deemed to be acquired from the decedent. Hence, only one-half will receive a new basis and the other one-half will keep the old basis. These principles may be illustrated by an example. Assume that the husband and wife purchased a marketable security for $10,000 out of their community property funds. The husband later dies and at the time the security is worth more than $25,000. If the asset were owned in joint tenancy, the wife's one-half of the asset would retain her old basis, namely $5,000 (1/2 times $10,000). If the asset were owned as community property, her one-half would receive a new basis of $12,500 (1/2 times $25,000). Hence, where community property source assets exceed their adjusted basis, it is normally advisable for such assets to be owned in community property form, rather than in joint tenancy.

§6.22   3.   Joint Tenancy May be a Poor Dispositive Device

There are at least three reasons why the joint tenancy method of holding title, except in very small estates, may be disadvantageous from an estate planning point of view. First, each of the joint tenants has given up the right of testamentary disposition. Circumstances may change and either tenant may later desire to leave the asset to someone other than the surviving joint tenant. Theoretically, either tenant can dissolve the joint tenancy. (See §6.23.) It may not, however, from a practical point of view, be feasible to dissolve the joint tenancy. The tenant may be incapacitated or not wish to hurt the feelings of the other joint tenant.

Second, from an income tax point of view, the holding of an appreciated asset in joint tenancy between husband and wife may be unwise. Where the spouse furnishing the consideration dies first, the appreciated asset would have received a higher basis if such spouse had been the sole owner because both halves would have been included in his estate, thereby receiving a new basis. I.R.C. §§1014(a) and (b). (But see §6.21 for a discussion regarding the advisability of making the non-contributing spouse a joint tenant where it is anticipated that such spouse will die first.)

Third, where the avoidance of estate taxes is an important consideration in the planning of one's estate, holding assets in joint tenancy prevents either joint tenant from leaving his share of the assets in such a way as to save such taxes. Upon the death of the first joint tenant, the asset will go outright to the survivor. This will cause the survivor's estate to be increased, and if the asset is income-producing, will also cause the survivor's taxable income to be increased. The joint tenancy holding will prevent the decedent from leaving his share to third persons or even to a bypass trust created by the decedent joint tenant for the benefit of the survivor. (See Chapter 5 on the use of a bypass trust).

It should be noted, however, that where the estate plan provides for a formula optimum marital deduction bequest (see §4.8) and a bypass trust, it is not necessarily disadvantageous from a tax point of view to hold certain assets in joint tenancy. The amount passing by joint tenancy will reduce the amount passing under the formula marital deduction clause, and an equivalent portion of the non-joint tenancy assets will fall into the residue of the estate and thereby go into the bypass trust. For example, if the estate owner's estate consists of $2,000,000 of non-joint tenancy assets, $1,400,000 will go into the marital deduction bequest and $600,000 into the bypass trust (see §4.8). On the other hand, if $400,000 of the $2,000,000 were held in joint tenancy, only $1,000,000 of the non-joint tenancy assets would go into the marital deduction bequest and $600,000 would still go into the bypass trust.

Some estate owners may wonder why an asset may not be owned in joint tenancy in order to avoid probate and then have the survivor, who will own the entire asset outright on the decedent's death, transfer all or part of such asset to a bypass trust created by the decedent joint tenant for the benefit of the survivor. One reason this may not be done is that, if the survivor receives the income from the bypass trust, such asset will, if transferred by the survivor to the trust, still be includable in the survivor's estate. See I.R.C. §2036. Moreover, if the bypass trust has beneficiaries other than the surviving joint tenant, the transfer by the surviving joint tenant to the bypass trust will be a taxable gift. For example, if the bypass trust provides that the survivor is to receive the income for life and, upon her death, the remainder is to go to the children, the transfer by the survivor to this trust will cause the then present value of the remainder interest to be taxed as a gift.

It should also be noted that the probate avoidance advantage of holding assets in joint tenancy is applicable only on the death of the first tenant. Unless the survivor makes other arrangements (and if the deaths occur closely in time it may not be possible to do so), the entire asset will be includable in the survivor's probate estate. If, on the other hand, the assets of a married couple are held as tenants in common or community property and the decedent's one-half goes into a bypass trust, only one-half of the assets will be subject to probate on the first death and only one-half on the death of the survivor. Moreover, if the survivor permits his or her share to go into the marital portion of a marital-residuary trust, only one-half of the asset will be subject to probate on the decedent's death and no probate will be required on the survivor's death.

§6.23 4. Dissolving the Joint Tenancy

If joint tenancy is not an acceptable method of holding title in a given case for estate planning purposes, consideration should be given to dissolving the tenancy prior to the death of either tenant. Before doing this, however, two factors should be thoroughly examined, namely, whether any gift tax consequences will result from the dissolution and, also, the mechanics which will be employed in effectuating the dissolution.

§6.24 a. Gift Tax Consequences

For the purpose of determining whether any gift tax consequences will exist upon the dissolution of the joint tenancy, the following circumstances should be reviewed:

1. Where the creation of the joint tenancy constituted a taxable gift, then upon the dissolution of such tenancy, care should be taken that the title is not reinvested in the original donor because a second taxable gift will be deemed to take place. For example, A out of his own funds purchased $50,000 of securities and put them in his name and B's name as joint tenants. Unless the "for convenience only" exception applied (see §6.17), this would have given rise to a taxable gift upon the creation of the tenancy. If, on the dissolution of this joint tenancy, title is reinvested in A, B will be deemed to have made a taxable gift to A of one-half of the value at the time of the retransfer.

2. Where upon the creation of the joint tenancy, there was no taxable gift because one of the exceptions discussed in §6.17 applied, then upon the dissolution the asset should be returned to the original contributing party. Otherwise, there will be a taxable gift to the extent that the non-contributing party receives an ownership interest through a new titleholding. For example, if "street name" securities were purchased by A, but put in joint tenancy with B, and upon the subsequent dissolution of the joint tenancy the account is transferred into a tenancy in common, A will be deemed to have made a taxable gift of one-half to B.

3. Since 1981, as a result of the unlimited gift tax marital deduction, there is no gift tax payable on the dissolution of a husband and wife joint tenancy. (See §2.42.)

§6.25 b. Methods of Dissolving the Joint Tenancy

The most common ways of dissolving a joint tenancy are by the parties' expressly changing title to another form, by an agreement or by using the "straw man" technique.

The simplest way to dissolve the joint tenancy is for the tenants to actually transfer the title to some other form as, for example, A and B holding title to real estate as joint tenants convey such real estate by deed to themselves as tenants in common.

It is, however, possible to change ownership by agreement. See *Siberell v Siberell* 214 Ca 767, 7 P2d 1003 (1932). This agreement may be either written or oral. For estate planning purposes, however, such agreements should always be in writing because of the problem of proof, particularly when dealing with the taxing authorities.

It is very common for husbands and wives to dissolve their joint tenancy holdings by an agreement. See "Tax, Legal and Practical Problems Arising From the Way in Which Title to Property is Held by Husband and Wife", (Panel Discussion) 18 *Univ of So Cal Tax Inst 35,* 109-126 (1966). Such agreements should, however, be entered into with great care to avoid unintended consequences. As a general rule, the agreement should *not* provide that *all* of the couple's assets constitute tenancy in common or community property regardless of how title is held. Such an agreement will automatically convert the ownership of assets which are one spouse's separate property. The conversion of separate property to tenancy in common or community property will put the transferring spouse in an unfavorable position in the event such spouse wishes to exercise the prerogatives of complete ownership of the assets, and particularly in the event of a divorce. A preferable agreement will specifically state that it applies only to jointly held assets and to none other.

If one party is not willing to dissolve the joint tenancy and transfer to some other form of titleholding, the other joint tenant may have to take action on his own. If the joint tenancy asset is in a form where it may be withdrawn by either tenant, such as a bank account, then the joint tenant who desires to terminate can withdraw his portion. However, if the asset is in a form where the consent of both parties is required to change the title, as would normally be the case with respect to joint tenancy real estate, it may be necessary to use a "straw man" technique. One joint tenant can convey his interest to a stranger (any cooperative person). This conveyance will sever the joint tenancy relationship. (See *Hammond v McArthur* 30 Ca2d 512, 183 P2d 1 [1947].) The stranger by prearrangement will then reconvey to the conveying joint tenant who will now hold his interest as a tenant in common with the other joint tenant. As a tenant in common, he may dispose of his interest by will. It may no longer be necessary, however, to use a "straw man" technique. The law may be moving in the direction of permitting a joint tenant to dissolve the joint tenancy by conveying his interest directly to himself as a tenant in common. See *Riddle v Harmon* 102 CaAp3d 524, 162 CaR 530 (1980).

§6.26   B.   Totten Trust

The deposit of money in a bank or a savings institution in the name of the depositor in trust for a beneficiary creates a revocable trust during the depositor's life and the proceeds are paid to the beneficiary upon his death. This type of bank account is not subject to probate, and is known as a "totten trust." See *In re Totten* 179 NYS 112, 71 NE 748 (1904).

During the depositor's lifetime, he has the sole control of the account and may withdraw it or change the beneficiary at will. From a tax and estate planning point of view, this form of holding title is similar to a bank account in joint tenancy created with one tenant's separate funds. The outstanding difference is that the noncontributing party has no right of withdrawal during the depositor's lifetime.

If the totten trust is not revoked during the depositor's lifetime, the beneficiary will receive the proceeds on death. It has been held that a will provision disposing of the bank account in a manner inconsistent with the beneficiary designation revokes the trust. See *Brucks v Home Federal Savings & Loan Assn* 36 Ca2d 845, 228 P2d 545 (1951). Where the estate planning objective is to bypass the beneficiary's estate, this form of ownership should not be used. (See §6.22.)

§6.27   C.   Disposition by Contract

Where the decedent during his lifetime enters into a valid contract, supported by consideration, providing for benefits to be paid after his death, such disposition is not considered to be testamentary in character. See *Estate of Howe v Howe* 31 Ca2d 395, 189 P2d 5 (1948). Hence, if benefits under such a contract are payable to a designated beneficiary, not the decedent's estate or personal representative, they are not subject to probate administration.

§6.28   1.   Life Insurance Contract

If a life insurance policy is payable to a named beneficiary other than the insured's estate, the proceeds are not subject to probate. Life insurance as well as other assets which may be disposed of by contract lend themselves very well to carrying out estate planning objectives without subjecting these assets to probate. Payments may be directed to a bypass trust to avoid death taxes in the beneficiary's estate and, also, to lower the beneficiary's income taxes. For a full discussion of the estate planning aspects of life insurance, see Chapter 10.

§6.29   2.   Deferred Compensation Contract

A deferred compensation contract is one entered into between an employer and an employee providing for payment of compensation after the period in which the compensation has been earned. One of the major reasons for this type of contract is to defer a portion of the employee's compensation to a year when he will normally be in a lower income tax bracket. Such a contract should name a beneficiary who will receive the deferred payments in the event of the employee's death prior to his having received full payment. In order to avoid probate, the named beneficiary should not be the estate of the employee. See *Estate of Howe v Howe* 31 Ca2d 395, 189 P2d 5 (1948). It is common to provide in a deferred compensation contract that the employee has the right to change the beneficiary. For a discussion of the tax consequences of this right, as well as the general tax considerations regarding a deferred compensation contract, see §§12.47 to 12.50.

§6.30   3.   Pension and Profit Sharing Plan Benefits

Another asset which is not subject to probate, unless payable to the employee's estate, is the death benefit payable under a pension or profit sharing plan established by the decedent's employer. For a fuller discussion of pension and profit sharing plans, see Chapter 13.

If the pension or profit sharing plan is a qualified plan under I.R.C. §401, the death benefit attributable to the employer's contribution is not includable in the employee's taxable estate provided it is not payable to the employee's estate and the recipient elects to forgo 10-year averaging and capital gain treatment for income tax purposes. I.R.C. §§2039(c) and (f). See §§13.16 and 13.17 for a discussion of 10-year income averaging and capital gain treatment regarding the proceeds of qualified plans.

In many instances it will be advantageous for the death benefit to be paid not to an individual, but to a bypass trust in order to minimize the death taxes on the survivor's death. Before planning for payment to be made to such a trust, care should be taken that the death benefit will not be considered as tantamount to payment to the employee's estate, and thereby cause inclusion of the otherwise exempt death benefit in the employee's taxable estate. Payment to either a testamentary or living trust created by the employee will not be included in his estate, if the trustee is not required to use the funds for the benefit of the estate, that is, to pay the employee's debts, expenses and taxes. Rev. Rul. 77-157, 1977-1 CB 279.

§6.31   4.   Payable-on-Death Securities

Certain securities such as United States savings bonds and sometimes mutual funds may be registered in a beneficiary form reading "A, payable on death to B." During A's life he is the sole owner, and upon his death the security goes to B without probate. The estate planning considerations in using this form of ownership are basically the same as those described in §6.26, dealing with totten trusts. See also §15.11 regarding the income tax election which should be considered on the death of a cash basis owner of United States savings bonds.

§6.32   D.   Funded Revocable Living Trust

One of the ways of avoiding probate, particularly in a married couple's estate where taxes are an important consideration, is through the use of a funded revocable living trust. This type of trust is such an important estate planning tool that Chapter 7 is devoted almost entirely to this device.

IV.   Recommended Reading

Bauer, "Legal Fees in Probate" 105 *Trusts and Estates* 850 (1966)

Casner, "Estate Planning - Avoidance of Probate" 60 *Columbia L Rev* 108 (1960)

Griffith, "Community Property in Joint Tenancy Form" 14 *Stan L Rev* 87 (1961)

Holdsworth, "How to Undo a Joint Tenancy, Thus Escape Numerous Tax and Non-Tax Complications" 2 *Estate Planning* 142 (1975)

Moore, "The Advantages of Probate" 10 *Univ of Miami Inst on Estate Planning* 400 (1976)

Straus, "Is the Uniform Probate Code the Answer?" 111 *Trusts and Estates* 870 (1972)

"Property Owned With Spouse: Joint Tenancy, Tenancy by the Entireties and Community Property," Report of Committee on Death Taxation of Estates and Trusts, Probate and Trust Division, 11 *Real Prop, Prob and Trusts J* 405 (1976)

"Tax, Legal and Practical Problems Arising From the Way In Which Title to Property is Held by Husband and Wife" (Panel Discussion) 18 *Univ of So Cal Tax Inst* 35 (1966)

Using A Revocable Living Trust

7

§7.1 I. Introduction

There are, in general, two forms of revocable living trusts, "funded" and "unfunded." The funded revocable living trust is funded, in whole or in part, with the estate owner's assets during his lifetime. Its prime purpose is to avoid probate as to those assets which are already in the trust at the time of the owner's death. The unfunded revocable living trust is funded only after the owner's death and will not avoid probate. It, nevertheless, may be an advantageous estate planning tool.

II. Funded Revocable Living Trust

§7.2 A. In General

A method for the estate owner to avoid probate and still retain maximum flexibility in disposing of his estate is to use a funded revocable living trust. The essence of this device is that the estate owner, during his lifetime, transfers assets to a trust reserving to himself during his lifetime all of the beneficial rights in the trust, including the right to revoke. Upon the grantor's death, the trust becomes irrevocable and the trust assets are administered and distributed in accordance with the provisions of the trust. Because legal title to the assets is held by the trustee, these assets need not be probated. In most states, all trust agreements are irrevocable unless specifically stated to be revocable. However, in some, a trust is revocable unless specified to the contrary. See *Scott on Trusts,* 3d Ed (1967) §330.1. To avoid problems, the trust instrument should clearly state whether or not it is revocable.

B. Typical Uses

§7.3 1. Probate Avoidance—Consistent with Tax Plan

It is usually a relatively simple matter to avoid probate. Assets may be placed in joint tenancy or, in certain instances, disposed of by contract. (See §6.2.) However, these methods are frequently disadvantageous from a tax point of view. See, for example, §6.22.

Where taxes are an important consideration, the use of a funded revocable living trust is frequently the only way of avoiding probate and at the same time saving taxes. The dispositive provisions taking effect after the grantor's death can be drafted in such a way as to reduce both estate and income taxes to the beneficiaries. For example, a husband and wife may desire to accomplish two objectives through estate planning. First, they wish to avoid probate. Second, they seek to eliminate the estate tax on the death of the first spouse to die, and also to minimize such tax on the death of the surviving spouse. They will not achieve both of these objectives unless they use a funded revocable living trust. To the extent that their assets are owned in joint tenancy, the surviving spouse will become the sole owner of the assets and the entire interest in such assets will then be included in the survivor's estate for death tax and probate purposes. (See §6.22.) On the other hand, if a spouse owns assets as his own, or the couple own their assets as tenants in common or as community property and an "A-B" trust plan is created under their wills to achieve their tax objectives, the interest of the first spouse to die will be subject to probate. (See §6.2.)

To carry out the couple's dual objective of avoiding probate and, also, precluding the decedent's interest in the assets from going outright to the surviving spouse so that such assets will be taxed again upon the surviving spouse's death, the couple should transfer their assets to a funded revocable living trust. The trust will typically provide that upon the death of the first spouse, it becomes irrevocable and is divided into two separate trusts, Trust "A" and Trust "B". That portion of the couple's total estate, consisting of the surviving spouse's interest in the assets plus that portion of the decedent's estate which equals the optimum marital deduction (see §4.8), will go into Trust "A". The balance of the estate (i.e., the non-marital deduction portion of the decedent's estate which will be approximate to the amount of equivalent exemption, see §2.25) will go into Trust "B". Upon the survivor's death the balance of Trust "A" will be taxed, but will not be subject to probate; the balance in Trust "B" will not be subject to either death taxation or probate. See §5.2 for a discussion of the "A-B" trust plan and §5.10 for a discussion of the use of the "B" trust to reduce income taxes.

§7.4 2. Lifetime Uses

In addition to utilizing a funded revocable living trust as a probate avoidance tool, such a trust has at least two other uses. First, where the grantor desires to have all or a portion of his estate managed for him during his lifetime, but does not desire to irrevocably give up control, he may create a funded revocable living trust and provide for an outside trustee, such as a corporate fiduciary, to manage the estate subject to the grantor's retention of all beneficial rights, including the right to revoke during his lifetime.

Second, the funded revocable living trust may serve as a vehicle for the management and control of the grantor's assets in the event of his legal incapacity. Since the title to these assets is in the trustee, no guardianship or conservatorship proceedings need be instituted to deal with the grantor's assets. The disadvantages of such guardianship or conservatorship proceedings, such as court costs, attorneys' fees, bonding costs, as well as the inflexibility of management when subject to court supervision, are all avoided. Even if the grantor at the time of the creation of the trust desires to manage his own assets and names himself as trustee, the trust can provide that in the event of his incapacity a successor trustee will assume the office. It will thereby be possible in the event of the grantor's subsequent incapacity for the title and the management of the assets to remain in the trust and to avoid a guardianship or conservatorship.

§7.5 C. During Life of Grantor

Where the funded revocable living trust is being considered as a device in a given case to avoid probate, account should be taken of various problems incident to creating and maintaining the trust during the grantor's life. A determination can then be made of whether the funded revocable living trust is a proper tool in the particular case.

§7.6 1. Expense and Nuisance

One of the major reasons for avoiding probate is to reduce the higher costs to the estate incident to the probate procedure. (See §6.7.) The estate planner should attempt to make an estimate of what the net cost savings will be and compare these savings with what the additional costs incident to creating and maintaining the funded revocable living trust during the grantor's life will be.

Using the principles detailed in §6.7, which the reader should review, the following is an analysis of the cost savings in a hypothetical estate.

Assume that there is a total estate of $1,000,000. The net estimated savings in using a funded revocable living trust, as compared to having the estate probated, are computed as follows:

Statutory or customary probate fee on death of estate owner (see §6.7) ($21,150 times 2 [assuming an outside executor])		$42,300
Less: Approximate tax savings resulting from deductibility on either estate tax or income tax return (see §15.15) of statutory probate fees and commissions (assume 40 per cent top bracket)		$16,920
Net after-tax cost of probate fees and commissions		$25,380
Less: Cost of after-death services which normally are compensated for as part of statutory fees and commissions (assume 50 per cent of probate fees and commissions)	$21,150	
Less: Approximate tax savings resulting from deductibility of these costs (assume 40 per cent top tax bracket)	$8,460	
Net cost		$12,690
		$12,690
Less: Estimated costs of drafting and setting up funded revocable living trust in excess of cost of preparing wills	$1,000	
Estimated cost of record keeping and other expenses incident to administering the trust where grantor is the trustee (assume $100 per year times hypothetical client's life expectancy of 20 years)	$2,000	
	$3,000	

Less: Approximate tax savings resulting from deductibility of these costs to the extent they are deductible. See I.R.C. §212; see also, *Sidney Merians* 60 T.C. 187 [1973] (assume 80 per cent is deductible and assume 40 per cent top bracket)	$ 960	
		$2,040
Net savings to estate from the use of a funded revocable living trust rather than a probate		$10,650

An important factor to be taken into account, in helping the estate owner to decide whether a saving of $10,650 is worth utilizing a funded revocable living trust, is the amount of nuisance there will be to the grantor in continuing the trust during his lifetime. Transfer agents, title companies and other institutions with whom the trust will have dealings in connection with investing and selling assets will frequently require documentary evidence of the existence of the trust and the trustee's powers. This can usually be satisfied by supplying certified copies of the trust. Sometimes, however, personnel at these institutions may not be familiar with revocable trusts and transactions may be held up until supervisory personnel or counsel for the institution pass upon the validity of the trust or the powers of the trustee. Whether a cost saving of $10,650, after considering the nuisance factor, makes the device worthwhile obviously depends to a large extent on the estate owner's inclination and philosophy with regard to time and money.

§7.7   2.   Transfer of Assets

In order to have the funded revocable living trust effectively avoid probate with respect to any asset owned by the grantor, it is necessary that legal title be actually transferred to the trust prior to the grantor's death. Title to all assets should be placed in the name of "A (name of trustee), Trustee under Trust Agreement dated (date of execution) between A (name of trustee) and B (name of trustor)."

Certain assets which are normally not subject to probate should also be made payable to the funded revocable living trust. In this way, these assets, such as life insurance proceeds (see §6.28), pension and profit sharing plan benefits (see §6.30) and deferred compensation contract benefits (see §6.29) will be subject to the dispositive provisions of the trust. If these proceeds or benefits are paid outright to an individual beneficiary, they become part of his taxable and probate estate, but where they are paid to a trust which has bypass provisions these consequences can be avoided. Where someone other than the insured is the owner of a life insurance policy on the life of one of the grantors (as, for instance, a child who owns a life insurance policy on the grantor-father's life), the trust should not be made the owner of the policy. If the grantor-father has the right to revoke the trust, or if he is a trustee, this could cause the policy to be taxed in his estate (see §10.42).

§7.8 a. Legal Problems Incident to Transfer of Certain Assets

The transfer of certain assets to a funded revocable living trust often presents legal problems and considerations. Some of these will now be discussed.

§7.9 i. Transfer of Partnership Interests

If a partnership interest is transferred to any person or entity without the consent of the other partners, the transferee does not become a partner, but merely the assignee of a partnership interest, thereby losing many of the rights which a partner normally has. See Uniform Partnership Act, §27(1). Moreover, partnership agreements frequently provide that partners may not transfer their interests without following the procedure set forth in the partnership agreement, such as first offering the interest to the other partners or obtaining their consent. Hence, if a partnership interest is transferred to a funded revocable living trust without first obtaining the consent of the other partners, a breach of the agreement may result. When a limited partnership interest is transferred, even if the procedure specified in the agreement is followed or the consent of the other partners is obtained, it will be necessary to amend the certificate of limited partnership to show the substitution of a new partner. See Uniform Limited Partnership Act, §24(2)(b).

§7.10 ii. Transfer of Stock Subject to Restrictions on Transfer

Normally, a buy-sell agreement among owners of a closely held business providing for the purchase of a deceased owner's stock interest upon his death will stipulate that none of the owners may during their lifetime dispose of their interest without first offering it to the others at the death price. The purpose of such a provision is to satisfy one of the necessary requirements in order to have the buy-sell price bind the taxing authorities for death tax purposes. (See Reg. §20.2031-2(h); see also §12.9.) An owner who transfers stock, subject to a buy-sell agreement restriction, to a funded revocable living trust should first obtain the consent of the other owners to the transfer unless the buy-sell agreement already permits such a transfer. Otherwise, he may be in default under the agreement.

The transfer of securities may be restricted by the requirements of the Federal Securities Act of 1933 where such securities have been issued or sold under an exemption to the registration requirements. There usually is no problem, however, where the owner transfers such securities to his funded revocable living trust. Only "sales" without registration are prohibited. See §5(a) of the Securities Act of 1933. A transfer to a revocable trust is not considered to be a sale. Requirements of state blue sky laws should also be studied to determine whether transfers of securities to the trust may be made under such laws.

Securities issued under the federal private offering exemption present another potential problem. The Securities and Exchange Commission has promulgated Rule 144 which requires that no sales by the issuee under this exemption may be made for a period of two years after acquisition. If during the two-year period the issuee transfers these securities to a funded revocable living trust, the question arises as to whether the trust may tack on the period during which the stock was held by the grantor in determining whether the two-year period was satisfied before the trust makes a sale. The answer is that the grantor's holding period may be tacked on in determining whether the security was held for two years by the trust. See S.E.C. Rule 144(d)(4)(F).

§7.11   iii.   Real Estate

Where real estate is transferred to a funded revocable living trust, should the trust obtain a new policy of title insurance or title guarantee in order to be insured with respect to defects in the title, or will the grantor's title policy or guarantee be sufficient? It has been this author's experience that title companies will generally treat the grantor's title policy as fully covering the property despite its transfer to the trust. Nevertheless, the practitioner will be well advised to examine the particular policy or guarantee.

Certain jurisdictions allow a homeowner's exemption for property tax purposes. The transfer of the grantor's home to a funded revocable living trust may cause the property tax assessor to deny the homeowner's exemption to the trust because the home is no longer owned by the resident. It is likely that the exemption will not be lost once the assessor is satisfied that the trust is revocable by the resident grantor, but local practice should be checked.

California (other jurisdictions may follow its lead) has adopted the well-known Proposition 13 which generally rolls back the base for computation of property taxes to the value of the property on March 1, 1975, plus an assumed increase of 2 per cent per year. However, wherever real property changes ownership subsequent to March 1, 1975, the property tax base of such parcel will be equal to the value of the property at the time of such change. For property tax purposes in California, transfer to a revocable living trust, however, does not constitute a change in ownership. California Revenue & Taxation Code §62(d)(2). Therefore, property taxes will not be increased as a result of the transfer.

The provisions of a deed of trust or mortgage on real estate should be examined before the real estate is transferred to a funded revocable living trust. Frequently, the deed of trust or mortgage will provide that a transfer of any kind (even if not a sale) is prohibited and if one takes place, the entire unpaid balance of the note secured by the deed of trust or mortgage becomes immediately due and payable. Financial institutions, such as savings and loan associations, normally will not contend that a transfer to a funded revocable living trust will cause the acceleration clause to come into effect. Moreover, it is doubtful that, even if a financial institution so contended, its contention would prevail. See *Tucker v Lassen Savings & Loan Assn* 12 Ca3d 629, 526 P2d 1169, 116 CaR 633 (1974). In the interest of caution and to prevent needless worry on the part of the grantor, the practitioner should consider obtaining express written permission from the lender before making a transfer of the encumbered property to a funded revocable living trust.

§7.12 iv. Interest in a Professional Practice

Where the estate owner owns a professional practice or is a partner in a professional partnership or a stockholder in a professional corporation, he may not transfer his interest in such professional practice or entity to a funded revocable living trust. Only the licensed professional may hold title to the practice or entity owning the practice. See, for example, California Corporations Code §13405. This type of asset will normally have to be probated.

§7.13 v. Bearer Securities and Tangible Assets

Where title to an asset is not registered, as is the case with bearer securities or tangible assets such as works of art, the title to such assets should be transferred to the funded revocable living trust by a written assignment. Otherwise, after the death of the grantor, claim may be made that the asset was not effectively transferred to the trust, which, if true, will subject it to probate.

§7.14 vi. Backstop Pour-over Will

In almost all instances where a funded revocable living trust is used as the basic device to dispose of the grantor's estate, it is advisable to supplement the plan with a pour-over will. Sometimes because of inadvertence or even inability to accomplish the transfer, it is quite common that at least a few assets may not be effectively transferred to the trust. Under a pour-over will, the grantor should leave the residue of his estate to the funded revocable living trust. In this way any assets which have not been transferred to the trust during the grantor's life, although they must first be probated, will augment the trust after death and be coordinated with the dispositive plan reflected in such trust. For a discussion of the validity of pour-overs, see §7.36.

§7.15 b. Tax Problems During the Grantor's Life

In creating the trust, there are normally no adverse tax consequences to the grantor. The grantor, for most tax purposes, is still treated as the owner of the assets transferred to the revocable trust. Accordingly, during his lifetime he is taxed on the income earned by the trust (I.R.C. §676); he is deemed to have made no taxable gift (Reg. §25.2511-2[c]); and upon his death the assets will be included in his gross estate (I.R.C. §§2036 and 2038). There are, however, several tax considerations involved in the transfer of certain types of assets to the trust (§§7.17 to 7.21).

§7.16   i.   Tax Reporting Requirements

A question to be considered is whether the grantor during his lifetime is required to file a trust income tax return, even though the income is taxable to him and not to the trust. Until quite recently, a trust income tax return (Form 1041) was required to be filed on behalf of the revocable trust, regardless of the fact that the income was taxable to the grantor. The Regulations now provide that a trust income tax return need not be filed and an employer identification number need not be obtained until the trust becomes irrevocable. Reg. §§1.671-4(b) and 301.6109-1(a)(2).

A fiscal year election for the funded revocable living trust may not be made during the grantor's lifetime. For the purpose of this election the first tax return is deemed to be the one filed at the time the trust becomes irrevocable (i.e., upon the grantor's death), and the fiscal year election must be made at that time, if at all.

§7.17   ii.   Stock in Subchapter S Corporation

The transfer of stock in a Subchapter S corporation to a funded revocable living trust in the past triggered lifetime tax consequences. Under the former rule, where any type of trust owned stock in a Subchapter S corporation, the election was lost. The Internal Revenue Code, however, now provides that where the grantor is treated for general income tax purposes as the owner of a trust, as is the case with respect to the grantor of a funded revocable trust (see §7.15), such a trust may own stock in a Subchapter S corporation without jeopardizing the election. I.R.C. §1371(f). For a discussion of the effect of the grantor's death on the Subchapter S election, see §7.31.

§7.18   iii.   Installment Obligations

At one time there was concern that the transfer of an installment obligation to a funded revocable living trust might be considered a disposition of the obligation under I.R.C. §453(b) and thereby result in a realization of the untaxed profit at the time of the transfer. This uncertainty has, however, been dispelled and the Internal Revenue Service now agrees that the transfer to a revocable trust does not constitute a disposition of the installment obligation. Rev. Rul. 74-613, 1974-2 C.B. 153.

§7.19   iv.   Capital Gains Exclusion on Sale of Residence

A capital gain exclusion of up to $125,000 is available to a person over the age of 55 who sells his home. I.R.C. §121. This exclusion is obtainable even where the title to the home is held by a funded revocable living trust. Letter Rul. 8007050.

§7.20   v.   "Flower" Bonds

Certain issues of United States government bonds are eligible for redemption at par for the purpose of applying the proceeds in payment of federal estate tax for which the estate of a deceased person is liable. Since these bonds frequently sell at a substantial discount from par, their use permits savings in the payment of federal estate taxes. While their low rate of interest detracts from their investment attractiveness, "flower" bonds may prove to be worthwhile purchases, particularly if acquired shortly before death. Such bonds are eligible for redemption, however, only where they are owned by the entity which is liable for the payment of the federal estate tax. The question therefore arises as to whether the funded revocable living trust should acquire "flower" bonds during the grantor's lifetime.

Where the bonds are owned by a funded revocable living trust, the requirements for the use of these bonds to pay federal estate tax are: (1) the trust must own the bonds prior to the grantor's death; and (2) either [a] the terms of the trust must specifically require the trustee to pay all or a pro rata part of the estate tax, or [b] the laws of the decedent's domicile must have an apportionment statute or case law requiring the trustee to pay the tax or the proportionate share thereof attributable to the trust. See 31 CFR §306.28(b) (1973). A typical apportionment statute provides that where the dispositive instrument is silent, each recipient of the decedent's assets is required to pay a ratable portion of the tax. See California Probate Code §970; Uniform Probate Code §3-916.

If there is no estate to probate or if the probate estate is insufficient to pay the federal estate tax, "flower" bonds held in the trust will qualify for redemption in an amount not exceeding the amount of insufficiency, even though the terms of the trust may not expressly require the trustee to pay the federal estate tax. However, where the probate estate is sufficient to pay the federal estate tax and the will expressly requires all taxes to be paid out of the probate estate, any "flower" bonds contained in the funded revocable living trust will not be eligible for redemption.

Accordingly, where a funded revocable living trust is the basic vehicle employed to carry out the estate plan, the following recommendations are in order: (1) the "flower" bonds should be owned by the trust; (2) the will should not require that all taxes be paid out of the probate estate; (3) the trust should specify that, to the extent that it owns "flower" bonds, these bonds shall first be used in payment of the estate tax, even that portion of the estate tax attributable to assets which are not contained in the trust. See Fleming, "Use of 'Flower Bonds' Being Restricted by Tighter Treasury Rules; Careful Planning Now Required" 2 *Estate Planning* 150 (1975).

Where "flower" bonds are eligible for redemption in order to use the proceeds to pay the federal estate tax, the bonds are included in the gross estate at their par value. Moreover, any "flower" bonds in the estate which could have been used to pay an estate tax deficiency, even if not so used, which have been sold in the interim, must be valued for estate tax purposes at par value. *Estate of Simmie v Commr* 69 TC 890 (1978) affd 632 F2d 93 (9th Cir 1980). When the bonds are redeemed, there will be no taxable gain on the redemption proceeds because the bonds receive a new basis equal to their federal estate value.

§7.21   vi.   Combining Community Property and Noncommunity Property Assets

Where community property assets are transferred to a funded revocable living trust by the grantor, it is important that these assets remain community property and be separately identified as such in the trust so that they will obtain the tax advantages of community property. These tax advantages are, first, that only one-half at the most will be taxed on the death of the first spouse, and second, where these assets have appreciated in value, both halves will receive a higher income tax basis on such spouse's death. For a full discussion see §7.25. If the grantors own both community property and separate property, it is also important that the assets be separately identified. This is to insure, in the event the trust is revoked during the joint lifetime of the spouses, that there will be distributed to each spouse the assets to which he or she is entitled.

§7.22   3.   Avoidance of Guardianship

To cover the possibility that the grantor may become legally incapacitated during his lifetime and thereby lose the ability to make withdrawals from the trust or revoke it, provision should be made for the trustee to use whatever funds are necessary for the grantor's support, medical care and general welfare. If this provision is not included, it may be necessary for the court to appoint a conservator or guardian who will have to obtain court permission to make withdrawals from the trust. Whether such permission can be obtained as being within the power of a conservator or guardian is subject to question.

D.   After Death of Grantor

§7.23   1.   Mechanics of Transfer

One of the advantages in using a funded revocable living trust to avoid probate is to afford the fiduciary the ability to buy, sell or distribute the trust assets much sooner than would have been the case if these assets had to be probated. Nevertheless certain steps must be taken by the trustee after the grantor's death so that he can deal with the assets.

If the grantor was the trustee during his lifetime, the first step is for the designated successor trustee to accept appointment as trustee. The living trust is not subject to automatic court supervision so no court proceedings are ordinarily necessary. However, if the successor trustee or trustees named in the trust are not willing or able to act and the trust instrument does not set forth a specific procedure for filling the vacancy, the court has the power to appoint a trustee. See *Scott on Trusts*, 3d Ed (1967) §108.2. The successor trustee will then need proof of the fact that he is the new trustee to use in notifying third parties with whom he will deal, such as transfer agents. If he is not court appointed, the grantor's death certificate and a certified copy of the trust will normally supply the needed proof. If he is court appointed, a certified copy of the order will be required.

The trustee must next obtain tax consents or releases so that he can deal with the trust assets. In certain states, there is an automatic lien which attaches upon the grantor's death to the trust assets because the trust was revocable by the grantor. For example, see California Revenue & Tax Code §14301. In those jurisdictions, the assets may not be sold or distributed unless the state taxing authority releases the lien or consents to the transfer.

There is also a lien for the federal estate tax imposed on assets which are included in a decedent's gross estate. I.R.C. §6324(a). Unlike the above described state inheritance tax lien, the property may be sold or transferred without the taxing authority's permission, but the federal estate tax lien remains on the property even after the sale or transfer until the tax is paid in full, unless the sale is to a bona fide purchaser. If real estate is to be sold, and the lien is a matter of record, the purchaser having notice takes subject to the lien. A title insurer will therefore request that the Internal Revenue Service furnish a release of lien on the particular property to be sold. See I.R.C. §6325.

§7.24 2. Creditors' Claims

Where assets are subject to probate, a general creditor must normally file his claim within a specified period of time depending on the requirements of the particular state. If such claim is not filed, the assets are thereafter not subject to the claim. Whether assets contained in a funded revocable living trust at the time of the grantor's death are subject to the claims of his general creditors for debts incurred during the grantor's life is not entirely clear. One line of reasoning is that the trust assets are not subject to the decedent's creditors unless at least one of two conditions is met. These conditions are, first, that the transfer was made by the grantor in fraud of creditors, and, second, that the transfer renders the grantor insolvent. See *Estate of Heigho v Heigho* 186 CaAp2d 360, 9 CaR 196 (1960). The first condition is a question of fact. The second arguably cannot be satisfied because the grantor retained the power to revoke the trust and hence, the trust assets were really his own, thereby leaving him solvent.

On the other hand, the *Estate of Camm v Brooks* 76 CaAp2d 104, 172 P2d 547 (1946), holds that where the grantor reserves the lifetime benefits from a trust, such as the income, the grantor's creditors may collect their debts after the grantor's death out of the assets which were payable to the grantor, even in the absence of the grantor's fraud or insolvency.

If, under state law, the trust assets are not subject to the decedent's creditors, the payment by the trust to such creditors is not deductible for federal estate tax purposes unless payment is actually made prior to the time for filing the federal estate tax return (including extensions). See I.R.C. §2053(c). Unless the particular state law is clear that assets in a funded revocable living trust are subject to the decedent's creditors, it is recommended that all of the creditors' claims which the trustee determines to pay actually be paid before the federal estate tax return is filed.

3.   Tax Considerations

§7.25   a.   Preserving Tax Benefits from Community Property Holdings

An asset owned as community property normally receives two beneficial tax characteristics. First, on the death of either spouse, only one-half of the asset is includable in the decedent's estate and by reason of the unlimited marital deduction, even this one-half will not be taxed if it passes to the surviving spouse (see §4.3). Second, upon the death of either spouse, both halves are deemed to be acquired from the decedent and receive a new basis equal to the federal estate tax value of the property. I.R.C. §1014(b)(6). Obtaining a new basis on both halves is advantageous where the asset has appreciated in value. For example, assume the adjusted income tax basis of a community property asset prior to the decedent's death is $10,000, and the federal estate tax value of both halves is $40,000. Even though only one-half of the federal estate value of the asset, or $20,000, is included in the gross estate, the asset receives a total new basis of $40,000.

Where husband and wife transfer community property assets to a funded revocable living trust in order to avoid probate, the question arises as to what portion of these assets are included in the estate of the first grantor to die and, also, whether both halves will receive a new basis on the death of such spouse. The answer to the questions depends upon whether the assets in the trust are deemed, for tax purposes, to retain their characteristics as community property or whether, by virtue of their being transferred to the trust, they are transmuted into another form of ownership. Under California substantive law, it is now clear that community property assets may be transferred to a funded revocable living trust and retain their character as community property provided the trust is drafted so as to satisfy certain statutory requirements. Under the statute, the following requirements must all be met:

1. The transfer to the trust must be made by both the husband and the wife.

2. The trust must be revocable during the joint lives of the husband and the wife.

3. The trust must provide that the assets, after transfer to the trust, shall remain community property and any withdrawal therefrom shall be community property. Hence, if the trust contains both community property and separate property, the community property must be identified as such.

4. The trust may not grant the trustee, during the joint lives of the husband and wife, any powers more extensive than those possessed by a husband or wife with respect to the community property.

5. The trust must be subject to amendment during the joint lifetime of husband and wife upon their joint consent. California Civil Code, §5113.5.

If the above requirements are met, the trustee may be any person, including either the husband or the wife or both.

The Internal Revenue Service has also issued example guidelines setting forth what the trust should provide in order for community property assets to be considered as having retained their characteristics as community property (see Rev. Rul. 66-283, 1966-2 C.B. 297). The trust approved in the Revenue Ruling contained similar provisions as are required under the California statute. The major difference was that the trust in the Revenue Ruling provided that, on the death of either spouse, the property was to be divided into two equal shares consisting of the community property interest of each and that the trust for the survivor's share was to be revocable by the survivor. This requirement of revocability of the survivor's share is not contained in the California statute, thereby permitting a forced widow's election. For a discussion of the widow's election, see §§5.15 to 5.31. Since state law establishes property rights for federal tax purposes, the state law governing community property rather than the Revenue Ruling will control if there is any inconsistency. Hence, in drafting funded revocable trusts to which community property will be transferred, the tax benefits of community property will be obtained providing all the requirements of state law are satisfied.

§7.26   b.   Loss of Probate Entity as Taxpayer

Where a funded revocable living trust is used, a potential income tax advantage incident to having a probate may be lost. (See, however, Ufford, "Income Taxation of the Funded Revocable Trust after the Death of the Grantor" 30 *The Tax Lawyer* 37, for a discussion of the taxability of the trust income after the grantor's death, but prior to the disposition provided in the trust instrument.) The probate estate is a separate income tax entity, so that all income earned by the estate which is not currently distributed is taxed to the estate. If the estate is in a lower income tax bracket than those beneficiaries who will eventually receive the estate income, there is a tax advantage in having a probate, because the income will be taxed at a lower rate during the probate period. The period of administration may continue for tax purposes only for such period as is actually required by the executor to perform the ordinary duties of administration. (See Reg. §1.641(b)(3); see also §15.32.)

The income tax advantage of a probate estate as a taxpayer may be illustrated by an example. If the net taxable income earned by the decedent's assets is $80,000 per year and it is all taxed to the surviving spouse as a single taxpayer, the federal income tax, using 1984 rates, will be $27,971. However, where, for example, by reason of preliminary distributions from the probate estate, one-half of the income is taxed to the surviving spouse and the other one-half to the probate estate, the total tax will be only $19,801 or a saving of $8,170 per year.

One might think it possible to accomplish at least a portion of the income tax saving by the use of a funded revocable living trust. The trust could provide that, upon the death of either spouse, the assets will be divided into separate trusts, the marital deduction portion in Trust "A" and the bypass portion in Trust "B". The surviving spouse will be entitled to all of the income from Trust "A". The trustee will have the discretion either to accumulate the income of Trust "B" or to pay it to the surviving spouse. By accumulating the Trust "B" income, it would appear at first blush that a similar income tax result as using the probate estate will be achieved; namely, that a portion of the income will be taxable to the surviving spouse and the other portion to the trust.

There are two major differences, however, between the two methods. First, by using either a maximum or optimum marital deduction clause (see §4.8), the chances are extremely remote that the estate will be divided equally between Trust "A" and Trust "B". To the extent the income from each fund is not equal to that of the other, the minimum income tax brackets will not apply and the total income tax will be greater than if the probate method were used. The second difference is that by accumulating the income in Trust "B" (rather than in the probate estate), such accumulated income when distributed in a later taxable year out of Trust "B" to the surviving spouse will be subject to the throwback rule. See I.R.C. §§665 to 667, inclusive. In general terms, the effect of the throwback rule is to require the distributee to pay in the year of distribution the tax that he would have paid if the average accumulated income had been added to his average income for three of the last five years, less the taxes on such income already paid by the trust. (See §8.45 for a summary of the throwback rule.) In contrast, the probate estate may distribute its accumulated income in a later taxable year without subjecting such income to the throwback rule, because probate estates are not subject to the rule.

§7.27   c.   Estate Tax Exemption for Proceeds of Qualified Retirement Plan Death Benefits

Death benefits payable under a retirement plan which are not payable to the employee's estate are not subject to probate. Moreover, if the retirement plan is a qualified plan under I.R.C. §401, the death benefit attributable to the employer's contributions is not includable in the employee's taxable estate, provided it is not payable to the employee's estate and further provided the recipient elects to forgo 10-year averaging and capital gain treatment for income tax purposes. I.R.C. §§2039(c) and (f). See §§13.16 and 13.17 for a description of 10-year income averaging and capital gain treatment regarding the proceeds of qualified plans. Therefore, the death benefit should not be made payable to the employee's estate, both from a probate as well as an estate tax point of view. Payment to a funded revocable living trust created to avoid probate will qualify for the federal estate tax exemption provided the trustee is not required to use the funds for the benefit of the decedent's estate, that is, to pay debts, expenses and taxes. See discussion in §6.30. It is, however, permissible to give the trustee discretionary authority to loan money or to purchase assets from the probate estate. In this way the probate estate can receive sufficient liquid assets to pay debts, taxes and expenses without causing the otherwise exempt death benefit to be taxable.

§7.28   d.   Death Expense Deduction

Whether there are differences between a funded revocable living trust and a probate estate in terms of the tax deductibility of expenses of administration incident to the grantor's death should be considered. Insofar as federal taxes are concerned, the deductibility of the expenses is generally the same whether they are expended by a probate estate or by a funded revocable living trust. They may be deducted on the federal estate tax return or on the estate income tax return as elected by the fiduciary. I.R.C. §642(g). For state inheritance tax purposes, however, the expenses of the trust may, in some states, not be deductible at all. In California, for example, there is no express inheritance tax deduction permitted for trustee fees. Only statutory probate fees and fees for dissolving joint tenancies and tax work are deductible. California Revenue & Taxation Code §§13988 and 13988.1.

§7.29   e.   Out-of-State Realty

Where the estate owner is a resident of one state and owns real property located in another state, there may be different state inheritance tax results if such real estate is placed in a funded revocable living trust, compared to leaving such property in the owner's name. Usually no inheritance tax is imposed by the state of the decedent's residence on real property located outside the state. The state where the real estate is located will tax such property.

Frequently, the tax imposed by the foreign state will be less than it would have been if imposed by the state of residence. Normally the decedent's estate is larger in the latter state and, therefore, is in a higher bracket. However, if the out-of-state realty by virtue of being transferred to a trust were then to be classified as personalty, it would become subject to inheritance tax in the state of residence. The law of the situs controls as to whether the real property has been converted to personalty. See *Estate of Tutules v Cranston* 204 CaAp2d 481, 22 CaR 427 (1962).

§7.30   f.   Federal Estate Tax Alternate Valuation

The next tax difference between the funded revocable living trust and the probate estate deals with the alternate valuation date election for federal estate tax purposes. When the alternate valuation election is made, the property, as a general rule, must be valued six months from the date of death. I.R.C. §2032. However, if any assets are distributed before the end of six months, these assets must be valued on the date of distribution. I.R.C. §2032(a)(1).

The personal representative of a probate estate can easily control the time that a distribution from the estate is made at least during the first six months. He can thereby help achieve a maximum utilization of the alternate valuation election. Suppose, however, that a funded revocable living trust is required to distribute assets on the death of the grantor. In that case, there has been concern that there would be no opportunity for utilizing the alternate valuation election, because the alternate valuation date and the date of death would be the same. Moreover, if the trust provides that upon the grantor's death the trust becomes irrevocable and the assets are then to be divided into two or more separate trusts (as, for example, separate trusts for the grantor's children), this division will be a distribution for purposes of the alternate valuation date. See Rev. Rul. 73-97, 1973-1 C.B. 404. However, this Revenue Ruling inferentially indicates that it is the date on which the physical division takes place which is the date of distribution and not the death of the grantor, even though the trust says that the division is to take place upon such death. In an "A-B" trust plan, the Internal Revenue Service has made it clear that where the trust is to be divided on the grantor's death into Trusts A and B, no distribution is deemed to take place for alternate valuation purposes until such time as the trustee makes a physical distribution of the assets into Trust B, as long as there is no unreasonable delay in the administration of the trust and the estate. Rev. Rul. 78-431, 1978-2 C.B. 230. Therefore, there is no substantial difference in obtaining the advantages of the alternate valuation election regardless of whether the assets are probated or whether they are administered in a funded revocable living trust.

§7.31 g. Stock in Subchapter S Corporation (After Grantor's Death)

A Subchapter S corporation is one which has elected to have its income taxed to its shareholders, thereby avoiding the corporate income tax. See §13.3. This election is available only to corporations meeting certain requirements, one of which is that, with certain exceptions, a trust may not be a stockholder. A revocable trust is one such exception (see §7.17).

After the grantor's death, the funded revocable trust becomes irrevocable and the requirements regarding its ownership of Subchapter S stock, as compared with those governing a probate estate, should be considered. Since the assets of the revocable trust are includable in the grantor's estate, the trust, regardless of the nature of the beneficial interests, may continue to own the stock of the Subchapter S corporation for two years after the grantor's death. I.R.C. §1371(e)(1)(B). A probate estate may own such stock during the entire period of administration, and the ownership of such stock may be continued by a trust to which the estate is distributed under the terms of the will for an additional 60 days thereafter. I.R.C. §1371(e)(1)(C). Which situation will be more favorable is, of course, difficult to predict in advance.

The Economic Recovery Tax Act of 1981 added a "qualified Subchapter S trust" to the type of trust which may own Subchapter S stock without causing the termination of the Subchapter S election. A qualified Subchapter S election is one where (1) all of its income is distributed to a citizen or resident of the United States, (2) at any given time there is only one income beneficiary, who, during his lifetime, is the exclusive beneficiary insofar as both income and principal distributions are concerned, and (3) the beneficiary makes an irrevocable election to be treated as the tax owner of the trust. I.R.C. §1371(g). This type of trust may own Subchapter S stock for as long as the above requirements are met. Accordingly, if the trust holding the Subchapter S stock after the grantor's or testator's death continues to meet the above requirements, it could continue to hold Subchapter S stock for an indefinite period, extending far beyond the two-year and 60-day requirements discussed in the preceding paragraph.

§7.32 h. Distribution by Fiduciary Which Gives Rise to a Taxable Loss

If the fiduciary is required by the terms of a will or trust to distribute a fixed sum to a beneficiary and he satisfies the distribution by distributing an asset in kind, the estate or trust will, under the general income tax rule, recognize gain to the extent that the asset has appreciated over its adjusted basis. *Suisman v Eaton* 15 FSupp 113 (DC Ct 1935), affd per curiam 83 F2d 1019 (2d Cir 1936), cert den 299 US 573, 57 SCt 37, 81 LE 422 (1936). However, if the asset on the date of distribution is worth less than its adjusted basis so that there is a loss on the transaction, the loss will be recognized if the distribution is from the probate estate, but will not be recognized if the distribution is from a funded revocable living trust. I.R.C. §267(b)(6); see also *Estate of Hanna v Commr* 320 F2d 54 (6th Cir 1963); Rev. Rul. 56-222, 1956-1 C.B. 155.

§7.33   i.   Personal Liability of Fiduciary

The problem of personal liability of an executor of a probate estate as opposed to that of a trustee, after the death of the grantor, of a funded revocable living trust should be considered. Both an executor and a trustee are personally liable if they make distributions to beneficiaries before the federal taxes are paid. 48 Stat 760 (1934), 31 USC c 6 §192 (1958); I.R.C. §6324(a)(2). The executor is normally protected in that the probate procedure does not require him to make distributions until the taxes are settled, or, at the very least, he can usually hold back a sufficient reserve against anticipated tax deficiencies. On the other hand, if a trust provides for immediate distributions upon death, the trustee may not be able to refuse to distribute even though he may have personal liability if he makes a distribution before the taxes are settled. This potential liability may deter a successor trustee from accepting his position. Such refusal may, in turn, seriously upset the grantor's plan for management of the trust assets after his death.

§7.34   4.   Conclusion as to Use of Funded Revocable Living Trust as a Device to Avoid Probate

No general overall conclusion can be drawn as to whether the funded revocable living trust as a device to avoid probate has more advantages or more disadvantages. As can be seen from the above discussion, however, it is important carefully to analyze and weigh both the general and tax advantages and disadvantages of the device in each specific instance before it is employed. The tentative conclusions drawn by the practitioner should, of course, be fully discussed with the estate owner and a memorandum made for the file summarizing such discussion. Otherwise, if a decision is made against using a funded revocable living trust, the beneficiaries, after the client's death, may assert that the estate planner did not give due consideration to the probate avoidance aspects of the estate plan.

III.   Pour-Over Will and Unfunded Revocable Living Trust

§7.35   A.   In General

The estate owner may, after careful analysis, decide, at least for the time being, not to use a funded revocable living trust to avoid probate. He may, however, wish to have his estate go into a trust after his death for the purposes of tax savings and/or management for his beneficiaries. Consideration should be given to creating a revocable living trust, and leaving it unfunded or nominally funded during the grantor's lifetime. The estate owner's will must then be drafted to provide that the estate pours over into the trust upon his death. Under this arrangement the initial probate of the grantor's estate will not be eliminated, but the expense, nuisance and other disadvantages of maintaining a funded revocable living trust during the grantor's lifetime will be avoided. (See §§7.6 to 7.21.)

The use of an unfunded revocable living trust, together with a pour-over will, may be a preferable choice over a testamentary trust where the estate owner is undecided at the time the estate plan is created whether to have his estate go through probate or be transferred to a funded revocable living trust. By creating the trust during his lifetime, he may fund it at any time prior to his death, without the need to have another trust drafted later on. If he should die prior to funding it, the initial probate will not be avoided, but the estate will pour over to the trust and his dispositive plan can be carried out in the same way as if he left his estate to a testamentary trust.

The unfunded revocable living trust may also be used later to partially fund the grantor's estate. For example, the grantor's real estate located in another state can be transferred to the trust in order not to subject the out-of-state realty to ancillary administration in another state. State inheritance tax consequences should, however, first be considered. See §7.29 for a discussion of the inheritance tax problem.

§7.36 B. Validity of Pour-Over

Under the Uniform Testamentary Additions to Trusts Act adopted in most states, a devise or bequest under a pour-over will to a living trust, even if unfunded, is valid, providing the trust is identified in the testator's will and its terms are set forth in a written instrument executed before or concurrently with the execution of the testator's will. Moreover, the devise or bequest is not invalid because the trust is amendable or revocable or even because the trust is amended after the execution of the will, or, for that matter, even after the death of the testator.

Although it is not required by the Uniform Act, many attorneys will recommend that a nominal consideration of perhaps 10 dollars be transferred to the otherwise unfunded trust in case the pour-over provisions have to be validated in a jurisdiction which has not adopted the Act. It is also common practice to make the trust the beneficiary of life insurance proceeds and death benefits under qualified retirement plans in order to coordinate these benefits with the estate owner's dispositive plan.

As added protection against a claim of invalidity, the pour-over will should provide that if the trust is invalid or has been revoked, its provisions are to be read into the will as a testamentary trust under the doctrine of incorporation by reference. This backstop provision is also useful where both husband and wife are grantors of the trust and one of them revokes the trust without the other's consent. The nonrevoking spouse will, unless and until a new estate plan is created, thereby have the dispositive provisions of the revoked trust in effect as a testamentary trust in the event of death. Under the doctrine of incorporation by reference, the incorporated document must be in existence when the will is executed. Accordingly, if a backstop provision is used, it is then important whenever the trust is amended subsequent to the date of the will to have the testator execute a codicil which incorporates by reference the amendment to the trust.

§7.37 C. Comparison with Funded Revocable Living Trust

The essential difference between the unfunded and the funded revocable living trust is that the latter will avoid probate, but the former will avoid the problems incident to maintaining the trust during the grantor's lifetime. (See §7.35.) In addition, if the trust remains unfunded at the time that the grantor becomes legally incompetent, the unfunded trust normally can no longer be used as a device to avoid a conservatorship or guardianship, since the grantor will lack the capacity to transfer his assets to it. (See §7.22.)

In analyzing the estate planning advantages and disadvantages of using an unfunded as compared to a funded revocable living trust, certain problems which may affect the willingness of a successor trustee to serve after the grantor's death should be considered. Where the estate owner wishes to manage his own estate during his lifetime, but desires that a corporate fiduciary become the successor trustee upon his death, it may be advantageous to use an unfunded rather than a funded revocable living trust. The corporation fiduciary may be reluctant to accept the successor trusteeship of a funded revocable living trust after the grantor's death because it may have a duty to investigate acts of the prior trustee and obtain redress for any breach of trust. If it does not do so, it will be liable. See *Scott on Trusts,* 3d Ed (1967) §223. An exculpatory clause relieving the successor trustee of this obligation and liability will be helpful, but it will be strictly construed against the successor trustee if the successor trustee has any reason to believe that the trust was mismanaged by the prior trustee. Where the trust is unfunded, mismanagement could not have occurred.

Another problem regarding the successor trustee's willingness to serve after the grantor's death is that the value of the assets, and, hence, the trustee fee, may be too small or the trust may be troublesome to administer. This possibility exists with respect to both funded and unfunded trusts. The only way to overcome the problem is to have the corporate trustee named as the trustee during the grantor's life. Frequently, corporate trustees will charge only a nominal fee, or sometimes no fee at all, during the period that the trust is unfunded.

§7.38   D.   Comparison with Testamentary Trust

Where the estate owner does not desire to avoid a probate, but wants his estate plan to provide for a continuing trust after his death, a decision must be reached as to whether this continuing trust should be created initially as a testamentary trust or as an unfunded revocable living trust. Until recently, there were many sharply defined advantages and disadvantages of each type of trust. There has, however, been a trend in many jurisdictions to eliminate many of the differences between the two. See, e.g., Uniform Probate Code §§7-101 to 7-307, inclusive. The characteristics of each type will be discussed together with the recent changes.

The following are disadvantages of a testamentary trust (and, conversely, advantages of revocable living trusts) which still exist in many states:

1. A testamentary trust is subject to the continuing jurisdiction of the probate court. Periodically court accountings should be filed. As a result, the fees of the trustee, particularly a corporate trustee, and its attorneys are usually higher for administering a testamentary trust than would be the case for administering a living trust.

2. A testamentary trust is a matter of public record and secrecy cannot be preserved.

3. A testamentary trust should not, for tax reasons, be made the beneficiary of a life insurance policy owned by someone other than the testator-insured. For example, a daughter may own life insurance on her father's life. The daughter may not make the father's testamentary trust the beneficiary of the life insurance policy, even though the daughter is the primary beneficiary of the trust. The father always has the right to revoke or amend his will. This right is tantamount to a right to change the beneficiary and is thereby considered an incident of ownership in the life insurance, causing the policy to be taxed in the father's estate. I.R.C. §2042(2). However, if a revocable living trust is used by the father, the trust provisions can specifically negate the right of the father to revoke or amend the living trust so as to in any way affect the life insurance policy or proceeds owned by the daughter payable to the trust.

The following are disadvantages of a testamentary trust which have been minimized by recent developments:

1. A testamentary trust had less flexibility than a living trust if the surviving spouse wished to transfer his or her assets to the "A" portion of an "A-B" trust in order to obtain management of the assets. See §5.2 for discussion of an "A-B" trust plan. In many jurisdictions, it is now possible to accomplish this objective because of the enactment of legislation permitting additions to testamentary trusts. (For example, see Cal Prob Code §1120.)

2. A testamentary trust lacked mobility. If the beneficiaries moved to anoth-

er state, it was not possible to move the trust to that state. Accordingly, it was thereby impossible for an out-of-state corporate trustee to be appointed, because corporate fiduciaries frequently cannot conduct business in states other than their own. Some states now permit the court to authorize the transfer of a testamentary trust to another jurisdiction. See, e.g., Cal Prob Code §§1139 to 1139.7, inclusive. The authorization is usually within the discretion of the court and the court has the power to direct the manner of transfer, approve the new trustee and impose such terms and conditions as may be just. A living trust may still, however, be more advantageous in regard to mobility. First, an out-of-state corporate fiduciary may be designated as the original trustee in the trust instrument, in effect creating the trust in another state, something which cannot be done with a testamentary trust. Second, even if the living trust is created in the estate owner's state, but has to be moved later on because the beneficiaries move, the trust instrument can provide for a transfer upon the terms and conditions stated therein, obviating the need for court approval.

3. In using a testamentary trust, it was not possible to have the estates of two persons, such as husband and wife, go into the same trust, say, for the benefit of the children. Consequently, there was a lack of unified administration. Only by creating a living trust could their objective be fulfilled. Unification of testamentary trusts created by two different persons for the benefit of common beneficiaries may now be achieved in some jurisdictions in substantially the same manner as may be accomplished with a living trust. See, e.g., Cal Prob Code §1120. It is possible for one person to leave all or part of his estate to a testamentary trust created by another person. The trustee under the latter person's will may petition the court for authority to accept additions to the trust from the first person's will upon the death of the first person. Moreover, if both persons in their wills create substantially identical trusts and both trusts have the same trustee, it may be possible in some states to combine the assets and administration of both trusts into a single trust. See e.g., Cal Prob Code §1133.

4. The federal estate tax exclusion for death benefits under qualified retirement plans was in doubt where payment was made to a testamentary trust under the employee's will, because it could have been considered the equivalent of payment to the employee's estate. Revenue Ruling 77-157, 1977-1 CB 279 now makes it clear that a payment to either a testamentary or a living trust will not cause inclusion of the otherwise exempt death benefit in the employee's taxable estate if the trustee is not required to use the funds for the benefit of the decedent's estate, that is, to pay debts, expenses and taxes.

The following are disadvantages of revocable living trusts (and, conversely, advantages of testamentary trusts) which have been minimized by recent developments:

1. The court had no continuing jurisdiction over living trusts. Hence, in the event of a controversy regarding the living trust, it was necessary to bring a lawsuit, usually an action for declaratory relief, in order to resolve the matter. In a testamentary trust, because of the probate court's continuing jurisdiction, it was possible to use simple and swift procedures such as obtaining instructions from the court.

2. There was no way for the trustee to file a court accounting and obtain a discharge. This sometimes inhibited a trustee selected by the estate owner from agreeing to act.

There is a trend, however, for states to permit the trustee or any beneficiary of a living trust to petition the court on a case-to-case basis to issue instructions, to settle accounts, to compel a trustee to submit accounts, and to grant the trustee powers not expressly contained in the trust instrument. See, e.g., Uniform Probate Code, §§7-102, 7-201. Hence, the advantage of a testamentary trust in this area is being narrowed.

Despite the elimination or narrowing of many of the differences between testamentary trusts and living trusts, it appears, at least to this author, that there are more advantages to living trusts than to testamentary trusts. At the very least, by establishing a living trust the estate owner retains the option of funding it prior to his death and thereby avoiding a probate. The use of the unfunded revocable living trust, when compared to a testamentary trust in many cases is the preferred estate planning tool.

IV. Recommended Reading

Bush, "Who Needs a Revocable Trust" 106 *Trusts and Estates* 17 (1967)

Casner, *The Revocable Trust, an Essential Tool for the Practicing Lawyer* (A.L.I. 1965)

Cohan and Hemmerling, *Inter Vivos Trusts - Planning, Drafting and Taxation* (McGraw-Hill Book Company/Shepard's Citations, Inc 1975)

Flemming, "One-Party Trusts" 2 *Univ of Miami Inst on Estate Planning* 300 (1968)

Friedman, "Special Types of Property in Revocable Trusts" 8 *Univ of Miami Inst on Estate Planning* 1700 (1974)

Halbach, "Trusts in Estate Planning" 2 *The Probate Lawyer* 1 (1975)

Landry, Gallo, Wyatt and Ufford, "Pre- and Post-Death Administrative and Tax Problems of Revocable Trusts" 1 *UCLA Estate Planning Inst* 121 (1979)

O'Connell, "Estate and Tax Planning Using a Revocable Trust Funded with Community Property" 1 *Estate Planning* 110 (1974)

Schwartz, "Revocable Trusts and California Marital Property" 20 *Univ of So Cal Tax Inst* 363 (1968)

Ughetta, "Practical Problems in Administering Revocable Trusts and Pour-

Over Wills Involving More Than One Jurisdiction" 113 *Trusts and Estates* 200 (1974)

Uri, "Flower Bonds Remain an Effective Method to Cut Estate Taxes" 52 *Journal of Taxation* 214 (1980)

"The Revocable Living Trust as an Estate Planning Tool", Report of Committee on Estate and Tax Planning, 7 *Real Prop, Prob and Tr J* 223 (1972)

Making Gifts

8

VII. Recommended Reading

§8.1 I. General Considerations in Making Gifts

Gifts can be an effective estate planning tool. They provide an estate owner with the opportunity to transfer assets to family members to save income and death taxes and also to reduce probate costs on his death. Since the enactment of the Tax Reform Act of 1976, which unified the previously separate estate and gift taxes, it is not as easy to reduce federal estate taxes in very large estates by making gifts as it formerly was. See §2.2. However, the Economic Recovery Tax Act of 1981 significantly increased the amount of the annual exclusion to $10,000 and eliminated the gift tax on interspousal gifts. As a result, gifts have once again become a most valuable estate planning tool.

Where the amount of the gift exceeds the amount of the annual exclusion and the available unified credit is not sufficiently large to eliminate the gift tax liability, a gift tax will have to be paid by the donor. For a discussion of how to compute the gift tax, see §§2.36 to 2.46.

It is sometimes possible to reduce the amount of the gift by making a "net gift." The donor, as a condition of the gift, may require the donee to pay the gift tax. The value of the gift will be reduced by the amount of the gift tax payable by the donee, which in turn reduces the total gift tax. Rev. Rul. 75-72, 1975-1 C.B. 310. In the case of a "net gift," however, the Internal Revenue Service maintains that if the gift tax paid by the donee exceeds the donor's adjusted basis in the gifted asset, such excess is taxable gain to the donor. The case law on this issue is split (compare *Johnson v Commr* 495 F2d 1079 (6th Cir 1974); *Hirst v Commr* 572 F2d 427 (4th Cir 1978); and *Owen v Commr* 81-2 USTC ¶9509 (6th Cir 1981); with *Deidrick v Commr* 643 F2d 499 (8th Cir 1981) cert granted 50 USLW 3244 (1982)) and it is likely that the question will soon be resolved by the Supreme Court.

A. Tax Advantages

§8.2 1. To Reduce Estate Taxes

By reason of the unification of estate and gift taxes, the amount of taxable gifts made by the estate owner after 1976 is added to the tax base in computing his estate tax. (See §§2.2 and 2.3.) Any gift taxes paid on the added back gifts are allowed as a credit against the estate tax. See §2.35. The effect of adding the taxable post-1976 gifts to the estate tax base and subtracting the gift taxes paid on such gifts is to tax such gifts at the marginal estate tax bracket. See §2.3.

A person who makes a taxable gift is really making a transfer of an amount which will eventually be subject to estate taxation. The gift tax which he pays is merely a prepayment of a portion of the estate tax. Despite this, there are at least three ways in which gifts can be useful tools in reducing estate taxes. (See §§8.3 to 8.5.)

§8.3   a.   Taking Advantage of the Nontaxable Portion of a Gift

Not the entire gift, but only the taxable portion, is added to the estate tax base for the purpose of computing the estate tax. I.R.C. §2001(b). Many gifts contain a nontaxable portion. Such portion consists of the amount of the gift qualifying for the $10,000 annual exclusion, the exclusion for tuition and medical care, the marital deduction, and the charitable deduction. (See §§2.39 to 2.44.)

Hence where A makes an outright gift of $50,000, only $40,000 is taxable, provided he has not already made previous gifts to that donee during the same year. The $10,000 is not taxable for gift tax purposes and is therefore not added back to the estate tax base. If the estate owner has sufficient potential donees to whom he is willing to make $10,000 annual gifts, he may over a period of years be able to effect a significant reduction of his estate. For example, a grandparent with three children and six grandchildren could reduce his estate by $90,000 per year.

The annual gift tax exclusion of $10,000 is, however, allowable only for a gift of a present and not a future interest. For an interest to be a present one, the unrestrictive right to the immediate use, possession or enjoyment of the asset must be given. For a discussion of the present interest exclusion, see §2.39.

A donor may wish to gift more than the amount of the annual exclusion in one year without making a taxable gift. A device sometimes used to accomplish this result is for the donor to sell an asset to the potential donee in exchange for a series of installment notes, payable in successive years, in amounts not exceeding the annual exclusion. Each year one of the notes is then forgiven. The Internal Revenue Service has held that where it is apparent the "donor" intends to forgive the notes in this manner, the transfer of the property will constitute a gift, rather than a bona fide sale, in the year of its transfer to the "donee." Rev. Rul. 77-299, 1977-2 C.B. 343. If the estate owner sells property to a son or daughter for $70,000 and takes back seven installment notes, each one of which the owner intends to forgive, the Service will contend that a gift of $70,000 was made in the year of the transfer rather than $10,000 gifts in each year when a note was actually forgiven.

Since 1981, direct payments of tuition and medical care do not constitute gifts. The estate owner may therefore reduce his estate by the amount which he expends for these purposes, as long as he is careful to pay the money directly to the educational institution or medical facility. See §2.41.

The amount of any gift made to a spouse is also excluded from the amount of gifts added back to the decedent's estate. In certain instances, it may be beneficial to make substantial gifts to one's spouse. For a full discussion of interspousal gifts, see §§8.14 to 8.16.

Where a married person makes a gift to a third party, it should be kept in mind that the gift can be treated as having been made one-half by each spouse. See §2.38 for a discussion of split gifts. If the gift is split, only the taxable portion of the decedent's spouse's one-half is added back to his estate tax base. For example, if A, a married person, gives $100,000 to X, only $50,000 (less the $10,000 annual exclusion, if applicable) is added back to A's estate tax base, if the gift was split with A's spouse. While not precisely spelled out in the Internal Revenue Code, there is little doubt that upon A's spouse's death, the other one-half of the gift (less the $10,000 annual exclusion, if applicable) will be added back to her estate. See I.R.C. §§2001(b), 2503 and 2513(a). Her estate may, however, be considerably smaller than A's. In that case only a small portion of the $100,000 gift will be taxed at A's estate tax rate. On the other hand, if her estate tax marginal bracket is higher than her husband's, splitting the gift will cause a larger estate tax.

§8.4   b.   Keeping Appreciation Out of the Estate

Another reason for making gifts is to keep future appreciation on the gifted assets out of the donor's estate. For example, assume the estate owner makes a gift, the taxable portion of which is $100,000. During the time the gift is in the hands of the donee, it appreciates in value so that at the time of the donor's death it is worth $300,000. Only the amount of the gift, i.e., $100,000, is added to the tax base. The $200,000 of appreciation is kept out. Gifting as a method of keeping appreciation out of the estate should be compared with other alternatives. See §8.47.

§8.5   c.   Keeping the Amount of the Gift Tax Out of the Estate

Another advantage in making lifetime gifts is that the amount of any gift tax paid will ordinarily not be taxed as part of the donor's estate. (See §8.7 for an exception to this rule where the amount of the gift is included in the gross estate because it was made within three years of death.) The fact that the gift tax is not "grossed up" will, particularly in larger estates, result in a net tax saving. This may be illustrated by an example. Assume an estate owner, who dies after 1986, with a net estate of $2,000,000. The federal estate tax will be $588,000. On the other hand, assume he made a gift of $750,000 during his lifetime, and retained $1,250,000. The gift tax of $55,500 which he paid will not be included in his estate. Hence, his estate tax base, instead of being $2,000,000, will be $1,944,500, resulting in an estate tax of $507,525 (after subtracting the gift tax). By making the gift, therefore, the total estate and gift tax will be $563,025, or a savings of $24,975, compared to where no gift was made.

§8.6   d.   Gifts Included in Gross Estate

Where a gift is made by the estate owner in such a manner that he retains certain prohibited benefits or rights in the property, or where certain gifts are made within three years of death, such gifts will be includable in his gross estate. (See §§2.12 to 2.15.) Gifts which are included in the gross estate, compared to gifts which are merely added to the estate tax base, lose some or all of the advantages of gift giving discussed in §§8.3 to 8.5.

§8.7   i.   Gifts Made within Three Years of Death

The Economic Recovery Tax Act of 1981, with a few limited exceptions, eliminated the inclusion in the donor's gross estate of gifts made within three years of his death. The exceptions are for gifts of life insurance and other transfers where the gifted property would otherwise be included in the gross estate under I.R.C. §§2036, 2037, 2038, 2041 or 2042, even if the decedent had retained the property. See §2.12. Although the statute is not entirely clear, it appears that all gifts of life insurance, but only those other transfers which require the filing of a gift tax return (i.e., those in excess of the $10,000 annual exclusion) are included in the estate. See I.R.C. §§2035(a), (b) and (d).

To the extent that the exception applies so that a gift made within three years of death is included in the gross estate, the value as of the date of death (or the alternate valuation date, if elected by the executor, see §2.16), rather than the value as of the date of the gift, is included. Thus, the amount of appreciation after the date of the gift is subject to estate tax. For example, where a life insurance policy worth $5,000 at the time of the gift has a face value of $100,000 at the time of death, it is unfortunately the latter amount that is includable in the estate.

The gift tax paid on any gifts made within three years of death will be included in the gross estate. I.R.C. §2035(c). This rule applies to the gift tax paid on all gifts made within three years of death, not merely those gifts included in the gross estate. In the example set forth in §8.5, if the donor died within three years of making the gift, the gift tax of $55,500 would have been included in his gross estate and the hoped-for $24,975 saving would have been nullified. The amount of gift tax paid by the decedent's spouse on gifts made by such spouse where the gift was "split," however, is not included in the decedent's estate. For a discussion of split gifts, see §§2.38 and 8.3.

§8.8   ii.   Other Lifetime Transfers Included in the Estate

Other lifetime transfers, in addition to certain gifts made within three years of death, may be included in the gross estate. These include transfers taking effect at death (see §2.13), gifts with possession or enjoyment retained (see §2.14), and transfers with a retained power to alter, amend, revoke or terminate (see §2.15).

With respect to these transfers, two of the advantages of making gifts are lost. First the entire transfer, and not merely the taxable portion (see §8.3), is included in the gross estate. In other words, there is no exception to the extent of the $10,000 annual exclusion. Second, the value of the gifted assets at the time of death, rather than at the time of the gift, is included in the donor's gross estate. Hence, the appreciation is taxed. (See §8.4.) Yet, unlike a gift made within three years of death, the amount of gift tax paid on these transfers is excluded from the donor's estate. (See §8.5.) For a full discussion of transfers in trust included in the estate, see §8.37.

§8.9 2. To Reduce Income Taxes

Another important tax reason for making gifts is to reduce the income taxes payable on the income earned by the gifted assets. This may be illustrated by an example. Assume an estate owner owns $100,000 of securities which earn $5,000 per year. He is in a 50 per cent income tax bracket and hence his net after tax yield is $2,500. If he gifts these securities to his son, who is only in a 20 per cent bracket, the son's after tax yield from the securities will be $4,000 per year. Additionally, the donor will not only save income taxes, but by making the gift, he will prevent his estate from being increased by the income from the gifted asset. Thereby his estate tax will tend to be less than if he had not made the gift.

If the gift is large enough, it will incur a gift tax which, as previously indicated, is in reality a prepayment of the estate tax. (See §8.2.) The gift may, however, be made and the income therefrom shifted to a lower bracket taxpayer without incurring a gift tax. This may be accomplished by having the donor retain a testamentary power of appointment over the principal. The result will be an incompleted gift of the principal and the avoidance of gift tax on the value of the principal. See I.R.C. §674(b)(3); Reg. §25.2511-2(c). The value of the principal may be computed by reference to Reg. §25.2512-9(f). See Appendix, Table VIII.

A possible drawback to this technique is that by retaining the power of appointment, the value of the principal at the time of the donor's death, rather than at the time of the gift, will be included in his estate. See I.R.C. §2038. This will result in an estate tax on the appreciation after the time of the gift. However, the donor may ameliorate this disadvantage by gifting a nongrowth asset, such as a bond or savings account.

§8.10 B. Nontax Advantages

There are at least five nontax reasons why an estate owner may wish to make gifts during his own lifetime. These are:

1. To enhance the wealth of the recipient: A wealthy estate owner may wish to see his children enjoy a higher standard of living.

2.   To secure the family against speculative activity and business risks: An estate owner may wish to make gifts to his spouse or children so that in the event of his bankruptcy or insolvency, his creditors may not go against the gifted assets. If, however, one makes such gifts after incurring liabilities, such gifts may be deemed to be in fraud of creditors and the creditors, to whom these liabilities are owed, may go against the gifted assets even in the hands of the donees.

3.   To relieve the donor of management problems: An elderly estate owner who has a sufficient other estate may wish to relieve himself of the burden of a troublesome asset by giving it away to younger family members.

4.   To remove assets from probate: Assets which are not owned by the estate owner at the time of his death are not subject to probate administration in his estate. (See §6.2.) Hence, even a deathbed gift will avoid probate.

5.   To bar rights of the spouse in the owner's estate: The laws of various states give a surviving spouse a statutory share in the decedent spouse's estate. The estate owner may make gifts prior to his death to defeat his spouse's statutory rights. He may wish, for example, to give a greater portion of his estate, than would remain after the statutory share, to his children of a prior marriage.

§8.11   C.   Disadvantages

Before a substantial gift is made, particularly one made primarily for tax reasons, the estate owner should be made aware of some of the serious disadvantages inherent in making gifts. To procure any tax advantage, a gift must be irrevocable. Once the gift is made it is possible the donor's circumstances may change, creating a need for either the principal or income from the asset given. Because the gift must be irrevocable, the donor may be in the extremely uncomfortable and disadvantageous position of having to rely on the donee or other persons for financial support.

Another concern when making gifts is the possibility of the death of the donee prior to the donor. The estate owner may find that, if the donee dies prior to the donor, the asset may go to persons whom the donor does not wish to benefit, such as in-laws. Even if the donee's estate plan provides for the return of the gifted asset to the donor, it may first be subject to an estate tax in the donee's estate, which would not have been the case if the gift had not been made.

Finally, gifts frequently cause family disharmony. Particularly where gifts are made to various members of the family, such as children, in unequal amounts or on unequal terms, jealousies and frictions may arise. In many instances it may not be possible, due to the nature of the owner's estate, for gifts to be made on a completely equal basis. Another cause for contention sometimes arising from a substantial gift is that it may engender loss of respect by the donee for the donor; because the donee, as a result of the gift, is no longer dependent on the donor.

§8.12 II. Legal Requirements for a Valid Gift

In order for a gift to accomplish the estate planning and tax advantages discussed in §§8.2 to 8.10, it is necessary not only that the gift be irrevocable, but also that it be a valid gift under state law. If the gift is not valid, the asset will still be deemed to be owned by the donor.

There are three basic requirements that must be fulfilled for a gift to be valid. First, there must be a clear intention on the part of the donor to make a gift. Second, there must be actual or constructive delivery of the subject matter. Third, the donee must accept the gift; where the gift is beneficial, however, acceptance is presumed. From a tax point of view, the second requirement, namely, that there be an actual or constructive delivery of the subject matter, does sometimes present a problem. Where the donor retains physical custody of the asset, as by leaving it in his own safe deposit box, this requirement will usually not be satisfied.

§8.13 III. To Whom Should the Gift Be Made

Once the estate owner decides that making a gift will be of benefit in terms of his estate planning objectives, he must then decide to whom the gift should be made. If the gift is made essentially for nontax reasons (see §8.10), it should be a relatively simple matter to determine to whom the gift should be made. However, if the gift is motivated primarily by tax reasons, alternative donees should be explored. Even in the latter event, the donor's nontax objectives should be carefully ascertained so that he does not do something for tax reasons which conflict with his underlying objectives (see §1.4). In the sections which follow, the spouse, the children and the grandchildren as potential donees are explored.

A. Spouse

§8.14 1. Gift Tax Avoidance

In order to accomplish certain estate planning objectives (see §§8.15 and 8.16), gifts from one spouse to the other should be considered. Either spouse, after 1981, may gift unlimited amounts to the other free of gift tax. I.R.C. §2523(a).

In the event the donor spouse does not wish to make outright gifts to the donee spouse, or gifts in trust where the donee spouse will have a general power of appointment permitting the donee to control the future disposition of the gifted asset, the donor may gift assets to a qualifying terminable interest property ("QTIP") trust. This type of gift, made after 1981, will qualify for the unlimited gift tax marital deduction. A qualifying income interest requires that the donee spouse be entitled to receive all the income from the property at least annually and that no person be able to appoint the property during the spouse's lifetime to anyone other than the spouse. If an election is made by the donor, there will be no gift tax at the time of the gift, but when the donee spouse either disposes of the qualifying terminable interest property during lifetime, or dies, such property will then be subject to gift or estate tax. See I.R.C. §§2044, 2519 and 2523(f). By making the gift to a "QTIP" trust, the donor spouse may give the donee spouse the income for life and provide that the remainder will pass to the children on the donee spouse's death. In this way, the donor does not surrender the power of future disposition of the gifted asset to the donee.

§8.15   2.   Estate Tax Savings

Where one spouse has no estate or a much smaller estate than the other spouse, interspousal gifts to the "poorer" spouse should be considered. The reason for considering such gifts is to avoid the loss of the marital deduction and the unified credit against the estate tax if the "poorer" spouse dies first. This may be demonstrated by an example.

Assume the husband has an estate of $1,500,000 and his wife has none, and both spouses live until at least 1987. If the husband dies first, he can leave an optimum marital deduction bequest of $900,000 to his wife. See §4.8. There will be no tax on his death, but $900,000 will be taxed on her death, resulting in an estate tax of $114,000. Each estate will receive the benefit of deducting the unified credit of $192,800. However, if the wife is the first to die, there will be no tax on her death, but there will be a tax of $363,000 on the husband's $1,500,000 estate upon his subsequent death. His larger estate is taxed at higher brackets and only one unified credit is deducted rather than two. As a result, an additional estate tax cost of $249,000 would have been incurred.

This additional cost of $249,000 could be avoided by the husband, during his lifetime, gifting $600,000 to the wife. There would be no gift tax cost (see §8.14) and on the husband's subsequent death, the federal estate tax would be $114,000, rather than $343,000, or a saving of $249,000. It may be that the couple would prefer that, if the wife dies first, the husband receive the lifetime benefits of the assets which he gifted to the wife. This objective may be fulfilled by the wife leaving her estate in the form of a bypass trust (see §§5.2 to 5.8) for the husband's benefit. As a result, the husband will receive the lifetime benefits without causing the assets to be included in his estate on his death.

If the husband, after making the gift to the wife, should die first, there is no adverse estate tax effect. Under the facts of the above example, there will be no estate tax on his death because the optimum marital deduction will be taken. Upon the wife's subsequent death, her estate will be $900,000, the estate tax on which will be $114,000.

Where each spouse's estate is already as large as the amount of the equivalent exemption (see §2.25), there is usually no estate tax advantage in one spouse gifting assets to the other. Regardless of which spouse dies first, there will be no estate tax because of the availability of the unified credit and the optimum marital bequest. On the death of the surviving spouse, the full unified credit will be available because of the size of such spouse's estate.

§8.16   3.   Income Tax Savings

In most cases, there is no income tax advantage in making gifts from one spouse to the other. Even where one spouse owns all the income-producing assets, the spouses may by filing joint income tax returns, achieve a splitting of the brackets for income tax purposes. In a few instances, however, income tax savings are obtainable through interspousal gifts.

The first such instance is where one spouse owns an appreciated asset and it appears likely that the other spouse will die first. By gifting this asset to the non-owner spouse, the asset will receive a new "stepped-up" basis on the donee spouse's death. See I.R.C. §§1014(a) and (b). For example, assume H owns an asset worth $100,000, with an income tax basis of $10,000. If he gifts this asset to his wife and she dies first, the asset, with the exception noted below, will receive a new basis of $100,000, even if she leaves it to the husband. If the husband had not gifted it to the wife, the asset, on her prior death, would have retained its basis of $10,000.

Where the couple resides in a community property state, the advantage of a "stepped-up" basis may be achieved by having each spouse gift his or her separate property to the community property. Both halves of the community property receive a new basis on the death of the first spouse to die. I.R.C. §1014(b)(6).

Gifts made in order to obtain a new "stepped-up" basis on the death of the donee spouse will fail to accomplish the intended result where such spouse dies within one year of the gift and the gifted asset passes from the decedent donee to the donor spouse. I.R.C. §1014(e). It is at present unclear whether the "stepped-up" basis will be denied where the decedent donee leaves the gifted asset to a bypass trust, of which the original donor spouse is a beneficiary. Resolution of this issue must await the issuance of regulations, Internal Revenue Service rulings, or judicial authority.

Another instance in which interspousal gifts could lead to an income tax saving is where the income from the gifted asset will be taxed at a lower bracket after the donee's death. For example, assume the husband is in a 50 per cent income tax bracket. He gifts an income-producing asset to the wife, who dies before he does. By having the wife leave this asset to a trust, with discretionary provisions, the income could either be accumulated or distributed to the children and thereby taxed at a lower income tax rate than if the income from the asset were received by the husband. For a discussion of discretionary trusts, see §§5.9 to 5.14.

B.   Children

§8.17   1.   Estate Tax Savings

If the purpose of the gift is to reduce estate taxes (see §§8.3 to 8.8), it is usually preferable to make gifts to the children rather than to the other spouse. Gifts made to the children will reduce the estate taxes on the death of each spouse, while a gift made from one spouse to the other will increase the estate of the surviving spouse. However, see §§8.15 to 8.16 for a discussion of where it is advisable to make interspousal gifts. The estate owner should make sure, however, that his spouse will not need the income from the gifted asset. If she will, the gift may be made to a trust where she will receive the income, with the remainder going to the children.

§8.18   2.   Income Tax Savings

As compared to interspousal gifts, gifts to children may frequently be used to advantage in saving income taxes. This may be illustrated by an example. Assume that the estate owner and his spouse have securities worth $90,000 which earn $3,600 per year. If they are in a 50 per cent bracket, the taxes on such income will be $1,800 per year. If they gave these securities in equal shares to three children, each child would have income of $1,200 per year, which would result in little or no income tax. For a discussion of the availability of the standard deduction and low income allowance where a dependent taxpayer receives unearned income, see §9.2.

§8.19   3.   Problems in Making Gifts to Children

The first problem in making gifts to children, particularly young ones, is that they may misuse the gift, thus dissipating a portion of the family wealth and causing pyschological discomfort to the estate owner. To some extent this problem may be solved by making the gift in trust (see §8.32). The second disadvantage is that the children may eventually have large estates and large incomes so that the estate and income tax advantages in making the gift turn out to be disadvantages. If the children already have estates of their own, consideration should be given to making gifts directly to the grandchildren or to a bypass trust for the child's lifetime with the remainder to the grandchildren. Any such trust with a value larger than $250,000 on the child's death will, however, incur the generation-skipping tax at that time. (See §5.37.)

C. Grandchildren

§8.20   1.   Avoiding the Generation-Skipping Transfer Tax

If the estate owner desires a portion of his estate to eventually go to his grandchildren, he may wish to consider giving it to them either outright or in trust. Unless the grandchildren are mature adults, the gift should normally be made in trust (see §8.32). This trust should not provide, however, that the income or other benefits go to the owner's child during his life because such a trust will be subject to the generation-skipping transfer tax upon the child's death. (See §§5.34 to 5.39.)

When making a gift, even in trust, to young grandchildren, it is possible that one or more of them may become very wealthy on their own or that as they become adults, they may be undeserving, while others are in great need. One of the ways of solving this problem is for the estate owner to give a person, perhaps his child, a special power of appointment to "sprinkle" income and principal among the grandchildren. As long as the power may be exercised only in favor of the grantor's lineal descendants who are in a younger generation than the holder of the power, this power will not cause the trust to be subject to the generation-skipping transfer tax. I.R.C. §2613(e).

§8.21   2.   Income Tax Savings

By giving assets directly to, or in trust for the benefit of, grandchildren, rather than to the children, there may be income tax savings if the grandchildren are in lower income tax brackets than the children are. For example, if the grantor is in a 50 per cent, the children in a 40 per cent, and the grandchildren in a 20 per cent bracket, greater income tax savings will be achieved by gifting the principal in such a way that the income will be taxed to the grandchildren rather than to the children.

IV.   Selection of Assets to Give

§8.22   A.   In General

Once the estate owner has decided on the particular donee or donees to whom to make gifts, he must next decide which of his assets to make the subject matter of these gifts. All too often insufficient consideration is given to this very important question. Before exploring the tax aspects, the donor must first decide whether a particular asset is best retained or given away. For example, if the asset is an income-producing one, will he need the income? If it is a growth asset, is it one which should be kept for his retirement in an inflationary era? If the asset is stock in a closely held corporation, would it interfere with the operation of the business if some of the stock were gifted? Only after the donor feels secure in giving away a particular asset, should his selection be considered from a tax point of view.

§8.23   B.   Tax Rules to Follow in Gifting Assets

There are various rules which should be taken into consideration by the estate owner before deciding which assets to make the subject matter of a gift. It is, however, emphasized that certain of these rules are not inflexible, but should be thought of as guidelines to follow absent countervailing factors. The following rules should be considered.

1.   Give taxable income-producing rather than nontaxable income-producing assets: Where one of the estate owner's objectives in making the gift is to reduce the income tax rate applicable to the income earned by the asset, then as much income as possible per a given dollar value of principal should be gifted. This may be illustrated by an example. Assume that the donor has two assets and must decide which one of the two to give. Each has a present fair market value of $50,000. One is a tax-free municipal bond yielding 8 per cent; the other a highgrade corporate bond yielding 15 per cent. If the donee is in a lower income tax bracket than the donor, the corporate bond should be gifted.

2.   Give growth, rather than nongrowth, assets: One of the tax reasons for making gifts is to keep future appreciation out of the donor's estate. (See §8.4.) It is evident that the gift of a growth asset will accomplish this objective much better than an asset which is likely to remain constant in value, such as a long-term note. It is, of course, not always possible to predict which assets will grow. What appears to be a growth asset may in fact decline substantially in value. One asset, however, which has a guaranteed growth factor, is a life insurance policy whose face value exceeds the present value of the policy. For a full discussion of the considerations in gifting a life insurance policy, see §§10.34 to 10.50.

3.   Give high basis, rather than low basis, assets: An asset acquired from a decedent receives a basis equal to the federal estate tax value of the asset. See §2.48. On the other hand, an asset which is gifted during the decedent's lifetime, and not included in the decedent's gross estate, retains the same basis for determining gain, depreciation, or depletion as it had in the hands of the donor. I.R.C. §1015. For a gift made after December 31, 1976, this basis may be increased by the portion of the gift tax paid on the amount of the excess of the fair market value over the donor's adjusted basis immediately before the gift. See §2.51.

   Because of the operation of the above rules, an asset worth more than its present basis will receive a higher basis if held by the decedent until death than if gifted during lifetime. Before selecting which assets to gift and which assets to retain, the estate owner should compute the comparative bases for each asset on the assumption that his death will occur in the near future. He then can decide which assets appear to be eligible for a significant "step-up" on death and which do not. Consideration may then be given to gifting those assets that have relatively high bases compared to their present values, and retaining assets that presently have low bases compared to their present values.

By way of example, assume A has two assets, each of which is a marketable security worth $100,000. The first has a basis of $10,000 and the second has a basis of $100,000. A should give away the second asset because the first will receive a higher basis if kept until death. In that way both assets will eventually receive a high basis. If, however, the low basis asset were given away, only the second would end up with a high basis.

Following the "give high basis, retain low basis" rule will not achieve a favorable result if the donee should predecease the donor. Where it is anticipated that the donee will die first, it would be advisable, if a gift is made at all, to gift the low basis asset to such donee. By having the donor retain the high basis asset, both assets will have a high basis on the donee's death. See §8.16 for a full discussion of the rule where the donee dies within one year of the gift.

4.   Do not give an asset which has a value less than its basis; rather sell the asset and gift the proceeds: When an estate owner dies with an asset worth less than its adjusted basis immediately prior to his death, the recipient will receive a new basis equal to the fair market value. By the same token, if such asset is gifted during the estate owner's lifetime, the donee's basis for determining loss is limited to the fair market value of the asset at the time of the gift. (See §2.51.) Hence, in either case, if the recipient sells such asset, he may not deduct the estate owner's "loss." To illustrate, if an asset worth $50,000 with a basis of $60,000 is either left on death or gifted during lifetime and then sold by the recipient, the $10,000 loss may not be deducted. In order to insure that the loss will not be wasted, the donor should sell such asset during his lifetime, deduct the loss on his return and gift the proceeds.

5.   Do not give to a trust property subject to an encumbrance for which the donor is personally liable: Where property is gifted to a trust on which there is an encumbrance for which the donor is personally liable, the income, to the extent that it may be used to make payments on the encumbrance, will be taxable to the donor rather than to the donee. See Reg. §1.677(a)-1(d). Moreover, because the trust income is attributable to the donor, there will also be an estate tax consequence. If the donor dies before the encumbrance is satisfied, the trust assets will be includable in his estate as a transfer with possession or enjoyment retained. See Reg. §20.2036-1(b)(2). Hence, the tax benefits from making the gift will be negated. As a result, most of the usual estate and income tax purposes in making a gift (see §§8.3, 8.4 and 8.9) will be unfulfilled. On the other hand, if the donor is not personally liable for the indebtedness, as would normally be the case where he purchased real property already subject

to a mortgage, the income of the trust will not be attributable to him for either income or estate tax purposes.

6. The gift should be more than a mere assignment of income: If only the income from an asset, aside from the income-producing asset itself, is gifted, the income will remain taxable to the donor. For example, where the owner of a bond makes a gift of the bond interest coupons, but retains the bond itself, he, and not the donee, will be taxable on the income. *Helvering v Horst,* 311 US 112 (1940). Hence, to shift the taxability of income to the donee, it is generally necessary that more than the income interest be gifted. However, if the income interest is for a substantial period of time, such as a life estate, the income will not be taxed to the donor. *Blair v Commr* 300 US 5, 57 SCt 330, 81 LE 465 (1937). Moreover, if the transfer is to a trust which lasts for a minimum of 10 years, the income will also not be taxable to the donor. See I.R.C. §673. For a full discussion of short term trusts, see Chapter 9.

7. Do not give an installment obligation: Where the estate owner sells an asset and receives less than the full selling price during the year of sale, he may decide to report any gain from the sale on the installment basis. The profit on the sale is then prorated over the period in which the payments are received, rather than all of it being subject to income tax in the year of sale. See I.R.C. §453. The installment note should not, however, be gifted. A disposition of the installment obligation will result in a realization of the entire untaxed profit at the time of the transfer. See I.R.C. §453(d).

8. Do not gift stock in a subchapter S corporation to a trust unless the trust is a "qualified Subchapter S Trust": An irrevocable trust whose income is not taxable to the grantor is ordinarily an ineligible shareholder. The corporation's election not to be taxed as a regular corporation will automatically be revoked whenever such a trust becomes a shareholder. See I.R.C. §§1371(a)(2), and (f). See §7.31 for a full discussion of a "qualified Subchapter S trust."

§8.24 V. Manner of Making Gifts

Once the estate owner has decided on the amount, the donee and the subject matter of the gift, he should then decide on the manner or form in which the gift should be made. Basically he has three choices. The gift can be made either outright, in trust, or, if the donee is a minor, under the Uniform Gifts to Minors Act. The general and tax considerations governing such choices are discussed in the sections that follow.

A.   Outright Gifts

§8.25   1.   Advantages

The most favorable characteristic of an outright gift is its simplicity. A trust instrument is not required and other documentation may be kept to a minimum. Another advantage of an outright gift is that the $10,000 annual gift tax exclusion is normally available since an outright gift is almost always a gift of a present interest. See I.R.C. §2503(b). For a discussion of the advantages in obtaining the $10,000 annual exclusion, see §§2.39 and 8.3.

§8.26   2.   Disadvantages

An outright gift compared to alternative gift forms may have the following disadvantages:

1.   Where the donee is a minor, the court may need to appoint a guardian of the minor's estate to manage and, where a sale is to be made, to sell the gifted asset. The guardianship method of holding assets for minor children is disadvantageous compared to either a custodianship under the Uniform Gifts to Minors Act or a trust. See §3.16 for the disadvantages of a guardianship.

2.   Even where the donee is an adult, but is either not capable of financial management or otherwise immature, the ownership by such donee of substantial assets may be unwise.

3.   Where the donee is the outright owner of the gifted asset, such asset will become part of his estate for estate tax purposes and the income therefrom will increase his income tax.

One or more of these disadvantages may be eliminated or ameliorated by the use of a gift under the Uniform Gifts to Minors Act or a gift to an irrevocable trust.

§8.27   B.   Gifts Under Custodian Statute

Most states have adopted the Uniform Gifts to Minors Act (or the revised Uniform Gifts to Minors Act). This act is designed as a simple, convenient and inexpensive method of making gifts to minors.

§8.28   1.   Legal Requirements

Under the Uniform Gifts to Minors Act, a gift of money, securities, life insurance policies, or annuity contracts can be made by having the donor place the asset in the name of a person called the custodian, who then holds the custodial property for the benefit of the minor. Gifts so made can be made only to one minor, and only one person at a time may be a custodian.

Legal title to the gift is vested in the minor. The custodian, unlike the trustee of a trust, has no title to the custodial property, but does have the right to hold and manage it under the provisions of the Act. During the minority of the minor, the custodian is required to pay to or for the benefit of the minor as much of the property as the custodian deems advisable for the support, maintenance, education and benefit of the minor. This payment may be made with or without regard to the duty of the custodian or any other person to support the minor and regardless of any other income or assets which the minor owns. When the minor attains the age of majority, which in most states is now 18, the custodianship terminates and the assets are owned outright by the minor.

Aside from tax considerations (see §§8.29 to 8.31), there are two main disadvantages to making gifts under the Act. First, it is available only for gifts of money, securities, life insurance and annuity contracts, but is not available for gifts of tangible personal property or real estate. Second, the custodianship terminates when the minor reaches his majority. The minor on attaining age 18 is probably not yet mature enough to deal wisely with the gifted assets.

2. Tax Consequences

§8.29 a. Income Tax

Generally, any income earned on assets gifted under the custodian statute is taxable to the minor, whether or not it is distributed or expended for his benefit. The Internal Revenue Service contends, however, that to the extent the income from the custodian account is used for the minor's support, the income is taxable to the person who is legally obligated to support him, namely the minor's parent. See Rev. Rul. 56-484, 1956-2 C.B. 23. To avoid this result, the income should either be retained in the custodianship account or used for nonsupport purposes. For a discussion of whether college education is within the duty of support, see §9.13.

§8.30 b. Gift Tax

A gift to the custodian is a completed gift for gift tax purposes. This type of gift is considered to be a gift of a present interest and, hence, qualifies for the gift tax annual exclusion. (See §2.40.) Accordingly, a gift under the custodian statute will satisfy one of the purposes for making gifts, namely, that gifts to the extent of the $10,000 annual exclusion are not added back to the tax base for the purpose of computing the estate tax. (See §8.3.)

§8.31   c.   Estate Tax

Where the donor is the custodian and dies while serving in that capacity before the minor donee attains his majority, the custodianship assets will be includable in the donor's estate. Rev. Rul. 59-357, 1959-2 C.B. 212. The reason is that the donor custodian has the right under the Uniform Act to terminate the custodianship. This right to terminate makes the transfer taxable under I.R.C. §2038. *Stuit v Commr* 452 F2d 190 (7th Cir 1971). Where an asset is included in the gross estate under I.R.C. §2038, neither the amount of the $10,000 annual exclusion nor the post-gift appreciation will escape estate taxation. (See §§8.4 and 8.8.) The donor should always name a third party as custodian in order to be sure to avoid includability in his gross estate.

C.   Gifts in Trust

§8.32   1.   Advantages

Gifts in trust can be useful where the donor does not desire to make either an outright gift or, where there is a minor donee, a gift under the custodian statute. A trust as a receptacle for gifts is the most flexible of devices. The trust can be structured to provide management for the beneficiaries who are too young or otherwise incapable of management and also, particularly where broad discretionary powers are given to the trustee, to provide for a flexible plan of distribution which will take into account the needs of the beneficiaries. For a complete treatment of all aspects of trusts, see Cohan and Hemmerling, *Inter Vivos Trusts, Planning, Drafting and Taxation* (McGraw-Hill Book Co/Shepard's Citations, Inc 1975).

§8.33   2.   Tax Consequences, in General

From a tax point of view, the trust to which gifts are made must be irrevocable; otherwise the gifts will be disregarded for all tax purposes. The assets and the income therefrom will be deemed to belong to the donor. The trust, if it does not interfere with the basic objective of the estate owner, in addition to being made irrevocable, should be structured so as to maximize the tax benefits in making gifts. Accordingly, it should qualify for the gift tax annual exclusion so this amount will not be added to the tax base (see §§8.34 and 8.35). Prohibited powers causing the assets to be included in the donor's estate (see §8.36) should be avoided, so that any appreciation will not enter into the computation of his estate taxes. Similarly, those powers and rights which cause the income from the trust to be taxable to the donor should also be avoided. (See §§8.38 to 8.41.)

3. Gift Tax

§8.34   a. $10,000 Annual Exclusion

In computing the gift tax, the donor is permitted to exclude from his taxable gifts annual exclusions of up to $10,000 per donee in each calendar year. (See §2.39.) Moreover, the amount permitted to be excluded is not added back to the tax base in computing the estate tax. (See §8.3.) However, the gifts must be gifts of a present interest in order to qualify for the annual exclusion. See I.R.C. §2503(b).

If a gift is made in trust, the principal is not a gift of a present interest because the donee does not have the unrestricted right to its immediate use, possession, or enjoyment. See Reg. §25.2503-3(b). However, where the trust provides that the income is to be paid currently to the income beneficiary, the value of the income interest is a present interest and qualifies for the $10,000 annual exclusion. The value of the income interest is computed by using the tables set forth in Reg. §25.2512-9(f), see Appendix, Table VIII. For example, where $100,000 is gifted to a trust which provides that the income is to be paid currently to A for A's life and upon A's death the remainder to B, and A is a male, age 50, 67.997 per cent of the gift, or $67,997, will be considered the value of the income interest. Since this amount exceeds the $10,000 annual exclusion (or even $20,000 in the event of a split gift, see §8.3), the full annual exclusion is available.

Despite the fact that the trust provides for income to be distributed currently, the annual exclusion may be disallowed if the income interest is, in fact, not a present interest. For example, the income interest will not be considered a present interest if the trust provisions direct that gains or losses be credited to or charged against income. Rev. Rul. 77-358, 1977-2 C.B. 342. The basis for this ruling is that, since losses will be chargeable to income, the amount of net income that will be distributed to the income beneficiary is unascertainable, as it cannot be accurately determined. Moreover, the exclusion may not be allowed where the gift to the trust consists of nonincome-producing assets, such as nondividend-paying corporate stock. Rev. Rul. 69-344, 1969-1 C.B. 225; *Stark v US* 345 FSupp 1263 (WD Mo 1972) affd per curiam 477 F2d 131 (8th Cir 1973) cert den 414 US 975, 94 SCt 290, 38 LE2d 218 (1973); but see *Rosen v Commr* 397 F2d 245 (4th Cir 1968). In any event, where the trust instrument requires that the income be accumulated, or the trustee is given discretionary powers over its payment, there is no gift of a present interest unless the trust qualifies as a Crummey trust (see §8.35) or a minor's trust (see §8.36).

§8.35   b.   Crummey Trust

By providing in the trust that the beneficiary is allowed to withdraw during each year the lesser of the amount of the annual exclusion or the value of the assets transferred to the trust during that year, the annual exclusion, even if there is otherwise no gift of a present interest, will be allowed. See *Crummey v Commr* 397 F2d 82 (9th Cir 1968). Therefore, where a donor transfers $100,-000 to a discretionary trust which permits the beneficiary to withdraw in the year of the gift the lesser of the gift or $10,000 (or $20,000 in the case of a "split" gift), the annual exclusion will be available. Moreover, according to the *Crummey* case, the gift will qualify as one of a present interest where the beneficiary has a right to withdraw, even if he is a young minor who cannot practically exercise his right to withdraw and even though no legal guardian is appointed.

The Internal Revenue Service, however, takes the position that any adult beneficiary must be informed of his right to withdraw and be given a reasonable time within which to make the withdrawal. Rev. Rul. 81-7, 1981-1 C.B. 474.

Where the beneficiary is given the right to withdraw annually more than the greater of $5,000 or 5 per cent of the value of the principal, which could be the case where he is given the right to withdraw the $10,000 annual exclusion amount, and the beneficiary fails to exercise this right, such failure will be considered a lapse for gift and estate tax purposes. As a result of such lapse, the beneficiary will be deemed to have made a taxable gift to the remainder beneficiary of the trust and also a transfer which may cause the assets which could have been withdrawn to be taxable in the beneficiary's estate. For a discussion of the tax effect of the lapse of a power which is not limited to $5,000 or 5 per cent, see §5.5. The lapse problem can be avoided in its entirety by limiting the beneficiary's right to withdraw to the lesser of (1) the amount of the annual exclusion or (2) the greater of $5,000 or 5 per cent of the principal of the trust. The gift tax problem, but not the estate tax problem, can also be solved by including a trust provision giving the beneficiary a special power to appoint the lapsed assets to third persons. See §5.8.

§8.36   c.   Minor's Trust

There is an exception to the rule that no present interest is created by a transfer to a discretionary trust if the transfer is to a so-called minor's trust. Congress recognized the necessity for such an exception because, if not for the exception, in order to obtain the exclusion, outright payments would have to be made to a minor.

The minor's trust must meet the requirements of §2503(c) of the Internal Revenue Code in order to qualify for the annual exclusion. Such section requires the trust to provide that both principal and income may be expended by, or for the benefit of, the donee before he becomes 21 and to the extent that such principal and income is not expended, it will pass to the donee on reaching age 21. In the event that the donee dies before reaching age 21, the trust is required to provide that the accumulated income and principal be payable to his estate or as he may appoint under a general power of appointment. I.R.C. §2503(c)(2)(B).

Despite the apparent wording of the statute that the trustee must have the above described power with respect to both principal and income, the courts and the Internal Revenue Service have held that the income interest alone may qualify for the annual exclusion. See *Commr v Herr* 303 F2d 780 (3d Cir 1962); Rev. Rul. 68-670, 1968-2 C.B. 413. The trust therefore may provide that the net income alone be either paid or accumulated in the trustee's discretion until the beneficiary reaches 21 years of age, at which time all undistributed income will be distributed to him or his estate. The value of the income interest will then qualify for the annual exclusion.

It should be noted that the minor's trust requirements are specifically geared to the beneficiary attaining age 21. This age continues in the statute despite the fact that most states have reduced the age of majority to 18. As a result, the minor's trust, although in many respects very similar to a gift under the Uniform Gifts to Minors Act, has an advantage over the latter type of gift. The assets will be subject to fiduciary management and control until the beneficiary reaches age 21 rather than age 18.

There could also be an income tax advantage in using a minor's trust, rather than a custodianship under the Uniform Gifts to Minors Act. Under the custodianship, the income is taxable to the minor whether or not distributed. However, under the trust arrangement, the income will be taxable to the minor or to the trustee, depending upon whether it is distributed or accumulated. (See §8.44). Hence, the trustee may be able to lower the income tax bracket by accumulating a portion of the income. Prior to the Tax Reform Act of 1976, any income accumulated in the minor's trust was subject to the throwback rule on eventual distribution, but this is no longer the case with regard to income accumulated prior to a beneficiary attaining age 21. (See §8.45.)

§8.37   4. Estate Tax

In gifting assets to an irrevocable trust, the estate owner should be careful to retain no prohibited benefits, rights or powers which will cause the trust assets to be included in his gross estate upon his death. If the trust assets are includable in his gross estate, there will be two adverse tax consequences. First, even the amount of the $10,000 annual exclusion will be includable in the gross estate (see §8.8). Second, the value of the asset at the time of death, rather than the value at the time that the gift was made, will be taxable. Accordingly, any appreciation after the time of the gift will be subject to estate tax (see §8.8).

What causes trust assets to be included in the estate owner's estate are *retained* benefits, rights or powers. If one is given benefits, rights or powers over trust assets by a third person, the assets are not taxed in the recipient's estate unless the benefit, right or power constitutes a general power of appointment. (See §2.8 for the definition of a general power of appointment.) For example, if A gifts assets to a trust and retains the income for life, the assets will be included in his estate. (See §2.14.) However, if A gifts assets to a trust, under which B receives the income for life, the trust assets are not includable in B's estate.

The prohibited retained benefits, rights or powers which cause a transfer to be included in the owner's gross estate are discussed in §§2.13 to 2.15. Basically, these prohibited transfers may be placed in one of two categories. The first is where the grantor retains a beneficial interest in the gifted assets, such as a reversionary interest (§2.13), a life estate (§2.14), or a power to revoke (§2.15). This category will not be reviewed here, but the reader is referred to the discussion in Chapter 2.

The second category is where the grantor has not retained any beneficial interest for himself, but merely a power to affect or rearrange the beneficial interest given to other persons. This category of powers is, for the most part, covered in I.R.C. §§2036(a)(2) and 2038 and will be discussed here.

§2036(a)(2) of the Internal Revenue Code causes inclusion in the gross estate where the donor has the right to designate the person who shall possess or enjoy the property or its income. §2038 of the Internal Revenue Code deals with retained powers to alter, amend, revoke or terminate the trust. The retention of these powers is prohibited whether the grantor holds them alone or in conjunction with any other person, even an adverse party. Moreover, even if the power is held by the grantor only in his capacity as a trustee or a co-trustee, it will nevertheless cause inclusion of the trust assets in his gross estate.

In most cases, the retention of these powers is not intentional and may easily be avoided by careful drafting. See generally Rabkin and Johnson, *Current Legal Forms With Tax Analysis,* Vol. 4 (Matthew Bender & Co 1981); Cohan and Hemmerling, *Inter Vivos Trusts, Planning, Drafting and Taxation* 185-199 (McGraw-Hill Book Co/Shepard's Citations, Inc (1975). A few examples of powers which will cause inclusion in the gross estate and which should be avoided are as follows:

1. The retained unlimited discretionary power to accumulate or distribute income or principal, or both, to a particular beneficiary will cause the value of the trust assets to be included in the gross estate. *US v O'Malley* 383 US 627, 86 SCt 1123, 16 LE2d 145 (1966); *Industrial Trust Co v Commr* 165 F2d 142 (1st Cir 1947). An example is where the trust gives the grantor the power, either alone or with anyone else, to make trust distributions without regard to an ascertainable standard to A, and on A's death the remaining trust assets will go to B.

2. The retained power to terminate a trust prior to the termination date specified in the trust agreement is also prohibited. *Lober v US* 346 US 335, 74 SCt 98, 98 LE 15 (1953). An example is where the trust will terminate when the beneficiary reaches age 35, but the grantor may distribute principal to him, without regard to an ascertainable standard, prior to that time.

3. The retained power to vote stock of a controlled corporation transferred to a trust causes the stock to be included in the grantor's gross estate.

I.R.C. §2036(b). A controlled corporation is defined as one in which the estate owner or related parties, as described in the constructive ownership rules of I.R.C. §318 (see §12.33), own 20 per cent or more of the corporate stock. I.R.C. §2036(b).

4.   The retained power to substitute a trustee with another trustee, which enables the grantor to appoint himself, causes the trustee's powers to be treated as if held by the grantor. If these powers are prohibited under I.R.C. §§2036, 2037 or 2038 (see §§2.13 to 2.15), they will cause the trust assets to be taxed in the grantor's estate. The Internal Revenue Service goes even further and takes the position that the trustee's powers will be deemed to be held by the grantor even where his power to substitute is limited to appointing a third person, or even a corporate trustee. Rev. Rul. 79-353, 1979-2 C.B. 325. However, in Rev. Rul. 81-51, 1981-1 C.B. 9, the Internal Revenue Service held that Rev. Rul. 79-353, insofar as it pertains to the substitution of one corporate trustee for another, is not to be applied to a transfer to an irrevocable trust made prior to October 29, 1979.

Certain powers are not considered broad enough to cause inclusion in the gross estate. The retained power to distribute to a third person under an ascertainable standard will not cause inclusion. *Jennings v Smith* 161 F2d 74 (2d Cir 1947). For instance, the grantor's right to distribute principal only if needed for the beneficiary's education is not prohibited. Moreover, the retention of administrative powers or control over the trust investments generally does not cause inclusion in the gross estate. *Old Colony Trust Co v US* 423 F2d 601 (1st Cir 1970). Additionally, the grantor may be given the power to allocate receipts and expenses between principal and income pursuant to a fiduciary standard. Because of these exceptions for administrative and investment powers, the grantor in many instances may be made a co-trustee, even where the trust contains discretionary powers regarding the distribution of income or principal. However, in that case the trust instrument must provide that all discretionary distribution powers be lodged solely in the other trustee.

§8.38   5.   Income Tax

The income earned by an irrevocable trust may be taxed in one of four ways. It may be taxed to the grantor, to a person who is neither the grantor nor a beneficiary of the trust, to the trust itself, or to the beneficiary of the trust. Since in many instances, a prime motive for gifting assets to the trust is to reduce income taxes, the trust should be structured in such a way that the income is taxable to the trust or to the beneficiary, but not to the grantor or any other person.

§8.39   a.   Avoiding Income Being Taxable to Grantor

The income earned by a trust will be taxable to the grantor in any one or more of the following situations:

1. The grantor, or any nonadverse party, has the power to revoke the trust. See I.R.C. §676.

2. The grantor, or any nonadverse party, has the right to control the beneficial enjoyment of the trust. See §8.38.

3. The grantor, or any nonadverse party, may exercise certain prohibited administrative powers. See §8.39.

4. The grantor, or any nonadverse party, has the power to recapture the income earned by the trust for himself or his spouse. See §8.40.

A "nonadverse party" is anyone who is not an adverse party. I.R.C. §672(b). An "adverse party" is a person having a substantial beneficial interest in the trust that would be adversely affected by the exercise or nonexercise of the particular power. A third party having a general power of appointment is considered to be an adverse party. I.R.C. §672(a).

If none of the above powers may be exercised for at least 10 years, the income will not be taxed to the grantor during such period. For a discussion of the 10-year reversionary interest rule, see §9.5.

§8.40   i.   Retention of Powers Affecting Beneficial Enjoyment

Where the grantor, or a nonadverse party, without the consent of an adverse party, retains the power to shift or dispose of the principal of the trust, the income earned by the trust will be taxable to him. I.R.C. §674(a). A prime example of the power to shift or dispose of trust assets is the power to "sprinkle" (i.e., distribute) to one or more beneficiaries in the grantor's discretion. There are, however, four exceptions to this rule. Without causing the income to be taxed to the grantor, he, or any nonadverse party, may have the power to shift principal:

1. By will (I.R.C. §674(b)(3)),

2. Among charitable beneficiaries (I.R.C. §674(b)(4)),

3. Among beneficiaries according to a reasonably definite standard set forth in the trust instrument (for example, the power to distribute principal to those named beneficiaries who are in college) (I.R.C. §674(b)(5)), or

4. To a current income beneficiary whose proportionate share of income will be reduced by the shifting of principal (for example, where A and B are each receiving one-half of the income, the power to distribute

principal to either of them will be permissible if the distributee's share of the future income is reduced by the same proportion as the distributed principal). (I.R.C. §674(b)(5)).

Similarly, where the grantor, without the consent of an adverse party, retains the power to affect who will receive the income, the income of the trust will be taxable to him. Here also there are four exceptions. The grantor will not be taxed on the income, if he has a power over income to:

1. Change beneficiaries by his will (I.R.C. §674(b)(3)),
2. Reallocate among charitable beneficiaries (I.R.C. §674(b)(4)),
3. Accumulate income during the legal disability of an income beneficiary or during the time such beneficiary is under age 21 (I.R.C. §674(b)(7)), or
4. Accumulate income that will ultimately be payable to the current income beneficiary or beneficiary's estate or appointees (for example, the power to accumulate income until the beneficiary reaches age 30 at which time such accumulated income is to be paid to him) (I.R.C. §674(b)(6)).

Where persons other than the grantor or his spouse are the trustees, certain additional powers may be exercised by these trustees, even if they are not adverse parties, and the income will not be taxed to the grantor. An "independent trustee" may shift beneficial interests among any beneficiaries. I.R.C. §674(c). An independent trustee is one who is not related to or subservient to the wishes of the grantor, such as a corporate trustee. Any other trustee (except for the grantor or his spouse) may shift income interests provided the power is limited to a reasonably definite external standard set forth in the trust instrument. I.R.C. §674(d). Hence the grantor's brother, for example, may act as trustee and be given power to distribute income to those beneficiaries who are in college. An independent trustee could be given an unlimited discretion to distribute income to any beneficiary, as for example, for the general welfare of the beneficiary.

§8.41   ii.   Administrative Powers

The retention of any of the following administrative powers will cause the income of the trust to be taxed to the grantor:

1. The power, exercisable by the grantor or a nonadverse party, without the approval or consent of an adverse party, which enables the grantor or any person to purchase, exchange or otherwise deal with or dispose of the corpus or income for less than an adequate consideration. I.R.C. §675(1).
2. The power, exercisable by the grantor or a nonadverse party, which enables the grantor to borrow the corpus or income, directly or indirect-

ly, without adequate interest or without adequate security, except where a trustee (other than the grantor) is authorized under a general lending power to make loans to any person without regard to interest or security. I.R.C. §675(2). Moreover, if the grantor borrows the principal or income and fails to completely repay the loan and any interest before the beginning of the taxable year, the income of the trust will be taxable to him. If the loan is made by an independent trustee, the foregoing requirement of repayment of the loan and all interest is not applicable. I.R.C. §675(3).

3.   Exercisable by any person in a nonfiduciary capacity:

   a.   The power to vote or direct the voting of stock or other securities of a corporation in which the holdings of the grantor and the trust are significant from the viewpoint of voting control;

   b.   The power to control the investment of trust funds either by directing investments or reinvestments, or by vetoing proposed investments or reinvestments, to the extent that the trust fund consists of stocks or securities of corporations in which the holdings of the grantor and the trust are significant from the viewpoint of voting control; or

   c.   The power to re-acquire the trust corpus by substituting other property of an equivalent value. I.R.C. §675(4).

§8.42   iii.   Income Held for Future Use of the Grantor

The grantor is also taxable on the income of a trust whose income, without the consent of an adverse party, may be distributed to him or his spouse, accumulated for the benefit of either, or applied to the payment of premiums on life insurance policies on his or her spouse's life. I.R.C. §677(a). To cause taxability, it is in most instances not required that the trust income be actually distributed for the prohibited purpose, but merely that there be a power to do so.

Where the trust income may be used to satisfy the grantor's obligation (as for example, his liability on a loan), such income is taxable to him on the theory that it is distributable to him. Reg. §1.677(a)-1(d). However, where income may be used in the trustee's discretion to discharge the grantor's obligation to support any person (other than his spouse), the income will not be taxable to the grantor unless the income is actually so applied or distributed. I.R.C. §677(b). To avoid taxability to the grantor, it is advisable, in a discretionary type trust, to give the trustee power to make distributions to the grantor's minor children for purposes other than support.

§8.43   b.   Avoiding Income Being Taxable to Persons Other Than Grantor or Beneficiary

In gifting assets to an irrevocable trust, the grantor should be careful to not only avoid the income's being taxed to him, but also to avoid its being taxed to a third person other than the trust or the beneficiary. There are two circumstances where the income will be taxed to such third person.

The first is where the third person has the power to withdraw or distribute income or principal to himself. The income will then be taxed to such person. I.R.C. §678(a)(1). For example, assume A creates a trust for the benefit of B, but gives to C (whether or not C is the trustee) the unlimited power to invade principal for himself. All the income will be taxable to C. Moreover, a power to distribute for the support of a person whom the holder of the power has a duty to support (as for example, minor children) will generally cause the income to be taxed to the third person obligor. However, if the third person holds such support power in the capacity of a trustee, the income will not be taxed to him, except to the extent distributions are actually made for support purposes. I.R.C. §678(c).

The second circumstance where the income will be taxed to a third person, is where it is used to satisfy the legal obligation of such person even though he has no power to direct that the income be used in this fashion. See Reg. §1.662(a)-4. Under this rule, where a grandfather creates a trust for the benefit of his minor grandchildren, whom his son (i.e., the grandchildren's father) is obligated to support, the income will be taxed to the grantor's son, to the extent it is so used, even if the son is not a trustee.

c.   Normal Rules of Trust Income Taxation

§8.44   i.   The Extent to which Income Is Taxable to the Trust and to the Beneficiary

Where the estate owner has carefully structured the trust so that the income will not be taxed to him or a third person (see §§8.39 to 8.43), the income will be taxed under the rules of trust income taxation. These rules are extremely technical and will only be summarized here.

In general terms, a trust is a separate income tax paying entity. The portion of the net income which is not currently distributed or required to be currently distributed is taxable to the trust. I.R.C. §641. The remaining portion of the net income is taxable to the beneficiary, in his taxable year during which the trust's taxable year ends. I.R.C. §662. The trust may choose any fiscal year ending on the last day of the month, even if the beneficiaries of the trust are on a calendar year. I.R.C. §441(e).

For purposes of illustration, assume a trust has a fiscal year ending January 31. The trust provides that all the net income is to be distributed at least annually to B, the beneficiary, who reports his income on a calendar year basis. During the fiscal year, the trust earns $10,000 of net income. The trust will not pay tax on this income on its own return. B will report the entire $10,000 as part of his income for the calendar year ending on December 31 following the end of the trust's fiscal year. If in this example the trustee had discretion to accumulate the income or distribute all or part of it to B and exercised its discretion by distributing $4,000, B would include only the $4,000 in his taxable income. The trust would pay the tax on the undistributed $6,000.

Because of the method used in taxing trust income, a discretionary trust may provide certain income tax benefits. A discretionary trust is one where the trustee has discretion to accumulate income and to distribute all or part of it to one or more of the beneficiaries. Income may thereby be distributed currently to persons who are in a low income tax bracket, or if the beneficiaries are in a high income tax bracket, the trust may retain all or part of the income and pay the current tax at a lower rate. When the accumulated income is later distributed, it may, however, be subject to the throwback rule (see §8.45). For a discussion of the discretionary powers which may cause the trust assets to be included in the grantor's estate or the income to be taxed to him, see §§8.37 to 8.40. Moreover, see §§5.10 to 5.14 for a fuller discussion of discretionary trusts.

§8.45   ii.   Effect of the Throwback Rule

The throwback rule was enacted to prevent discretionary trusts from being used to accomplish too great a tax advantage for the beneficiary (see §8.44). The throwback rule is extremely technical. See I.R.C. §§665 to 667. All of its aspects will not be covered here. However a brief explanation of the history, theory and present method of computing the tax under the rule is presented. For a fuller discussion of the original theory of the throwback rule, see Cohan, Brown, Carr, Cornfeld, Hemmerling & Weinstock, "Accumulation Trusts and Charitable Remainder Trusts" 23 *Univ So Cal Tax Inst* 501 (1971).

The original theory of the throwback rule was to tax income which was accumulated in one year and distributed to a beneficiary in a subsequent year in roughly the same manner as if the income had been distributed to the beneficiary currently instead of being accumulated in the trust. Under this theory if a discretionary trust in a given year earned $10,000 of income and paid $2,000 of income tax, if the beneficiary in that year was in a 50 per cent bracket, and if the beneficiary eventually received a distribution of the accumulated income, he would have had to pay an additional tax of $6,000 (50 per cent times [$10,000, plus $2,000]), less the $2,000 of taxes which the trust had already paid, or a net additional tax of $4,000.

Starting in 1969, the taxpayer was in most instances given an option of using one of two methods in computing the additional tax under the throwback rule. He could use the exact method or the short-cut method. Under the exact method, the accumulated income was thrown back to the year it was earned, as in the previous example. Under the short-cut method the additional tax was computed on an arbitrary averaging basis. In either case no income accumulated prior to 1969, which is distributed after 1973, was, or is, subject to the throwback rule.

The Tax Reform Act of 1976 made three major changes. First, the distribution of income accumulated before the beneficiary attained age 21 (or before he was born) is no longer subject to the throwback rule. Second, the distribution of accumulated capital gains to any beneficiary is also no longer subject to the throwback rule. Finally, the taxpayer may no longer use the exact method as an option in computing his additional tax, but must use a new form of the short-cut method. See I.R.C. §667(b).

Under the new short-cut method, the additional tax on the accumulation distribution is computed on the basis of the five immediately preceding taxable years of the beneficiary. However, the year with the highest taxable income and the year with the lowest taxable income in this five-year period are eliminated and therefore the additional tax, in reality, is computed on a three-year period.

After the three-year period has been determined, the accumulation distribution is divided by the number of years over which the accumulation income was earned and this portion is then added to the beneficiary's taxable income in each of the three years. Hence, if the accumulated income is attributable to six different years, then one-sixth of the amount distributed would be added to the beneficiary's taxable income in each of the three years. The additional tax is then computed with respect to these three years and the average additional tax for the three-year period is determined. This amount is then multiplied by the number of years to which the trust income relates, as, for example, six years. The tax as computed is then offset by a credit for any taxes previously paid by the trust with respect to the distributed income. The remaining tax liability is due and payable in the same year as the tax on the beneficiary's other income in the year of distribution.

These complicated rules may be illustrated by an example. Assume the beneficiary receives a $10,000 accumulation distribution in 1978, representing undistributed net income earned by the trust during the years 1972 through 1977. The trust paid $2,000 tax on such income. The beneficiary had taxable income of $24,000 in 1972, $25,000 in 1973, $26,000 in 1974, $27,000 in 1975, $28,000 in 1976, and $29,000 in 1977.

Under the required method of computation, the three-year base period would be the years 1974, 1975 and 1976 (1973 and 1977 are eliminated because they are the lowest and highest years). The $10,000 accumulation distribution, after adding the taxes of $2,000 paid by the trust, is divided by six (the number of years during which the income was earned by the trust), resulting in $2,000 ($10,000 plus $2,000 divided by six). This average distribution of $2,000 is added to the beneficiary's taxable income for 1974, 1975 and 1976, resulting in taxable income as adjusted of $28,000, $29,000 and $30,-000, respectively. Assume the average increased tax for each of such years is $1,000 per year. This average increased tax is multiplied by six (the number of years during which the accumulated income was earned), resulting in $6,000 ($1,000 times six). From the total increased tax is then subtracted the $2,000 of taxes already paid by the trust, resulting in a net additional tax payable on the beneficiary in 1978 of $4,000 ($6,000 minus $2,000).

Where a beneficiary's income with the passage of time is increasing, it may be disadvantageous from an income tax point of view to accumulate rather than distribute income. The reason is that the accumulated income is taxed at the beneficiary's marginal income tax rates for the three-year base period close to the time he received the income. If he had received the income earlier when he was in a lower bracket, there would have been less tax on such income. On the other hand, even if the ultimate tax is greater, the fact that the payment is deferred, at no interest cost, may more than compensate for the higher tax.

§8.46   d.   Sale by Trust Within Two Years

An estate owner who is in a high income tax bracket may contemplate selling an asset at a gain, in which case the gain will be taxed at a high rate. From an income tax planning point of view, he might be better advised to gift the asset to a trust and have the trust make the sale in which case it will be taxed at a lower rate. The Internal Revenue Code, however, somewhat restricts this planning device. A special tax is imposed on a trust that sells assets within two years after such assets have been transferred to it by gift (i.e., a transfer for less than full consideration). The trust's tax is generally the amount of the additional tax that the estate owner would have paid if he had sold the asset in the year in which the trust did. I.R.C. §644.

For example, assume a taxpayer, with a capital gain bracket of 20 per cent, gifts a capital asset to the trust worth $20,000 more than its adjusted basis. If the trust sells the asset within two years at a price equal to its value at the time of the gift, it will pay a capital gains tax of $4,000, computed on the taxpayer's bracket of 20 per cent, rather than on its own bracket which may have been less. If, however the asset is sold for less than its value at the time of the gift, the gain is computed on the amount of the actual gain, but based on the transferor's marginal bracket.

VI.   Alternatives to Gifts

§8.47   A.   In General

As indicated in §8.4, one of the main reasons for making gifts, since the unification of estate and gift taxes in 1976, is to keep appreciation out of the estate. The price which the estate owner pays when he makes a gift to achieve this objective is that he loses the economic benefit of the asset during his lifetime. There are other methods which may be used to freeze, or sometimes even reduce, the value of an asset, which permit the estate owner to retain all or part of the benefit of the frozen asset during his lifetime.

Several of these methods are discussed in other chapters, namely, private annuities (Chapter 11), corporate and partnership recapitalizations and restructures (Chapter 12), sales of an asset (Chapter 12) and transfers to charitable remainder trusts (Chapter 14). Other alternatives are sales of a remainder interest (see §8.48) and grantor annuities (see §8.49).

§8.48   B.   Sale of a Remainder Interest

This is a novel and relatively untested technique, designed to go beyond freezing the value of an asset. Its objective is to eliminate the asset completely from the estate owner's gross estate. To accomplish this aim, the estate owner sells a remainder interest in an asset, usually to a family member, for adequate and full consideration, retaining the life interest. Either the life interest may be held as a legal life estate or the entire property may be transferred to a trust whereby the estate owner retains the income or beneficial enjoyment for his life. On the estate owner's death, the asset goes to or for the benefit of the remainderman.

On the estate owner's death, provided "adequate and full consideration in money or money's worth" was paid for the remainder interest, the asset will not be includable in his estate. I.R.C. §2036(a). Although there is no clear-cut authority on the subject, it is this author's opinion that adequate and full consideration means an amount equal to the value of the remainder interest on the date of the sale. (See *Estate of Christ v Commr* 480 F2d 171 (9th Cir 1973); but see two earlier cases, *US v Past* 347 F2d 7 (9th Cir 1965) and *Estate of Lillian B Gregory v Commr* 39 TC 1012 (1963). Also see *US v Allen* 293 F2d 916 (10th Cir 1961), which at first blush appears to contradict the author's opinion, but which on closer examination deals only with a transfer in contemplation of death, and is not on point. See *US v Heasty* 370 F2d 525 (10th Cir 1965) for an explanation of the *Allen* case.)

The value of the remainder interest is determined by reference to the Treasury Department's valuation tables regarding life estates and remainder interests. Reg. §20.2031-10. Under these tables, the remainder interest will normally be worth significantly less than the value of the entire asset.

To illustrate the above, the value of a remainder interest to a male age 55 is only 38.224 per cent of the total value of the property. See Appendix VIII, Table A(1). As a result, such person could sell an asset worth $1,000,000 for $382,240, which would be adequate and full consideration therefor. Upon his death the transferred asset would not be included in his estate; merely the consideration which he received, to the extent he had not consumed it, would be included. Assuming no change in values had occurred between the date of the sale and the time of death, the seller's estate would have been reduced by $617,760.

Care should be taken to insure that the estate owner does not sell the asset for less than the value of the remainder interest. If he does, a different rule applies. The fair market value of the entire asset at the time of his death, less the value of the consideration received, will be included in his estate. I.R.C. §2043(a). To be certain that sufficient consideration is paid, the property sold should be accurately appraised and the consideration, if not paid entirely in cash, should be worth the full sales price.

The income tax consequences of the sale of a remainder interest should not be overlooked. There will be taxable gain to the seller to the extent the sales price for the remainder interest exceeds that portion of the basis of the asset allocable to the remainder interest. The seller should also take into account the fact that he will continue to receive the income from the property during his lifetime, so the device, compared to a gift, will not reduce his income. In addition, upon the seller's death, the purchaser's income tax basis for the asset will be an amount equal to the purchase price of the remainder interest. This amount, in many cases, will be less than what the purchaser's basis would have been if the asset had been included in the seller's estate and the purchaser had inherited it. In some cases, it also will be less than what the basis would have been if the purchaser had received the asset by gift. For the computation of basis where property was inherited, see §2.48 and for the computation of basis of property acquired by gift, see §2.51. A careful analysis should be made in each case to determine whether the projected estate tax saving is more than outweighed by the income tax disadvantage.

§8.49   C.   Grantor Annuity

An innovative method of making a "gift" is available, which is not subject to gift tax and, hence, the amount is not added to the estate tax base. This device may be called a grantor annuity. The donor transfers assets to an irrevocable trust which provides for a fixed rate of return to be paid to the donor for a fixed period of time. At the end of that period the trust terminates and the trust assets are distributed to the remaindermen donees, for example, to the donor's children. The value of the gift is computed by referring to the valuation tables set forth in Reg. §20.2031-10. See Appendix, Table VIII, Table B. These tables are predicated on a 6 per cent interest factor. A sufficiently higher rate of return could be required to be paid to the donor by the trust, so that the value of the donor's annuity will equal the value of the assets transferred. As a result, the gift tax value of the gift to the remaindermen donees will be nil. During periods of high interest rates, the trust assets can easily be invested to return more than 6 per cent.

To illustrate, assume a father transfers $100,000 to an irrevocable trust. The trust provides that 12 per cent of the value of the assets at the time of such transfer (i.e., $12,000) is to be paid each year to the donor for a period of 13 years, after which time the remaining trust assets are to be distributed to the children. Using this payout rate, the value of the father's annuity would be at least $100,000. See Appendix VIII, Table B ($12,000 times 8.8527 equals $106,232). The value of the gift to the children will therefore be nil. After 13 years, they will receive the trust assets as a nontaxable gift, and, on the father's subsequent death, this gift will not be added back to his estate tax base.

If the father, however, should die prior to the expiration of the trust term, the trust assets would be included in his gross estate under I.R.C. §2036. (See

§2.14.) This technique is therefore most appropriate where the donor is relatively young and healthy.

VII. Recommended Reading

Bolmuth, "Is It Still Economical to Make Lifetime Gifts?" 117 *Trusts and Estates* 165 (1978)

Brogan, "Use of Grantor Trusts Imperiled by Maze of Disparate Income and Estate Tax Rules" 44 *Journal of Taxation* 69 (1976)

Capouano and Rinsky, "Planning Gifts to a Spouse to Obtain Maximum Tax Benefits Under the New Law" 46 *Journal of Taxation* 73 (1977)

Cohan and Hemmerling, *Inter-Vivos Trusts: Planning, Drafting and Taxation* (McGraw-Hill Book Company/Shepard's Citations, Inc (1975)

Cornfeld, "New Laws on Accumulation Trusts Require Practitioners to take Prompt Action" 45 *Journal of Taxation* 331 (1976)

Costello, "Capital Gains Realized by Trusts: Taxation to Persons other than the Trustee" 22 *The Tax Lawyer* 495 (1969)

Edwards, "How to Transfer Property to Minor Children" 3 *Estate Planning* 13 (1975)

Flannery, "The 'Sprinkler Trust' and Its Inherent Federal Income Tax Problems: Fulfilling of Legal Support Obligations" 54 *Taxes* 483 (1976)

Halbach, "Trusts in Estate Planning" 2 *The Probate Lawyer* 1 (1975)

Heckerling, "Taxing the Grantor Who Remains Trustee-Custodian for a Minor" 1 *Tax Advisor* 443 (1970)

Hess, "Effective Lifetime Gift Program Can Reduce Income and Estate Tax of Donor" 1 *Estate Planning* 134 (1974)

Horvitz, "How the Nature of Trust Property Can Kill the Gift Tax Exclusion" 113 *Trusts and Estates* 490 (1974)

Simons, "Drafting the Crummey Power" 15 *Univ of Miami Inst on Estate Planning* 1700 (1981)

Stitler, "Estate Planning Changes Necessitated by Statutory Reduction of the Age of Majority" 1 *Estate Planning* 2 (1973)

Weinstock, "Beyond Freezes: Planning to Reduce the Taxable Estate" 16 *Univ of Miami Inst on Estate Planning* 500 (1982)

Wentworth, "Accumulation Trust: A Step Toward Simplification" 117 *Trusts and Estates* 621 (1978)

"Tax Consequences of Gifts of Encumbered Property in Trust" Report of Committee on Income Taxation of Estates and Trusts, 8 *Real Prop, Prob and Tr J* 371 (1973)

Using a Short-Term Trust

9

§9.1   I. Introduction

The short-term trust is an estate planning tool to save income taxes. It can be employed instead of an outright gift or permanent trust where the estate owner does not desire to part with the principal permanently. The usefulness of a short-term trust was affected negatively in some respects by the unification of the estate and gift tax under the Tax Reform Act of 1976 (see §§2.2 and 9.12), but it is enhanced by the increase in the annual exclusion to $10,000 under the Economic Recovery Tax Act of 1981. This chapter will discuss the purpose of a short-term trust, how it is taxed, when it should be used and several problems which are unique to this device, and then it will be compared with alternative planning tools.

A short-term trust, sometimes called a "Clifford" trust, is an irrevocable trust which is required to last, with the exceptions discussed in §9.5, for at least 10 years. If properly set up, the income during the term of the trust will belong to the income beneficiary and, depending upon the provisions of the trust, may be either currently distributed or accumulated in the trustee's discretion. If the income is currently distributed, it is taxable to the beneficiary in the beneficiary's taxable year in which ends the taxable year of the trust during which the income was earned. I.R.C. §652. If the income is accumulated, it must be distributed to the income beneficiary no later than the termination date of the trust. Accumulated income when earned will be taxable to the trust (I.R.C. §662), but upon distribution it will be subject to the throwback rule in the hands of the beneficiary. For discussion of the throwback rule, see §8.45.

§9.2   II. Basic Purpose of Short-Term Trust

The basic purpose of a short-term trust is to permit the grantor to shift temporarily some of his income to a taxpayer who is in a lower income tax bracket than he is, without the necessity of the grantor's permanently giving away the assets subject to the trust. Not only will the taxes be reduced on the income, but the grantor will be able to utilize certain of his capital for other purposes.

The purpose of the trust may be better understood by an example. Assume the estate owner is in a 50 per cent income tax bracket. He furnishes his mother, who has only $1,500 of taxable income, with $4,500 per year for her support. The estate owner may not deduct the $4,500 which he pays to his mother, which results in his paying a tax of $2,250 on this amount. If the $4,500 were taxable to his mother rather than to the estate owner, it would incur an income tax of approximately $500, resulting in an annual saving of $1,750.

Moreover, as long as the estate owner is giving his mother $4,500 per year, his investments must earn $9,000 in order to net the required $4,500. If these investments earn at the rate of 10 per cent per year, the estate owner is committing assets with a value of $90,000 to support his mother. On the other hand, if the estate owner were to transfer $50,000 of these assets to a short-term trust for his mother, $5,000 per year would be distributed to the mother, who, after paying taxes of $500 would thereby earn the required $4,500. The estate owner could therefore devote the remaining $40,000 of assets to other endeavors.

It should be noted that the mother in the above example is not a dependent of the taxpayer, because she had over $1,000 of her own taxable income. If the proposed beneficiary of the trust, however, is a person who qualifies as a dependent of another (see I.R.C. §151(e)), the tax which such beneficiary would pay on the same trust income used in the example would be greater. The reason is that the standard deduction and low income allowance is not allowed with respect to unearned income of a taxpayer who qualifies as a dependent of another. I.R.C. §141(e). No person, however, other than a child under age 19 or a fulltime student, could qualify as a dependent where the trust income is in excess of $1,000. See I.R.C. §151(e). However, even in the case of a child, where the benefit of the low income allowance and standard deduction is lost, the tax bracket of the estate owner will usually be higher than that of the child so it is still advisable to shift income.

It should be clear that if a grantor in a high income tax bracket is using some of his after tax income for the benefit of a lower bracket taxpayer, he would be well advised to consider transferring income-producing assets to a short-term trust.

III. Tax Rules

§9.3 A. Income Taxes

Under the tax rules governing short-term trusts, the income earned during the term of the trust is not taxed to the grantor provided that all of the following requirements discussed in §§9.4 to 9.7 are satisfied.

§9.4 1. Irrevocable Gift of the Income

The first requirement necessary to avoid having the income taxed to the grantor is that the gift of the income must be irrevocable. This means that the trust cannot be made revocable and, additionally, that the income cannot be accumulated or applied for the grantor's or the grantor's spouse's benefit. See I.R.C. §§676 and 677. The trust must provide that any accumulated income be distributed to the income beneficiary, and not to the grantor or his spouse, upon the termination of the trust.

§9.5   2.   Reversionary Interest Rule

The second requirement relates to the duration of the trust. The grantor must not have a reversionary interest in either the principal or the income which may reasonably be expected to take effect in possession or enjoyment within 10 years from the date of the transfer to the trust. I.R.C. §673. This does not mean that the trust cannot, under any circumstances, terminate prior to the end of 10 years from the date of the transfer. If the terminating event is reasonably not expected to occur within 10 years, then the reversionary interest rule is satisfied. For example, where the reversionary interest is to take effect on the death of the grantor, the grantor is not taxable on the income if his life expectancy is more than 10 years. See Reg. §1.673(a)-1(c).

An exception to the 10-year rule provides that the measuring term of the trust may be the life of the income beneficiary, even if such beneficiary's life expectancy is less than 10 years. I.R.C. §673(c). Accordingly, it is possible to create a short-term trust for the benefit of an elderly relative and have the principal returned upon the relative's death without awaiting the expiration of the 10-year period.

The 10-year period is not measured from the date of the trust, but from the date that the assets were transferred to it. I.R.C. §673(a). It is therefore imperative that all assets which are to be transferred to the trust are actually transferred prior to the commencement of the 10-year time period.

If the trust is already in existence and there are less than 10 years remaining prior to the termination date, the trust term should be irrevocably postponed for at least 10 years from the date of postponement before transferring additional assets to it. Apart from the transfer of additional assets, there could be another reason for postponing the term of the trust for 10 more years. The estate owner may realize that he will still be in a high income tax bracket at the end of the initial term and can part with the trust principal for a longer period. For example, assume a short-term trust, set up to last for 10 years, has already been in existence for four years. The estate owner by extending the term for 10 more years (or a total of 14 years), can avoid having the income taxable to him during any of the 14 years. If, however, he extends the term for only nine years (or a total of 13 years), the income earned during the last three years will be taxable to him. I.R.C. §673(d).

§9.6   3.   Control of Beneficial Enjoyment

The beneficial enjoyment of the principal or income must not be subject to the control of the grantor, except as permitted under certain statutory exceptions. For example, where the grantor retains the power either to add beneficiaries to those named in the trust instrument, to vary the proportions in which the corpus or income is to be paid to specified beneficiaries, or to accelerate or postpone the time when distributions are to be made, beneficial enjoyment of the trust is considered subject to the donor's control. I.R.C. §674 sets forth certain powers of beneficial enjoyment which may be retained by the grantor or which may be exercised by a third party trustee without causing the income to be taxed to the grantor. For a discussion of these powers, see §8.40.

§9.7   4. Prohibited Administrative Powers

The presence of certain administrative powers which may be exercised primarily for the grantor's benefit will cause the trust income to be taxed to the grantor. Such powers include the power to deal with the trust for less than an adequate consideration, the power to borrow trust funds without sufficient interest or security and other general powers of administration, if exercisable by anyone acting in a nonfiduciary capacity. Examples of such general administrative powers are the power to vote stock of a corporation in which the holdings of the grantor of the trust are significant in terms of voting control, or the power to reacquire trust property by substituting other property. I.R.C. §675. For a discussion of these powers, see §8.41.

5. Capital Gain Problem

§9.8   a. Description of the Problem

One of the major income tax problems arising from the use of a short-term trust is that, unless the trust provides to the contrary, capital gains will be treated as principal and, hence, will be taxable to the grantor during the term of the trust. See I.R.C. §677(a)(2). This may work a hardship on the grantor since the gains themselves must ordinarily remain in the trust until the termination date and the grantor in the interim may not have sufficient funds outside the trust to discharge his tax obligations.

For example, assume the estate owner transfers assets with a basis of $50,000 to the trust. The assets retain the same basis in the hands of the trust. They are then sold by the trust for $110,000. The capital gains tax on the gain of $60,000 is payable currently by the grantor, but the net proceeds of the sale are not returned to the grantor; they must remain in the trust until the termination date.

§9.9   b. Possible Solutions

There are several possible solutions to the short-term trust capital gain problem which may be considered.

The most direct solution is to have the trust instrument specifically provide that capital gains are to be treated as income. In this case, the gains will belong to the income beneficiary and be taxable to him or to the trust, depending upon whether the gain is currently distributed or accumulated. Either way, the funds will be available to the one who is required to pay the tax. This solution, however, presents other problems. First, the grantor may be willing to part with the ordinary income from the assets transferred to the trust for a period of 10 years, but may not desire that the income beneficiary receive the gain realized on their sale during the trust term because he is not willing to give away any portion of the principal. He still might be willing to permit the income beneficiary to receive any appreciation in the value of the asset from the time that it is transferred to the trust. For example, assume the asset has a basis of $50,000 and a fair market value of $100,000 when it is transferred to the trust. It is later sold by the trust for $140,000. The trust provides that the amount of the sale proceeds in excess of the fair market value of the asset when transferred to the trust will be treated as income and the balance of the gain as principal. The income beneficiary will thereby receive $40,000 ($140,000 minus $100,000) and $50,000 ($100,000 minus $50,000) will be added to principal for eventual return to the grantor. The grantor's tax liability for the capital gain will be limited to the tax on $50,000.

Another problem with allocating gains to income arises when appreciated assets are transferred to a short-term trust and capital gains are allocated in the trust instrument to the income beneficiary, because there may be adverse gift tax consequences. Where appreciated properties are transferred to a short-term trust requiring gains to be allocated to income, where the grantor is not the trustee, the Internal Revenue Service has indicated that there is an immediate taxable gift of the amount of the unrealized appreciation. See Rev. Rul. 72-571, 1972-2 C.B. 533. For example, assume an asset has a basis of $70,000 and a fair market value of $90,000 at the time of transfer to the trust, and that all capital gains are allocated to income. There will be a taxable gift by the grantor at the time of the transfer to the trust not only of the income interest in $90,000 (see §9.10), but also of the total unrealized appreciation of $20,000. On the other hand, if the grantor is also the trustee, then no immediate gift of the unrealized appreciation occurs, but the capital gains will probably be considered additional gifts in the year they are realized by the trust, on the theory that it is not until the grantor decides to sell the capital asset that he has put the gift beyond recall. See Bush, "Short-Term Trusts: Advantages and Dangers" 27 *NYU Inst on Fed Tax* 317, 326 (1966).

The second possible solution to the capital gain problem where such gains are allocable to principal is to reduce the risk of the appreciated assets being sold. The trust instrument could prohibit any sale of assets during the trust term, but a prohibition could turn out to be too inflexible. Circumstances could change during the 10-year period making a sale necessary.

Rather than a complete prohibition of sales, the grantor could be made the trustee or be given a veto power over sales. If he is a trustee, he will be able to control the sale of assets and thereby limit his income tax liability for capital gains. This solution, however, also has disadvantages. The grantor-trustee, by failing to sell assets which should be sold in the best interests of the income beneficiary, may thereby commit a breach of his fiduciary duty and suffer liability. It would therefore appear advisable that the grantor retain a veto power over sales rather than be made a trustee. He should not, however, retain any veto power over sales of stock in a controlled corporation because this is a prohibited administrative power under I.R.C. §675(4).

A possible, but untested, solution where capital gains are allocable to principal is to draft the trust instrument to permit the grantor to withdraw currently the amount necessary to meet his tax liabilities on the amount of any gain. One might think that this power to withdraw prior to the end of 10 years will cause at least a portion of the trust ordinary income to be taxable to the grantor from the inception of the trust. However, under Rev. Rul. 66-161, 1966-1 C.B. 164, it appears that the only portion of the ordinary income of the trust taxable to the grantor is the income attributable to realized gains and not the portion of such income attributable to the unrealized appreciation present in the trust assets. Assuming this interpretation of the ruling is correct, once the grantor withdraws an amount equal to his tax liability on the realized gain, such amount will earn no further ordinary income. He will have been permitted to withdraw the necessary amount without adverse tax consequences.

The last suggested solution is to permit the grantor to borrow funds from the trust to pay the tax. With this arrangement, it is necessary to have an independent trustee, who is unrelated to the donor, make the loan on an arm's length basis, and insist on adequate interest and security. If these requirements are not satisfied, the grantor will be deemed to have a prohibited power and the income of the trust will be taxable to him. See I.R.C. §675(3).

§9.10 B. Gift Taxes

The transfer of assets to a short-term trust results in a taxable gift to the extent of the value of the income interest in such assets. The income interest is taxable even where nonincome-producing assets are transferred to the trust, as long as the trustee has the power to reinvest. Rev. Rul. 79-280, 1979-2 C.B. 240. Where the duration of the income interest is readily ascertained, such value is determinable by reference to the applicable table in Reg. §25.2512-9(f). (See Appendix, Table VIIIB) For example, if a transfer is made to a short-term trust for a period of 10 years, under the Table, 44.1605 per cent of the fair market value of the assets transferred is the value of the income interest. Where the income of the trust is distributable currently, or if the beneficiary is a minor and the trust otherwise meets the requirements of a minor's trust as set forth in I.R.C. §2503(c), then the $10,000 annual exclusion applicable to gifts of a present interest will be allowed in computing the amount of the taxable gift. (See §§2.39 and 2.40.) By reason of the $10,000 annual exclusion, it is possible to contribute as much as $22,644 to a 10-year trust without causing the gift to be taxable.

Where the trust instrument provides that capital gains are allocable to income and capital losses to principal (see §9.9), the value of the reversionary interest will be considered to be incapable of determination. Consequently, the entire value of the assets transferred to the short-term trust will be treated as a taxable gift, even if the income is currently distributable. See Rev. Rul. 77-99, 1977-1 C.B. 295.

§9.11   C.   Estate Taxes

The commuted fair market value of the grantor's reversionary interest at the time of his death is includable in his gross estate for estate tax purposes. See Reg. §20.2031-10(A). This value will be determined by reference to the applicable table set forth in Reg. §20.2031-10(f). (See Appendix, Table VIIIB.) For example, if the grantor dies three years before the expiration of a 10-year trust term, 83.9619 per cent of the then fair market value of the trust assets will be includable in his estate. It should be noted, however, that a discounted value in the reversionary interest is not always present. Where the trust is to terminate on the grantor's death, or where the grantor retains a power over the income requiring such interest to be includable in his estate, such as the power to accumulate, the entire value of the trust assets will be taxable in his estate.

§9.12   IV.   Considerations in Deciding Whether a Short-Term Trust Is Appropriate

The first factor which must be considered in determining whether to create a short-term trust in a given situation is whether the estate owner can afford to part with his capital during the term of the trust. By way of example, a high income tax bracket professional person could perhaps save substantial income taxes by transferring his relatively small capital estate to a short-term trust. If he should become disabled or if his practice should for some other reason fall off, he may need his capital for his own support. Hence, the creation of a short-term trust in this instance might be too risky.

The second factor to consider is whether the income tax savings from a short-term trust are outweighed by other tax planning factors. By reason of the unification of the estate and gift tax under the Tax Reform Act of 1976 (see §2.2), there is now an estate tax cost in making a gift to a short-term trust. Assume the estate owner transfers $100,000 of assets to the trust for a 10-year period. The value of the income interest, or $44,161 ($100,000 times 44.1605 per cent, see Appendix, Table VIII B), is a taxable gift. This amount (less the annual exclusion, if applicable, see §9.10) is added to the tax base to compute the estate tax and credit is given for any gift tax paid. (See §2.3.) Therefore, the gift of the income interest is ultimately taxed at the estate tax rate. In addition, the value of the principal in the trust is still part of the owner's estate. Hence, $144,161 (assuming no annual exclusion) is, in effect, taxed for estate tax purposes, but the grantor only owns $100,000 worth of assets. This estate tax cost should be measured against the anticipated income tax savings on the income earned on the $100,000 for 10 years.

Finally, before creating a short-term trust, a determination should be made of whether the setup costs, attorneys' fees, administrative costs, tax return preparation fees, trustee fees and the like are worth the amount of income taxes saved.

V. Specific Uses

§9.13 A. For Children

One of the most common uses of a short-term trust is to benefit the grantor's minor children. Where the trust income is used for purposes other than a minor child's support, the device will effectively shift the taxability of the income away from the grantor. The estate owner should be made aware that to the extent the income of the trust is used for the support of a minor child, it will be taxable to the grantor-parent. I.R.C. §677(b). What constitutes support, as opposed to luxuries and other non-support items, is a matter of state law. No clear-cut guidelines exist as to whether expenditures for such items as private school, music lessons, and summer camp constitute support payments. A question also exists as to whether the trust income may be used for the college education of the grantor's minor child without causing such income to be taxed to the grantor as support income. In recent years many jurisdictions have reduced the age of majority from 21 to 18. In those states, parents no longer have a duty to support or educate their children who are 18 or older. Since, in almost all instances, the major portion of one's college education takes place after age 18, the problem is not as serious as it previously was, but still exists to a limited extent.

Several suggestions are in order when the short-term trust is used as a vehicle to provide a college education for the grantor's minor children. The most obvious, but perhaps least desirable method, from a practical point of view, is to forgo using the trust income to finance the children's college education while they are minors, but only to use the trust income to finance their education after they have attained their majority. Another alternative is to distribute the trust income directly to the minor, who is then free to expend it for whatever purpose he sees fit, hopefully, for his college education. Even if the minor chooses to expend the distribution on his education, the income apparently will not be taxable to the grantor because it is the minor's own funds. In an effort to ensure that the expenditure will, in fact, be used for the intended purpose, i.e., college education, and still avoid inclusion in the grantor's income, it has been suggested that the trust income be distributed to a custodian for the minor under the Uniform Gifts to Minors Act, who will then use the custodianship funds to defray the education expense. Schneider and Crestol, "Combined Short-Term Trust and Custodian Account: An Effective Family Gift Vehicle" 24 *The Journal of Taxation* 224 (1966); see, also, "Is the Trust-Custodian Plan Workable? Readers and Authors Disagree" 25 *The Journal of Taxation* 19 (1966).

When the income of a short-term trust is used to pay for the expenditures of an adult child, the income, as previously indicated, will ordinarily not be taxed to the grantor because there is no legal duty to support such child. The grantor, however, should not contractually obligate himself to make such payments. If he does, the trust income used to pay for such items will be taxable to the grantor on the ground that his legal obligation was discharged. Reg. §1.677(a)-1(d).

Another factor to be considered in creating a short-term trust to pay education expenses of an adult child is the provision in the Economic Recovery Tax Act of 1981 dealing with the gift tax consequences of direct payments of tuition (see §2.41). Such payments are no longer treated as taxable gifts. Unless the income tax savings in using a short-term trust clearly outweigh the gift and estate tax cost (see §9.12), the estate owner should consider making direct payments of tuition for his child and funding a short-term trust only for other educational and support purposes.

§9.14 B. For Other Relatives

A short-term trust for an adult relative, whom the grantor is not legally obligated to support, is free from the support problem mentioned with regard to a trust for the grantor's minor children. (See §9.13.) Thus, it is an excellent device to be used by a high income tax bracket estate owner who is contributing to the support of an adult family member, such as an aged parent.

One might initially conclude that where trust income is used to support a parent of the grantor who has no other source of income, the income will be taxable to the grantor on the theory that such income has been used for the support of a person whom he is legally obligated to support. I.R.C. §677(b). However, for tax purposes no legal obligation exists where the parent must first use his own resources. See Reg. §1.662(a)-(4). In the usual case, a child has a duty to support a parent only where the parent has insufficient resources of his own. The trust income will constitute the parent's own resources and may then be used to support him without having such income taxable to the grantor.

By way of caution, it should be noted that the trust income distributed to or used for the parent's benefit will be considered part of the parent's gross income. If such gross income exceeds $1,000, the estate owner will not be able to claim the parent as a dependent on his income tax return. I.R.C. §151(e).

§9.15 C. Financing Life Insurance on the Life of One Other than the Grantor or His Spouse

Where the income of a trust may be used without the approval of an adverse party for the payment of premiums on life insurance policies on the life of the grantor or his spouse, such income will be taxable to the grantor. I.R.C. §677(a)(3). Where, however, the policy is on someone else's life, trust income may be used to pay the premiums without taxability to the grantor. The short-term trust is an excellent vehicle to finance the latter type of life insurance purchase.

By way of example, if the grantor wishes to provide his son with a policy of life insurance on the son's life, it would be less costly tax-wise for the grantor to set up a short-term trust. The trust could use its income to purchase the policy for the son, rather than have the higher bracket father pay the premiums himself. Upon the termination of the trust, the life insurance policy would be distributed to the son, and the trust principal would revert to the father.

§9.16 D. Avoiding Penalty Taxes on Closely Held Corporate Earnings

A high income tax bracket estate owner may own stock in a corporation which has unreasonable accumulated earnings (see I.R.C. §531) or is a personal holding company (see I.R.C. §541). In either case, the corporation may wish, or be required, to pay a dividend in order to avoid the applicable penalty tax. The dividend will be taxed at high rates to the estate owner. To avoid the high dividend tax, the estate owner could create a short-term trust to which he would transfer a portion of the stock in the closely held company. The trust would then receive a portion of the dividend which would be taxed at lower rates. The grantor may, if he wishes, go one step further and transfer to the trust his shares in a second class of stock, such as preferred, so that the dividend can be paid only on the stock owned by the trust and none paid on the stock retained by the grantor. For a discussion of recapitalizing the stock of a corporation, see §§12.39 to 12.44.

It should be noted, however, that in the *Estate of Smith v Commr* 292 F2d 478 (3d Cir 1961) cert den 368 US 967, 82 SCt 438, 7 LE2d 395 (1962) where the dividend was declared before the gift of the stock was completed, the dividend was held taxable to the donor, since the right to receive the dividend had accrued to him when it was declared. There is also a danger that once the circumstances giving rise to the corporate penalty tax have transpired, even though no dividend has yet been declared, a transfer of the stock may not shift the dividend to the donee. See Rev. Rul. 60-331, 1960-2 C.B. 189. Accordingly, it is best to create the short-term trust and transfer stock to it well before there is any existing penalty tax problem.

§9.17 E. Leaseback of Assets

Short-term trusts have on occasion been used to receive assets from the grantor and then lease them back to him. In this way the grantor hoped to receive a rent deduction for the rent which he paid to the trust and have the rental income taxed to the trust or the income beneficiary at lower rates. Upon the termination of the trust, the leased assets would revert to the grantor.

For a time it was thought that this device would work, at least where the trustee was an independent trustee. See *Skemp v Commr* 168 F2d 598 (7th Cir 1948). However, recent decisions have disallowed the rent deduction to the grantor, even where the trustee was independent. *Perry v US* 520 F2d 235 (4th Cir 1975) cert den 423 US 1052, 96 SCt 782, 46 LE2d 641 (1976); *Mathews v*

Commr 520 F2d 323 (5th Cir 1975) cert den 424 US 967, 96 SCt 1463, 47 LE2d 734 (1976); but see *Quinlivan v Commr* 599 F2d 269 (8th Cir 1979) cert den 44 US 996, 100 SCt 531, 62 LE2d 426 (1979). Using a short-term trust as a leaseback vehicle is a risky tool at the present time.

VI. Selecting Assets to Transfer to Short-Term Trust

§9.18 A. In General

A few rules may be used to advantage in choosing which assets to transfer to a short-term trust.

1. Transfer assets which, for a given principal value, earn the greatest amount of taxable income. For example, assume there are two assets, each worth $50,000; one throws off a taxable yield of 12 per cent per year, the other is tax-sheltered real estate. The first asset should be transferred to the trust because there is no purpose in transferring tax-sheltered income to a lower bracket taxpayer.

2. Transfer assets which, for a given principal value, have the higher income tax basis. Following this rule will tend to ameliorate the capital gains tax problem described in §9.8.

3. Do not transfer encumbered assets. Using trust income to pay the principal portion of encumbrances will be deemed to enhance the corpus of the trust. Hence, this income will be taxed to the grantor.

§9.19 B. Transferring a Partnership or Other Business Interest

Transferring a partnership or other business interest to a short-term trust may create tax problems. The first is that there is too close an identity between the grantor's ownership of the property and control over the income. It is probably too risky to transfer a family partnership interest to a short-term trust because the partnership income may be taxable to the grantor. See 2 Willis, Pennell and Postlewaite, *Partnership Taxation* (Shepard's/McGraw-Hill 3d Ed 1981) §172.08. If closely held corporate stock is transferred to the trust, the grantor should not have the power to vote the stock unless he is the trustee; otherwise, the trust income will be taxable to him. See I.R.C. §675.

Stock in a Subchapter S corporation should not be transferred to a short-term trust because it will disqualify the corporation from continuing under the Subchapter S election. I.R.C. §§1371(a)(2) and (e).

VII.   Alternatives to Using a Short-Term Trust

§9.20   A.   Municipal Bonds

The first alternative is the purchase of municipal bonds, the interest from which is not subject to federal income tax. The grantor can thus earn tax-free income without the necessity of making a gift of the income interest, which gift may entail a gift and estate tax cost. Nevertheless, it should be noted that when the grantor gifts the income earned from the municipal bonds, he may be making a taxable gift at that time. Particularly if split with the donor's spouse, this gift, when contrasted with a gift to a short-term trust, will rarely exceed the annual gift tax exclusion. In some cases, there may not be a taxable gift at all. If the income is used by a parent for the support of a minor child, no gift arises because the expenditure is in discharge of the parent's legal obligation; neither is the gift taxable if it consists of a payment on behalf of a donee directly to an educational institution for tuition or to a health care provider for medical services. I.R.C. §2053(e).

The purchase of municipal bonds also provides added flexibility in that the donor need not make an irrevocable commitment to gift the income, but may change his mind as his desires or circumstances change. A drawback of the municipal bond alternative is the lack of investment diversification. Municipal bonds are a poor hedge against inflation and many of them have depreciated in value in recent years.

§9.21   B.   Interest-Free Loan

The estate owner, instead of gifting to a short-term trust, may make an interest-free loan to a family member. The donee can then invest the proceeds of the loan in income-producing assets. If the device is successful, the donor will have accomplished the objective of shifting income to a lower bracket taxpayer without making an irrevocable gift for even a 10-year period. There are, however, two potential problems.

First, the question arises as to whether a reasonable amount of interest on the loan will be regarded as a taxable gift and, if so, when the gift is deemed to be made. The Internal Revenue Service has ruled that the amount of interest which would reasonably have been earned on the loan is a taxable gift. Rev. Rul. 73-61, 1973-1 C.B. 408. The date on which the gift is deemed to have been made depends, according to the ruling, on the nature of the loan. If the loan is for a fixed term, the gift consists of the assumed reasonable interest for the entire term and such gift is deemed to have been made on the date of the loan. On the other hand, if the loan is a demand loan, only the assumed interest for each calendar year is considered to be a gift during that year. A demand loan, because of the availability of the annual gift tax exclusion, will result in a smaller gift. For example, if an interest-free demand loan of $100,000 is made and a reasonable rate of interest is 12 per cent, the annual interest will be

$12,000. The net gift for the year, after subtracting the $10,000 annual gift tax exclusion, is $2,000. If the loan is unpaid for five years, the gifts will total $10,000. However, if the loan is for a fixed term of five years, the total assumed reasonable interest of $60,000 ($12,000 times 5) will be considered a gift in the year in which the loan is made. After subtracting the $10,000 annual gift tax exclusion, the total gift is $50,000, or $40,000 more than the gift made in the case of a demand loan.

The Tax Court has held that an interest-free *term* loan gives rise to a taxable gift. *Estate of Meyer B Berkman* TC Memo 1979-46. However, the Circuit Court in *Crown v Commr* 585 F2d 234 (7th Cir 1978) affg 67 TC 1060 (1977) held that there is no taxable gift involved in an interest-free *demand* loan. The Internal Revenue Service is expected to contest this result in other circuits. Consequently, until the matter is resolved, estate owners should be cautious in making even demand interest-free loans where the reasonable annual interest will exceed the annual exclusion.

The estate owner who makes an interest-free loan, even if it is a demand loan, should not permit the statute of limitations on the collection of the note to expire. Otherwise the lender will be deemed to have made a taxable gift of the uncollected principal in the year in which the statute of limitations runs out. *Estate of Lang v Commr* 613 F2d 770 (9th Cir 1980). In those jurisdictions where the statute of limitations begins to run from the date of issuance of a demand note (rather than from the date of demand), the estate owner should make certain that he receives a new note for the unpaid balance prior to the expiration of the statutory period. See California Commercial Code §3122(b) and California Civil Procedure Code §337.

The second possible problem is whether the income earned by the borrower from the loan proceeds may be taxed to the lender. Although the Internal Revenue Service apparently has not raised this issue in the context of a gift type interest-free loan (as opposed to an employee or shareholder interest-free loan), it may do so in the future. See Roth, "Can Lender be Charged with Receiving Taxable Income as a Result of an Interest-Free Loan?" 52 *Journal of Taxation* 136 (1980).

VIII.   Recommended Reading

Berall, "How to Deal with the Capital Gains Problem of the Settlor of a Short-Term Trust" 7 *Estate Planning* 86 (1980)

Bush, "Short Term Trusts: Advantages and Dangers" 24 *NYU Inst on Fed Tax* 327 (1966)

Calleton, "Dangers in Misuse of the Short Term Trust: Guidelines for Employing This Valuable Device" 3 *Estate Planning* 200 (1976)

Costello and Klepetko, "Short-Term Trusts: The Vintage Year is Here" 9 *Real Prop, Prob and Tr J* 232 (1974)

Hull and Kaster, "Interest-Free Loans are not Gifts, But Problems Remain in Their Use" 6 *Estate Planning* 66 (1979)

Pinney, "Benefits Still Available from Short-Term Trusts Despite Recent Developments" 6 *Estate Planning* 266 (1979)

Rossbach, "Tax Planning for the College Education of Minors" 2 *Univ of Miami Estate Planning Inst* 600 (1968)

Somers, "Income Tax Aspects of Short-Term Trusts" 4 *Real Prop, Prob and Trust Journal* 188 (1969)

Wiggins, "Use of Short-Term Trust to Build Up Tax—Sheltered Fund for Education of Children" 1 *Estate Planning* 246 (1974)

Life Insurance

10

§10.1   I.   Use of Life Insurance in Estate Planning, in General

Life insurance is one of the most important estate planning tools. It can create an estate, provide liquidity, fund business and employment agreements, and provide fringe benefits for employees.

§10.2   A.   Estate Creation

Life insurance may be used to create an estate where one does not otherwise exist or to supplement an estate which is too small to meet the needs of the insured's family in the event of the insured's death. This use of life insurance is most common in the case of a young estate owner with a spouse and children to support and educate. In this type of estate the life insurance on the estate owner's life may frequently be the major, if not the sole, asset to provide for the family's support.

§10.3   B.   Liquidity

Life insurance is a very useful tool in providing an estate with liquidity to pay death taxes, expenses of administration and, until other assets can be liquidated, immediate living expenses of the insured's family. This use of life insurance is most common in larger estates where the size of the estate is sufficient for the family's support, but where the necessity of having to liquidate assets within a short period of time to pay taxes and expenses could be very disruptive.

§10.4   C.   Funding Business and Employee Agreements

Life insurance is often an excellent vehicle to fund business buy-sell agreements, providing for the purchase of a decedent's interest in the business upon his death. See § 10.53, and for a comprehensive discussion of buy-sell agreements, see §§12.7 to 12.34. Insurance may also be used to fund agreements between an employer and an employee providing for benefits on the employee's retirement or death. In order to fund for retirement, it is necessary to use a whole life form of life insurance, rather than term life insurance, so that the cash values may be converted to retirement income. See §§10.6 to 10.10 for a discussion of the types of life insurance policies, and see §10.54 for a discussion of employee agreements.

§10.5   D.   Fringe Benefits

Life insurance is useful in providing tax-favored employee fringe benefits, such as group life insurance, split-dollar life insurance and benefits under qualified pension and profit sharing plans. (See §§10.56 to 10.58.)

§10.6   II.   Types of Life Insurance Policies

It is beyond the scope of this book to examine in detail the numerous types of life insurance. Generally speaking, however, there are four types of life insurance, which form the basis of many different policies imaginatively created by the life insurance industry.

§10.7   A.   Term Insurance

This form of insurance is pure insurance against the risk of dying during a specified period. Frequently, the policy may be renewed at the end of the specified period, but the premium for the renewal period will be based on the insured's age at the time of renewal. When the term expires and the insurance is not renewed, the policy will seldom have any value. Term insurance, when first issued, has the lowest premium of any type of life insurance policy for a given age, but the premiums increase in each subsequent renewal period. After a period of time they will become more expensive than premiums payable on other forms of life insurance. One form of term insurance, called decreasing term, has a premium which does not increase, but the face amount of insurance decreases with the passage of time.

§10.8   B.   Ordinary Life Insurance

This form of life insurance differs from term in that the insurance exists for the entire period of the insured's life and is not restricted to the contingency of his death during a specified term. Typically, a level insurance premium is paid for this type of policy, and the same premium which is payable at the age of issue continues throughout the insured's lifetime. Because of this level premium, during the early years of coverage the insured's payments are greater than the actuarial risk and a reserve develops, part or all of which is credited to the policyholder. The portion credited may be used by the policyholder as a cash value, which he will receive upon surrender of the policy or which he may borrow at interest during the continuance of the policy. Alternatively, it may be used to provide a paid up policy for a reduced face amount or to purchase term insurance for the full face amount for a period of time depending on the insured's age and the amount of cash value. Ordinary life insurance is a form of permanent insurance because as long as the insured continues to pay the premiums the insurance will remain in force.

§10.9   C.   Limited Pay Life Insurance

This form of life insurance is a level premium permanent life insurance policy. It differs from an ordinary life insurance policy in that the premiums are not payable during the insured's entire lifetime, but rather for a limited period such as 5, 10, 15, 20 or 30 years. The premiums, during the paying period, are greater in amount than comparable ordinary life policy premiums, because the total premiums necessary to carry the policy for the insured's lifetime are condensed into a shorter period of time.

§10.10   D.   Endowment Insurance

An endowment life insurance policy is similar to a limited pay life insurance policy in that level premiums are paid for a specified period of time. The distinguishing feature, however, is that the premiums for a given face amount of insurance are higher so that the cash value increases at a more rapid pace. At the expiration of the premium paying period, the cash value will equal the face amount of the policy. Even if the insured is still living at that time, the policy will mature and the face amount of the policy will be paid to him.

III.   Death Taxation

§10.11   A.   General Rule of Includability

Life insurance proceeds are generally includable in the insured's estate for death tax purposes. I.R.C. §2042. If, however, the insured possesses none of the incidents of ownership at the time of his death and the policy is not payable to or for the benefit of his estate, the proceeds will be excludable. (See §10.12.) However, even where the life insurance proceeds are not includable because the decedent did not have any of the incidents of ownership and the policy was not payable to or for the benefit of his estate, the proceeds may, depending upon the facts of the particular case, be included in the gross estate for some other reason. For example, if the decedent gratuitously transferred all rights in the policy within three years of his death, the proceeds would be includable as a gift made within three years of the decedent's death under I.R.C. §2035(d)(2). (See §10.13.)

Even if the insured possesses none of the incidents of ownership, the life insurance proceeds will be included in his estate where the policy is payable to or for the benefit of his estate. I.R.C. §2042(1). A policy is payable for the benefit of the insured's estate where the beneficiary is required to use the proceeds to pay the decedent's taxes or other obligations of his estate. Reg. §20.2042-1(b)(1). Also see §10.49.

§10.12   B.   Exception Where Insured Does Not Possess Incidents of Ownership

Unless a life insurance policy is payable to the insured's estate or for the benefit of the insured's estate, the policy will not be includable in his gross estate if he does not possess at the time of his death any of the incidents of ownership in the life insurance policy. If the insured has any incident of ownership, it is immaterial whether he may exercise it alone or whether the consent of another person is required. I.R.C. §2042(2). The term "incidents of ownership" is not limited in its meaning to ownership of the policy in the technical legal sense. The term really has reference to the right of the insured or his estate to the economic benefits of the policy. Thus, it includes the power to change the beneficiary, to surrender or cancel the policy, to assign the policy, to revoke an assignment, to pledge the policy for a loan or to borrow the cash surrender value. Reg. §20.2042-1(c)(2). These powers, set forth in the Regulations, are not intended to be all-inclusive as to what constitutes an incident of ownership. For example, the mere right to change the time or manner of payment of proceeds to the beneficiary by electing, changing or revoking settlement options, has been held to be a taxable incident of ownership. *Estate of Lumpkin Jr v Commr* 474 F2d 1092 (5th Cir 1973). Moreover, the Internal Revenue Code specifically provides that more than a 5 per cent reversionary interest is an incident of ownership. I.R.C. §2042(2). A "reversionary interest" includes a possibility that the policy or its proceeds may return to the insured or become subject to a power of disposition by him. For a discussion regarding designating the insured as a contingent owner of the policy, see §10.42. The possibility that the insured might receive the policy or its proceeds by inheritance through the estate of another person is not, however, considered to be a reversionary interest. In order to determine whether or not the value of a reversionary interest exceeds 5 per cent of the value of the policy, see the actuarial tables (Appendix, Table VIII) and principles set forth in Reg. §20.2031–10. See also §10.42.

An incident of ownership may also be possessed by the insured in an indirect way, causing the life insurance proceeds to be taxed in his estate. For example, the insured may be deemed to have an incident of ownership where he is the trustee of a trust which owns the life insurance on his life (see §10.41), or where he is the owner of a corporation that owns a policy on his life which is payable for a noncorporate purpose (see §10.57).

§10.13   C.   Gift Made Within Three Years of Death

As previously indicated, even where the insured does not possess at the time of his death any of the incidents of ownership, the policy proceeds may nevertheless be includable in his estate as a gift made within three years of the decedent's death under I.R.C. §2035. The transfer within three years of death rule was virtually eliminated by the Economic Recovery Tax Act of 1981, but transfers of life insurance policies are still subject to the rule. I.R.C. §2035(d)(2); see §2.12. Where a decedent, within three years prior to his death, makes a gratuitous transfer of a life insurance policy on his life, the full amount of the death proceeds are includable in his gross estate. In addition, the §2035(b) exclusion from the gross estate, of gifts not in excess of the $10,000 annual exclusion, is not applicable to a gift of a life insurance policy. See §8.7. For example, the insured gifts a $100,000 life insurance policy with a gift value (see §10.18) of $8,000 to a child. The insured dies within three years of the gift. The $100,000 death proceeds are includable in the insured's estate.

A gift of a life insurance policy may be includable in the insured's gross estate within the scope of the above rule in one of at least two circumstances: first, where the policy itself is assigned by the insured to a third party within three years of the insured's death (see §10.14), and second, in a few select instances where the insured paid premiums on the policy within three years of his death, notwithstanding the fact the policy either was never owned by the insured or was assigned by him prior to three years before his death. See §10.15.

§10.14   1.   Transfer of Policy within Three Years of Death

Where a life insurance policy is transferred by the insured within three years of his death, the transfer is automatically included in the insured's gross estate. I.R.C. §2035.

Even where a policy is originally issued to someone other than the insured, for example, his wife or children, the proceeds may still be includable in his estate as a gift made within three years of the decedent's death. This situation arises where the insured pays the premiums and dies within three years of issuance of the policy. See *Bel v US* 452 F2d 683 (5th Cir 1971) cert den 406 US 919, 92 SCt 1770, 32 LE2d 118 (1972); *Detroit Bank & Trust Co v US* 467 F2d 964 (6th Cir 1972) cert den 410 US 929, 93 SCt 1364, 35 LE2d 590 (1973).

Where the policy is includable as a gift made within three years of the decedent's death and the donee paid premiums after the transfer, only a portion of the proceeds will be taxable in the insured's estate. In that case, the amount of proceeds includable in the insured's estate is limited to the amount produced by multiplying the face value of the policy by the ratio of the premiums paid by the insured to the total premiums paid. See *Estate of Silverman v*

Commr 521 F2d 574 (2d Cir 1975) (1975-2 U.S.T.C. ¶13084) affg 61 TC 338 (1973). For example, if a father transfers a $50,000 life insurance policy on his life to his son within three years of death and if the father before the transfer paid $9,000 of premiums and the son after the transfer paid $1,000 of premiums, 90 per cent or $45,000 of the proceeds will be includable in the father's estate.

§10.15   2.   Payment of Premiums

Where the life insurance policy itself is transferred more than three years before death, but the insured continues to pay premiums during the three-year period before death, the question arises as to what is includable in the insured's estate as a gift made within three years of death. In the past, the Internal Revenue Service attempted to include a proportionate part of the proceeds in the insured's estate based on the ratio of the premiums paid within three years of death to the total premiums paid on the policy. In 1971, after the uniform rejection of this contention by the courts, the Internal Revenue Service changed its position and conceded that, with respect to most types of policies, the payment of a premium is not tantamount to the transfer of a proportionate part of the proceeds. See Rev. Rul. 71-497, 1971-2 C.B. 329. This revenue ruling states, however, that if premiums are paid on accidental death policies or one-year term policies, the entire proceeds will be includable in the insured's estate. The Internal Revenue Service has also ruled, though, that the payment of premiums within three years of death on a one-year group term life insurance policy which was automatically renewed by such payment does not result in the proceeds being taxed in the insured's estate. Rev. Rul. 82-13, I.R.B. 1982-2, 9.

Where only the premiums paid by the insured, rather than a proportionate part of the proceeds, are deemed to be the gift made within three years of death, such premiums are no longer included in the gross estate since the enactment of the Economic Recovery Tax Act of 1981. I.R.C. §2035(d). However, to the extent the yearly premiums paid since 1976 (even if more than three years prior to the death) exceed the annual gift tax exclusion, such excess will be added back to the taxable base. (See §2.3.)

§10.16   D.   Death of Noninsured Owner

If the insured is not the owner of the policy and the owner dies before the insured, the then value of the policy will be included in the owner's estate. If the policy is paid up, its value is established through the sale of comparable contracts by the insurance company. See Reg. §20.2031-8(a)(1). For example, if at the time of the owner's death a comparable paid up policy on the insured's life at his then age would cost a single premium of $10,000, the value of the policy will be deemed to be $10,000, and that amount will be included in the owner's estate. If the policy is one on which further premiums are to be paid, the value may be approximated by adding to the interpolated terminal reserve value at the owner's death the unused portion of the premiums paid prior to the owner's death. See Reg. §20.2031-8(a)(2). The interpolated terminal reserve value is the reserve in the policy adjusted to the date of the owner's death. The amount of this value should be obtained from the insurance company. Any loans outstanding on the policy are deductible in computing the value of the policy.

§10.17   IV.   Gift Taxation

The transfer of all of the ownership rights in a life insurance policy results in a taxable gift to the transferee. Moreover, if the donor continues to pay the premiums on the policy after he has given it away, the amount of premiums paid will also constitute a gift to the new owner. For the effect of a taxable gift on the ultimate estate tax, see §2.2. For gifts to a spouse, see §2.42.

§10.18   A.   Valuation of Life Insurance Policy

The value of the policy for gift tax purposes is determined in the same manner as for estate tax purposes on the noninsured owner's death, substituting the date of the gift for the date of death. See §10.16 for a statement of the rules used in determining the value of the policy. See Reg. §25.2512-6. If at the time of the gift the insured is no longer insurable, this may be a factor in valuing the policy for gift tax purposes. See *Estate of James Stuart Pritchard v Commr* 4 TC 204 (1944).

§10.19   B.   Payment of Premiums

To the extent that anyone other than the owner of the life insurance policy pays the premiums, the payor will be making a taxable gift to the owner each time a premium is paid. For example, if the insured transfers the ownership of a policy to his son and continues to pay premiums of $5,000 per year on the policy, he is making a gift of $5,000 per year to his son.

§10.20   C.   Annual Gift Tax Exclusion

In computing the gift tax, the donor is permitted to exclude from his taxable gifts up to $10,000 given to each donee in each calendar year. However, the gifts must be gifts of a "present interest" to qualify for the annual exclusion. See I.R.C. §2503(b).

The gift to one person of the outright ownership of a life insurance policy will qualify as a gift of a present interest. However, if the gift of the policy is to more than one person, it will not qualify because no single owner can exercise all of the ownership rights without the consent of the other co-owners. See *Ryerson v US* 312 US 405, 61 SCt 656, 85 LE 917 (1941); *Spyros P Skouras v Commr* 14 TC 523 (1950) affd 188 F2d 831 (2d Cir 1951). Moreover, a gift of a policy to a trust where the trustee has authority to retain the policy until the insured's death is usually not a gift of a present interest, because no beneficiary will receive the proceeds until a future date. Rev. Rul. 69-344, 1969-1 C.B. 225. For the effect of "Crummey" provisions, see §10.47. Also see Rev. Rul. 76-490, 1976-2 C.B. 300, which states that where a trust which owns a life insurance policy provides for the outright distribution of the insurance proceeds free of trust upon the insured's death, the payment of premiums by the insured may qualify for the $10,000 annual gift tax exclusion.

When the gift of a policy does not qualify as a present interest, the payment of premiums on such policy by someone other than the owner will also fail to qualify for the $10,000 annual exclusion. Hence, if the policy is transferred by the insured to his two children as equal owners and the insured pays the premium directly to the insurance company, the premium payments will constitute gifts of a future interest. However, if the insured makes outright gifts of money or other assets to his children and they voluntarily pay the premiums on the insurance policy, the gifts will constitute gifts of a present interest.

V. Income Taxation

§10.21   A.   General Rule of Excludability

The proceeds of a life insurance policy payable by reason of the insured's death are generally not subject to income tax. I.R.C. §101(a). However, if the owner acquired the policy in a "transfer for valuable consideration" (see §10.22) or if the proceeds are paid out as a death benefit under an exempt employees' retirement plan (see §10.58), all or a portion of the proceeds may be includable for income tax purposes. Where life insurance is used to fund a deferred compensation agreement and the proceeds are payable to the employer, the employer's receipt of the proceeds does not cause inclusion in the employer's income. However, the payment of the death benefit by the employer to the employee's estate or beneficiary may be includable in the payee's income. (See §10.54.)

§10.22   B.   Transfer for Value Rule

If a transferee of a life insurance policy acquires the policy for a valuable consideration, the proceeds paid on the insured's death are subject to income tax. I.R.C. §101(a)(2). The amount includable will be the net proceeds of the policy less (1) the amount of valuable consideration paid by the transferee and (2) the premiums paid by the transferee.

The transfer for value rule may be illustrated by an example. A purchases a $50,000 policy on B's life from B for $4,000. A then pays $6,000 in premiums. When B dies, the amount includable in A's income will be $40,000, which is the amount paid by the insurance company, less A's investment. This amount will be taxable as ordinary income and not as capital gain.

The transfer for value rule does not apply where the purchaser, whether or not he is the insured, acquired the policy directly from the insurance company. For example, if the insured's son is the applicant owner of the policy, the rule will not apply even though he pays all of the premiums. Moreover, the rule does not apply where the transferee obtains the policy by way of gift or through any transaction where he keeps the same income tax basis as the transferor had in the policy. See I.R.C. §101(a)(2)(A).

Even where the transfer for value rule otherwise applies, there are several statutory exceptions. If the transferee is the insured, a partner of the insured, a partnership in which the insured is a partner, or a corporation in which the insured is a shareholder or officer, the proceeds will not be included in the transferee's income. I.R.C. §101(a)(2)(B). For example, if A is a partner of B, the insured, and A acquires the policy for a valuable consideration from B, when B dies the proceeds will not be included in A's income. It should be noted that the above exceptions do not include members of the insured's immediate family or persons who are the insured's co-stockholders in a corporation.

§10.23   C.   Settlement Options

A settlement option may be selected either by the insured, or if the insured has not exercised his right, by the beneficiary. The settlement options in common use are an interest option, an installment option for a fixed period, an installment for life and a "special" option.

§10.24   1.   The Interest Option

Under this option, the proceeds of the policy on the death of the insured are left with the insurance company and interest is paid periodically on these proceeds. All or part of the proceeds may be withdrawn at a future date.

§10.25   2.   Installments for a Fixed Period

The proceeds of the insurance policy, plus earnings on such proceeds, are payable in installments over a designated period, until completely paid (e.g., $100 per month for 20 years).

§10.26   3.   Installments for Life

The proceeds, plus earnings on the proceeds, are payable in installments over the life of the beneficiary. This option usually guarantees certain minimum payments regardless of when the beneficiary dies (e.g., $100 per month for life, but in any event, for 10 years certain).

§10.27   4. Special Options

Sometimes the insurance company will agree to provide a tailor-made option to fit the needs of the beneficiary. For example, the option might provide for payments of $100 per month until the proceeds are completely paid, except that during the time the beneficiary is in attendance at college, $200 per month shall be paid. While these special options frequently add some degree of flexibility, the insurance company will not undertake to act as a trustee and make discretionary decisions generally made by a fiduciary.

§10.28   5. Interest Portion

The interest portion of the amounts payable under each of the settlement options is taxable income to the beneficiary. I.R.C. §101(d). For example, if the proceeds are $20,000 and $1,200 per year is payable for 20 years, or a total of $24,000, 20/24th (or $1,000) of each payment will be deemed to be a return of principal and 4/24th (or $200) of each payment will be taxable interest.

Where an installment for life is selected, the interest portion and the return of principal portion are determined by dividing the proceeds by the beneficiary's life expectancy. For example, if the proceeds are $20,000, the option provides for payments of $1,200 per year for life, and the beneficiary's life expectancy is 25 years, $800 ($20,000 divided by 25) of each payment is excludable from income as a return of principal and the balance of $400 per year is taxable interest. Reg. §1.01-4(c). The beneficiary's life expectancy must be determined under the mortality table used by the insurance company. The portion of each payment which is excludable remains the same regardless of whether the beneficiary outlives his life expectancy. If the settlement option is a joint and survivor option, which provides for payments for the life of more than one beneficiary, the interest portion and the excludable portion are determined in a similar manner. The proceeds, however, are divided by the life expectancy of such beneficiaries as a group. Reg. §1.101-4(d).

Where the beneficiary is the surviving spouse of the insured, I.R.C. §101(d)(1)(B) allows such beneficiary to exclude from the gross income each year the first $1,000 of the interest portion of the payments received during such year. This interest exclusion is applicable only where an installment option (as opposed to an interest option) is selected. I.R.C. §101(c). The Regulations make it clear that the payment of an insignificant amount of principal, together with interest, is not considered an installment option, but rather an interest option. Reg. §1.101-3(a). Where the surviving spouse switches from the interest option to an installment option the $1,000 interest exclusion becomes applicable from and after the commencement of payments under the latter option. Rev. Rul. 65-284, 1965-2 C.B. 28.

§10.29   D.   Policy Loans and the Interest Deduction

From an estate planning point of view, a policy owner, for a variety of reasons, may desire to borrow all or a portion of the cash value from his life insurance policy. For example, he may wish to use the proceeds to make an investment which he anticipates will earn more than the interest on the loan payable to the insurance company. This interest rate varies, with 5 per cent being customary on older policies, but with much higher rates on more recent policies. Alternatively, he may desire to reduce the net cost of the premiums by using the loan proceeds to pay for them in whole or in part. Another reason for borrowing is to reduce the value of the policy preparatory to making a gift of it, so the gift taxes will be less. The gift of a life insurance policy which has been borrowed upon by the donor does not ordinarily subject the donee to the transfer for value rule. (See §10.22.) Where the policy loan is less than the actual value of the policy at the time of transfer, the policy has the same basis in whole or in part in the donee's hands as it had in the donor's hands and, therefore, the transfer for value rule is not applicable. Rev. Rul. 69-187, 1969-1 C.B. 45.

Regardless of the owner's reason for borrowing on his life insurance policy, it will reduce the cost of his loan if he is permitted an income tax deduction for the interest charges. There are generally two circumstances where the interest payments, whether made to the insurance company or to another lender, are not deductible.

First, where interest is paid or accrued on indebtedness incurred to purchase or continue in effect a single premium life insurance policy, the interest payments are not deductible. I.R.C. §264(a)(2). For this purpose, a single premium policy is defined as one on which substantially all of the premiums are paid within four years from the date of purchase, or on which an amount is deposited with the insurance company for the payment of a substantial number of future premiums. I.R.C. §264(b).

The second circumstance where the interest deduction is not allowed is where interest is paid on a loan made pursuant to a plan of purchase of life insurance which contemplates a systematic borrowing of part or all of the increase in the cash value of the policy. I.R.C. §264(a)(3). This rule, however, does not apply to contracts purchased before August 7, 1963. Moreover, there are four exceptions to this rule even if the policy is purchased after that date (see I.R.C. §264(c)). If any one of the four following exceptions applies, the interest payments will be deductible.

1. Seven-year exception: If no part of four of the annual premiums due during the seven-year period, beginning with the date of payment for the first premium on the policy, is paid by a loan, the deduction will be allowed. Once the seven-year exception has been satisfied and the seven-year period has expired, there is no longer any limit to the amount that may be borrowed to pay premiums on the policy. Thus, under this exception, any three of the first seven annual premiums may be bor-

rowed and the interest deduction taken, provided the remaining premiums during the seven-year period are paid with nonborrowed funds.

2. $100 per year exception: If the total amount of interest on the loans paid during the year does not exceed $100, such amount will be deductible.

3. Unforeseen event exception: If the loan is incurred because of an unforeseen substantial loss of income or an unforeseen substantial increase in the taxpayer's financial obligations, a deduction will be allowed even though the loan is used to pay premiums on the policy. An event is not "unforeseen" if it could have been foreseen at the time that the life insurance policy was purchased. Reg. §1.264-4(d)(3).

4. Trade or business exception: If the indebtedness was incurred in connection with the taxpayer's trade or business, the interest deduction will not be denied despite the fact that the indebtedness was incurred as part of a plan of systematic borrowing on life insurance policies. Borrowing to finance business life insurance, such as keyperson, split-dollar or stock retirement plans, is not considered to be incurred in connection with the taxpayer's trade or business. Reg. §1.264-4(d)(4).

§10.30   E.   Surrender or Exchange of Policies

When a life insurance policy is surrendered prior to the insured's death, the cash value, minus the premiums and other amounts paid for the policy, is includable as taxable income. By way of an example, assume that A purchases an endowment policy in the face amount of $50,000. He pays $30,000 in premiums and thereafter surrenders the policy, receiving its cash value in the amount of $40,000. His taxable income from the transaction will be $10,000. This income will be ordinary income and not capital gain.

It is possible for the policyholder to defer his gain, if any, on the surrender of his policy by electing within 60 days not to receive a lump sum payment, but rather to receive an annuity from the insurance company. I.R.C. §72(h). The annuity payments will then be taxed when received in accordance with the formula described in §11.8. Because of this option it is possible to convert a permanent life insurance policy into retirement income without the necessity of paying an immediate income tax on the gain.

The Internal Revenue Code also provides that no gain or loss will be recognized on the following exchanges: (1) A life insurance policy for another life insurance policy or for an endowment or an annuity contract; (2) An endowment contract for an annuity contract or for an endowment contract under which payments will begin no later than payments would have begun under the contract exchanged; (3) An annuity contract for another annuity contract. I.R.C. §1035(a). The cost basis of the new policy will be the same as the cost basis of the old policy, plus any premiums paid and less any dividends received after the exchange. Unless the exchange is one described above, the gain (i.e., the value of the new policy minus the premiums and other consideration paid on the old policy) will be taxable.

VI. Estate Planning Considerations in Designating the Owner and Beneficiary of a Life Insurance Policy

§10.31   A.   Small Estate

If a person's estate is under $600,000, and it is anticipated that such person will live until at least 1987 without a significant increase in the estate, taxes are usually not an important consideration. Hence, insurance ownership considerations as tax-saving devices are not significant. Typically, in a small estate the insured will be designated as the owner of the life insurance policy. However, even in such an estate, it is important to correctly designate the primary and contingent beneficiaries of the policy.

§10.32   1.   Coordinate the Beneficiary Designation With the Dispositive Plan

Life insurance is an asset which should normally be paid to the same persons who will receive the balance of the insured's estate. In accomplishing this objective, it is almost always disadvantageous to make the policy payable to the estate of the insured. Such a beneficiary designation will subject the policy proceeds to probate.

In some instances, it is advisable to designate a beneficiary of a life insurance policy who is not otherwise provided for in the insured's will or other dispositive document. For example, if the insured wishes to provide for a child of a previous marriage or a collateral relative, he could do so through an insurance policy without complicating the dispositive provisions of his will.

In advising the owner of a small estate regarding his insurance beneficiary designations, consider the following fact situation. A young married couple has two children. Their estate, including life insurance, is about $200,000. The husband desires to leave his entire estate to his wife, and if she does not survive him, then to his two children. Who should be named beneficiary of the life insurance policies on his life?

In an estate of this size, the wife, in most instances, should be made the direct primary beneficiary. Provided the wife has at least a minimum of financial capability, payment to a trust to provide asset management for the wife is ordinarily not feasible. A corporate trustee's fees will be expensive in relation to the size of the trust. Moreover, there are no important tax considerations which require the use of a trust to save taxes upon the subsequent death of the wife. Even if the wife is not financially capable, payment to her under a settlement option should be considered as an alternative to payment to a trust. (See §10.33.)

The real problem present in an estate of this nature is the selection of the contingent beneficiary. If the proceeds of the policy are payable directly to minor children, the insurance company will require the appointment of a guardian for each child receiving the proceeds. The guardianship method of holding funds for minor children is generally disadvantageous compared to other alternatives. (These disadvantages are described in detail in §3.16.)

A more acceptable alternative to the payment of the proceeds to a guardian is the payment thereof to a trust for the benefit of the insured's minor children. (For the advantages of a trust, see §3.18.) If the trust device is used, the trust may be a testamentary trust or a living trust. For a discussion of each type, see §§7.35 to 7.38.

§10.33   2. Trust Versus Settlement Option

If in a small estate the beneficiary of the policy is an adult, for example, the insured's wife, who is not capable of financial management, the election of a settlement option should be considered. For a discussion of the different kinds of settlement options and their tax consequences, see §§10.23 to 10.28.

The selection of a settlement option is usually, by the terms of the policy, not available to a fiduciary, but only to an individual acting in his own right. It is, therefore, necessary to decide whether the proceeds should be payable to a trust as opposed to an individual who can select a settlement option. The advantages usually cited for the use of a settlement option over a trust are the following:

1. There is a guaranteed fixed income which is subject to little or no risk.

2. There is no direct management fee.

3. If an installment option is selected, the $1,000 interest exclusion of the surviving spouse will be available. (See §10.28.)

The advantages usually cited for the use of a trust beneficiary over the selection of a settlement option are:

1. The trust is more flexible. The trust can provide that the beneficiary is to be supported in accordance with changing needs and circumstances, rather than in accordance with a fixed schedule of payments.

2. Where a trust is used, the insured can control the ultimate disposition of the proceeds by designating a remainder beneficiary. On the other hand, if a settlement option is selected, even by the insured, he may lose this control. The policy beneficiary, if he lives long enough, will receive the entire proceeds and will thereby have full power of disposition over such proceeds.

3. The trust is a hedge against inflation. If the principal is wisely invested, it should, in inflationary times, increase in value, while the principal under a settlement option is normally payable with fixed dollars.

4. The rate of return is usually greater where a trust is used.

5. In the event the policy beneficiary becomes incompetent, a guardian or conservator would have to be appointed to collect and manage the

settlement option payments. Such a procedure is expensive and inflexible. However, if a trust is used, the proceeds can be used for the beneficiary's benefit by the trustee without the appointment of a guardian or conservator.

It may be possible to obtain some of the advantages of both a settlement option and a trust. Ordinarily, a trust will invest in both equity securities and fixed income obligations. If a portion of the insurance proceeds are left with the insurance company under one of the settlement options, this amount can substitute for the portion of the trust estate which would normally be invested by the trustee in fixed income obligations. The trust under this plan would provide that the trust assets be invested largely in equity securities. The rate of interest payable by the insurance company may be somewhat less than the interest normally received by the trust from fixed income obligations. However, viewing the settlement option and the trust as a whole, there would be a balanced portfolio, the trustee's fee will be payable on only a portion of the estate, and it will be possible to obtain the $1,000 interest exclusion for the surviving spouse.

While settlement options are more frequently used in small estates, they can also be used in larger ones.

If the marital deduction is important to the insured's estate, care should be taken in the selection of a settlement option to preserve the marital deduction. See Chapter 4. If the insured does not select the settlement option, but leaves the choice up to his wife, the proceeds will ordinarily qualify for the deduction, provided the wife's right to select is not so restricted as to result in her having only a non-qualifying terminable interest. Where the insured selects the option, the marital deduction will, as a general rule, be available as long as all amounts payable under the option are payable only to the surviving spouse, and she has a general power of appointment over any potential remainder of the proceeds. I.R.C. §2056(b)(6).

§10.34   B.   Planning to Exclude Proceeds from Gross Estate

Where the estate is large enough to be concerned with death tax consequences, serious consideration should be given to designating someone other than the insured as the owner of the policy. Where a new life insurance policy is being purchased, the person whom the insured wishes to be the owner can purchase the policy as the owner-applicant. Where the insured already owns one or more policies on his life, he should consider transferring the ownership. In either event if none of the incidents of ownership are possessed by the insured at the time of his death, the policy is not payable to or for the benefit of the insured's estate, and the transfer is not made within three years of the insured's death, the proceeds will normally be excluded from his estate. (See §§10.12 and 10.13.)

Where the insured owns several life insurance policies on his life, thought should be given to the selection of the particular policy or policies to be transferred. It is advisable to transfer policies with the lowest gift value (see §10.18) in relation to the face value. If the total yearly gifts are less than the amount of the gift tax annual exclusion, they will incur no gift tax and the amount of the gifts will not, through the operation of the unified estate and gift tax (see §2.2), be taxed at death at the estate tax rates. Even if the value of the gifted policies exceeds the annual exclusion, only the excess is, in effect, still taxed at the estate tax rates. This excess should be kept to as low an amount as possible. Term policies usually have nominal value, i.e., only the unearned portion of the premium. A policy which contains an accidental death benefit may be advantageous to transfer because its gift value is low in relation to its face value. If there are several ordinary life policies, the most recently acquired will usually have a lower gift value to face amount ratio and should be transferred first. A paid up policy will have a high ratio and its transfer should be avoided. It is possible to reduce the gift value of a policy by having the insured borrow the cash value prior to the transfer.

§10.35 1. Make Sure That Insured Rids Himself of All of the Incidents of Ownership

If the insured wishes to make someone else the owner in order to eliminate the proceeds from his taxable estate, it is necessary that all of the incidents of ownership should be assigned to the new owner. The assignment form supplied by the insurance company should be examined by counsel to ensure that it effectively assigns as a gift all of the ownership rights, without exception. To avoid the transfer for value problem (see §10.22), the assignment should not be for consideration, but should be gratuitous.

§10.36 2. Who Should Pay the Premiums?

Where the premiums on the non-insured owned life insurance are paid by the insured during the three-year period before the insured's death, the question arises as to whether any portion of the proceeds of the policy is includable in the insured's estate as a gift made within three years of death. See I.R.C. §2035. Unless the policy is an accidental death policy or a one-year term policy, the proceeds will not be includable in the gross estate. See Rev. Rul. 71-497, 1971-2 C.B. 329. See also §10.15 for a full discussion.

Aside from the question of whether the payment of premiums by the non-owner insured will cause the proceeds of the life insurance policy to be included in his estate, it should be remembered that the insured will be making a taxable gift to the owner each time a premium is paid (see §10.19).

Where the non-insured spouse is the owner of a life insurance policy on the insured spouse's life and after the transfer of ownership the premiums are paid out of community property, another problem arises. Unless the intention of both spouses is to the contrary, that portion of the proceeds which is equal to the portion of the total premiums paid out of the community property is deemed to be community property. *Modern Woodmen of America v Gray* 113 CaAp 729, 299 P 754 (1931). For example, if the wife owns a life insurance policy on her husband's life which was issued 10 years prior to his death, she was made the owner six years before his death and thereafter the premiums were paid out of community property, then 60 per cent of the policy, will be deemed to be community property. Accordingly, if the wife dies first, she will not be able to dispose of the husband's one-half community property interest in the policy, since such interest belongs to him. This may be disadvantageous because it will increase his taxable estate. There are two ways of avoiding this potential tax problem. The first is to have the wife pay all of the premiums on the wife-owned life insurance on the husband's life out of her separate property. If she has no separate property, a tax-free gift can be made to her of a portion of the community property. See §2.42. Another way to solve the tax problem is to have the husband and wife enter into an agreement providing that no portion of the policy or its proceeds shall be community property despite the fact that the premiums may be paid from that source. Such an agreement will effectively change the character of the property to the wife's separate property. See *Perkins v West* 122 CaAp2d 585, 265 P2d 538 (1954).

§10.37   3.   Who Should Be the Beneficiary of the Non-Insured Owned Policy?

Generally, if anyone other than the non-insured owner is the beneficiary, such owner will be deemed to have made a taxable gift on the insured's death in the amount of the death proceeds. See *Goodman v Commr* 156 F2d 218 (2d Cir 1946). The simplest way of avoiding this gift tax consequence is to have the non-insured owner designated as the beneficiary. (See §10.39 for a discussion, in the context of wife-owned life insurance, of the considerations in designating a trust as beneficiary of the policy.)

VII.   Who Should be Made the Owner?

§10.38   A.   Wife Ownership

Prior to the enactment of the Economic Recovery Tax Act of 1981, a frequently used estate planning tool was to have the wife[1] own the life insurance policies on her husband's life. The primary purpose of making the wife the owner of the life insurance was to keep all of the proceeds out of the husband's estate, since the maximum marital deduction was generally limited to 50 per

---

[1] For the purpose of this discussion, the husband will be deemed to be the insured and the wife, the owner. The same principles will apply if the wife is the insured and the husband is the owner.

cent of the decedent's estate. As a result of this limitation, if the insured-husband were the owner, only one-half of the proceeds of the life insurance could pass to the wife free of estate tax on the husband's death.

The new unlimited marital deduction for decedents dying after 1981 (see §2.22) has eliminated the estate tax advantages of having the wife own the insurance policies on her husband's life. The husband's estate can now deduct the full amount of the life insurance proceeds paid to his wife as beneficiary without incurring any federal estate tax liability on his death. In most instances, the husband will therefore be well advised not to transfer the ownership of the policy to the wife. In relatively large estates, making the children or an irrevocable trust the owner and the beneficiary of the life insurance should be explored. In this way, the insurance proceeds may be excluded from the estates of both husband and wife. See §§10.44 to 10.50.

Many life insurance policies were transferred to wife ownership prior to 1982. A careful analysis should be made to ascertain whether the wife should remain the owner of these policies. From a non-tax point of view, she may wish to retain the ownership rights because life insurance is a valuable asset. From a tax aspect, however, it may be preferable to make the children or an irrevocable life insurance trust the owner, thereby keeping the proceeds out of the wife's estate, as well as out of the estate of the husband. If she does not wish to transfer ownership to the children or to an irrevocable trust, should she, from a tax point of view, transfer ownership to the husband? Where the husband's estate plan leaves a maximum or optimum marital deduction bequest to the wife (see §4.8), there would usually be no advantage in such a transfer. The proceeds will enhance the wife's estate whether she or her husband owns the policy. Where, however, the husband's estate is less than the amount of the equivalent exemption (see §2.25), there could be some advantage in the husband owning one or more of the policies. He could then designate a bypass trust (see Chapter 5) as the beneficiary of all or a portion of the proceeds. In this way, the wife will receive the lifetime benefits of such proceeds, but they will escape estate taxation on the death of both spouses.

The wife may decide to retain the ownership of a life insurance policy on the husband's life. It is then necessary to consider who should be the beneficiary of such policy and to whom such policy should be transferred if she predeceases the husband. (See §§10.39 to 10.43.)

§10.39 1. Who Should be the Beneficiary of the Wife-owned Policy?

Generally, if anyone other than the wife is the beneficiary, she will be deemed to have made a taxable gift on the insured's death in the amount of the death proceeds. See §10.37. The simplest way of avoiding this gift tax consequence is to have the wife designated as the beneficiary.

Frequently, however, the designation of the wife as the outright beneficiary of the policy which she owns on her husband's life does not conform to the general estate plan covering the couple's other assets. Where the objective is to obtain management for the wife after the husband's death and/or probate reduction or avoidance, as well as death tax savings on the wife's death if she survives her husband, the estate plan may include an "A-B" trust created in the form of a living revocable trust, which is funded either during life or through a pour-over will. (See §§5.2, 7.1 and 7.37.)

§10.40   a.   Possibility of Gift Tax to Wife

In considering whether to designate the above-described trust (see §10.39) as the beneficiary of the wife-owned life insurance policies, certain problems are encountered. The first question is whether this will cause any gift tax consequences to the wife upon the death of the insured husband. Since the rights of the wife in the "B" (residuary) trust are typically limited to a lifetime interest, any portion of the proceeds flowing into such trust will result in the wife's making a taxable gift to the remainder beneficiaries at the time of the insured's death. The amount of the gift will depend upon the wife's age. For example, if she is 45 years of age at the time of the husband's death, then 19.731 per cent of the proceeds of the policy will constitute a taxable gift to the remaindermen. Reg. §20.2031-10(f). See Appendix, Table VIII.

The gift may be avoided in one of two ways. The wife may be given a special power of appointment over the "B" trust. This will prevent there being a taxable gift of the proceeds upon the husband's death. See Reg. §25.2511-2(c). Avoiding the gift in this manner will not, it should be noted, remove the proceeds of the life insurance from inclusion in the wife's estate for death tax purposes. See I.R.C. §§2036 and 2038. Moreover, the trustee will, as a practical matter, have to segregate the life insurance proceeds and the investments thereof from the other assets in the "B" trust. If there is commingling and poor recordkeeping, the Internal Revenue Service may contend that all of such assets are includable in the wife's estate on her subsequent death.

The more usual way to avoid this taxable gift is to have all of the proceeds of the policy payable to the "A" (marital) trust, provided the wife has a general power of appointment in this trust (see §4.14). This will not prevent the proceeds from being taxed in the wife's estate; but, since all of the "A" trust assets will be so taxed, there is no necessity in keeping separate records of the insurance proceeds. Payment to the "A" trust may be accomplished by the policy beneficiary designation expressly providing for the entire proceeds to be paid to the "A" trust. Alternatively, the policy may be made payable to the trust generally, but the trust itself will provide that all of the proceeds of the life insurance policies owned by the wife are to be allocated entirely to the "A" trust.

§10.41   b.   Possible Taxation in Husband's Estate

Designating the revocable trust as the beneficiary of the wife-owned insurance (see §10.39) may create the possibility of causing the policy to be taxable in the husband's estate even if he is the first to die. If the husband's estate plan does not provide for the maximum or optimum marital deduction (see §4.8), such inclusion could cause an estate tax on his death. The possibility of inclusion may come about in one of three ways. First, the policy proceeds will be taxable in the husband's estate if the trustee is required to use the proceeds to pay the husband's death taxes or other obligations of his estate. Reg. §20.2042-1(b)(1). Second, it arises where the wife-owned policy is payable to a revocable trust which has any incidents of ownership in the policy and where the husband is either a trustee or a co-trustee of the trust. Reg. §20.2042-1(c)(4) states that where the insured is a trustee of a trust which owns a life insurance policy, the proceeds will be taxed in the insured's estate. Such taxability may arise even though the trustee has no beneficial interest in the trust. *Rose v US* 511 F2d 259 (5th Cir 1975); *Terriberry v US* 517 F2d 286 (5th Cir 1975) cert den 424 US 977, 96 SCt 1484, 47 LE2d 748 (1976) (75-2 U.S.T.C. ¶ 13088); cf. *Estate of Fruehauf v Commr* 427 F2d 80 (6th Cir 1970); *Estate of Skifter v Commr* 468 F2d 699 (2d Cir 1972). Accordingly, the trust provisions should carefully negate the trust having any of the incidents of ownership in the policy or, alternatively, the husband should not act as a trustee or co-trustee of the trust.

The third possibility of taxability in the husband's estate arises if the trust provides that during the joint lifetime of the spouses it can be revoked or amended either by the husband alone or in conjunction with the wife. (See §7.25 for a discussion of the requirement that a funded trust be revocable by both spouses in order to preserve the community property characteristics for stepped-up basis purposes of community property assets in the trust.) This right on the part of the husband, either alone or in conjunction with the wife or any other person, may be considered an incident of ownership in the policy because by the exercise of this right the beneficiary of the policy could, in effect, be changed. See Reg. §§20.2042-1(c)(1) and (2); but see *Estate of Margrave v Commr* 618 F2d 34 (8th Cir 1980). Accordingly, the proceeds of the life insurance policy will be included in his estate. There are two alternative solutions to this problem. First, a separate, revocable trust may be created by the wife that she alone has the power to revoke or amend. Her wife-owned insurance will be made payable to this trust. This solution has the disadvantage of complexity in terms of non-unified trust administration and double record-keeping. The alternative is to make the second policy payable to the regular revocable living trust, but this trust should clearly provide that the husband shall at no time have any right to alter, amend or revoke the trust in such a manner as to in any way affect any life insurance policies or the proceeds thereof which are the separate property of the wife and that such right shall belong solely to the wife.

§10.42   2. Who Should Get the Policy if the Wife Predeceases the Husband?

Where the wife is the owner of the policy, planning is required to cover the possibility that the wife predeceases the insured husband. For a full discussion of the considerations which must be considered in planning for the possibility of the wife's dying first, see Weinstock, "What If The Wife Dies First?" 28 *Univ of So Cal Tax Inst* 55 (1976).[2] If the wife should die first, the policy, unless a contingent owner is designated, will pass under the wife's will. Normally, in the estate plan considered here (see §10.39), the residue of the wife's estate will pour over from her will into the revocable living trust which will thereby become the owner of the policy. If the husband is the trustee of the trust he will be considered as having the incidents of ownership in the policy and upon his subsequent death the policy proceeds will be taxed in his estate. Reg. §20.2042-1(c)(4); *Estate of Harry R Fruehauf v Commr* 50 TC 915 (1968). This result may be avoided by having someone other than the husband act as trustee, at least as to that portion of the trust which consists of the wife-owned life insurance policies.

Even if the husband were not the trustee, any portion of the policy allocable to the marital deduction trust would once again be taxable in the husband's estate upon his subsequent death. It therefore would be advisable for the trust to provide that any wife-owned policy be allocated entirely to the bypass trust. While the marital deduction would not be obtainable on the value of the policy on the wife's death, the proceeds would bypass the husband's taxable estate on his later death.

Another possible solution to the problem of the wife predeceasing the husband is for the wife to bequeath the policy to someone other than the husband, for example, the children. This will eliminate the policy proceeds from the husband's estate. However, unless the estate is much larger than average, the husband may not be willing to lose the economic benefit of the policies if his wife should predecease him.

Designating a contingent owner of the policy should not be overlooked in planning for the possibility of the wife's dying first. If the policy passes under the wife's will, it will be subject to probate and the cash value will have to be inventoried. Probate of the policy may be avoided by having the wife designate those persons who would otherwise receive the policy under the wife's will as the contingent owners of the policy.

In certain instances, the wife may be willing to name the husband as the contingent owner, fully realizing that if she dies first the policy will be in the husband's estate. However, care should be taken to avoid the possibility that the proceeds are includable in the husband's estate if, in fact, he is the first to die. Where the insurance policy is originally owned by the husband and the contingent ownership designation is put into effect at the time that the husband assigns the incidents of ownership in the policy to the wife, such contingent ownership may arguably constitute a reversionary interest which, if worth more than 5 per cent, will cause the inclusion of the proceeds in the husband's estate. However, if the wife, as a right of her ownership, can cash the policy or remove the husband as the contingent owner, the argument should fail. See

---

[2] A portion of the material in §10.42 is taken from the cited article with the permission of Matthew Bender & Company, Inc., the copyright holder.

Reg. §20.2042-1(c)(3); see also Rev. Rul. 79-117, 1979-1 CB 305. In any event, if the wife, as the original owner or sometime after acquiring ownership, designates the husband as contingent owner and reserves the right to change such contingent owner, this certainly should remove these grounds for inclusion in the husband's estate.

§10.43   3. Simultaneous Death

Where the wife owns a life insurance policy on the husband's life, of which she or the "A" trust is the beneficiary (see §10.39), and the husband and the wife die simultaneously, the tax consequences may differ from those where one or the other spouse survives.

In the case of simultaneous deaths, the insured is ordinarily deemed to survive the beneficiary, unless there is a stipulation in the policy or other instrument changing the presumption. See Uniform Simultaneous Death Act §5. Therefore, where there is no contrary survivorship designation, only the value of the unmatured life insurance policy, namely the interpolated terminal reserve plus the unused portion of the premium (see §10.16), but not the proceeds, will be taxed in the wife-owner's estate. Rev. Rul. 77-181, 1977-1 C.B. 272. Unless the death proceeds are payable to the insured-husband's estate, it does not appear that the proceeds will be taxed in his estate either.

On the other hand, if the presumption of the Uniform Simultaneous Death Act is changed by the policy terms or by other means of designation and the wife is presumed to be the survivor, the death proceeds will be includable in her estate (see Rev. Rul. 77-48, 1977-1 C.B. 292), but the interpolated terminal reserve value plus the unused portion of the premium will be excluded.

§10.44   B. Ownership by Children or Irrevocable Life Insurance Trust

One of the drawbacks in making the wife the owner or the beneficiary of the life insurance policies on her husband's life is that if she is the second to die, the proceeds will become part of her estate. In order to avoid the proceeds being taxable on the husband's death and/or on the wife's death, it is necessary to make someone other than the husband or the wife the owner of the policies. In many instances, a married couple will plan their estate so that there will be no estate taxes on the death of the first spouse to die (see §4.8). Instead, the tax on the entire estate, except for the portion contained in the bypass trust, will be deferred until the death of the surviving spouse. As a result, life insurance in larger estates may not be necessary for liquidity purposes until the death of the spouse who dies second.

In order to help defray the cost of the tax when the surviving spouse dies, a relatively little used type of life insurance, known as a joint life policy, will probably become much more popular in the future. Under this type of policy, both the husband and the wife are the insureds, but the proceeds are not paid until the death of the survivor of them.

Nevertheless, one should not entirely dismiss the utility of the traditional type of life insurance policy, which is payable on the death of the insured spouse. In this way, if the estate is planned to anticipate the payment of some estate tax on the first death, in order to avoid a much larger tax on the second death, or if the surviving spouse chooses to effect a similar result through a qualified disclaimer, liquid funds will be available to pay the tax on the first death. See §4.8.

Regardless of the type of life insurance policies, consideration should be given to designating either the children or an irrevocable insurance trust for the children's benefit as the owner of the life insurance policies.

§10.45   1. Ownership by Children

There are generally four disadvantages to making the children the outright owners of the life insurance policies. These disadvantages are:

(a)   The children may be immature and misuse their rights of ownership. For example, they may cash the policies prior to the insured's death and use the cash for their own purposes. If a child is a minor, the Revised Uniform Gifts to Minors Act, as adopted in many states, permits insurance policies to be held by a custodian for the benefit of such minor. §1(c) Revised Uniform Gifts to Minors Act. This gives the custodian complete control over the policy until the minor reaches his majority. To avoid the policy's being included in the estate of the donor, someone other than the donor should be designated as the custodian. See Rev. Rul. 59-357, 1959-2 C.B. 212.

(b)   After the death of the insured, the children may not be willing to use the proceeds for estate liquidity purposes. This is particularly true where the children are not the primary beneficiaries of the estate.

(c)   If the children are the owners of the policies, the proceeds will become part of their estate for estate tax purposes and the income therefrom will increase their income taxes during their lifetime.

(d)   If the children are the owners, they cannot permit any portion of the proceeds to be available for the wife's lifetime use, without gift tax consequences.

These disadvantages may be eliminated or ameliorated by the use of an irrevocable insurance trust.

§10.46   2.   Ownership by Irrevocable Insurance Trust

An irrevocable insurance trust is a trust created to acquire and own one or more life insurance policies. The trust may be funded with other assets, in addition to the life insurance policies, to provide a source of funds to pay the life insurance premiums, or it may be unfunded in which case the grantor or another person will have to pay the premiums to keep the policies in force.

a.   General Tax Consequences

§10.47   1.   Gift Taxes

The transfer of life insurance policies to the trust will constitute a taxable gift. See §10.17 for discussion of the value of an insurance policy for gift tax purposes. In computing the gift tax the $10,000 present interest exclusion will usually not be allowed. Unless the trust is funded and thereby pays the premiums, their payment by other persons will constitute additional gifts of a future interest. (See §10.19.) However, if the trust provides that the insurance proceeds are to be paid out free of trust upon the insured's death to the trust beneficiary or his estate, the payment of premiums may qualify for the $10,000 annual gift tax exclusion. Rev. Rul. 76-490, 1976-2 C.B. 300.

Where the trust is funded with other assets, they, too, will be subject to gift tax. If the income from these other assets may be used to pay the premiums, then no annual exclusion will generally be allowed. (See §10.20.) If, however, under the terms of the trust, the beneficiary is allowed to withdraw during each year the lesser of the amount of the present interest exclusion or the value of the assets transferred to the trust during that year, the present interest exclusion will be allowable. See *Crummey v Commr* 397 F2d 82 (9th Cir 1968). Where the gift which gives rise to the withdrawal right is the life insurance policy itself, or the premium payments, and the trust has no other assets, the withdrawal right may be satisfied by the trust assigning its interest in the insurance policy to the beneficiary. See Letter Ruls. 7947008, 8006109 and 8021058. For a discussion of Crummey trusts, see §8.35.

§10.48   ii.   Income Taxes

If the income of a trust is or may be used to pay the premiums on a policy of life insurance on the life of the grantor or his spouse, the grantor is taxable to the extent of the premium payments. I.R.C. §677. On the other hand, if the grantor of the trust already is the owner of a life insurance policy on the life of someone other than himself or his spouse, he may transfer it to an irrevocable insurance trust, and the income of the trust will not be taxable to him. Moreover, where the trust is unfunded, but merely holds the life insurance policies, it will ordinarily have no income so the problem of taxability to the grantor will not exist.

Where a policy on which there is a loan (see §10.29) is transferred to an irrevocable unfunded insurance trust, another income tax problem is created, since only the owner of the policy can obtain an interest deduction. Where the trust is unfunded, this deduction will not be of any benefit to the trust because it will not have any other income to offset the interest deduction.

It may be possible to avoid the loss of the interest deduction by structuring the trust so that it is a "defective grantor trust." Such a trust is one where the grantor is treated as the "owner" of the trust for income tax purposes (see I.R.C. §§674 through 677 and see §§8.39 through 8.42), and thereby the trust's deductions will become his deductions. The grantor, in making himself the income tax "owner" should, however, be careful to avoid the trust assets being included in his gross estate by reason of his retention of certain benefits, rights or powers over the trust assets. See I.R.C. §§2036, 2037, 2039 and 2042; see also §8.37. Several examples of trust provisions which should make the grantor the income tax owner, but not the estate tax owner, are:

1. Permitting the income of the trust to pay the life insurance premiums (I.R.C. §677(a)(3)),

2. Making the grantor's spouse a permissible distributee of trust income (I.R.C. §§677(a)(1) and (2)),

3. Giving an independent trustee the right to add beneficiaries to the trust (I.R.C. §§674(a) and (c)), and

4. Giving the grantor's spouse, parent, brother or sister the discretionary power to distribute income and principal (I.R.C. §§674(a), (b) and (c)).

The Internal Revenue Service has issued several favorable income tax letter rulings regarding one or more of the above defective grantor trust provisions. See Letter Ruls. 8008085, 8014078 and 8103074. However, in Revenue Procedure 81-37, I.R.B. 1981-34, 72, the Service stated that, until it re-examines the entire subject, no more rulings will be issued regarding the tax consequences of the defective grantor trust provisions used in a Crummey-type irrevocable life insurance trust. Until the matter is clarified, caution should be exercised.

Another possible way to avoid the loss of the interest deduction is by dividing the ownership of the policy between the wife as her separate property and the trust. The wife will own the cash surrender value of the policy, and the trust will own the pure insurance portion of the policy. See §10.57 for a discussion of the split-dollar policy in the corporate context. In this way, the wife will remain the debtor-obligor since the loan is against the cash value, and she can claim the interest deduction on the couple's joint income tax return.

§10.49 iii. Death Taxes

Unless the transfers to the trust have been made within three years of the grantor's death, the life insurance policies will ordinarily be kept out of his estate. For a discussion of the problems incident to a gift of a life insurance policy made within three years of death, or the payment of premiums thereon within three years of death, see §10.13. In order to avoid death taxation, the insured should not act as a trustee of the irrevocable life insurance trust. (See §10.41.) Care must be taken in drafting the trust to avoid requiring the trustee on the insured's death to pay any death taxes or other obligations of the insured's estate. See Reg. §20.2042-1(b). If the trustee, however, has no enforceable legal obligation to pay, but only discretionary power to loan the proceeds to or purchase assets from the insured's estate, the insurance proceeds will not be includable in the insured's estate.

§10.50 b. Who Should be the Beneficiaries of the Irrevocable Life Insurance Trust?

The grantor should not be a beneficiary of the trust because this will cause all or a portion of the trust assets to be taxed in his estate. See I.R.C. §2036. Caution should also be used to ensure that any other beneficiary is not, in fact, the grantor of the trust; otherwise the trust assets may be includable in the beneficiary's estate. Obviously, the person who transfers a life insurance policy to the trust will be considered a grantor. If the policy is community property at the time of transfer, then the spouse of the owner will also be considered a grantor as to one-half. Anyone who transfers other assets to the trust or pays the premiums on the life insurance policies contained in the trust will also be considered a grantor. Here, again, if any of the other assets or the source of funds used to pay the premiums is community property, then both spouses will be grantors. Thus, where the life insurance policy is on the husband's life, there is usually only one situation where it will be safe to make the wife a beneficiary of the trust; that is where the life insurance is the husband's separate property and all premiums are paid out of his separate property funds. The wife, since 1981, may gift her interest in the husband's policy to him, without giving rise to a taxable gift. See §2.42. If the wife owns an interest in the husband's policy, the children or other relatives, but not the wife, should be made the beneficiaries of the trust.

The reciprocal trust doctrine may also cause the proceeds to be taxed in the grantor's estate, even if the grantor is not a beneficiary of the trust which he created. See *US v Estate of Grace* 395 US 316, 89 SCt 1730, 23 LE2d 332 (1969). This doctrine will be invoked where there are two trusts, one created by each spouse, in which the non-grantor spouse is given the income for life. When each spouse dies, the assets in the trust created by that spouse will be included in that spouse's estate. Accordingly, where the husband and wife each own insurance policies and wish to create irrevocable life insurance trusts, the wife, for example, can be made a beneficiary of the husband's trust, but the husband should not be made a beneficiary of the wife's trust.

§10.51   VIII.   Advisability of Life Insurance on the Life of the Wife

It is sometimes overlooked that there may be a liquidity problem upon the death of the wife. Whenever she has an estate of her own, or where the estate is community property, and she does not leave to her husband a maximum or optimum marital deduction bequest, there may be an estate tax on her death. In these instances, there may even be a greater need for liquidity than if the husband dies first. For example, if the husband is active in a closely held business, arrangements will frequently have been made, perhaps through a buy-sell agreement, to sell the husband's interest on his death. This sale will help make the husband's estate liquid. However, where the wife is not active in the business, a sale of her interest on her death will usually not be provided for because the husband would lose voting power or even control of the closely held business.

Moreover, where, for reasons of health or age differences, it appears likely that the wife will be the surviving spouse, and the husband's estate plan provides for a maximum or optimum marital deduction bequest, the estate tax burden will be much greater on the wife's death than on the husband's. The estate plan should take this into account and attempt to insure that there will be sufficient liquid funds available on her death.

One of the best ways of avoiding the liquidity problem if the wife dies first is to have her obtain adequate life insurance on her life. To maximize the available proceeds, the ownership of this life insurance should be planned in such a way so that the proceeds will be kept out of the wife's estate. This may be done by making such persons as the children, or an irrevocable life insurance trust the owner of the policies. (See §10.44.)

§10.52   IX.   Business Life Insurance

The purpose of §§10.53, 10.54 and 10.55 is to highlight the role of life insurance in buy-sell agreements, and in employee agreements and to fund for the loss of key persons. However, for a full discussion of the business aspects of estate planning, see Chapter 12.

§10.53   A.   Use in Buy-Sell Agreements

Life insurance is an excellent vehicle to fund business buy-sell agreements providing for the purchase of the decedent owner's interest in a corporation or a partnership upon his death. See §§12.7 to 12.34 for a full discussion of buy-sell agreements. This vehicle is advantageous to buyers, whether the business or the surviving co-owners, because they will be supplied with funds necessary to consummate the purchase. For example, assume A and B each own a 50 per cent interest in a closely held business. If either one dies, it will be very difficult to generate sufficient funds from the business itself, without severely contracting the company, in order to buy out the interest of the deceased owner. The use of life insurance to fund a buy-sell agreement is also advantageous to the seller's estate because his estate will then not be dependent upon the ability of the buyer to pay the full purchase price. If little or no insurance is available and most of the purchase price is paid with a long-term note, the decedent's estate is taking a business risk that the note will not be paid, while at the same time it is not sharing in the profits of the business. The use of life insurance eliminates this unfair situation.

There are two types of buy-sell agreements, a cross-purchase agreement (the co-owners agree to purchase the deceased owner's interest) and an entity agreement (the business entity agrees to purchase the deceased owner's interest). For a full discussion of the tax and other considerations in using each type, see §§12.23 to 12.34. Whenever life insurance is used to fund a buy-sell agreement, whether a partnership or a corporate one, it is important to coordinate the ownership and beneficiary designations of the life insurance policies with the type of agreement which is used. Where the agreement is a cross-purchase agreement, each shareholder should own and be the beneficiary of a policy on each of the other shareholders' lives. If, on the contrary, there is a cross-purchase agreement but the corporation pays the premiums and is the owner and beneficiary of the policies, there will be tax consequences with which to contend. The payment of the premiums may be taxed as a dividend to the shareholders. Moreover, on the death of a shareholder, if the proceeds are distributed to the surviving shareholders or if the corporation uses the insurance proceeds and purchases the stock itself, such distribution or purchase may be taxed as constructive dividends to the surviving shareholders. See Rev. Rul. 59-184, 1959-1 C.B. 65; Rev. Rul. 58-614, 1958-2 C.B. 920.

On the other hand, where the buy-sell agreement is in the form of an entity agreement, the life insurance policies should be made payable to the business entity. Otherwise, the business will not have the necessary funds to fulfill its obligations. In that event, it may be necessary for the owners to loan the proceeds to the business and they might be unwilling to do so.

The subject of disability insurance, at least in any great detail, is beyond the scope of this chapter. The estate planner will want to consider the problem not only of death, but of a prolonged and serious disability of a partner or stockholder. Frequently, a buy-sell agreement will provide for a buyout in the event of such disability. To fund this buyout, the purchase of disability insurance may be advisable. Regardless of whether the buyout agreement is an entity agreement or a cross-purchase agreement, premiums paid for the disability insurance are not deductible. See I.R.C. §265(1); Rev. Rul. 66-262, 1966-2 C.B. 105. When the beneficiary owner of the disability policy (the nondisabled owners of the business in the event of a cross-purchase agreement, and the business itself in the event of an entity agreement) receives the disability income payments, such payments are not subject to income tax. See I.R.C.

§104(a)(3); Rev. Rul. 66-262, 1966-2 C.B. 237. If the payments are then used by the beneficiary-owner to buy out the interest of the disabled owner, such payments will normally not be deductible by the buyer and will be capital gain to the seller.

§10.54 B. Use in Employee Agreements

Life insurance may be used to fund an agreement between an employer and an employee providing for benefits on retirement or death. These agreements, which may be called deferred compensation contracts, should be distinguished from benefits under qualified pension or profit sharing plans which receive certain tax advantages. (See §§13.8 to 13.18.) For the general and tax characteristics of nonqualified deferred compensation agreements after the death of an employee, see §§6.29 and 12.45 to 12.50.

Using life insurance to fund a deferred compensation agreement will provide a source of funds to make the required payments to the employee. Permanent insurance should be used because this type of insurance will provide a death benefit in the event of the employee's death before retirement or, alternatively, a cash value which can be converted into an annuity upon retirement. It may also be worthwhile to have the life insurance policy contain a waiver of premium provision, excusing the obligation of the employer to pay premiums during any period that the insured is disabled. The employer can then use the funds thereby saved to continue all or a portion of the employee's salary during his diability.

In order to avoid having the employee pay any income tax until he receives the benefits under the agreement, the employee should have no vested right in the insurance policy, but should have a mere contractual right to receive payments from the employer. Accordingly, the employer should be the owner and the beneficiary of the life insurance policy. See Rev. Rul. 68-99, 1968-1 C.B. 193; Rev. Rul. 72-25, 1972-1 C.B. 127. In this way the premiums paid on the policy by the employer will not be income to the employee, nor will they be deductible by the employer. When the policy is cashed during the employee's lifetime, any gain on the policy will be taxable to the employer, but the employer will be able to deduct the payments made to the employee. If the policy proceeds are paid by reason of the employee's death, they will not be includable in the employer's income, and the payments made to the employee will be deductible. In either case, the payments to the employee, or his beneficiary or estate in the event of his death, will be included in the taxable income of the recipient.

For a discussion of the death tax consequences of employee deferred compensation agreements, see §12.47.

§10.55 C. Key Person Life Insurance

This is life insurance which a business will purchase on the life of one or more of its key employees. Its major function is to provide monetary compensation to the business for the loss of the key person or persons. From an estate planning point of view, it may also be used to fund an agreement with a key employee (see §10.54), or if the key person is a major stockholder, a stock redemption agreement under I.R.C. §303 (see §§12.35 to 12.38).

X. Use of Life Insurance in Connection with Employee Fringe Benefits

§10.56 A. Group Life Insurance

Group term life insurance receives certain favored tax treatment. The premiums paid are deductible by the employer. The cost of coverage up to $50,000 is excludable from the employee's income. I.R.C. §79(a). This exemption is not available, however, unless (1) the coverage is on the life of an employee, who must render personal services in that capacity; (2) the coverage is group term life insurance under the Regulations; and (3) the insurance is carried directly or indirectly by the insured's employer. Reg. §§1.79-(a) and (b). The cost of coverage in excess of $50,000 is taxable to the employee. This taxable cost is not the actual cost, but is computed under Reg. §1.79-3(d)(2). In many instances, the computed cost is less than the actual cost, so it may provide an opportunity for the employee to have more than $50,000 of coverage at little extra expense.

In other respects, a group term life insurance policy usually has the same general tax characteristics as any other policy of life insurance. See §§10.11 to 10.30 inclusive. Group term life insurance should, however, not be used to fund a shareholder's buy-sell agreement because of two potential problems. First, the company may be denied a deduction for premium payments on the ground that the premiums are not related to its trade or business. Secondly, if the shareholders reciprocally name each other as beneficiaries of their insurance policies, or reciprocally agree to apply the proceeds to the purchase of their stock, the proceeds may be taxable for income tax purposes under the transfer for value rule. (See §10.22.)

For death tax purposes it is possible for an employee to assign to another all his incidents of ownership in group term life insurance as long as both the policy and state law permit an absolute assignment of all of the insured's interest in the insurance policy upon termination of employment. Rev. Rul. 69–54, 1969–1 C.B. 221 For a discussion of the payment of the premiums on a group term life insurance policy within three years of death, see §10.15.

Group term life insurance, in order to qualify for the income tax exclusion of the cost of coverage up to $50,000, must form part of a plan of group insurance that meets certain requirements. These requirements are very technical in nature and the estate planner should study I.R.C. §79 and the Regulations thereunder. In general terms, the plan must make term life insurance available to all of the employees, or to a class or classes of employees determined on the basis of factors which preclude individual selection. For example, the amounts of insurance made available to the covered employees must be based on an objective factor such as salary, years of service, or position with the company. Normally, a plan must provide protection for at least 10 full-time employees at some time during the calendar year. Groups of less than 10 employees may be covered if certain antidiscrimination requirements of the Regulations are met. (See Reg. §§1.79-1(b)(1)(iii), (d)(1)-(5).) The latter requirements are generally (1) all full-time employees must be covered; (2) the amount of protection for employees must be computed either as a uniform percentage of salary or on the basis of brackets under which no bracket exceeds two and one-half times the next lower bracket, and the lowest bracket is at least 10 per cent of the highest bracket; (3) medical evidence from a medical examination may not be used to determine eligibility for coverage or the amount of coverage. If the group term life insurance does not meet the requirements of a plan of group insurance, then the full amount of the premium paid by the employer will be taxable to the employee as additional compensation.

In addition to the income tax benefits of group term life insurance, this type of insurance is a valuable estate planning tool in that it often enables persons to obtain insurance at lower rates than such insurance would be available, if at all, under an individual policy.

Some group life insurance plans also provide for permanent life insurance benefits. The portion of the premium attributable to the permanent life insurance benefit is includable in the insured employee's income. See Reg §§1.79-0 and 1.79-6. Usually there is an allocation in the policy which has been approved in advance by the Internal Revenue Service. Thus, the insured employee has income imputed to him in the amount of the portion of the premium not allocated to the term insurance, and he receives ownership of the cash value of the policy. In many cases, after the first year the income tax on the portion of the premium taxable to him is usually less than the cash value that he owns. After four out of the first seven annual premiums have been paid without borrowing, the employee may borrow on the policy and deduct the interest charged on the loan. See §10.29.

As a supplement to many group insurance plans, a retired lives reserve fund has been used. This is a fund held by the insurance company, to which the employer pays the premiums, which enables employees to continue their group term life insurance after retirement. The claimed tax advantages of such a fund are that the employer, in most instances, will be permitted to deduct the premiums, the employee need not include such premiums in income and, after retirement, the employee does not receive taxable income by reason of the continuation of the group term life insurance. The Internal Revenue Service, however, has temporarily suspended the issuance of rulings on retired lives reserves because it is making an "extensive study" of the subject. Rev. Proc. 80-22, 1980-1 C.B. 654.

§10.57   B.   Split-Dollar Life Insurance

Split-dollar life insurance is ordinary life insurance purchased by either the employer or the employee and held pursuant to a contract where the employer and the employee each pay a portion of the premiums and they share in the death proceeds. Generally, the employer pays that portion of the premium equal to the annual increase in the cash value, and the employee pays the balance of the premium. On the death of the employee, an amount equal to the cash value will be payable to the employer and the balance (which consists of the "term" portion of the proceeds), to the employee. Because of the ever-increasing cash value, the employee's portion of both the premiums and the proceeds will decrease with each succeeding year that the policy is in force.

There are, however, hybrid plans where the portion of the premium paid by the employer and the employee and the amount received by each on the death of the employee vary. For example, the policy may contain a "fifth dividend" or "increasing term insurance" option which, for an additional premium, will result in the death proceeds being equal to the face amount of the policy, plus the cash value; thus, the employee's portion will be the original face amount of the policy.

There are two planning objectives which may be achieved through a split-dollar life insurance program. First, it usually enables the employee to achieve a lower after-tax cost for insurance protection than he could have if he purchased the insurance on his own. Second, it enables the employer to provide a fringe benefit to a key employee and, at the same time, build up a fund in the form of the cash value of the insurance policy which can be used for corporate purposes when needed.

The income tax characteristics of a split-dollar life insurance policy are set forth in Rev. Rul. 64-328, 1964-2 C.B. 11. In general, these characteristics with respect to policies issued after November 13, 1964, are as follows:

1. The value of the economic benefit, to the extent paid for by the employer, is taxable to the employee. The economic benefit is the current insurance protection under the policy, plus other benefits such as dividend options. The current insurance protection, in turn, is determined by use of the Internal Revenue Service one-year term rates (called P.S. 58 rates, see Appendix, Table X). See also Rev. Rul. 55-747, 1955-2 C.B. 228.

2. The employer is not allowed a deduction for any portion of the premium which it pays.

3. On the death of the employee, the proceeds received by either the employee or the employer are not subject to income tax.

For death tax purposes the employee may assign his portion of the policy to another owner in order to avoid having the proceeds taxed in his estate. In terms of estate inclusion, however, a possible problem exists where the employee owns over 50 per cent of the stock in the employer-corporation. Reg.

§20.2042-1(c)(6) requires the inclusion in the stockholder-employee's estate of the total proceeds under a policy if the corporation has any of the incidents of ownership in the policy and the policy is payable for a noncorporate purpose. Unless the portion of the policy payable to the employee, or the employee's assignee, is deemed to be for a corporate purpose, the Internal Revenue Service may attempt to tax the proceeds in the employee's estate. In order to attempt to negate this argument, it is recommended that no portion of the policy be owned by the corporation. Any "interest" which the corporation wishes to have in the policy to secure that upon the employee's death it will be reimbursed for the premiums which it has paid should be in the form of a collateral assignment by the employee. At the very least, if the corporation is designated as an "owner," its rights of ownership should be restricted to that portion of the policy securing the repayment of the loan. Rev. Rul. 76-274, 1976-2 C.B. 278; *Estate of Alfred Dimen v Commr* 72 TC 198 (1979).

Where the employee's policy has been assigned to a third person, the value of the economic benefit (see item 1 above) is nevertheless includable in such employee's taxable income. In addition, each time a premium is paid by the employer, the employee is deemed to have made a taxable gift of the value of the economic benefit to the third person owner of his portion of the policy. See Rev. Rul. 78-420, 1978-2 C.B. 67.

§10.58   C.   Pension and Profit Sharing Plans

This section will summarize briefly the considerations in using life insurance to fund pension or profit sharing plans. For a full discussion of the general tax and estate planning aspects of such plans, see §§13.8 to 13.21.

One of the advantages of using the contributions to a qualified pension or profit sharing plan to purchase life insurance on the employee-participants' lives is to guarantee the employee an annuity upon retirement at the rates at the time of purchase rather than at the rates in effect when the employee retires. Annuity costs have increased and probably will continue to increase because of longer life expectancies not yet reflected in the annuity tables currently used by many insurance companies.

The types of life insurance policies which generally have to be purchased are ordinary life policies or other policies that will have cash values, so that they may be used for retirement income on the employee's retirement. For a discussion of the types of life insurance policies, see §§10.6 to 10.10.

Since the primary purpose of a qualified pension or profit sharing plan is to provide for retirement benefits and not death benefits, the latter must be merely "incidental." See Reg. §§1.401-1(b)(1)(i) and (ii). Subject to many technical exceptions and variations, the life insurance death benefit is generally deemed to be "incidental" in a qualified pension plan if it will not exceed 100 times the monthly retirement benefit to which the participant would have been entitled under the plan if he had lived to retirement. Hence, if the retirement benefit is $1,000 per month, the death benefit may not exceed $100,000. See Rev. Rul. 68-453, 1968-2 C.B. 163. The death benefit is "incidental" in a money purchase pension plan or in a profit sharing plan if less than 50 per cent of the aggregate employer contributions and forfeitures that have been allocated to the employee is generally all that may be used to purchase life insurance. See Rev. Rul. 60-84, 1960-1 C.B. 159. Insurance death benefits under an employee stock ownership plan (see §13.13) will be considered "incidental" if the aggregate premiums do not exceed 25 per cent of the value of the participant's account. See T.I.R. 1413 (Nov. 4, 1975).

If the life insurance purchased is "incidental," then the employer may deduct the contributions which are made to the qualified plan. Subject to one exception, the portion of the employer's contributions made to the plan to purchase life insurance which is "incidental" does not constitute taxable income to the employee-participants. The exception is that the net term cost of the life insurance, determined under the P.S. 58 rates (see Appendix, Table X), will constitute taxable income to the insured participant. See Rev. Rul. 55-747, 1955-2 C.B. 228. Generally, this amount is small in comparison to the overall contributions of the employer. On the employee's retirement or death, the cash value of the insurance contract, less the amount of the employer's contributions which have previously been taxed to the employee, will be subject to income tax. The remaining life insurance proceeds received by reason of the employee's death will be excludable from gross income. See I.R.C. §101(a).

XI. Recommended Reading

Brawerman and Holcomb, "How to Use Life Insurance in Community Property Estate Planning" 20 *Univ of So Cal Tax Inst* 495 (1968)

Chapman, "Life Insurance as a Planning Tool: The Life Insurance Policy" 34 *NYU Inst on Fed Tax* 723 (1975)

Corcoran, "How to Use Spouse-Owned Life Insurance" 51 *Taxes* 363 (1973)

Denenberg, "Implementing an Irrevocable Life Insurance Trust: An In-Depth Analysis" 42 *Journal of Taxation* 42 (1975)

Eliasberg, "Contemplation of Death and the Estate Taxation of Life Insurance" 111 *Trusts and Estates* 690 (1972)

Eliasberg, "IRC Section 2042 - The Estate Taxation of Life Insurance: What is an Incident of Ownership?" 51 *Taxes* 91 (1973)

Jones, "Valuation Techniques Required by Gift of Community Property Life Insurance" 51 *Journal of Taxation* 100 (1979)

Kanter, "New Approaches to Split Dollar" 111 *Trusts and Estates* 790 (1972)

Keydel, "Irrevocable Life Insurance Trusts: 1981 Update" 4 *UCLA Estate Planning Inst* _____ (1981)

Lawthers, "Income Tax Aspects of Transfers of Life Insurance Policies and of Various Forms of Settlement Options" 22 *NYU Inst on Fed Tax* 1299 (1964)

Morgan, "Split Dollar Insurance — New Developments Suggest Planning Techniques That Save Taxes" 58 *Taxes* 269 (1980)

Munch, *Federal Taxation of Insured Pensions* (Matthew Bender and Co 1975)

Salem and Schmalbeck, "Group-Term Life Insurance: IRS Creates New Solutions, Questions and Challenges" 51 *Journal of Taxation* 130 (1979)

Schlesinger, "How to Use Life Insurance in Estate Planning" J.K. Lasser, *Estate Tax Techniques* 799 (Matthew Bender and Co 1972)

Sullivan, "Life Insurance: Incidents of Ownership Held by Trustee may Bring Proceeds into his Estate" 2 *Estate Planning* 250 (1975)

Wark, "IRS Rulings Hint 'Super' Life Insurance Trust Okay for Gift, Income and Estate Tax Saving" 54 *Journal of Taxation* 162 (1981)

Annuities

11

§11.1   I.   In General

An annuity may be defined as an agreement to pay a person (the annuitant) a fixed sum at periodic intervals as long as the person lives. In one sense, it is the opposite of a life insurance policy, which insures against the risk of dying too soon. The annuity contract insures against the risk of living too long so that one's estate is used up before death. The annuity may be a commercial annuity, i.e., one purchased from an insurance company or similar organization (see §11.2) or a private annuity, i.e., one resulting from the sale of assets usually by one family member to another (see §11.12).

§11.2   II.   Commercial Annuities

A commercial annuity may be purchased for a single premium, in which case the annuity payments frequently commence immediately. Sometimes, however, even where the annuity is purchased with a single premium, the annuity payments may commence at some future date, such as the date on which the annuitant reaches age 65. The annuity may also be purchased on the basis of monthly or other periodic premiums. In the case of such an annuity, the annuity payments will usually commence at a future date. Often an annuity will result from the transformation of a life insurance policy, such as an ordinary life, limited pay or endowment policy. Prior to the insured's death, the cash value in the policy may be converted into an annuity, either in accordance with the policy terms or in exchange for an annuity contract.

A.   Types

§11.3   1.   Straight Life Annuity

A straight life annuity provides for annuity payments for the annuitant's lifetime. Upon his death the annuity payments will cease, even though the cost of the annuity has not yet been returned. For example, A for $10,000 purchases a lifetime annuity with payments of $100 per month. A dies one year after the starting date of the annuity. No further payments are made after his death.

§11.4   2.   Refund Annuity

A refund annuity is similar to a straight life annuity, except that, if the annuitant dies before the consideration paid for the annuity has been returned, the insurance company will refund the balance to the annuitant's beneficiary or estate. For example, A for $12,000 purchases an annuity providing for annuity payments of $100 per month. A dies one year after the starting date of the annuity. The insurance company will refund $10,800 to A's beneficiary or his estate. The premium for this type of an annuity is more expensive than for a straight life annuity with the same monthly or other periodic payments.

§11.5   3.   Life Annuity with Term Certain

This type is a variation that combines the straight life annuity and the refund annuity. It provides for annuity payments to be made during the annuitant's entire lifetime, but if the annuitant dies before the expiration of the term specified in the annuity agreement, for example, one, five or ten years, the payments will continue until the expiration of such fixed term. The premiums for this type of annuity are more costly than those for a straight life annuity.

§11.6   4.   Joint Life and Survivorship Annuity

Under this type of an annuity the payments are made during the joint lives of two persons, typically husband and wife, and then continue for the life of the survivor. The annuity contract may be written so that each annuity payment will be either in the same amount during the life of the survivor as it was during the joint lives, or in a reduced amount. If the annuity payment during the life of the survivor is in a reduced amount, the premium for the annuity will be less than where the annuity payments during joint lives continue for the survivor. In either event, however, the premiums paid for this type of annuity will exceed those paid for straight life annuity. A joint life and survivorship annuity may also contain a refund feature (see §11.4) or provide a term certain (see §11.5).

§11.7   B.   Nontax Advantages and Disadvantages in Purchasing an Annuity

The most important reason for purchasing an annuity is to ensure the annuitant an "income" for the rest of his lifetime without the burdens and risks of management. Frequently, elderly persons become very concerned that their estate will be dissipated prior to their death. Moreover, in advancing years, the burdens of management become difficult, if not impossible. An annuity will help to solve these problems and concerns.

There are two major disadvantages in purchasing an annuity as compared to other investments. In the usual type of annuity where the annuity payments are fixed in amount, continuing inflation presents a serious problem. The annuity will be paid for with "expensive" dollars, and the insurance company will pay it back with "cheap" dollars. In recent years insurance companies have developed a so-called variable annuity, where theoretically, at least, the payments will keep better pace with inflation. The second major disadvantage of an annuity is its lack of flexibility. The annuitant may be faced with extraordinary expenses in any given month or other period, but the annuity payments will be made in accordance with the prearranged fixed schedule.

C. Taxation

§11.8   1. Income Tax

The income taxation of annuities is governed by §72 of the Internal Revenue Code and the Regulations thereunder. These rules are quite detailed and, particularly in the case of refund, term certain and joint and survivorship annuities, there are complex nuances. However, the income tax principles applicable in most cases may in general terms be more easily illustrated by reference to a straight life annuity.

The basic rule is designed to return the purchaser's investment in equal tax-free amounts over the payment period and to tax the balance of the amounts received. As a result, each payment is in part a nontaxable return of cost and in part taxable income. In order to determine the nontaxable part, the "exclusion ratio" for the annuity contract must be determined. Such ratio is, in turn, determined by dividing "the investment in the contract" by the "expected return."

In general, the "investment in the contract" is the premium cost or other consideration paid for the contract. If the annuity has not been purchased directly but rather results from the conversion of a life insurance policy, the "investment in the contract" will be the premiums paid on the life insurance policy. However, if the life insurance policy is surrendered and the insured fails to elect within 60 days from the surrender of the policy to receive an annuity, he will first have to pay the tax on any gain (see §10.30) In such case, his investment in the contract will be the amount of cash value in the insurance policy.

The "expected return" is in general the total amount that the annuitant can expect to receive under the contract. It is computed by multiplying the sum of one year's annuity payments by the life expectancy of the annuitant or annuitants. The life expectancy multiple must be taken from the annuity tables prescribed by the Treasury Department. See Reg. §§1.72-5 and 1.72-9.

The following is an example of how an annuity payment is taxed. A, a male, age 65, purchases a straight life annuity paying $500 per month. The purchase price of the annuity is $70,000. The investment in the contract is, therefore, $70,000. The expected return is A's life expectancy of 15 years (see Reg. §1.72-9, Table I) times $500 (the monthly payment) times 12 (the yearly payment) or $90,000. The exclusion ratio is 77.777 per cent ($70,000 ÷ $90,000). Hence, 77.777 per cent of each monthly payment of $500, or $388.89, is excluded from A's income, and the balance, or $111.11, is taxable. Even if A outlives his life expectancy of 15 years, the amount excluded will remain the same during each year of his life. Conversely, if A dies before the end of his 15-year life expectancy, he will not recover his cost for income tax purposes.

§11.9   2.   Gift Tax

One may purchase an annuity and make a gift of it to another person. If the donor gives it away immediately after the purchase, the value of the gift for gift tax purposes is the premium paid for the annuity. However, if the donor makes the gift at a later date, the value of the gift is the single premium the insurance company would charge at that time for a comparable annuity. The value of an annuity on which premiums are still to be paid is the terminal reserve, adjusted to the date of the gift, plus the unearned portion of the last premium payment. See Reg. §25.2512-6. The gift of an annuity policy, to the extent that its value exceeds the gift tax annual exclusion and deductions will, through the operation of the unified estate and gift tax introduced by the Reform Act of 1976, be taxed at the estate tax rate, less the gift tax paid on the gift. (See §§2.2, and 2.3.) Since the value of an annuity policy tends to increase with the passage of time, there is a tax incentive to gift these policies, despite the unification of the estate and gift taxes. (See §8.4.)

One may also incur gift tax by purchasing a joint life and survivorship annuity. The amount of the gift is the cost of the annuity less the portion of the cost attributable to a single life annuity for the purchaser. For example, a donor purchases for $15,198 a joint and survivor annuity contract which provides for the payment of $60 per month to the donor during his lifetime, and then to his sister for such time as she may survive him. The premium which would have been charged by the company for an annuity of $60 monthly payable during the life of the donor alone is $10,690. The value of the gift is $4,508 ($15,198 less $10,690). Reg. §25.2512-6. If the donor reserves the right to change the survivor beneficiary, there will be no taxable gift.

Where one spouse purchases a joint life and survivorship annuity and designates the other spouse as the survivor beneficiary, the gift tax marital deduction is not allowed because the gift is one of a non-qualifying terminable interest. Reg. §25.2523(b)-(1)(c)(2).

§11.10   3.   Estate Tax

A straight life annuity is not subject to death taxation in the annuitant's estate because it ceases on the annuitant's death, and there is no residual value left. However, refund annuities, term certain annuities and joint life and survivorship annuities are subject to death tax, to the extent of the present value of the annuity to be paid after the annuitant's death. If the amount to be paid after the decedent's death is payable to his estate, the entire amount is included in his gross estate under I.R.C. §2033. Where such amount is payable to a named beneficiary, under an annuity purchased after March 3, 1931, it is includable in his estate only to the extent of the portion of the purchase price which the decedent paid. See I.R.C. §§2039(a) and (b). For example, if A and B each contribute 50 per cent of the purchase price of a joint life and survivorship annuity, and A dies first, only one-half of the then present value of the survivor's benefit will be included in A's estate.

§11.11   D.   Tax Deferred Variable and Investment Annuities

Under the general income tax rule governing annuities, the annuity owner will pay no income tax until the annuity contract is surrendered or until annuity payments are made under the contract. I.R.C. §72(a). Hence, all withdrawals prior to the starting date of the annuity will normally be tax-free until the annuity owner has recovered the cost of the annuity.

In recent years two types of annuity contracts have been developed to take advantage of the income tax deferral rule (see §11.8), a variable annuity and an investment or "wraparound" annuity. Under both of these contracts, the annuity premiums are invested, and the annuity owner may withdraw all or a portion of his premiums prior to the starting date. Unless the entire contract is surrendered beforehand, the annuity payments will begin on the starting date. The amount of the annuity payments will depend, in part, on the then market value of the unwithdrawn investments made with the annuity premiums. Under a variable annuity, the insurance company makes and controls the investments; while under an investment or "wraparound" annuity, the owner himself, within limits, determines and controls the investments which are made.

Both of these contracts have been structured to implicitly encourage the owner to make current withdrawals. The claimed income tax benefit is that until the sum of the withdrawals exceeds the total premiums paid, the amounts withdrawn will not be taxable as income, despite the fact that what is being withdrawn may be, in effect, the investment earnings.

While the purported tax consequences of the variable annuity appear to have received Internal Revenue Service approval, the tax consequences of the investment or "wraparound" annuity generally have not. The income earned on the assets in the latter type of annuity is currently taxable to the owner. See Rev. Rul. 81-225, IRB 1981-41, _____; Rev. Rul. 80-274, 1980-2 C.B. 27; Rev. Rul. 77-85, 1977-1 C.B. 12.

On the other hand, when the owner of the annuity contract dies, the beneficiary should receive a stepped-up basis with respect to an investment or "wraparound" annuity, but will not receive a stepped-up basis with respect to amounts contributed after October 20, 1979, for a variable annuity. Consequently, the amounts received by the beneficiary in excess of the amounts contributed by the decedent under an investment or "wraparound" annuity will be included in the beneficiary's income under the annuity rules. Rev. Rul. 79-335, 1979-2 C.B. 292. See §11.8.

§11.12   III.   Private Annuities

A private annuity is an annuity contract which is entered into between the annuitant and someone other than an insurance company or entity regularly engaged in the business of issuing annuity contracts. For a definition of an annuity, see §11.1. A private annuity is usually in the form of an elderly family member's transferring assets to a younger family member who makes an unsecured promise to pay a lifetime annuity to the transferor. For the considerations to be used in determining the amount of the annuity payment, see §11.14. One of the primary purposes of the private annuity device in estate planning is to reduce the estate owner's potential death tax liability by eliminating assets from his estate during his lifetime. It may have other estate planning advantages and disadvantages as well. (See §§11.17 to 11.19.)

A. Taxation

§11.13 1. Death Taxation

Generally, nothing will be taxed in the annuitant's estate because nothing remains to be paid after the annuitant's death. However, if the purchaser is a trust or the payments to be made by the purchaser are conditioned upon the income from the transferred property, the transaction may be treated as a transfer with income retained and will, therefore, be includable in the transferor's estate under I.R.C. §2036. See *Estate of Ambrose Fry v Commr* 9 TC 503 (1947).

§11.14 2. Gift Taxes

Unless at the time of the transfer the value of the annuity is less than the value of the property transferred, there will be no gift tax on the transaction. The value of the annuity is determined actuarially by reference to the annuity tables set forth in §25.2512-9 of the Regulations. By way of example, assume a 65 year old father transfers assets with a fair market value of $100,000 to his son for a private annuity. The annuity factor at his age is 8.0353. The yearly annuity payments, therefore, should be $12,445 ($100,000 ÷ 8.0353). If they are less than $12,445, the then present value of the difference will constitute a taxable gift. If, for example, they are $2,000 per year less, the value of the gift will be $16,071 ($2,000 × 8.0353). It is possible, however, to avoid an immediate gift by setting the annuity payments in a sufficiently large amount in the agreement (i.e., $12,445 per year), but leaving it up to the father to make yearly gifts to the son. If these yearly gifts are less than the gift tax annual exclusion and other deductions, they will not be included in the tentative tax base in computing the annuitant's estate tax. (See §§2.3 and 2.36 to 2.43.)

3. Income Taxes

§11.15   a.   Of the Transferor—Annuitant

The receipt of the annuity payments will be partially taxable and partially tax-free under the annuity rules of I.R.C. §72. (See §11.8.) However, where appreciated property is transferred in exchange for the annuity payments, the private annuity agreement may be thought of as a two-step transaction: (1) a sale of property, and (2) a purchase of an annuity with the sale proceeds. The transferor realizes no gain at the time of transfer, and no tax is then payable because the promise of the transferee to pay the annuity is a "naked," un-secured promise and therefore does not have a value that can be ascertained for income tax purposes. Accordingly, the annuitant will be taxed on the gain as it is received over a period of time. Rev. Rul. 69-74, 1969-1 C.B. 43. A part of each payment will then be excluded from taxable income, a part will be taxed as capital gain, and the balance will be taxed as ordinary income.

The above income tax rules may be illustrated by an example. Assume a father, age 65, transfers to his son an asset having a basis of $60,000 and a fair market value of $100,000. The son agrees (by way of an unsecured promise) to pay the father $12,445 per year for life. The income taxability of the payments to the father is computed by reference to the formula described in §11.8, as follows:

1.   Exclusion ratio $=\dfrac{\text{investment in contract}}{\text{expected return}}$

$$\dfrac{\$60,000}{15 \text{ (father's life expectancy under Reg. §72.9, Table I)} \times \$12,445}$$

$$\dfrac{\$60,000}{\$186,675} = 32.1414\%$$

2. $4,000.00 ($12,445 × 32.1414 per cent) of each annual payment will be excluded from the father's taxable income for the rest of his life.

3.   During the first 15 years that the annuity payments are made, $2,666.67 ($40,000 [the profit] ÷ 15 years [the father's life expectancy]) will be taxed as capital gain. If the father lives more than 15 years, this portion of the annuity payment will thereafter be taxed as ordinary income.

4.   During the first 15 years of the annuity, the balance, or $5,778.33 ($12,-445 minus [$4,000.00 plus $2,666.67]) will be taxed as ordinary income. After the first 15 years, the entire annuity payment, less the amount excluded (see Step (2)), is taxable as ordinary income, or $8,445.00 will be taxable as ordinary income.

Where the annuity is not for a "naked" promise, but is secured, the above formula is not used. The entire gain is taxable at the time of the transfer. *212 Corporation v Commr* 70 TC 788 (1978).

§11.16 b. Of the Transferee—Payor

The private annuity transaction also results in income tax consequences to the transferee—payor. The income earned from the property belongs to him and will increase his income for tax purposes. He will not, however, be allowed an income tax deduction for payments made to the annuitant. Rev. Rul. 72-81, 1972-1 C.B. 98. These payments are considered to be payments on the purchase price of the property, and even if they exceed the present value of the property because the annuitant lives too long, no part will be deductible as interest. *Rebecca Bell v Commr* 76 TC No 21 (Feb 17, 1981). The payments, including the "interest" element, will, however, increase the transferee—payor's basis in the property. The rules for computing the basis in the property are set forth in Revenue Ruling 55-119, 1955-1 C.B. 352. These rules may best be illustrated by using the facts in the example set forth in §11.15:

1. If the son retains the asset until after his father's death, his basis will be the total of the annuity payments which he made, minus the depreciation taken by him on the property. Assuming the father dies at the end of 10 years and the total depreciation during such 10 years is $40,000, the son's basis will be $84,450 ($12,445 times 10 minus $40,000).

2. If the son sells the asset prior to his father's death, his basis for computing gain will be the total payments made by the son up to the time of the sale, plus the then present value of the remaining payments to be made under the private annuity contract. Hence, if the son, in the example set forth in §11.15, sells the asset at the end of 10 years, his basis will be computed as follows:

Payments actually made ($12,445 times 10)	$124,450
Present value of remaining payments (9.6 [father's life expectancy at age 75, see Reg. §72.9, Table I] times $12,445)	119,472
Total	$243,922
Less depreciation	40,000
Son's basis for gain	$203,922

The son's basis for computing loss will be the payments actually made up to the father's death, less the depreciation taken by the son. Using the above example, such basis will be $84,450 ($12,445 × 10 minus $40,000).

After the son makes the sale, the continuing annuity payments made by him to his father are taken into account in recomputing his gain or loss. If the sale was made at a gain, then upon his father's death if the actual payments result in a lower basis than the one used at the time of the sale, the son will have additional gain, all taxable in the year of the father's death. Alternatively, if the actual payments result in a higher basis, he will have a loss. If the sale was originally made at a loss, then each additional payment will increase the amount of the loss.

§11.17   B.   Estate Planning Considerations

The estate planning advantages and disadvantages of a private annuity transaction may be summarized as follows:

§11.18   1.   Advantages

1.   The asset transferred will be kept out of the owner's estate.

2.   Where the owner needs "income" during his lifetime, the annuity payments can be used to satisfy this need.

3.   A portion of the annuity payments will be excluded from the owner's taxable income.

4.   The private annuity may be used as a device to provide the estate owner with more liquidity during his lifetime. The asset transferred will immediately receive a new income tax basis to the purchaser equal to the then present value of the annuity payments to be made. Hence, where the asset is nonincome-producing, the purchaser could sell the asset at its then fair market value without paying an immediate capital gains tax and convert the asset to one producing income. The owner, without using a private annuity, could not have made a sale of the underlying asset to a third party without the payment of a capital gains tax, which would have reduced the after-tax net proceeds.

5.   When compared to a gift, the private annuity transaction results in no gift tax, unless the actuarial value of the annuity payments is less than the fair market value of the property. Moreover, if the owner had made a gift rather than a sale under a private annuity, the receipt by him of payments from the donee may have constituted a transfer with a retained life estate, causing the gifted assets to be included in his estate under I.R.C. §2036.

6.   When compared to selling the property for a fixed price on the installment basis, nothing will be included in the owner's estate at the time of his death. Under the installment sale the unpaid balance of the purchase price would have been included in his estate.

§11.19   2.   Disadvantages

1.   The owner may live too long and the annuity payments will tend to increase his estate beyond what it would have been if he had kept the transferred asset.

2.   The purchaser, if the owner lives too long, will have paid out more than the value of the asset.

3. The purchaser may not deduct any portion of the payments which he makes, even if they exceed the fair market value of the asset. Under an installment sale, however, the amounts paid in excess of the purchase price would have been deductible as interest.

4. If the owner dies substantially before the expiration of his life expectancy, the purchaser may receive a much lower income tax basis for the property than would have been the case if the owner died still owning it. For a discussion of income tax basis after death, see §2.48. The receipt of a lower basis may offset the advantage of keeping the asset out of the owner's estate.

5. Where a private annuity is entered into to provide "income" for the owner, it should be remembered that the promise to pay the annuity must be unsecured. (See §11.15.) The owner, thereby, may have difficulty in collecting on the contract and his objective may be unfulfilled. Moreover, if the purchaser should die before the owner, the obligation would become a burden of the purchaser's estate. It might then be even more difficult to enforce, particularly if the transferred asset were the major asset of the purchaser's estate and he left a family which had been dependent upon him for support. Whenever the owner is dependent upon receiving the annuity payments for his own support, he should consider these possible consequences before entering into a private annuity transaction.

IV. Recommended Reading

Ekman, "Utility of Private Annuities in Estate Planning" 27 *NYU Inst on Fed Tax* 421 (1969)

Malloy and Bufkin, "Critical Tax and Financial Factors that Must be Considered when Planning a Private Annuity" 3 *Estate Planning* 2 (1975)

Miller and Corleto, "The Use of Annuities in Estate Planning", J.K. Lasser, *Estate Tax Techniques* 757 (Matthew Bender and Co 1971)

Sackett, "Using Private Annuities Today" 49 *Journal of Taxation* 48 (1979)

Handling a Business Interest

12

§12.1   I.   Introduction

Where a major asset of the owner's estate consists of an interest in a closely
held business, several special estate planning problems exist. These problems
may be characterized as follows:

1. There is a problem in estimating the amount of death taxes with any
    degree of certainty because of the underlying difficulty in valuing a
    closely held business interest (see §12.2);

2. There is normally a greater need for liquidity in an estate containing a
    closely held business interest because such interest is rarely liquid;

3. Where the estate owner is actively employed by the closely held business, there is a need to replace the owner's salary income from this source to provide for his family's support after his death;

4. Where the owner is a key person in the business, the preservation of the business itself after the owner's death may be in jeopardy.

This chapter will deal with the question of valuing an interest in a closely held business and, then, describe certain estate planning tools which may be used to solve the above-described problems.

II. Valuation of a Closely Held Business Interest for Death Tax Purposes

§12.2   A.   General Factors

Revenue Ruling 59-60, 1959-1 C.B. 237 sets forth eight factors to be taken into account in valuing a closely held business interest for tax purposes. These factors are:

1. The nature of the business and its history. Is it a high-risk business? Does it fluctuate or is it stable?

2. The general outlook for the entire economy, this particular industry, and this particular company.

3. The book value of the company.

4. The earning capacity of the company.

5. The dividend-paying capacity of the company, recognizing that in a closely held business the capacity to pay dividends, rather than the actual dividend-paying history, is important.

6. The existence of goodwill.

7. Recent sales of shares of stock of the company.

8. The market price of publicly traded stock in similar industries.

In applying the above factors in valuing a given business interest, it is important to keep in mind that all of the factors cannot be given equal weight. Unfortunately, the revenue ruling does not detail the weight to be accorded to each factor in any given situation.

The best evidence of fair market value is the price of recent sales of stock of the company. If there are no such sales, the most common method of determining the value of most closely held corporations is by computing the fair market value of the net tangible assets and then adding to it the value, if any, of the goodwill.

B.   Tangible Assets

§12.3   1.   Applicability of Book Value

The starting point for valuing the tangible assets is their book value as shown on the balance sheet. An examination should then be made of each asset in order to determine whether the book value is a proper indication of the fair market value of such asset and, if not, the amount by which the fair market value exceeds or is less than the book value. Cash, accounts receivable and often inventories will usually be accepted at their book value. On the other hand, assets such as machinery and equipment, patents and real estate, unless recently purchased, will frequently have values different from book value. In difficult cases it will be necessary to employ appraisers in order to ascertain the fair market value of this latter category of assets.

§12.4   2.   Special Election to Value Real Estate Used in a Closely Held Business or for Farming

In an inflationary economy, real estate is often worth substantially more than its book value. As a general rule the fair market value of real estate must be determined for tax purposes based upon its highest and best use. For example, if a business owns a warehouse in an area which was until recently an outlying one, but now borders on a major shopping center, the real estate may be much more valuable for retail store purposes than for a warehouse.

Under the Tax Reform Act of 1976, as amended by the Economic Recovery Tax Act of 1981, the executor may, if certain designated requirements are met, elect to value real estate used as a farm or other closely held business in accordance with its actual use rather than based on its highest and best use. See I.R.C. §2032A.

The major requirements which must be satisfied before the election can be made are as follows:

1. The property must pass to or be purchased from the estate by a "qualified heir." This term is defined as a member of the decedent's family, including the decedent's spouse, parents, children, stepchildren, and spouses and lineal descendants of those individuals, or a trust for the exclusive benefit of such persons. I.R.C. §§2032A(b)(1)(A)(ii), (e)(1), (2), (9) and (g).

2. The decedent or a member of his family must have owned the property and have materially participated in the operation of the farm or business for five out of the eight years preceding the earlier of (1) the date of death, (2) the date on which the decedent became disabled, or (3) the date on which the decedent began receiving social security. I.R.C.

§2032A(b). A special participation requirement applies for certain surviving spouses. See I.R.C. §2032A(b)(5)(A).

3.   The real property must have been used as a farm or in a trade or business on the date of the decedent's death and for five out of eight years just prior to the decedent's death. I.R.C. §2032A(b).

4.   The value of real and personal property used in the business must make up at least 50 per cent of the adjusted value of the decedent's gross estate and the qualifying real property must make up at least 25 per cent of the adjusted value of the decedent's estate. Adjusted value of the estate means the gross estate less indebtedness attributable to such property. I.R.C. §§2032A(b)(1)(A), (B) and (3).

If the valuation election is made, the executor can elect to have the assets valued as follows:

1.   Farms: A qualifying farm is valued by dividing the excess of the average annual gross cash rental for comparable farm purpose land, over the average annual state and local real estate taxes for such comparable land, by the average annual effective interest rate for all Federal Home Loan Bank loans. I.R.C. §2032A(e)(7). However, since 1981, if cash rentals for comparable land in the same locality are not available, the use of net-share rentals is allowed. The amount of a net-share rental is equal to the value of the produce received by the lessor of comparable land on which the produce is grown during a calendar year minus the cash operating expenses (other than real estate taxes) of growing the produce paid by the lessor. I.R.C. §2032A(e)(7)(B).

2.   Closely held business real estate: In general, this real estate is valued by applying the following factors: Capitalization of income, capitalization of fair rental value, assessed land values, comparable sales, and any other factor fairly valuing the property. I.R.C. §2032A(e)(8).

In no event may the valuation election result in a reduction of more than $700,000, for decedents dying in 1982, and $750,000, in 1983 and thereafter, from the fair market value of the property based on its highest and best use. I.R.C. §2032A(a)(2).

The application of the valuation election to real property owned by a partnership or corporation, rather than by the decedent personally, will be prescribed by regulations to be promulgated by the Treasury Department. See proposed Reg §20.2032A–3(b).

If the election is made and the real property is subsequently disposed of to outsiders (i.e., nonqualified heirs) or the qualified use of the property ceases, then all or part of the tax savings is recaptured. A premature disposition occurs if the property is disposed of within 10 years of the decedent's death and the qualified heir is still alive. A premature cessation of use takes place if (a) the property ceases to be used for the very use under which the property qualified for the special valuation (i.e., farm or closely held trade or business), or (b) during any eight-year period after the decedent's death there are periods aggregating three years or more where there is no material participation in the operation of the farm or other business by the qualified heirs. However, the commencement of the eight-year period is extended for the lesser of (1) the time that no qualified heir is using the qualified real property, or (2) two years after the decedent's death. On a recapture, the amount of additional tax, which would have been payable if the election had not been made, is under the general rule then required to be paid. However, no more than the excess of the value received from the property over the special valuation is recaptured.

§12.5   C.   Goodwill

The existence of goodwill must be determined and the amount thereof, if any, must then be valued. Goodwill may be thought of as the ability of a going concern to earn more than a fair rate of return on its tangible assets. One way to determine the value of goodwill is to use a formula approach.

Revenue Ruling 68-609, 1968-2 C.B. 327 sets forth the ingredients of such a formula, but cautions that the formula approach should not be used if there is better evidence available from which to determine the value of the goodwill. Under the formula approach, as described in the revenue ruling, the following steps should be taken:

1. Compute the average annual value of the tangible assets used in the business. In computing such average, a period of years (preferably not less than five) immediately prior to the valuation date should be used.

2. Determine the percentage return which the average annual value of tangible assets should earn. This percentage should be the percentage prevailing in the industry involved or, if the industry percentage is not available, a percentage of 8 per cent or 10 per cent may be used. The 8 per cent rate should be used with respect to businesses with a small risk factor and stable and regular earnings; the 10 per cent rate should be applied to businesses in which the hazards of the business are relatively high.

3. Multiply the average annual value of the tangible assets (Step (1)) by the percentage return (Step (2)). The product will be the average annual earnings of the tangible assets.

4. Determine the average annual earnings of the business for the period of time used in Step (1). In computing such earnings, the actual earnings of the business should be adjusted to eliminate abnormal transactions. For example, salaries and rents paid to shareholders should be adjusted to the extent they are unreasonably high or low. In the case of proprietorships and partnerships, a reasonable amount for services performed by the owners should be deducted. In arriving at an annual average of such adjusted earnings, those years which abnormally depart from the average should be eliminated.

5. Deduct the amount arrived at in Step (3) from the amount in Step (4). The excess, if any, is deemed to be the average annual earnings from the intangible assets of the business.

6. Capitalize the average annual earnings from the intangible assets (see Step (5)), if any, by using an appropriate capitalization rate. The quotient will be the value of the goodwill. Factors that influence the capitalization rate include the nature of the business, the risk involved, and the stability or irregularity of earnings. The greater the risks and irregularities, the higher the capitalization rate should be. Revenue Ruling 68-609 suggests that, unless better evidence is available, a 15 per cent capitalization rate should be applied to a business with a small risk factor and stable and regular earnings, and a 20 per cent rate of capitalization should be applied to a business in which the hazards are relatively high.

Using a simple example, assume the average annual value of XYZ company's tangible assets during the past five years is $1,000,000. The industry, in which XYZ Company operates, normally earns 8 per cent of the value of its tangible assets. XYZ Company's average annual earnings for the past five years are $200,000. The risk factor is average. The value of the goodwill may be computed as follows:

(1)	Average annual value of the tangible assets	$1,000,000
(2)	Multiplied by the industry percentage return	8%
(3)	Presumed average annual earnings from the tangible assets	$ 80,000
(4)	Average annual earnings of XYZ COMPANY	200,000
(5)	Excess of (4) over (3) (average annual earnings from intangible assets)	$ 120,000
(6)	Divided by capitalization rate (assumed to be 17 1/2%) 17 1/2%	
	GOODWILL	$ 685,714

§12.6   D.   Interest of Owner

Once the value of the entire business is ascertained by adding the value of the goodwill to the value of the tangible assets, the next step is to determine the value of the particular interest in the company held by the estate owner. In many cases it is necessary only to divide the total value by the portion which the owner owns in order to arrive at the value of the owner's interest. However, if the owner's interest is a minority interest in a corporation, this procedure would result in too high a valuation because such owner usually has no power to compel the liquidation of his interest so that he may receive his proportionate share of the assets. Accordingly, where a minority interest in a closely held corporation is owned, it is frequently possible to discount the value of the interest for the fact that it is a minority. *Laird v Commr* 85 F2d 598 (3d Cir 1935).

Where the owner, together with other family members, owns a majority interest, the Internal Revenue Service has taken the position that no minority discount will be allowed. Rev. Rul. 81-253, I.R.B. 1981-43, 10. However, in *Estate of Bright v US* ____F2d____ (5th Cir 1981) (81-2 USTC ¶13,436), the court disagreed with the Service and held that an interest should be valued as a minority interest, if the decedent owned less than a majority interest, without regard to the holdings of other family members.

III.   Buy-Sell Agreements

§12.7   A.   In General

Where there is more than one owner of a closely held business, the use of a buy-sell agreement will be helpful in solving many of the problems involved in planning the estate of a business owner. (See §12.1.)

A buy-sell agreement is an agreement which provides that on the death of an owner of a closely held business his interest will be purchased. If the interest is to be purchased by the surviving owners, the agreement is called a cross-purchase agreement. If the interest is to be purchased or redeemed by the business, it is referred to as an entity agreement.

§12.8   B.   Purpose

Buy-sell agreements, whether of the cross-purchase or entity type, have certain purposes in common. One of the main purposes is to assure an uninterrupted, conflict-free continuation of the business after the death of the deceased co-owner. The estate and the decedent's family will usually require funds for taxes, administration expenses and income. From a tax as well as a financial point of view, the business may not be able or willing to distribute earnings to nonemployee owners. The ensuing conflict may be injurious to the business. By purchasing the interest of the deceased owner, the surviving owners will eliminate this source of conflict.

Second, a buy-sell agreement provides a method whereby the decedent's estate will receive cash or other liquid assets on the death of the decedent rather than an unmarketable interest in a closely held business. In the case of so many closely held companies, dividends are rarely paid on the stock and the owner of less than a specified percentage (in many states, 50 per cent) of the stock will usually not have a right to liquidate the corporation and have its assets sold. Hence, the interest may not only be unmarketable, but, for all intents and purposes, it may be next to worthless to the decedent's family and yet, for death tax purposes, it may have a substantial value.

The third purpose which a properly drafted buy-sell agreement fulfills is that it will fix the estate tax valuation of the decedent's closely held business interest. Absent such an agreement, the decedent's estate will be faced with the very difficult problem of ascertaining the value to be placed on the decedent's business interest and having such value accepted by the taxing authorities. (See §12.2.) If one of the goals of planning is to eliminate future uncertainty, then this is an area where much can be accomplished. Valuation questions, particularly where the estate is not liquid, should be avoided if at all possible.

When the business owner dies leaving a maximum or optimum marital deduction bequest (see §4.8) to his surviving spouse, there will be no estate tax on his death. In such instance, there is no major benefit from a buy-sell agreement which fixes the estate tax value. However, if his spouse does not survive him, or when the surviving spouse dies, the importance of fixing estate tax value cannot be overemphasized.

§12.9 C. Making the Price Binding for Tax Purposes

The price set either specifically or by formula in a buy-sell agreement negotiated at arm's length will be accepted as the value of the business interest for estate tax purposes if:

1. The estate of the decedent is bound by the agreement to sell his interest; and

2. The purchaser (whether it is the surviving owners or the entity) is obligated to purchase the decedent's interest, or, at the very least, has an option to do so; and

3. The business interest could not have been disposed of during the lifetime of the decedent without first offering it to the entity or individuals who have the right to purchase at the decedent's death at a price no higher than the one fixed for the purchase at death; and

4. The price specified in the agreement was fair and adequate at the time that the agreement was made. See Reg. §20.2031-2(h); Rev. Rul. 59-60, 1959-1 C.B. 237.

Where, however, the agreement is between closely related parties so that it is really a device to pass the decedent's interest to the natural object of his bounty for less than full value, the agreed price, even if the above requirements are met, will ordinarily not be binding for tax purposes. Reg. §20.2031-2(h). Brothers and sisters are not usually considered to be natural objects of each other's bounty. See *Estate of Bischoff v Commr* 69 TC 32 (1977).

§12.10 D. Selecting the Method of Determining the Price

There are three major alternative methods which owners of a closely held business frequently use to set the price in a buy-sell agreement at which the decedent's interest will be purchased and sold. These methods are a predetermined price, perhaps subject to periodic review, a price determined by appraisal or arbitration, and a price determined by formula.

§12.11   1.   Predetermined Price Subject to Periodic Review

One of the ways of setting the price in the buy-sell agreement is to agree upon a specified price. For example, the agreement could provide that, in the event of a stockholder's death, his shares will be purchased for $50 per share regardless of when his death occurs. While such an agreement has the virtue of simplicity, it could work a hardship. In all likelihood, the value of the company will undergo a substantial change from the time that the agreement is entered into until the decedent's death. The predetermined price will be either too high or too low. As a result, most buy-sell agreements which utilize a predetermined price also provide for a periodic review by the owners. Such agreements specify that the owners shall review the price, say, every year, and initial an exhibit to the agreement indicating either a new price which will be in effect for the next year or an agreement to continue the old price for such year.

This method of setting and reviewing the price in an agreement has merit, in that the owners are usually in the best position to know the true value of the business. Its major drawback is that, particularly as time goes on and the price is reviewed, the owners may not bargain with each other in good faith. For example, one of the owners may be in poor health and the other will attempt to argue for a lower price. This disadvantage may be ameliorated to some extent by inserting a backstop provision in the agreement stating that if the price previously agreed to has not been changed or reconfirmed within a specified period prior to the death of one of the owners, a new price may be established on such death by arbitration or appraisal. (See §12.12.)

§12.12   2.   Price Determined by Appraisal or Arbitration

Another method for determining the price is for the agreement to provide neither a fixed price nor one determinable by formula, but rather to set forth a procedure for the appointment of an appraiser or arbitrator who will set a price based on the fair market value of the business at the time of death. The disadvantage, however, is that it is difficult for the owners prior to their death to know with any degree of assurance what the purchase price will be. Hence, it is difficult for them to plan their estates without a reasonable estimate of what the taxes and expenses and, thereby, the sufficiency of their estates, will be.

§12.13 3. Price Determined by Formula

The third method for setting the price is by the agreement providing a formula by which the price will be determined upon the death of the decedent. Various formulas are in common use.

One formula sometimes used is to determine price based on the book value of the company at the time of the decedent's death (or, for accounting convenience, at the end of the month or accounting period immediately following or preceding the owner's death). Book value, when used all by itself, is frequently not a good measure of a company's value. There are two reasons for this. First, book value represents historical cost (adjusted for depreciation) and may bear little or no resemblance to the true fair market value of the assets on the company's books. Second, inherent in a company's value is its earning capacity which often cannot be measured by an examination of the assets shown on the balance sheet.

Another formula sometimes used in arriving at the price is one based on a capitalization of earnings. By way of example, this formula may require that the average annual net earnings of the business for a specified period be divided by an agreed upon capitalization rate, say, 20 per cent, and the quotient will equal the value of the business. This method is more sound than a book value approach in many enterprises, particularly those where earnings are the major element of value. However, in other cases, such as a company whose assets will be sold or liquidated shortly after an owner's death or a company which has a deficit in earnings, the value of the tangible assets rather than the ability to earn continuing income is a more important factor, and the capitalization of earnings method should not be used.

The best type of formula in most instances is one which takes into account both the fair market value of the tangible assets and the earning capacity of the corporation, the latter of which can be referred to as goodwill. For a description of such a formula, see §12.5.

E. Paying the Purchase Price

§12.14 1. Through Life Insurance

The buy-sell agreement should prescribe the method whereby payment of the purchase price will be made on the death of one of the owners. Funding the payment, in whole or in part, with life insurance on the lives of the owners should always be considered. In this way, when an owner dies, the estate will receive immediate payment and the purchaser will not have to raise funds. Where the parties are insurable, this method is in most cases the most advantageous. See §10.53 for a full discussion of the use of life insurance in funding a buy-sell agreement.

§12.15   2.   Through a Sinking Fund

The purchase price to be paid under the buy-sell agreement may be funded by the business setting aside into a sinking fund an annual amount while the owners are still alive. If the owners live long enough, sufficient money may be available to pay the purchase price in cash. Where payments to the sinking fund are made out of current earnings, two problems must be contended with. First, the payments may be a greater drain on the company's resources than the payment of life insurance premiums. Second, setting aside a portion of a corporation's earnings to fund a buy-sell agreement may constitute an unreasonble accumulation of earnings, subjecting the corporation to the accumulated earnings tax. See §12.33 for a fuller discussion. Where the payment of the purchase price is funded by life insurance and the premiums are less than the amount set aside to the sinking fund, the possible impact of the accumulated earnings tax is less severe.

§12.16   3.   Through Long-Term Payout

Where the entire purchase price under the buy-sell agreement is not funded by life insurance or a sinking fund, at least a portion of the purchase price, in most instances, will have to be paid by a promissory note providing for installment payments to be made over a period of time. In planning the provisions of an agreement dealing with a long-term payout, two considerations should be kept in mind.

First, the agreement should provide for adequate security in the event of a default on the note. The note may be secured by a pledge of the decedent's stock or business interest, or other assets agreed to by the parties. Where the buy-sell agreement, however, is in the form of a stock redemption agreement (see §12.7), there is a potential danger in securing the note with the decedent's stock, because the Internal Revenue Service may argue, particularly if the note is a long-term one, that there is not a complete redemption of the decedent's stock. See Rev. Proc. 72-9, 1972-1 C.B. 719; see also §12.33 for a discussion of the tax consequences where the redemption is not in complete termination of the shareholders' interest.

Second, the note should provide for a reasonable rate of interest on the unpaid balance. Where the note provides for an interest rate of less than 9 per cent per year, an interest rate of 10 per cent per year will be imputed. Reg. §1.483-1(c)(2). (These rates are subject to change by the Secretary of the Treasury, see I.R.C. §§483(b) and (c)(1)). The effect of imputing interest is that for income tax purposes the payor may deduct and the recipient must include the imputed amount; otherwise, such amounts would be treated as nontaxable and nondeductible principal payments.

§12.17 F. Disadvantages of Buy-Sell Agreements

Although buy-sell agreements are beneficial more often than not, the question of whether there are any possible disadvantages in a given situation should always be considered. The existence of one or more of the following factors may call for the use of a different planning tool in an estate containing a closely held business interest.

§12.18 1. Forecloses Alternative where Estate Keeps Business and Insurance

From the viewpoint of the decedent, it may be possible for his estate, at no increased cost, to receive both the business interest and the value thereof. Instead of entering into a buy-sell agreement to be funded with life insurance, each co-owner could obtain the desired amount of life insurance on his own life, make his spouse the beneficiary or assign the ownership thereof to another family member or to an irrevocable life insurance trust in order to keep the proceeds out of his taxable estate. (See §§10.34 to 10.50.) Upon his death his family will have both the business interest and a greater amount of insurance proceeds because no estate tax will be payable on the life insurance proceeds. While the apparent advantage of this alternate arrangement is tempting, it should be realized that the problem caused by the uncertain estate tax valuation of the business interest (see §12.1) is not solved. Also see §12.8 for a discussion of the estate tax situation where a maximum or optimum marital deduction bequest is left to the spouse. Moreover, the lack of a buy-sell agreement is discomforting from the viewpoint of the surviving owners. They will still be subject to the potential conflicts arising from having to deal with the decedent's estate and family. (See §12.8.)

§12.19 2. Owner's Lifetime Rights Are Restricted

As is indicated in §12.9, in order for the buy-sell price to be binding on the Internal Revenue Service in setting the estate tax value of such interest, it is necessary that the agreement provide that no owner can sell his interest without first offering it to the business entity or the co-owners at a price not in excess of the death price. Complying with this requirement could be troublesome in that it restricts the owners from freely alienating their ownership interest during lifetime. Particularly where the death price is not determined under a realistic formula, this disadvantage may outweigh many of the advantages in having a buy-sell agreement.

§12.20 3. Price May Become Unrealistic

Another possible disadvantage of a buy-sell agreement is that the purchase price, even if a realistic formula has been used, may become unrealistic at the time of death. The economy or the industry in which the company operates may radically change. The ground rules which the owners have in mind in setting up the buy-sell formula may become antiquated. Yet, it may be impossible to amend the agreement because of the failure of all the parties to agree to a change. If one of the owners dies, the price set in the agreement may be extremely unfair and yet it is not only binding on the Internal Revenue Service for tax purposes but also legally binding on the parties to the agreement.

§12.21   4.   Forecloses Alternative of Liquidation

The next disadvantage inherent in a buy-sell agreement is that it forecloses what in certain instances may be a preferable alternative, namely, that the business be liquidated on the death of any of the owners. Assume two relatively elderly individuals are the owners of the business and both of their services are needed in its operation. On the death of either one, it may be impossible for the remaining owner to assume the entire burden of the operation of the business. In this type of a situation, it may be preferable for the business to be liquidated on the death of the first owner and the proceeds divided rather than have a buy-out of the interest of the first owner to die.

§12.22   5.   Forecloses Alternative of Retaining Business Interest for Family Member

In certain instances a buy-sell agreement is not appropriate because the decedent's business interest should continue for the benefit of a family member rather than be sold. For example, if the decedent has a child who is active in the business or who will probably enter the business, he may wish to preserve his business interest for the child's benefit. In this situation, a recapitalization of the company into various types of ownership interests in order to protect different categories of family members may solve at least some of the problems usually solved by a buy-sell agreement and still preserve the interest for the decedent's child. (See §§12.39 to 12.44.)

§12.23   G.   Form of Agreement

Once the usefulness of a buy-sell agreement becomes apparent in a given situation, the form of the agreement, that is, whether the agreement should be a cross-purchase agreement or an entity agreement, must then be determined. (See §12.7.)

§12.24   1.   Partnership Buy-Sell Agreement

In a partnership the major tax difference between a cross-purchase and entity agreement is in the treatment of goodwill. Where a cross-purchase agreement is used, the portion of the purchase price attributable to goodwill is treated as a capital transaction. Such portion is accordingly not considered part of the deceased partner's distributable income and is not, even indirectly, deductible by the surviving partners. On the other hand, when an entity agreement is used, the partners have a choice. If the agreement states that a specific amount is to be paid for goodwill, such payment is treated as a capital transaction. If the agreement, on the other hand, is silent as to goodwill, the portion of the purchase price allocable to goodwill will, under I.R.C. §736, be considered an income item which will be taxable as ordinary income to the deceased partner's estate and be deductible by the remaining partnership and, hence, in effect, by the surviving partners. For a full discussion of the use of §736 in tax planning a partnership buy-sell agreement, see 2 Willis, Pennell and Postlewaite, *Partnership Taxation* (Shepard's/McGraw-Hill 3d Ed 1981) §145.04.

§12.25   2.   Corporate Buy-Sell Agreement

In a buy-sell agreement providing for the buy-out of a deceased stockholder's shares in a corporation, there are several important factors to consider in deciding whether to use a cross-purchase agreement or an entity agreement (i.e., a stock redemption agreement).

a.   Where Stock Redemption is Preferable

§12.26   i.   More Economical

It is sometimes more economical, after considering the income tax consequences, for the corporation, rather than the shareholders, to pay the purchase price under a buy-sell agreement or, if the agreement is to be funded with life insurance, the policy premiums. If the shareholders must have additional funds from the corporation in order to pay the required amounts, it would be less expensive for the corporation itself to make the payments where either of the following conditions is present:

1. The first condition is where the corporation cannot make any additional payments to the shareholders without such payments being taxable to the shareholders as a dividend. For example, assume the shareholders are employees of the corporation, but they are already being paid the maximum amount of salaries which can be deducted as reasonable compensation under the Internal Revenue Code. See I.R.C. §162(a)(1). In this instance any increase in salary will normally be taxable as a dividend. This will cause double taxation of the amounts necessary for the shareholders to receive in order for them to pay the purchase price or the insurance premiums. On the other hand, if the corporation, provided it is obligated under the agreement to purchase the interest of the deceased shareholder, pays either the purchase price or the insurance premiums, these payments will not be taxable to the shareholders.

2. The second condition is where the corporation is in a lower tax bracket than the individual shareholders. Here, also, it will be more economical tax-wise for the corporation to fund the purchase price. This may be illustrated by an example. If the shareholders are all in a 50 per cent income tax bracket and each shareholder, under a cross-purchase agreement, needs $1,000 to pay the life insurance premiums on the lives of his co-owners, $2,000 must be paid to each shareholder in order for him to have the required $1,000 after taxes. If the corporation, on the other hand, is in a 15 per cent top bracket (the lowest corporate bracket in 1983 and thereafter), and under a stock redemption agreement it owns the life insurance policies on the lives of all the shareholders, it will need to earn only $1,176.42 for each $1,000 of premiums. Under these facts, the corporation should pay the premiums. Conversely, if the shareholders are in a lower income tax bracket than the corporation and their salaries may be increased without the increase being taxed as a dividend, it would be less expensive for the shareholders to pay the premiums under a cross-purchase agreement.

§12.27　ii.　Numerous Shareholders

A second instance where a stock redemption agreement is usually preferable to a cross-purchase agreement is where there are numerous shareholders and the buy-sell agreement is to be funded with life insurance. If there are only two shareholders, only two policies of life insurance will be needed under either form of agreement. However, if the corporation has, for example, 10 shareholders, then under a stock redemption agreement there will be 10 policies of life insurance owned by the corporation. Under a cross-purchase agreement, each of the shareholders will own nine policies, one on each of his fellow shareholders' lives, or a total of 90 policies. The practical problems of dealing with so many policies may call for the use of a stock redemption agreement.

§12.28　iii.　"Transfer for Value" Rule

Another advantage usually present in using a stock redemption agreement rather than a cross-purchase agreement with respect to corporate stock is that the "transfer for value" rule under I.R.C. §101(a)(2) may be avoided. See §10.22 for a discussion of the "transfer for value" rule. Under a cross-purchase agreement, on the death of one shareholder, the remaining shareholders will normally wish to purchase from the decedent shareholder's estate the life insurance policies owned by the estate on the surviving shareholders so that the buy-sell agreement can continue in force on the death of the next shareholder to die. Such purchase, however, will result in the death proceeds of such life insurance policies being included in the taxable income of the surviving shareholders under the above-cited "transfer for value" rule. While this rule makes exception for transfers of life insurance policies to the insured, to a partner of the insured, to a partnership in which the insured is a partner or to a corporation in which the insured is an officer or shareholder, there is no exception for a transfer from a shareholder to a fellow shareholder. See I.R.C. §101(a)(2)(B).

§12.29   iv.   Appreciated Assets

A fourth situation where a stock redemption agreement may be advantageous compared to a cross-purchase agreement is where it is desirable to pay for the decedent's stock with appreciated corporate assets. Frequently a corporation may have assets which can be used to acquire the stock of a deceased shareholder, such as marketable securities or income-producing real estate. Under §311(d) of the Internal Revenue Code, it is possible for a corporation to distribute appreciated assets to a shareholder's estate in complete redemption of the estate's stock, without the corporation itself realizing any gain (except for depreciation recapture) on the distribution. To avoid such gain, the estate is required to have owned at least 10 per cent of the outstanding stock of the corporation for at least 12 months prior to the distribution. See I.R.C. §311(d)(2)(A).

Accordingly, if the corporation has securities worth $100,000 with an adjusted basis of $40,000, by paying out these assets it can avoid recognizing the $60,000 gain which it would have if it had sold the securities and used the proceeds to purchase the stock. Moreover, the basis of the property received by the shareholder's estate from the corporation will be its fair market value at the date of distribution. See I.R.C. §301(d)(1). Therefore, in the preceding example, the new basis of the securities to the shareholder's estate will be $100,000. As a result, the appreciation will permanently escape income taxation. It should be noted, however, that, where corporate assets are to be used, the stock redemption agreement should not provide for a fixed price but merely that certain assets be distributed in redemption of the stock; otherwise, there could arguably be a realization of gain to the corporation on the theory that there is a liquidation of an indebtedness in a specific amount. See Reg. §1.311-1(e)(1). If the use of corporate appreciated assets to purchase the decedent's interest is desirable, it will be necessary to use a stock redemption agreement rather than a cross-purchase agreement because, under the latter type of agreement, corporate assets are not involved in the transaction.

§12.30   b.   Where Cross-Purchase Agreement is Preferable

In certain situations a cross-purchase agreement may be preferable to a stock redemption agreement.

§12.31   i.   State Law Restrictions on Redemption

In using a stock redemption agreement, it is necessary to satisfy certain requirements of state law before the redemption can be made. For example, in many states, stock may be redeemed only out of earned or other specifically designated types of surplus; in other states, only out of retained earnings, or out of capital, only if certain balance sheet ratios are maintained. It should be noted that funding the buy-sell price with life insurance will usually create the needed surplus or retained earnings. Absent the use of insurance, however, it is necessary, where state law causes a redemption problem, to utilize a cross-purchase agreement or, at the very least, to provide in the stock redemption agreement that, if the corporation cannot legally redeem all of the decedent's stock, the surviving shareholders be either compelled or have the option to purchase such stock.

§12.32   ii.   Unequal Ownership

Another situation in which it may be unwise to use a stock redemption agreement rather than a cross-purchase agreement is where the stock owner-ship is held very unequally. If one shareholder, for example, owns 80 per cent of the stock while the other owns only 20 per cent, under a stock redemption agreement the 80 per cent shareholder will, in large part, be using his own money to buy himself out. In effect, he will be making a gift of a substantial portion of the business to the other shareholder. Under a cross-purchase agreement, each shareholder will typically use his own funds to purchase or fund for the purchase of the others' stock, so this disadvantage will be eliminated.

§12.33   iii.   Tax Consequences

In certain instances, a cross-purchase agreement is preferable to a stock redemption agreement because using the latter type will result in adverse tax consequences.

One tax disadvantage which is present in a stock redemption agreement is that the surviving shareholders, after the death of the decedent, will have a lower income tax basis for their stock than would have been the case if a cross-purchase agreement were used. To illustrate, let us assume that A and B each own 50 per cent of the stock of a corporation and that the income tax basis of each of their 50 per cent interests is $10,000 and that the fair market value of each 50 per cent interest is $250,000. Under a stock redemption agreement, if A dies, B's basis for 100 per cent of the stock of the corporation will remain at $10,000 because he still owns the same shares which he owned prior to the redemption. On the other hand, under a cross-purchase agreement, his basis for 100 per cent of the stock of the corporation after the purchase from A's estate will be $260,000 because he will have purchased the other 50 per cent for $250,000. If it appears likely that the surviving shareholder will sell the business after the death of the other shareholder, serious consideration should be given to structuring the buy-sell agreement in the form of a cross-purchase agreement.

In deciding whether to use a cross-purchase agreement or a stock redemption agreement, it is also necessary to consider the potential income tax consequences to the decedent shareholder's estate. In most instances it will make no difference which form of agreement is used because in either case the sale will result in no gain or loss to the estate because the estate will have received a new basis for the stock equal to its federal estate tax value. I.R.C. §§1014(a) and (b). Even if the sales price for some unusual reason differed from the federal estate tax value, any resulting gain or loss would normally be capital in nature.

While in the usual situation the payment by the corporation to the estate in redemption of the stock will be treated as a capital transaction, there are circumstances where it will be taxed as a dividend. I.R.C. §302 provides that the redemption payment will not be considered a dividend if it completely terminates the stockholder's interest in the corporation (§302(b)(3)), if it is substantially disproportionate (§302(b)(2)), or if it is not essentially equivalent to a dividend (§302(b)(1)). If, however, none of these three exceptions applies, the proceeds of the redemption will, to the extent that the corporation has earnings and profits, be taxable as a dividend to the deceased shareholder's estate rather than as a capital transaction.

In order for the redemption to terminate completely a shareholder's interest, all of his stock must be redeemed by the corporation. In order to have a substantially disproportionate redemption, the shareholder, immediately after the redemption, must own less than 50 per cent of the corporation's voting stock, and the percentage of voting stock which he owns in the corporation after the redemption must be at least 20 per cent less than his percentage was prior to the redemption.

In determining the number of shares a shareholder owns after a redemption, for the purpose of satisfying the disproportionate redemption or complete redemption tests, the rules of constructive ownership set out in I.R.C. §318 are to be applied. This section provides, in part, that a living shareholder is deemed to own not only his own stock, but also the stock owned by his spouse, his children, his grandchildren and his parents. Also, and of particular importance to the problem at hand, stock owned by a beneficiary of a decedent's probate estate is considered to be owned by the estate, and stock owned by such estate is considered as owned proportionately by its beneficiaries, regardless of whether or not they are related to the decedent. As a consequence, if one of the beneficiaries of the deceased stockholder's estate owns stock in the corporation, the estate will be considered, under §318, as owning such stock.

By way of example, if all the stock of the corporation is owned in equal shares by a father and a son and the son is the sole beneficiary of the father's estate, all of the son's shares will be deemed to be constructively owned by the father's estate. See Rev. Rul. 56-103, 1956-1 C.B. 159. Moreover, the possible effect of a double attribution should be considered. If, in the above example, the mother, rather than the son, were the sole beneficiary of the father's estate, the son's stock would, in the view of the Internal Revenue Service, nevertheless be attributed to the father's estate. The reason for this is that the son's stock is attributed to his mother, under the family attribution rules, and the stock which she owns is once again attributed to the father's estate, under the estate attribution rules. See *Thomas G Lewis v Commr* 35 TC 71 (1960); Rev. Rul. 59-233, 1959-2 C.B. 106. In both of the above examples, the shares actually owned by the father's estate could not be redeemed as a complete termination of its interest or as a substantially disproportionate redemption. (See, however, item (3) below).

If there has been neither a complete nor substantially disproportionate redemption, it appears unwise to rely, at least from a planning point of view, on the third exception to the dividend rule, namely that the redemption is not essentially equivalent to a dividend. The Internal Revenue Service and the courts have generally, but not without exception, applied the attribution rules of §318 in determining whether the redemption is not essentially equivalent to a dividend. *Bradbury v Commr* 298 F2d 111 (1st Cir 1962); *Thomas G Lewis v Commr* 35 TC 71 (1960); cf. *Estate of Arthur H Squier v Commr* 35 TC 950 (1961).

If a §318 problem exists, but a stock redemption agreement is otherwise desirable, consideration should be given to eliminating the problem by one of the following methods:

1. The shareholder should make no other shareholder of the corporation a beneficiary of his probate estate. Moreover, because of the possibility of a double attribution of ownership, the shareholder should make no prohibited family member of the other shareholder a beneficiary of his estate. It should be noted that a remainderman, who has no interest in the property until after the death of the life tenant, is not considered a beneficiary. Reg. §1.318-3(a), Ex(2). Nor is the beneficiary of an inter vivos trust created by the decedent or a beneficiary of a life insurance policy on his life deemed to be a beneficiary of the decedent's probate estate for the purposes of §318. Accordingly, it is possible to provide for the related shareholder and still circumvent the dividend problem.

2. The estate-beneficiary attribution rules can be avoided if the legacy of the shareholder beneficiary, providing he is not a residuary legatee, is satisfied before the stock redemption takes place. (Rev. Rul. 58-111, 1958-1 C.B. 173; Rev. Rul. 60-18, 1960-1 C.B. 145).

3. The attribution rules could be waived where the decedent shareholder leaves his stock to a family member who will agree to have such stock redeemed by the corporation. For example, in the above father-son illustration, the father's estate could distribute its shares to the mother. She could then have all of her stock redeemed. Provided the requirements of I.R.C. §302(c) are met, the mother could then waive the application of the family attribution rules. Therefore the son's stock would not be attributed to the mother and redemption of her shares would

result in a complete termination of her interest in the corporation. Rev. Rul. 79-67, 1979-1 C.B. 128.

The family attribution rules, in most instances, may be waived for the purpose of determining whether a redemption is complete with respect to a shareholder if all of the following conditions are met:

a. The distributee (the shareholder from whom the stock is being redeemed) has no interest in the corporation other than as a creditor after the redemption.

b. The distributee does not acquire any such interest within 10 years from the date of the redemption.

c. The distributee files an agreement, promising to notify the Internal Revenue Service of any such acquisition within 10 years and to retain the necessary records so that the appropriate deficiency may be assessed and collected.

The Internal Revenue Service has consistently maintained that only the family attribution rules may be waived, not the estate attribution rules. In the above example, it would be necessary to have the father leave his stock to the mother, so that she, rather than the estate, would be the redeeming shareholder. Several court decisions have, however, permitted an estate (and also a trust) to waive the family attribution rules. See *Crawford v Commr* 59 TC 830 (1973); *Rogers P Johnson Trust v Commr* 71 TC 941 (1979); *Rickey, Jr v US* 592 F2d 1251 (5th Cir 1979).

4. Partial relief from the dividend problem may be obtained by qualifying the redemption under §303 of the Internal Revenue Code. For a discussion of §303, see §12.36.

5. If no other solution is available, a cross-purchase agreement entered into by the individual stockholders, rather than a stock redemption agreement between the shareholders and the corporation, should be used in the first instance.

The last possible tax disadvantage to be mentioned in using a stock redemption agreement, as compared to a cross-purchase agreement, is that the funding of the purchase price may result in the imposition of the accumulated earnings tax. See I.R.C. §531. There are several cases dealing with this question, but the answer is not entirely clear. See *Emeloid Co v Commr* 189 F2d 230 (3d Cir 1951); *Pelton Steel Casting Co v Commr* 251 F2d 278 (7th Cir 1958) cert den 356 US 958, 78 SCt 995, 2 LE2d 1066 (1958); *Mountain State Steel Foundries Inc v Commr* 284 F2d 737 (4th Cir 1960). Without attempting a detailed review of the areas of uncertainty, it appears from these cases that where the stock redemption serves a reasonable need of the business, apart from its benefit to the surviving shareholders, the accumulation of funds to provide for the redemption will furnish no basis for the imposition of the I.R.C. §531 tax.

§12.34   c.   Correlating Life Insurance

Where life insurance is used to fund a corporate buy-sell agreement, it is important that the ownership and beneficiary designations of the life insurance policies be coordinated with the particular type of agreement that is used. For example, where a stock redemption agreement is used, the corporation and not the individual stockholders should be the owner and beneficiary of the policies. For a full discussion, see §10.53.

IV.   Use of §303 Redemption

§12.35   A.   The Problem

The major asset of a shareholder's estate may very well be his stock in a closely held corporation and there may be no other liquid assets. The corporation may have liquid assets, or the ability to convert assets into cash. Unless there are co-owners with whom to enter into a buy-sell agreement (see §12.7), it will be necessary that the shareholder's estate be able to utilize the corporation's liquidity to pay death taxes and expenses. The problem is, however, that most distributions from a corporation to a shareholder or his estate will, to the extent of the corporation's earnings and profits, be taxable as a dividend. See I.R.C. §§301(c) and 316.

Section 303 of the Internal Revenue Code permits a decedent shareholder, providing certain requirements are met, to redeem that portion of his stock which does not exceed in value the sum of the federal and state death taxes and funeral and administration expenses, without the proceeds being taxable to his estate as a dividend. It should be kept in mind that even if the redemption qualifies under §303, and is thereby treated as a sale of stock, there may be a taxable capital gain on the redemption to the extent that the redemption proceeds exceed the federal estate tax value of the stock.

§12.36   B.   Qualifying Under §303

In order to qualify under §303, the decedent's stock in the closely held corporation must, under the Economic Recovery Tax Act of 1981, with respect to decedents dying after December 31, 1981, have a value of more than 35 per cent of the excess of his gross estate over the sum of the debts, losses, funeral and administration expenses allowed as deductions in the estate. Neither the marital deduction nor the charitable deduction enters into the calculation. Gifts made within three years of death are, since 1981, generally not includable in the gross estate (see §2.12). However, such gifts are included for the purpose of making the §303 qualification calculation. I.R.C. §2035(d)(3). To illustrate, assuming the decedent's gross estate is $1,000,000, there are $100,-000 of gifts made within three years of death, not otherwise included in the gross estate, and the sum of the debts, losses, funeral and administration expenses is $50,000, the value of the decedent's stock will have to total more than $367,500 (35 per cent times [$1,100,000 minus $50,000]) to qualify. If the decedent owns more than 20 per cent of the stock of two or more corporations, such corporations can be combined in meeting the 35 per cent requirement.

In planning to take advantage of a §303 redemption, it is important that the estate owner during his lifetime refrain from making gifts of stock in the corporation that could reduce his ownership below the 35 per cent requirement. By the same token, it may be advisable to make gifts of other assets which are projected to grow rapidly to help ensure that the value of the stock in the closely held corporation will constitute no less than the above-stated percentage of the estate. By way of illustration, if a shareholder's sole assets consist of stock in a corporation worth $400,000 and gross real estate holdings worth $500,000, the stock would, if his death occurred now, safely qualify for a §303 redemption. However, if the shareholder gifted one-half of his stock, or if the real estate holdings doubled in value, the ability to qualify under §303 would be placed in jeopardy. Hence, if the shareholder desires to make gifts during his lifetime, he should make them from his real estate holdings and not from the stock. For a discussion of the reasons for making gifts, see §§8.3 to 8.5, 8.9 and 8.10.

If the estate owner leaves an unlimited or optimum marital deduction bequest to a spouse (see §4.8), the federal estate tax will be eliminated. In that event, only that portion of the stock which does not exceed the amount of state death taxes and funeral and administration expenses may be redeemed. A §303 redemption may be valuable as a tool to withdraw corporate funds without the withdrawal being taxed as a dividend. See §12.38. In light of this, it is possible that the estate owner may wish to refrain from using the unlimited or optimum marital deduction and thereby increase the amount of the §303 redemption.

Once the 35 per cent requirement is satisfied, it is necessary to meet the next requirement of §303, namely, that the shareholders whose stock is redeemed have borne at least a portion of the decedent's death taxes, funeral or administration expenses. I.R.C. §303(b)(3). Hence, in the pre-death planning of a §303 redemption, care should be taken that the stock to be redeemed is owned by a person or entity which is liable for these items. For example, if the stock is owned in joint tenancy or by a funded revocable trust, the decedent's will should not provide that all taxes and expenses be paid out of the probate estate. Similarly the stock should not be redeemed from a marital deduction trust which is not liable for the payment of taxes.

Lastly, in order to qualify under §303, the redemption must ordinarily take place within four years of the decedent's death. I.R.C. §303(b)(1). However, the time will be extended for as much as 15 years from the date of death where the election has been made to defer the payment of estate tax under I.R.C. §§6166 and 6166A. (See §12.51.) However, for any distributions made more than four years after the date of death, §303 generally provides relief from the dividend tax only to the extent of death taxes and funeral and administration expenses paid within one year after the distribution. See I.R.C. §303(b)(4).

§12.37   C.   Unreasonable Accumulation of Surplus Considerations

Where a §303 redemption is to be used as a method of providing liquidity in the shareholder's estate, the corporation may desire to fund the redemption either through savings or through the purchase of a life insurance policy on the stockholder's life. In this connection, it is important to consider whether this use of corporate funds will be considered an unreasonable accumulation of surplus under I.R.C. §531. An accumulation of funds to redeem stock of shareholders at death under §303 has sometimes been denied treatment as a reasonable corporate accumulation purpose. *Youngs Rubber Corp v Commr* 21 TCMemo 1593 ¶62,300 (1962) affd 331 F2d 12 (2d Cir 1964); see also *Pelton Steel Casting Co v Commr* 251 F2d 278 (7th Cir 1958) cert den 356 US 958, 78 SCt 995, 2 LE2d 1066 (1958). I.R.C. §537 gives limited relief in the case of redemptions at death by providing that a redemption qualifying under §303 also qualifies as a reasonable business need. However, anticipatory accumulations prior to death are not sheltered by this provision because it applies only to accumulations beginning with the year of death.

§12.38   D.   Using §303 Even if Liquidity is Not Needed

Once the requirements of §303 are met, it is usually not necessary that the proceeds of the redemption be actually used to pay the death taxes and funeral and administration expenses. Hence, even if such items have already been paid, a §303 redemption may be used solely as a tool to withdraw corporate funds without the payment of a dividend tax. For example, assume a corporation has been accumulating a portion of its earnings during the shareholder's lifetime in order to avoid paying dividends and incurring double taxation. If the shareholder's estate qualifies for a §303 redemption, these earnings, to the extent permitted under §303, may be paid out after the shareholder's death in the form of redemption proceeds, which are not taxable as a dividend, regardless of whether or not the shareholder's estate needs such proceeds for liquidity purposes. When the §303 redemption takes place more than four years after the decedent's death, the distribution proceeds generally must not exceed the death taxes, funeral and administration expenses actually paid within one year after the redemption. (See §12.36.)

If the estate of the deceased shareholder does not need cash in order to pay the death taxes and other expenses, or if the corporation is not liquid enough to make such payment in cash, the redemption proceeds may be paid by a note (see Rev. Rul. 65-289, 1965-2 C.B. 86) or with other assets. Where assets which have appreciated in value over their income tax basis are distributed, the consequences could be very beneficial. Under §311(d) of the Internal Revenue Code, the corporation can use appreciated assets to redeem stock under §303 without the corporation's realizing any gain (except for depreciation recapture) on the distribution. The decedent's estate will receive a basis equal to the then fair market value of the distributed appreciated assets. See §12.29 for an illustration of the tax advantages of using appreciated assets in a redemption of stock.

V. Recapitalizing Stock of Closely Held Company

§12.39 A. Introduction

Most closely held corporations have a single class of outstanding stock, which is common stock. If there is more than one shareholder and the shareholders are agreeable to having a buy-sell agreement covering all of a deceased shareholder's stock, the single stock structure is usually satisfactory. However, if there is only one shareholder, or even several shareholders but they do not desire their stock to be sold on death because, for example, they wish to have their family members continue in the business, a recapitalization into a multi-stock structure may accomplish certain estate planning objectives.

§12.40 B. Purpose of the Recapitalization Plan

The following objectives may be accomplished through a multi-class stock structure:

1. The present value of the stockholder's interest may be frozen and the future growth removed from his estate. For example, the estate owner may retain a class of stock which has a fixed value and give away, during his lifetime, stock with a nominal value, but which will increase in value as the company grows.

2. Different classes of stock may be given to different donees, depending upon whether or not the donees are active in the business. For example, a nonvoting, fixed dividend-paying stock may eventually be left to a child who is not active in the business. A voting stock, which represents the equity interest in the business, may be left to a child who is active in the management.

3. If there is to be a §303 redemption (see §§12.35 to 12.38), it will be possible on the estate owner's death to redeem all or a portion of a particular class of stock which does not affect the voting control of the corporation.

§12.41   C.   Typical Plan of Recapitalization

The recapitalization of the stock of a corporation to achieve the estate planning objectives described in §12.40 may be illustrated by describing a typical plan. Assume XYZ Corporation is owned entirely by A. The corporation, which has a present fair market value of $1,000,000, has one class of stock outstanding. A has a son who is active in the business and a daughter who is not. Under the plan of recapitalization the corporation issues 10,000 shares of preferred stock, 990 shares of nonvoting common stock and 10 shares of voting common stock in exchange for all of the present outstanding stock of the corporation.

The preferred stock under the assumed plan will have the following characteristics:

1.   Each share will have a par value of $100 per share, and a redemption price of $110 per share.
2.   Each share will pay a 12 per cent noncumulative dividend per year.
3.   The preferred stock will be nonvoting, except that it may vote to liquidate the company if preferred dividends are in arrears for more than one year.
4.   In the event of the liquidation of the company for any reason each share will receive $110 per share, before anything is paid to the common stock.

The nonvoting common stock will have the following characteristics:

1.   Each share will have a par value of one dollar per share.
2.   Each share will be entitled to share on an equal basis with each share of voting common in any dividends or liquidation proceeds paid to the common stockholders.
3.   This class of stock will be nonvoting.

The voting common stock will have the same characteristics as the nonvoting common stock, except that each share of the former will have one vote.

One of the reasons for assigning the above characteristics to each class of stock is to attempt to peg the value of each class for tax purposes. The preferred stock will have a value at the time of issuance of approximately $1,000,000, the present value of the company. As the company prospers and increases in value, the preferred stock in all likelihood will not be worth more than $1,100,000, its liquidation value. At the time of issuance, each class of common stock will have only a minimal value because the entire value of the company is represented by the preferred stock. If the company's value in the future exceeds $1,100,000, the entire excess will be represented by the value of the common stock. As between the voting and nonvoting common, the Internal Revenue Service may argue that the voting common should be valued at a premium because this stock has the vote, which is a valuable right. See *Estate of Lee v Commr* 69 TC 860 (1978) nonacq 1980-1 CB 2.

Under the typical plan, the estate owner will retain the preferred stock and the voting common stock. At the time of issuance, he will give the nonvoting common to his children. This gift, using the above example, may be accomplished without much risk of gift tax cost because the nonvoting common has little or no value in excess of the gift tax annual exclusions. In his will he can give the voting common stock to his child, who is active in the business. The preferred stock can go to the residue of his estate, which provides for an "A-B" trust, primarily for the benefit of his wife, and on her death for the children. This disposition will enable the child, who is active in the business, to control the company. The preferred stock may be used for a §303 redemption (see §§12.35 to 12.38) without affecting the child's voting control. Moreover, the wife and other children, through the trustee of the "A-B" trust, can force the company to pay dividends on the preferred, on the threat of causing the liquidation of the corporation.

Substantial estate taxes will be saved, by reason of the above plan. Using another example, assume on the estate owner's death, the company is worth $2,000,000. It is likely that the preferred stock will have a value of approximately $1,100,000. The remaining $900,000 of value will be assigned to the common stock. If each share of voting and nonvoting common is held to be of equal value, the voting common will be worth $9,000 ($900,000 times 10/1,000), and the nonvoting common, $891,000 ($900,000 times 990/1,000). Even assuming that each share of voting common stock, because it has voting rights, is worth 100 per cent more than each share of nonvoting common stock, the voting common will be worth $18,000, and the nonvoting common, $882,-000. Based on the latter assumption, the total value of the preferred and voting common stock included in the estate owner's estate will be $1,118,000. If he had not recapitalized the stock and not gifted the nonvoting common, a total value of $2,000,000 would have been included.

A similar plan may be used to freeze a partnership interest. Since a partnership does not issue stock, the partnership agreement would create two classes of partnership interest. The frozen interest would correspond to preferred stock, and would be limited as to income and the amount to be received from any sale or dissolution of the partnership. The nonfrozen interest would receive all residual distributions. All the future growth in the value of the partnership will thereby belong to the nonfrozen interest.

D. Special Tax Problems Incident to Reorganization

§12.42   1.   Income Tax

The issuance of the new classes of stock in exchange for the old ordinarily will not be a taxable event. The issuance will normally constitute either a tax-free dividend or a tax-free recapitalization. See I.R.C. §§305(a) and 368(a)(1)(E).

A concern, although a remote one, is that the issuance of the preferred stock may be taxed as a dividend under I.R.C. §305(b). In the plan described in §12.41, however, there is no disproportionate distribution as is required for taxability under I.R.C. §305(b). Nevertheless, the Internal Revenue Service could contend that, under the step-transaction doctrine, the issuance of the preferred stock is the first step in a rearrangement of each stockholder's interest. See 8 *Real Prop Prob & Tr J* 223, 248 (1973).

Although it is unlikely that there will be an income tax incurred with respect to the issuance of the stock, the preferred stock, issued in exchange for common stock, will be tainted under I.R.C. §306. Thus, if any of the preferred shares are sold to third persons, any gain, to the extent of the corporation's earnings and profits at the time of issuance, will be taxed as ordinary income. I.R.C. §306(a)(1). Where such stock is redeemed (i.e., sold back to the corporation), the proceeds to the extent of the corporation's earnings and profits at the time of the redemption will be taxed as a dividend. I.R.C. §306(a)(2). However, this taint does not apply where the shareholder's entire stock interest in the corporation stock is sold or redeemed at one time. See I.R.C. §306(b)(1).

The §306 taint is also removed on the shareholder's death. I.R.C. §306(c)(1)(C) includes, in the definition of §306, stock which has an income tax basis determined by reference to the shareholder who initially received such stock. Because inherited assets receive a new basis equal to their federal estate tax value, they are therefore not covered by the definition.

The problem caused by I.R.C. §306, during the estate owner's lifetime, applies only where the preferred stock is issued in exchange for already outstanding common stock. I.R.C. §306(c)(1). To avoid the problem, the estate planner should consider the advisability of having various classes of stock issued at the time of the incorporation of the business.

§12.43   2.   Gift Tax

As is indicated in §12.41, it is unlikely that a gift of the nonvoting common stock, issued in the typical plan of recapitalization, will give rise to a gift tax. Where the characteristics of the preferred stock are not carefully planned, however, the company's value may exceed the value of the preferred stock. See *Estate of Lee v Commr* 69 TC 860 (1978). In that event, the nonvoting common stock may have substantial value and give rise to a gift tax. Even if that is the case, the gift nevertheless may be advisable from an estate planning point of view. Where the company grows in value, the value of the nonvoting common stock will increase while the value of the preferred stock will not. The amount of appreciation in the value of the nonvoting common stock will be excluded from the estate owner's estate. See §8.4.

§12.44   3.   Estate Tax

One of the major purposes of the recapitalization plan is to enable the estate owner to give away the growth interest in the company at little or no gift tax cost and, at the same time, keep such growth out of his estate. The estate owner should therefore refrain from retaining any right in the gifted stock which will cause this stock to be includable in his estate. See §§2.13 to 2.15. If the voting stock (unlike the stock in the example in §12.41) is gifted, the donor should not retain any voting rights. Prior to the Tax Reform Act of 1976, it was permissible for the donor to retain the right to vote the gifted stock, as long as he did not retain the income or the right to designate to whom the income would be paid. *US v Byrum* 408 US 125, 92 SCt 2382, 33 LE2d 238 (1972). Under the present tax law, however, the retention of the right to vote the stock in a "controlled" corporation causes its inclusion in the donor's gross estate. I.R.C. §2036(b). A "controlled" corporation is one in which the estate owner or related parties, as described in the constructive ownership rules of I.R.C. §318 (see §12.33), own 20 per cent or more of the corporation. I.R.C. §2036(b).

VI. Use of Deferred Compensation Contracts

§12.45 A. Purpose

Where the estate owner is an active employee in a closely held business, his death will normally terminate his salary income. In order to replace this lost income, a deferred compensation contract is a worthwhile estate planning tool.

§12.46 B. In General

A deferred compensation contract is an agreement entered into between an employer and an employee providing for the payment of compensation after the period in which the compensation has been earned. The deferred payout period may commence on any given date, which is usually the time of the employee's retirement or death. For example, the contract may provide for payment of 50 per cent of the employee's salary for 10 years following his attaining age 65 or his death, whichever occurs first. Such a contract should name a beneficiary who will receive the deferred payments in the event of the employee's death prior to his having received the payments himself. For the use of a deferred compensation contract as a method of avoiding probate, see §6.30.

C. Tax Considerations

§12.47 1. Death Tax

If the employee dies before all of the deferred payments have been made, the commuted value of the remaining payments to be made on or after his death is includable in his gross estate. See I.R.C. §2039(a) and *Estate of Wadewitz v Commr* 339 F2d 980 (7th Cir 1964). For example, if at the time of the employee's death $25,000 per year is to be paid for five years, or a total of $125,000, the commuted value will be $105,310. See Reg. §20.2031-10(f), Appendix, Table VIII.

Where the contract is drafted in such a way that no deferred payments are payable to the employee during his lifetime, but there is only a death benefit payable on his death to a named beneficiary, it is possible that the value of the death benefit is not includable in the employee's estate. See *Estate of Fermin D Fusz v Commr* 46 TC 214 (1966); *Kramer v US* 406 F2d 1363 (Ct Cl 1969); cf. *Estate of Harry Fried v Commr* 54 TC 805 (1970). In determining whether the contract provides for deferred payments to the employee during such employee's lifetime, the payments under a qualified retirement plan (see §§13.8 to 13.18) are not considered. Moreover, any payments which are payable to an employee under a disability plan after retirement but prior to death are also not considered. See *Estate of Schelberg v Commr* 612 F2d 25 (2d Cir 1979).

The reader should be aware, however, that the Internal Revenue Service is continuing to attempt to include the death benefit payments in the employee's estate, particularly where the employee retained certain rights or benefits in the contract. See Rev. Rul. 78-15, 1978-1 C.B. 289. One of the factors to be considered in determining whether the death benefit will be taxable in the employee's estate is whether or not he has the right under the contract to revoke and change the beneficiary. If he does, it is more likely that the proceeds will be includable in his estate. See I.R.C. §2038(a)(1); Rev. Rul. 76-304, 1976-2 CB 269 Hence, it is advisable in the "death benefit only" type of contract for the employee not to have the right to change the beneficiary. It should be remembered that where the beneficiary is a living trust which the employee during his lifetime has the right to revoke, he thereby will indirectly have the right to revoke the beneficiary, even if the contract specifically excludes such right. If one wishes to utilize a revocable living trust (see Chapter 7) in a given estate plan and name this trust as the death beneficiary under the deferred compensation contract, the trust should provide that the employee's right to revoke the trust does not extend to any death proceeds payable under the deferred compensation contract.

§12.48   2.   Gift Tax

In its continuing efforts to prevent "death benefit only" contracts from escaping taxation, the Internal Revenue Service contends that the employee who does not retain any rights or benefits in the contract during his lifetime (see §12.47) has made a completed gift of the contractual benefits to the irrevocable beneficiary at the time the contract is made. Rev. Rul. 81-31, 1981-1 C.B. 475.

§12.49   3.   Income in Respect of a Decedent

Payments made under a deferred compensation contract after the decedent's death, whether or not the value of these payments is includable in the decedent's estate, will be subject to income tax in the hands of the recipient as items of income in respect of a decedent. (See §2.50.) However, the first $5,000 received will ordinarily be excludable as an employee death benefit if the contract provides only for death benefits. See I.R.C. §101(b). If the commuted value of the payments is includable in the gross estate for estate tax purposes, the estate tax attributable to such payments may be taken as a deduction on the recipient's income tax return. I.R.C. §691(c).

§12.50   4.   Deductibility by Corporation

The amount of deferred compensation paid to the deceased employee's beneficiary will, under general income tax rules, be deductible by the corporation only if such payments constitute reasonable compensation, after considering the other compensation paid to the employee for the period during which he performed his services. See I.R.C. §162(a)(1). In order for the corporation to obtain a deduction, it is also necessary to show that a business end was served. If these requirements are not met, the payments made to an employee stockholder may be disallowed as a dividend. In structuring the deferred compensation agreement, the payments should therefore be set at a reasonable level.

VII.   Election to Defer Payment of Estate Tax with Respect to Closely Held Business Interest

§12.51   A.   Introduction

Where an interest in a closely held business or farm constitutes more than a designated percentage of the estate and certain other requirements are met, the executor may elect to pay a portion of the estate tax in deferred installments. If certain requirements are met, and the decedent dies after 1981, the deferred payments may be extended over a 15-year period (see §12.52). The fact that an election to defer the payment of the tax may be available should be taken into account in determining the liquidity needs of the estate owner.

B.   Decedents Dying After 1981

§12.52   1.   In General

If the requirements described in §§12.53 and 12.54 are met, the payment of that portion of the estate tax attributable to the estate owner's interest in a closely held business or farm may be made over a 15-year period. The executor may elect to defer completely the tax for a period of up to five years and then to pay the tax in up to 10 equal annual installments. I.R.C. §6166(a). Interest is payable at the rate of 4 per cent per year on the portion of the deferred estate tax attributable to the first $1,000,000 of closely held business or farm property. Interest on the remaining portion of the deferred estate tax is payable at the rate generally applicable to tax deficiencies, which is currently 20 per cent. See I.R.C. §6621; Rev. Rul. 81-260, I.R.B. 1981-44, 19.

2. Requirements

§12.53   a.   Percentage Requirements

The first requirement to qualify for the election to defer the tax for 15 years has to do with the value of the closely held business interest included in the decedent's gross estate. Such value must be at least 35 per cent of the value of the gross estate reduced by the expenses, indebtedness and losses of the estate. For example, if the gross estate is $1,000,000, and the expenses, indebtedness and losses total $200,000, the value of the business interest must be at least $280,000 (35 per cent times [$1,000,000 minus $200,000]) in order to qualify for the election. In computing the gross estate for the purpose of determining whether the 35 per cent test is met, it is necessary to include gifts made within three years of death, even though such gifts are not otherwise includable. I.R.C. §2035(d)(3). (See §2.12.)

Where the estate owner owns more than one business, the value of each business in which the decedent owns at least a 20 per cent interest may be aggregated to determine if the 35 per cent rule is satisfied. I.R.C. §6166(c). Hence, if the decedent's gross estate is $1,000,000, the expenses, indebtedness and losses total $200,000, and the estate owner owns 100 per cent of a business worth $200,000 and 10 per cent of a business worth $2,000,000, the election cannot be made because only the $200,000 of value can be counted. For a discussion of special attribution of ownership rules regarding the 20 per cent requirement, see §12.54.

§12.54   b.   Must Constitute a "Closely" Held Business

The second requirement to qualify for the election is that the interest which the decedent owns must be in a business which is, in fact, closely held. This requirement is satisfied if the decedent is:

1.   A sole proprietor;

2.   A partner in a partnership with no more than 15 partners, or where at

least 20 per cent or more of the capital interest in the partnership is owned by the decedent; or

3. A stockholder in a corporation with no more than 15 stockholders, or where 20 per cent of the voting stock of the corporation is owned by the decedent. I.R.C. §6166(b)(1).

4. In determining whether or not there are more than 15 partners or stockholders, all partnership or stock interests owned by the decedent's brothers and sisters, spouse, ancestors and lineal descendants are deemed to be owned by the decedent. I.R.C. §6166(b)(2)(D). In determining whether the 20 per cent test of requirements (2) and (3) is met, the decedent is deemed to own partnership or stock interests owned by his brothers and sisters, spouse, ancestors and lineal descendants as well as those interests actually owned. I.R.C. §6166(b)(7). However, in order to include the stock of these family members, the stock in the closely held corporation may not have a market on a stock exchange or in the over-the-counter market. If it is necessary to include the partnership interests or stock not actually owned by the decedent to meet the 20 per cent test, the 4 per cent rate of interest on a portion of the estate tax and the five-year moratorium is not available (see §12.52).

Implicit in the above requirement is that an active trade or business, rather than a passive investment type activity, be conducted by the entity. The Internal Revenue Service has ruled that the management of investment type assets does not constitute a trade or business. See Rev. Rul. 75-365, 1975-2 C.B. 471; Rev. Rul. 75-366, 1975-2 C.B. 472; Rev. Rul. 75-367, 1975-2 C.B. 472; and Letter Rul. 8136022.

§12.55   3.   Time for Making the Election

The election to pay the tax in installments must be made within the time for filing the federal estate tax return, namely nine months from the date of death, including any extension of time granted for the filing of the return. I.R.C. §6166(d). If the election is not made in connection with the filing of the estate tax return, but a deficiency in estate tax is assessed, the election to pay the deficiency in installments may be made not later than 60 days after the issuance of notice and demand by the Treasury Department for payment of the deficiency. I.R.C. §6166(h).

§12.56   C.   Decedents Dying Before 1982

For decedents who died prior to 1982, the election to pay estate taxes in installments was somewhat different than the election for decedents dying after 1981. See §§12.51 to 12.55 for a discussion of the election applicable to decedents dying after 1981.

Where the decedent died prior to 1982 there were two elections to be considered. One election permitted the deferral of tax up to 15 years, and is similar to the election described in §§12.51 to 12.55. The major difference is that in order to qualify for the 15-year election, the value of the closely held business was required to exceed 65 per cent (rather than 35 per cent) of the value of the gross estate reduced by the expenses, indebtedness and losses of the estate.

The other election permitted the deferral of tax up to 10 years. If that election was made, interest was payable on the entire unpaid portion at the rate generally applicable to tax deficiencies, which is currently 20 per cent. See I.R.C. §6621; Rev. Rul. 81-260, IRB 1981-44, 19.

In general, the requirements for the 10-year payout election and for the 15-year payout election were similar, with the following major differences:

1. The interest in the closely held business must have represented at least 35 per cent of the gross estate or 50 per cent of the taxable estate. I.R.C. §6166A(a).

2. In order to aggregate two or more businesses to determine whether the 35 per cent or 50 per cent tests were met, the decedent must have owned more than 50 per cent of the value of each separate business. I.R.C. §6166A(d).

3. If the decedent's interest was in a partnership or corporation, there must have been either no more than 10 partners or stockholders, or the decedent must have owned at least a 20 per cent interest. I.R.C. §6166A(c).

§12.57   D.   Pitfalls in Planning to Use Election

While the possibility of qualifying for the deferred payment elections should be considered in planning the estate of an owner of a closely held business, it is usually desirable to make alternate liquidity arrangements. The following are reasons why this should be done:

1. Because of changing values, the nonbusiness assets in an estate may appreciate more rapidly than the business interests, so that at the time of death the percentage requirement will not be satisfied.

2. Except for the 4 per cent interest rate payable on the portion of the estate tax attributable to the first $1,000,000 of closely held business value, the interest rate is adjustable yearly by the Treasury Department in accordance with changes in the prime rate charged by banks. I.R.C. §6621. Although this interest rate is currently 20 per cent, the rate in effect at the time of the payment controls rather than the one in effect at the time the obligation arises. Hence, for planning purposes it is impossible to know the eventual interest cost.

3. The portion of the estate tax attributable to the first $1,000,000 of closely held business value, on which the 4 per cent interest rate is

payable, decreases each year from 1982 to 1987, as the unified credit increases (see §2.25). That portion is a maximum of:

Year	Amount
1982	$283,000
1983	$266,500
1984	$249,500
1985	$224,000
1986	$190,000
1987 & thereafter	$153,000

Hence, in larger estates the bulk of the deferred portion of the estate tax will bear interest at the current interest rate, rather than the special 4 per cent rate.

4. The election to pay the tax in installments is terminated and the unpaid balance must be paid immediately in the event of a disposition of more than 50 per cent of the decedent's interest in the closely held business or the withdrawal of money or other assets from the business in excess of 50 per cent of the value of the business. In many instances, because of these rules, the decedent's estate is effectively prevented from selling the business for a small cash down payment and the balance on a note. If such a sale is made, the deferred payout of tax election will be terminated and, since the sale proceeds are not in liquid form, the estate will not have the means to pay the tax in full.

5. Depending on the probate procedures in the jurisdiction governing the decedent's estate, there may be practical difficulties in closing the estate prior to the payment of the final installment of the estate tax.

VIII.   Considering Disposition of Business Interest before Death

§12.58   A.   In General

Where the estate planning tools previously discussed in this chapter cannot adequately solve the estate planning problems caused by the closely held business interest, or such solutions do not accord with the estate owner's objectives, the estate owner may wish to consider selling his business interest while he is still alive. In the event of sale during the owner's lifetime, the business interest will not be part of his estate. By carefully structuring the sale, the proceeds will be more liquid and easier to value than the business would have been. There could be an income tax disadvantage, however, in selling the business prior to the estate owner's death. If the business is held until death, it will receive a new income tax basis equal to the federal estate tax value thereof. I.R.C. §§1014(a) and (b). Accordingly, if the business is worth more than its income tax basis, the income tax cost of selling the business will be greater if sold during life than if sold after death.

§12.59 B. Outright Sale for Cash

By making a cash sale, the estate owner receives the full purchase price at the time of sale and he is, thereby, not concerned about the ability of the purchaser to pay any deferred balance. However, the outright sale, from a tax point of view, may be disadvantageous, since the net profit will be subject to immediate income tax. Where the business interest has been held for over one year, the gain will usually, but not always, be taxed as a long-term capital gain. For circumstances where the gain will be taxed as ordinary income, see §§341 (sale of stock of a collapsible corporation) and 1245 and 1250 (recapture of depreciation) of the Internal Revenue Code. Even though capital gain rates are lower than ordinary income tax rates, the capital gains tax, for federal purposes, could be as high as 20 per cent. See I.R.C. §1202. If, for example, the estate owner started the business with a nominal investment and then sold it for $1,000,000, the income tax on the gain could be as large as $200,000, leaving the owner with an after-tax net of only $800,000, a substantial reduction in the value of his worth.

§12.60 C. Installment Sale

As an alternative to selling his business interest for cash, the estate owner should consider selling his interest on the installment basis. The profit on the sale is then prorated over the period in which the payments are received, rather than all of it being taxed in the year of the sale. See I.R.C. §453.

Since all or a portion of the income tax is deferred, the estate owner will have a greater initial amount of capital to use for the production of income than he would have had if the sale had been for all cash. For example, assume he sells his business for $1,000,000 in cash and, after payment of taxes, nets $800,000. If he can invest at 12 per cent, he will earn $96,000 per year. However, if the sale were made on the installment basis for, say, no cash down, the entire $1,000,000 note would, at least initially, be earning interest, assuming a rate of 12 per cent, amounting to $120,000 per year.

An installment sale is also a useful device in selling the business to a family member. The estate owner, by way of example, can sell his business interest to his son at a purchase price which reflects the fair market value of the interest. The purchase price could be paid with a very low down payment and the balance on a long-term installment note, providing for a reasonable rate of interest. This transaction will have the following estate planning advantages:

1. Although the value of the installment note at the time of death will be included in the estate owner's gross estate, any appreciation in the value of the business subsequent to the sale will be excluded.

2. Since the sale is made at fair market value, there will be no gift tax at the time of the sale.

3. The estate owner may further reduce his estate by forgiving portions of the installment note each year to the extent of the $10,000 annual exclusion. But see Rev. Rul. 77-299, 1977-2 C.B. 343.

§12.61   D.   Other Types of Sales

The estate owner may sell his business interest to a family member in return for the family member's promise to pay the seller an annuity for the rest of the seller's life. For a full discussion of private annuities and the tax consequences of this type of transaction, see §§11.12 to 11.19.

Alternatively, the estate owner may sell a remainder interest in his business holdings. For a discussion of a sale of a remainder interest, see §8.48. A sale of a remainder interest in closely held corporate stock, contrasted with such a sale of high yield income-producing assets, is advantageous. When the estate owner for full consideration sells a remainder interest in any asset, such asset will be removed from his gross estate. However, the consideration which he receives for the sale, together with the income earned from the asset over the rest of his lifetime, will enlarge his estate. In many instances, stock in a closely held corporation does not pay a dividend. See §13.3. As a result, the seller's estate will not be increased by reason of the right to receive the income from the transferred stock, as it would have been if the asset had been income-producing.

§12.62   E.   Disposition by Tax-Free Merger

As an alternative to selling his business interest in an income taxable transaction, the estate owner may consider exchanging his business for stock in another corporation. Where the exchange is structured as a reorganization under §368(a) of the Internal Revenue Code, the gain on the sale will not be recognized at the time of sale. I.R.C. §354(a)(1). The stock received in exchange for the business interest will have the same income tax basis as the business interest had. Hence, if the newly acquired stock is sold before death, gain will be recognized at that time.

For example, assume A owns all of the stock of ABC Co., a closely held corporation. This stock has a basis of $10,000 and a present value of $1,000,-000. A exchanges ABC Co. stock for shares of XYZ Corporation, currently selling for $1,000,000, in a transaction which qualifies as a tax-free reorganization. At the time of the exchange, A's profit of $990,000 ($1,000,000 minus $10,000) is not taxable. A's basis for the XYZ stock remains at $10,000, so that when he sells such stock, any amount realized in excess of $10,000 will be taxable at that time. However, if A retains the XYZ stock until his death, his estate or beneficiaries will receive a stepped-up basis for the stock.

In order for the exchange to qualify as a tax-free reorganization, many technical requirements must be satisfied. In very general terms, however, a tax-free reorganization is either a statutory merger or consolidation (I.R.C. §368(a)(1)(A)), an exchange of stock for voting stock of the acquiring corporation (I.R.C. §368(a)(1)(B)), or an exchange of the assets of a corporation for voting stock of the acquiring corporation (I.R.C. §368(a)(1)(C)).

Where the acquiring corporation's shares are publicly traded, they may have to be registered under the federal Securities Act of 1933. See §5(a) of the Securities Act of 1933. Where they are not registered, but are issued under the private offering exemption, they are subject to Rule 144 of the Securities and Exchange Commission, which restricts the transfer of such shares. (See §7.10.) Because the costs of registration are very high, most stock issued in exchange for closely held business stock or assets is not registered. The estate owner should be aware of the possibility that the unregistered shares which he receives may substantially decline in value before he may legally sell them.

IX. Planning for Possibility that Wife Owning a Community Property Interest Dies Before her Husband

§12.63 A. In General

A frequent assumption used in estate planning is that the husband will die before the wife. Particularly where the wife owns a community property interest (see §§4.34 to 4.36) in a closely held business in which the husband is active, the estate planner must take into account the possibility that the wife may die first. For a full discussion of the considerations which should be taken into account in planning for the possibility of the wife's dying first, see Weinstock, "What If The Wife Dies First?" 28 *Univ of So Cal Tax Inst* 55 (1976).[1]

§12.64 B. Estate Tax Considerations

Generally, the wife's community property interest in a closely held business is valued for estate tax purposes on her death on the same basis as it would have been had her husband died first. (See §§12.2 to 12.5.) There are, however, two apparent instances where the value on the wife's death will be different from the value on the husband's death.

The first situation is where there is a buy-sell agreement providing that, on the husband's death, his interest will be purchased, or at least is subject to a binding option of purchase, by the business or by the other co-owners. The price set forth either specifically or by formula in the buy-sell agreement will, if the requirements set forth in §12.9 are met, be accepted on the husband's

---

[1] Some of the material in §§12.64 to 12.68 is taken from the cited article with the permission of Matthew Bender & Company, Inc., the copyright holder.

death as the value of the business interest for death tax purposes. Where the wife dies first, however, and the buy-sell agreement triggers a sale only upon the husband's death, the buy-sell price will not be binding for death tax valuation purposes on the wife's death because there is no binding obligation that her interest be sold at the contract price. Where the buy-sell agreement restricts the sale of the wife's community property interest during the husband's lifetime and also is subject to a binding obligation of sale on the husband's death, it may be argued that on the wife's prior death, the buy-sell price, while not determinative of valuation, is at least one factor to be considered. The rationale for this argument is that the wife's interest at the time of her death could not have been sold for more than the death price. See Rev. Rul. 189, 1953-2 C.B. 294.

Another circumstance where the value of the wife's community property interest in the business on her prior death will be different than it would have been on the husband's death is where no buy-sell agreement exists and the husband's services are an important attribute of the business's goodwill. On the husband's death, the business will, for valuation purposes, be deemed to have suffered a diminution in value. See *Newell v Commr* 66 F2d 102 (7th Cir 1933). However, where the wife dies first and her services are not important to the value of the business, the valuation in her estate will be higher.

§12.65   C.   The Wife's Disposition Planning

If the wife leaves her entire estate, including her community property interest in the closely held business, outright to the husband, this will eliminate the estate tax on the wife's death, but will increase the husband's estate for death tax and probate purposes. In order to lessen this negative result, the wife should consider leaving no more than an optimum marital bequest to her husband (see §4.8) and at least the amount of the equivalent exemption to a bypass trust, which is for the husband's benefit but escapes taxation in his estate (see §5.2).

Care should be taken that any buy-sell agreement entered into by the husband does not prevent the wife from leaving her community property interest in the business to a bypass trust. Such an agreement should be drafted so as to permit a disposition of such interest, on the wife's prior death, to a trust for the benefit of the husband and other beneficiaries in her family.

In planning and drafting the bypass trust, which is to receive the wife's community property interest in the business, the following factors should be considered.

§12.66   1.   Who Is to be the Trustee?

Normally, the husband will desire to be named as the trustee of the bypass trust so that he may more effectively control the business interest. Whether or not he may serve as a trustee from a tax point of view depends to a large extent upon the substantive provisions of the trust. If he is to receive all of the income and, even in addition, has power to invade principal for himself limited by an ascertainable standard, a "five and five" power, and a power to dispose of principal to third parties (but not to himself, his creditors, his estate or the creditors of his estate), the husband will normally suffer no adverse tax consequences by virtue of acting as the trustee. (See §§5.4 to 5.6.)

Alternatively, the bypass trust can be a discretionary trust, i.e., one where during the husband's lifetime the trustee has broad discretion to accumulate and/or to distribute (i.e., "sprinkle") the income and principal to himself and other persons, such as the children. A discretionary trust may result in the trust income being taxed at a lower rate, but it is not feasible tax-wise for the husband to serve as a trustee of such a trust if he is also a beneficiary. (See §§5.10 and 5.14.)

It would appear to be better planning in those estates in which the major asset is an interest in a closely held business that the bypass trust not be a discretionary trust so that the husband may act as the trustee. The fact that the income tax advantages of a discretionary trust will be lost is probably not a serious consideration. More than likely, little or no dividends will be paid on the closely held stock. Hence, there will be no significant amount of income to sprinkle.

§12.67   2.   The Availability of the Subchapter S Election

If the closely held corporation, whose stock is to go into the bypass trust, has elected under Subchapter S, such election will be lost unless the trust is a "qualified Subchapter S trust." See §7.31 for a full discussion.

§12.68   3.   Trust Management May be More Cumbersome than Outright Ownership

Even if the husband is to act as the trustee of the bypass trust, his control of the business interest will not be as secure as outright ownership would be. The remainder beneficiaries of the trust may, for example, complain if the trust does not diversify its investments, but rather holds the business interest as its major asset. This problem can perhaps be minimized by carefully drafting the trust provisions. The trustee can be given an unqualified right to retain nonincome-producing assets. However, if the business did so poorly that the value of the stock dropped sharply, the trustee might nevertheless be liable for mismanagement.

Unless the husband is willing to assume fiduciary responsibilities with respect to the business interest, it may be best to attempt to avoid having the wife's community property interest in the business going into a bypass trust. The wife may consider two alternatives where the business interest will not go into a trust, but at the same time not unduly increase the husband's estate. The first alternative, if she has separate property, or an interest in other community property assets, is to leave her community property interest in the business as part of an outright marital deduction bequest to the husband and then leave an equivalent amount of her separate property and other community property to the bypass trust. The second alternative is to leave her community property interest in the business outright to the husband upon the condition that he transfer an equivalent amount of his interest in other community property assets to the bypass trust. The fulfilling of this condition will not be treated as a sale or exchange for income tax purposes. See §5.2.

X. Recommended Reading

Abbin, "Using the Multi-Class Partnership to Freeze Asset Values for Estate Planning Purposes" 52 *Journal of Taxation* 68 (1980)

Albin, "Gift, Estate and Income Tax Exposure for Recapitalizing Closely Held Companies" 10 *Univ of Miami Inst on Estate Planning* 1200 (1976)

Barcal, "IRS' Active' Trade or Business Requirement for Estate Tax Deferral: An Analysis" 54 *Journal of Taxation* 52 (1981)

Berall, "Recapitalizing Close Corporations May be Planning Solution for Major Stockholder" 3 *Estate Planning* 96 (1976)

Bittker and Eustice, *Federal Income Taxation of Corporations and Shareholders* (Warren, Gorham and Lamont, Inc, 3d Ed 1971, supplemented currently)

Blum, "A Practitioner's Guide to the Making of Estate Tax Deferral Decisions" 49 *Journal of Taxation* 266 (1978)

Burns, "How to Avoid Estate Tax on Proceeds Paid from Corporate Death Benefit Plan" 4 *Estate Planning* 112 (1977)

Dant, "Courts Increasing Amount of Discount for a Minority Interest in a Business" 43 *Journal of Taxation* 104 (1975)

Darling, "Effect of Installation Sales on Estate Planning" 11 *Trusts and Estates* 534 (1972)

Faber, "Avoid Tax Problems in Planning Recapitalizations" 119 No 1 *Trusts and Estates* 67 (1980)

Freeman, "Combining the Use of Corporations, Partnerships and Trusts to Minimize the Income and Transfer Tax Impact on Family Businesses and Investments" 57 *Taxes* 857 (1979)

Hardy, "Valuation: A Financial Planning Tool for Closely Held Corporations" 113 *Trusts and Estates* 584 (1974)

Herwitz, "Stock Redemptions and the Accumulated Earnings Tax" 74 *Harv L Rev* 866 (1961)

Kanter, "Freezing Future Estate Growth: Estate Planning Challenges and Opportunities" 113 *Trusts and Estates* 132 (1974)

Kelley and Ludtke, *Estate Planning for Farmers and Ranchers* (Shepard's/McGraw-Hill 1980)

King, "What Ingredients Should a Buy-Sell Agreement Contain to be Effective for Tax Purposes?" 12 *Taxation for Accountants* 78 (1974)

Lee, "Partnership Taxation in the Estate Situation" 114 *Trusts and Estates* 154 (1975)

Mastry, "Corporate Distributions of Appreciated Property" 56 *ABA Journal* 1210 (1970)

Meyer, "Redemption of Stock in the Close Corporation to Pay Death Taxes: IRC Section 303" 27 *NYU Inst on Fed Tax* 401 (1969)

Nassau, "Buy-Out Agreements in Planning the Estate of a Stockholder—Employee of a Closely Held Corporation" 31 *NYU Inst on Fed Tax* 1029 (1973)

Osach, "New Election Extends Estate Tax Payment up to 15 Years; Ten-Year Discretionary Rules also Eased" 4 *Estate Planning* 86 (1977)

Rosenberg, "Paying the Estate Tax in Installments: Working with Section 6166" 39 *Journal of Taxation* 302 (1973)

Rustigan, Lentz & Olsen, "Problems in Valuing Stock of a Close Corporation: a Panel Discussion" 23 *NYU Inst on Fed Tax* 1261 (1965)

Stechel, "Restrictive Buy-Sell Agreements can Limit Estate Tax Value of a Business Interest" 44 *Journal of Taxation* 360 (1976)

Starkey, "Valuation of Closely-Held Stock: Book Value v. Capitalization of Earnings" 2 *Estate Planning* 37 (1974)

Willens, "Recent Decisions Permit Trusts and Estates to Waive Attribution Rules" 51 *Journal of Taxation* 208 (1979)

"The Estate Freezing Rage" (Panel Discussion) 15 *Real Prop, Prob and Tr J* 21 (1980)

Employee Benefits

13

I. Introduction

§13.1   A. Role of Fringe Benefits in Estate Planning

The proper use of employee fringe benefits is important in estate planning. This is particularly true in planning the estate of a business owner who has considerable influence in initiating and structuring the type of employee fringe benefits which his company will adopt. The subject should, however, not be overlooked in the case of nonowner employees who participate in fringe benefit programs adopted by their employer.

Employee fringe benefits are important from an estate planning point of view both in terms of lifetime benefits, such as retirement income, as well as benefits which are paid on an employee's death. In many cases employee benefits are extremely valuable because the tax laws are designed to foster these benefits, affording them favorable treatment.

§13.2   B. Types of Employee Fringe Benefits

Certain employee fringe benefits have already been discussed in this book. Group life insurance, split-dollar life insurance, and the life insurance aspects of qualified pension and profit sharing plans have been discussed in §§ 10.56 to 10.58, and the use of deferred compensation contracts, in §§ 12.45 to 12.50. This chapter deals with the estate planning attributes of medical benefit plans (see §§ 13.4 and 13.5), group legal services plans (see § 13.6), the noninsurance aspects of qualified employee and individual retirement plans (see §§ 13.7 to 13.21), and the $5,000 income tax death benefit exclusion (see § 13.22).

§13.3   C. Requirement of Employment Relationship

Except for participation in a group legal services plan (see § 13.6) and self-employed and individual qualified retirement plans (see §§ 13.19 and 13.20), the various fringe benefits discussed in this chapter are in the nature of "employee" benefits. The estate owner who wishes to participate must be an employee of a business. A sole proprietor or a partner is usually not considered an employee for these purposes. If a nonincorporated business owner wishes to obtain for himself the requisite employment relationship, he should consider incorporating his business and becoming an employee thereof. For many years persons practicing a profession were not permitted to incorporate. In the last 15 years, however, these people have been able to incorporate under the Professional Corporation Acts of the various states.

Before incorporating in order to obtain employee status, the business owner should be made aware of the other general and tax considerations in incorporating his business. The major nontax advantage is the limited liability enjoyed by a corporate stockholder for the debts of the business, as opposed to the unlimited liability of sole proprietors and general partners. Insofar as tax considerations are concerned, the corporation is a separate tax entity. Its net income is subject to corporate rates of tax, which at present start at 16 per cent and go up to 46 per cent. By 1983, the lowest rate will be 15 per cent. See I.R.C. § 11. Hence where the business owner is in a high individual income tax bracket, the business net income may be taxed at lower rates than would have been the case where such net income had been earned by him as a sole proprietor or partner. For a comprehensive treatment of the corporate income tax, see Bittker, Boris I. and Eustice, James S. *Federal Income Taxation of Corporations and Shareholders,* (4th ed 1979, currently supplemented).

On the other hand, there are disadvantages in incorporating. The cost of incorporating and maintaining the corporation, increased social security and employment taxes, annual corporate registration fees, special franchise taxes and the like must be taken into account. In addition, to the extent that corporate earnings cannot be paid out in the form of a reasonable salary, they ordinarily cannot be paid to the corporate owner except as a dividend. When paid as dividends such earnings are subjected to double taxation. See I.R.C. §§ 162(a)(1) and 301(a) and (c).

Where dividends are not paid, the corporation could be subject to the tax on unreasonably accumulated earnings (see I.R.C. §531), which, for certain personal service corporations, are in excess of $150,000 and for all others, in excess of $250,000. (I.R.C. §§535(c)(2) and (3).) Undistributed earnings of personal holding companies are also subject to the personal holding company tax. I.R.C. §§541 to 547.

A Subchapter S corporation generally avoids the dividend problem because the corporate earnings are taxed directly to the shareholders. See I.R.C. §§ 1371 to 1379. This type of corporation, however, is ordinarily not a feasible solution where the purpose of incorporating is to obtain the benefits of a qualified retirement plan for the owner. While a shareholder employee of such a corporation satisfies the requisite employment relationship, such a corporation is subject to the limitation of a self-employment retirement plan with respect to any shareholder employee who owns more than 5 per cent of the stock of the corporation. See I.R.C. §§ 1379(b) and (d); see also § 13.19.

II.   Medical Reimbursement Plans

§13.4   A.   Income Tax Consequences

A valuable employee fringe benefit is an employer financed accident and health plan. In general, an accident and health plan is an arrangement for the payment of medical benefits to employees in the event of personal injuries or sickness. One plan may cover one or more employees, or there may be different plans for different employees or classes of employees. The plan may either be insured or noninsured. Reg. § 1.105-5(a). As long as the plan covers employees, the employer's contributions to the plan are deductible and neither such contributions nor any benefits paid under the plan are includable in the employee's gross income. See I.R.C. §§ 105 and 106. Hence where a medical plan is an insured one, the premiums paid for the medical insurance are deductible by the employer and are not income to the employee. Moreover, the payments made by the insurance company to pay the employee's expenses covered by the plan are also not income to the employee. Similarly, if instead of an insured plan, the employer agrees to reimburse its employees for medical expenses, either in whole or in part, such reimbursement is deductible by the employer and is not income to the employee.

§13.5   B.   Application to Owner-Employee of Closely Held Corporation

An uninsured medical plan (i.e., one where the benefits are not provided by a licensed insurance company) will not qualify for favorable tax treatment unless it meets nondiscrimination requirements similar to but somewhat less structured than those imposed on qualified pension plans. (See §13.9.) Where such a plan is discriminatory in favor of an owner or other highly paid employees, the amounts paid under the plan will be includable in such persons' gross income.

While there are no requirements that an insured medical reimbursement plan be nondiscriminatory, it is required that the plan be for the benefit of the employees. Accordingly, where the only participants in the insured plan are stockholder-employees, there is a danger that the employer's payments under the plan will be considered to have been made by virtue of the stockholder, and not the employee, relationship. If that is the case, the payments may be disallowed as deductions to the corporation and be taxable to the shareholder-employees as dividends. See *Larkin v Commr* 394 F2d 494 (1st Cir 1968); *Samuel Levine v Commr* 50 TC 422 (1968); cf. *Bogene Inc v Commr* 27 TCMemo 1968-147, ¶ 68,147 (1968). It is therefore advisable in structuring an insured medical reimbursement plan to include employees other than the shareholders, although, perhaps, it is not necessary that these employees receive substantially similar benefits as long as their benefits are significant.

§13.6   III.   Group Legal Services Plan

The Tax Reform Act of 1976 introduced a new form of employee fringe benefit on an experimental basis. It is effective for a trial period ending before 1985. I.R.C. § 120 excludes from the employee's income amounts contributed by the employer to a qualified group legal services plan for employees (or their spouses or their dependents). While the Code does not specifically cover the point, the employer's contributions to such a plan should also be deductible. See Reg. § 1.162-10 (for analogous deductions).

In order for the group legal services plan to be qualified, it must fulfill several requirements. These requirements are designed to insure that the tax-free fringe benefits are provided on a nondiscriminatory basis and minimize the possibility of tax abuse through misuse of the plan. See proposed Supplemental Report of the Committee on Finance, U. S. Senate, on additional Committee Amendment to H. R. 10612 (July 20, 1976), pp. 39 to 41.

A qualified group legal services plan must be a separate written plan of an employer for the exclusive benefit of its employees or their spouses or dependents. The plan must supply the employees, their spouses, and dependents with the payment of personal (i.e., nonbusiness) legal services. I.R.C. § 120(b). The amounts contributed by the employer under the plan may be paid only (1) to insurance companies, (2) to special types of trusts, (3) as prepayments to providers of legal services under the plan, or (4) to a combination of these three permissible types of payment arrangements. I.R.C. § §120(c)(5); 501(c)(20).

In order to qualify, a group legal services plan must also meet requirements with respect to nondiscrimination in contributions, benefits and eligibility for enrollment. The plan may not discriminate in favor of employees who are officers, shareholders, self-employed individuals or highly compensated personnel. I.R.C. § 120(c)(2).

Unlike most fringe benefits (see § 13.3), a self-employed proprietor or partner who has earned income may participate in the plan, as if he were a common law employee. I.R.C. § 120(d). A limit, however, is placed on the proportion of the amounts contributed under the plan which can be for employees, whether or not they are self-employed, who own more than 5 per cent of the stock or of the capital or profits interest in the employer corporation or unincorporated trade or business. The aggregate of the contributions for those employees and their spouses and dependents must not be more than 25 per cent of the total contributions. I.R.C. § 120(c)(3).

§13.7   IV.   Cafeteria Plans

Normally, where an employee is given a choice by the employer of accepting either nontaxable fringe benefits or additional taxable benefits (such as group life insurance in excess of $50,000, see §10.56), the receipt of either will result in taxable income. However, where the choice is given under a so-called cafeteria plan, the employee will not be taxed to the extent he elects to receive an otherwise nontaxable fringe benefit (such as group term life insurance up to $50,000 coverage, disability benefits, accident and health benefits and group legal services to the extent such benefits are otherwise excludable from gross income). The plan must qualify under complex nondiscrimination requirements. If the plan is discriminatory in favor of employees who are officers, shareholders or highly paid personnel, then all benefits (whether initially taxable or nontaxable) will be includable in the income of such persons. I.R.C. §125.

V.   Qualified Retirement Plans

§13.8   A.   Corporate Plans

The subject of qualified retirement plans is extremely technical and detailed. It is beyond the scope of this book to consider all the technical rules and requirements governing the qualification and operation of qualified plans. The Employee Retirement Income Security Act of 1974, called "ERISA," contains numerous labor law and tax requirements, many of which will not be referred to here. The purpose of this chapter is merely to describe the tax advantages and estate planning aspects of retirement plans and in order to do this, to summarize only in general terms certain of the technical requirements.

§13.9   1.   Requirements for Qualification

In general a qualified retirement plan must meet the following requirements:

(a)   There must be a definite plan which is communicated to the employees. Reg. § 1.401-1(a)(2).

(b)   The plan must be for the exclusive benefit of the employees or their beneficiaries and none of the plan assets may be diverted for any other purpose. I.R.C. §401(a)(2).

(c)   The plan must not discriminate in favor of certain employees. This requirement will be satisfied if either of two alternate tests is met. The first test is that the plan must cover 70 per cent or more of all employees who meet the minimum participation standards set forth in (d) below, or 80 per cent of all eligible employees, if 70 per cent of all employees meeting the minimum standard are eligible under the plan. I.R.C. §410(b)(1)(A). The second test is that the plan covers employees under a classification found by the Internal Revenue Service not to discriminate in favor of stockholders, officers or highly paid employees. I.R.C. §410(b)(1)(B).

(d)   The plan must set forth certain minimum standards for participation by employees. Under this requirement it may not exclude any employee who is at least 25 years old and has at least one year of service. I.R.C. §410(a)(1)(A). The plan may, however, require three years of service if it provides 100 per cent immediate vesting for participants. I.R.C. §410(a)(1)(B)(i).

(e)   The plan must also meet certain minimum vesting standards. Vested amounts are amounts not forfeited by an employee in the event his employment is terminated. These requirements are as follows: (1) There must be complete vesting of the employee's normal retirement benefit on reaching normal retirement age; (2) There must be complete vesting of all the employee's own contributions at all times; (3) In addition, one of the following four requirements must be met or exceeded: (i) full vesting on a five to fifteen year graduated standard with 25 per cent vested after five years of service, 50 per cent after 10 years; and 100 per cent after 15 years, (ii) 100 per cent vesting after 10 years of service, (iii) 40 per cent vesting after four years of service increasing to 100 per cent after 11 years, or (iv) full vesting under the "Rule of 45." I.R.C. §411(a). Under this rule an employee with at least five years of service must be 50 per cent vested when his age and years of service equal 45 and then for each additional year of service, he must be another 10 per cent vested, so that after an additional five years, the employee must be 100 per cent vested. I.R.C. §411(a)(2)(C).

(f)   In addition to the above requirements, the plan in operation cannot discriminate in favor of officers, shareholders or highly compensated employees, and if it does, the plan will be disqualified even if it was initially qualified.

§13.10   2.   What is a Profit Sharing Plan?

A profit sharing plan is a retirement plan which provides that the employer will contribute a percentage of the company's net profits to the plan. The percentage need not be fixed in advance, but may be decided by the employer each year. Even in the rare instances where it is fixed in advance, if there are no profits, no contribution can be made. The plan must provide a definite predetermined formula for allocating the contributions made to the plan among the employees, usually in proportion to their compensation, but adjustments may be made for the cost of the employer's social security contributions. Reg. § 1.401-1(b)(1)(ii).

A profit sharing plan is the most flexible from the employer's point of view, because of the lack of a fixed obligation to make contributions On the other hand, since no fixed benefit is payable to the employee upon retirement, he cannot plan his retirement income too far in advance. The precise retirement benefit payable to each employee depends entirely on the amount the employer decides to contribute and the earnings of the plan.

3.   What is a Pension Plan?

§13.11   a.   Defined Benefit Plan

A defined benefit pension plan is one which provides for the payment of definitely determinable benefits to the employee over a period of years, usually for life, after retirement. These retirement benefits generally are measured by, and based on, such factors as years of service and compensation received by the employee. The determination of the amount of the retirement benefits and the contributions to provide such benefits are not dependent upon profits. In most instances, the employer's contribution must be determined actuarially, so that the amounts contributed will be sufficient to fund the predetermined retirement benefits. Reg. § 1.401-1(b)(1)(i).

From the employer's point of view the defined benefit pension plan may be the most rigid of the plans because there is a relatively fixed commitment to annually contribute the amount necessary to fund the predetermined retirement benefits. Where, however, the owner-employees of a small company are elderly, in comparison to the nonowner-employees, the use of a defined benefit pension plan may be advantageous to the owner-employees. The reason is that a greater than proportionate amount of the contribution can be allocated to the accounts of the owner-employees where this amount is actuarially necessary to fund their retirement benefits. From the employee's viewpoint, the defined benefit plan assures a predetermined amount of retirement benefits, so he can more easily plan for his retirement.

§13.12   b.   Money Purchase Pension Plan

A money purchase pension plan, similarly to a profit sharing plan, has no defined retirement benefits. (See § 13.10.) However, it differs from a profit sharing plan in that the employer's contributions are based on a fixed percentage of the compensation paid to the covered employees. This fixed percentage must be paid even if there are no profits.

§13.13   4.   What are Employee-Stock-Ownership and Stock Bonus Plans?

An employee-stock-ownership plan (frequently called an "ESOP") and a stock bonus plan are similar to a money purchase pension plan and profit sharing plan, but the contributions are not necessarily dependent upon profits as is the case with a profit sharing plan. Such plans are designed to invest primarily in securities of the employer corporation and eventually to distribute a portion of the corporate ownership among the employees. This type of plan may be a helpful tool to be used by owners of closely held stock.

It is possible to use an ESOP (but not a stock bonus plan) as a means to raise working capital for the employer, and, at least indirectly, to pay for such working capital on a tax deductible basis. This can be accomplished by having the ESOP borrow funds, based upon the guarantee of the employer, and then use such loan proceeds to purchase stock from the employer. The stock will then be held by the plan for later distribution to the employees. The employer then uses the sale proceeds for its own business purpose, such as working capital. Each year the company's tax deductible contributions to the ESOP can be used to repay the loan. In effect then, the employer repays the loan with tax deductible money.

Another important characteristic of both an ESOP and a stock bonus plan is their ability to purchase stock from the employer's stockholders, thereby giving this stock a ready market. If not for such ability, a stockholder of a nonpublic corporation would not have any market for his shares. In that event, if he or his estate desired to make a sale, the corporation, itself, would be the only prospective buyer. Unless the purchase by the corporation constituted a complete or substantially disproportionate redemption of the stockholder's stock, there would be a taxable dividend problem for the stockholder or his estate (see § 12.33 for a discussion of the dividend problem). The availability of the ESOP or a stock bonus plan as an alternative independent purchaser for the stock should eliminate this problem. Provided the guidelines set forth in Revenue Procedure 77-30, 1977-2 C.B. 539 are followed, the purchase by an ESOP or stock bonus plan of a stockholder's stock will not result in a taxable dividend to the stockholder.

The purchase of the stockholder's stock by such plans instead of a redemption by the corporation also results in a tax advantage to the corporation. Where the stock is redeemed, there is no tax deduction to the corporation. However, the corporation, by contributing funds to the ESOP or the stock bonus plan, will be able to deduct its contribution.

5. Tax Aspects of Qualified Plans

§13.14 a. Employer's Contributions

The employer's contributions to a qualified retirement plan are, within prescribed limits, deductible. These limits vary considerably, depending upon whether the plan is a profit sharing plan, a pension plan, or an employee-stock-ownership or bonus plan. They are extremely technical and are not discussed in any detail here. In very broad terms, however, the employer's contributions to a money purchase pension plan are limited to 25 per cent of the compensation of the covered employees, but to a profit sharing plan or an employee-stock-ownership or bonus plan are limited to 15 per cent of the compensation of the covered employees. See I.R.C. § 404(a)(3). With respect to an ESOP, however, there is also an investment tax credit allowed, which is allowed until 1983 when it will be replaced by a payroll-based tax credit. I.R.C. § 44G. The contribution to a defined benefit pension plan is limited to the amount actuarially necessary to fund the plan. See I.R.C. §404(a)(1). For the limitation on deductible contributions for a 5 per cent or more stockholder of a Subchapter S corporation, see § 13.3. In certain instances where an employer has more than one type of plan, the employee's contributions are subject to higher limits, as for example, up to 25 per cent of compensation where there is both a profit sharing plan and any type of pension plan. See I.R.C. § 404(a)(7).

In addition to the overall limitations on the deductibility of contributions by the employer, the amount of contributions to or benefits payable from a plan with respect to any individual employee is also limited, the exact amount and nature depending on the type of plan. Consequently, very highly paid employees will not be able to receive enormous retirement benefits. If these limits are exceeded, the plan will be disqualified. I.R.C. §415(a). In very general terms, the Internal Revenue Code limitation regarding the annual benefits payable under a defined benefit pension plan is the lesser of $75,000 or 100 per cent of the participant's average compensation for his three consecutive highest paid years. I.R.C. § 415(b). The limitation regarding the annual contribution which may be made to a defined contribution plan, such as a profit sharing or money purchase pension plan, is the lesser of $25,000 or 25 per cent of the participant's compensation. I.R.C. §415(c). The $75,000 and $25,000 limits, however, are adjusted annually by the Treasury Department to reflect changes in the cost of living. I.R.C. §415(d). At this time they are $136,425 and $45,475, respectively.

§13.15   b.   Taxability of Plan Earnings

The contributions paid into the plan may, subject to certain restrictions, be invested in different types of assets. For the use of insurance in funding a qualified retirement plan, see §10.58. The earnings from the plan investments are not subject to income tax while they remain in the qualified retirement plan. I.R.C. §501(a). This is true even with respect to earnings from the employee's own contributions to the extent they may be made to the plan. The nontaxability of the income permits the plan assets to grow at a much more rapid rate than an individual's own earnings which he saves for his retirement. For example, if an employee, in a 50 per cent income tax bracket, without a qualified retirement plan, puts a portion of his compensation aside to fund for his retirement, the net earnings would be subject to income tax. Assuming a 12 per cent return, the after-tax yield would only be 6 per cent per year. On the other hand, if such employee's retirement was funded through a qualified plan, the full 12 per cent per year would be retained until retirement.

c.   Taxability of Employee Benefits

§13.16   i.   Income Tax

The employer's contributions to the plan, although deductible by the employer, are not taxable income to the employee when made. This tax deferral is important. For example, if $10,000 is paid as additional salary to an employee in a 50 per cent income tax bracket, all he retains after taxes is $5,000, which he may then invest for his retirement. On the other hand, if the $10,000 is contributed to a qualified plan, the full $10,000 will be invested for his retirement. This, coupled with the fact that the investment earnings in the qualified plan are also tax-free (see §13.15), results in a much faster rate of growth for funds in a qualified plan. Where the plan permits, the employee may make contributions of his own, but such contributions are not deductible by him, unless the exception described in §13.20 is applicable.

Under certain plans, if the nondiscrimination requirements are met, the employee may be given the option of taking a share of the employer's contribution either in cash or having it paid to the profit sharing trust. If it is paid to a profit sharing trust, the contribution is not taxable income to the employee when made, even though an election could have been made to take it in cash. See I.R.C. §§401(k)(3) and (4).

When the qualified plan benefits are paid to the employee, which would normally happen upon his retirement, death, or other termination of his employment, the amounts received, to the extent they are attributable to the employer's contributions, are taxable to the employee. The manner in which these amounts are taxed depends on the form in which they are received, that is, either as an annuity or as a lump sum. A lump sum is defined as a distribution within one taxable year of the recipient of the balance in the employee's account. I.R.C. §402(e)(4)(A). An annuity is any payment of benefit which is not a lump sum.

Where the amounts are paid in the form of an annuity, they are taxed, to the extent of the employer's contributions, as ordinary income in the year received. Hence if all contributions were made by the employer, and the employee is to receive $20,000 per year, the entire amount will be taxable as ordinary income when received. However, if the employee contributed a portion of the contributions, the payments will be taxed as an annuity, with the employee's contribution constituting the investment in the contract. For the rules governing the income taxation of an annuity, see §11.8. However, if the employee's contribution was small enough so that it will be recovered within three years, the employee will exclude the retirement payments from his income until the amount of his contribution is recovered; thereafter the remaining payments will be taxed as ordinary income. I.R.C. §72(d)(1).

If the benefits are paid in the form of a lump sum, the income taxability is more complicated. First of all, if the lump sum payment is transferred within 60 days to an individual retirement account (see §13.20) or to a new employer's qualified plan, the "rollover" distribution is tax-free. I.R.C. §402(a)(5). The surviving spouse of an employee may also roll over a lump sum distribution into an individual retirement account. Since this privilege is available only to a surviving spouse and not to a trust or to other beneficiaries, consideration should be given to having the estate owner designate his spouse as beneficiary of the qualified retirement plan death benefit. See I.R.C. §§402(a)(7) and 408(d)(3). Where there is no "rollover," that portion of the lump sum distribution that is attributable to the employee's contributions is not taxed. The portion that is allocable to employer contributions made prior to 1974 is treated as long-term capital gain. I.R.C. §402(a)(2). The balance of the distribution is treated as ordinary income, but is subject to a special 10-year averaging election. I.R.C. §402(e).

The distribution with respect to which the 10-year averaging election is made is taxed in what is usually a favorable way. In general terms, 50 per cent of the first $20,000 of the distribution (i.e., up to $10,000), reduced, however, by 20 per cent of the amount by which the distribution exceeds $20,000, is excluded. The balance is taxed by computing a tax, using the rates for single taxpayers and as if the employee had no other income, on one-tenth of the distribution. This tax is then multiplied by 10 and the total is added to the tax on the employee's other income for the year. I.R.C. §402(e). This averaging method could be very advantageous, because the effective rate on the distribution may often be much lower than the employee's top tax bracket.

Where the employee would rather not have the pre-1974 portion of the lump sum distribution taxed as a long-term capital gain, he may elect to treat the entire amount as ordinary income, subject to the special 10-year averaging election. I.R.C. §402(e)(4)(L). It is sometimes advantageous to elect the 10-year averaging method rather than capital gain treatment, because capital gain is a tax preference item, subject to the alternative minimum tax. I.R.C. §56(a).

Any payments made after the decedent's death, whether received as an annuity or as a lump sum, are treated as income in respect of a decedent and, as such, are taxed to the employee's beneficiary in the same manner that they would have been taxed to the employee if he had lived to receive the payments. For a discussion of income with respect to a decedent items, see §2.50. As an income with respect to a decedent item, the amount of a death benefit distribution subject to the special 10-year averaging election must first be reduced by the estate tax deduction attributable to the distribution. I.R.C. §691(c)(5). For a discussion of the estate tax deduction attributable to an income in respect of a decedent item, see §2.50. To the extent that the $5,000 employee's death benefit exclusion is not otherwise used, it is available, at least with respect to a lump sum distribution under the qualified retirement plan received after the employee's death. See §13.22, for a discussion of the $5,000 exclusion.

§13.17   ii.   Estate Tax

Any payments received from a qualified retirement plan after the employee's death, to the extent attributable to the employer's contributions, are generally excluded from the employee's gross estate. I.R.C. §2039(c).

There are, however, two major exceptions to the exclusionary rule. First, the exclusion is specifically denied if the recipient receives a lump sum distribution and computes the income tax thereon by using 10-year averaging or capital gain treatment. I.R.C. §§2039(c) and (e). See §13.16 for a description of 10-year averaging and capital gain treatment. Where the recipient is the employee's spouse, there will be no estate tax payable even if 10-year averaging or capital gain treatment is elected because the distribution will qualify for the marital deduction. I.R.C. §2056(a). The second exception is that the payments may not be made to or for the benefit of the employee's estate. Hence, they should be made payable to a named beneficiary rather than to the decedent's probate estate. Where a trust is the beneficiary, the estate tax exclusion will not be denied unless the proceeds are required to be used by the trustee to pay death taxes, debts or other expenses. Rev. Rul. 77-157, 1977-1 C.B. 279. However, the trustee, may be given discretionary authority to loan money to or purchase assets from the probate estate.

In the past where the employee's vested benefit in a qualified retirement plan was community property, one-half of the amount of such benefit was included in the gross estate of the employee's spouse where such spouse died first. However, in 1972, the estate tax exclusion was amended to insure that the portion of the predeceased's spouse's share, attributable to the employer's contributions, was excluded from the gross estate. I.R.C. §2039(d).

§13.18   iii.   Gift Tax

The gift of an employee's interest in a qualified retirement plan, to the extent that such interest is attributable to the employer's contributions, is excluded from gift tax. I.R.C. §§2517(a) and (b). Whether such a gift may, as a practical matter, be made by the employee in many cases is doubtful. Commonly, a retirement plan will contain a spendthrift provision preventing a participant from transferring his interest.

Prior to the enactment of the Tax Reform Act of 1976, a somewhat different gift tax problem was present where the employee's interest in a qualified plan was community property. Where the employee predeceased his spouse and the entire death proceeds were payable to a third party, for example, a child, the surviving spouse was deemed to have made a gift of his or her community property interest in the plan at the time of the employee's death. See Rev. Rul. 75-240, 1975-1 C.B. 315. I.R.C. §2517(c) now excludes the value of the nonemployee spouse's community interest in the plan from gift taxation, to the extent attributable to contributions by the employer. As a result, the employee, with the consent of his spouse, can now designate the children, or a trust for their benefit, as the beneficiary of both halves of the community property interest in the plan death benefit. Such benefit will not be subject to estate tax on the employee's death (see §13.17) and also will not be included in or added back to the surviving spouse's taxable estate.

B.   Individual Plans

§13.19   1.   Self-Employed Plans

For many years, the tax benefits of qualified retirement plans were available only to common law employees. Self-employed persons, such as sole proprietors and partners, even those whose income was attributable to personal services, were not eligible. However, self-employment retirement plans, sometimes called "HR-10" plans or "Keogh" plans, have been permitted since 1963. With many technical exceptions, such a plan, at least from an estate planning point of view, is generally similar to a corporate plan. The major difference is that generally a maximum of only $15,000 or 15 per cent of earned income, whichever is the lesser, of the annual contribution made with respect to an owner-employee is deductible. I.R.C §404(e)(1). Where the HR-10 plan, however, is a defined benefit plan, rather than a defined contribution plan, greater amounts may be contributed and deducted. See I.R.C. §401(j)(6). An owner-employee is defined as a sole proprietor or a partner who owns more than 10 per cent of the capital or profit interest in the partnership. I.R.C. §401(c)(3).

Prior to 1977, another disadvantage of a self-employed plan, as compared to a corporate plan, was that death benefits were not excluded from the gross estate. The Tax Reform Act of 1976 eliminated this disadvantage and death benefits are now generally excludable on the same basis as they are under corporate plans. I.R.C. §2039(e).

§13.20   2.   Individual Retirement Plans

The Economic Recovery Tax Act of 1981 substantially liberalized the rules applicable to the establishment of and contributions to an individual retirement account, commonly called an "IRA." Whether or not an employee is covered by another corporate or self-employed plan, he may create an IRA. Annual contributions to the IRA will be deductible, for income tax purposes, to the extent of the lesser of $2,000 or 100 per cent of his earned income for the year. Alternatively, an employee may now make voluntary tax deductible contributions to his qualified employer plan (see §13.8), provided the total amount contributed to both the IRA and the qualified employer plan does not exceed the lesser of $2,000 or 100 per cent of earned income limit.

The "spousal IRA" provisions introduced by the Tax Reform Act of 1976 have been expanded to allow greater contributions to be made for the benefit of a nonworking spouse. When such contributions are made, the maximum deduction allowable on the couple's joint return for contributions to the working spouse's and the spousal IRA is limited to the lesser of $2,250 or 100 per cent of the compensation includable in the working spouse's income. I.R.C. §219(c).

Except for the limitation on contributions to an IRA plan *and* the fact that the 10-year averaging election (see §13.16) is not available to distributions, the income tax benefits of such a plan are generally similar to a self-employed plan. (See §13.19). For the IRA to be excluded from the decedent's gross estate, the proceeds may not be payable in a lump sum, but must be payable as an annuity which lasts for a period of at least 36 months from the decedent's death.

§13.21   C.   Estate Planning Considerations

The following considerations should be taken into account in order to properly coordinate the estate owner's interest in a qualified retirement plan with his estate plan:

1.   Consider maximizing the death benefit. Where the employee has a large estate and does not need all of his retirement income for his support, he should consider having the post-retirement payments stretched out over as long a period as possible. The advantage is that any portion of the retirement benefit remaining unpaid on his death will be excludable from the gross estate under I.R.C. §2039(c). However, the exclusion will not be allowed if the recipient of the death benefit elects 10-year averaging or capital gains treatment (see §13.17).

   On the other hand from an income tax point of view, there is an advantage in receiving a lump sum payment, even though such payment will be includable in the employee's estate. The lump sum payment qualifies for 10-year averaging and under certain circumstances for long-term capital gain. (See §13.16). Hence, the beneficiary should carefully weigh the competing factors before deciding on the manner in which to receive his retirement benefits.

2.   Consider whether or not to designate a charity as the recipient of the death benefit. The death benefit, unless 10-year averaging or capital gain treatment is elected, is excludable from the gross estate. Hence from an estate tax point of view, it is inadvisable, in that instance, to make a charity the death beneficiary, because the charitable deduction will be wasted. However, it may nevertheless be advisable to so designate the charity in order to avoid income tax on the payments. The estate owner may then leave other assets not subject to income tax to noncharitable beneficiaries.

3.   To the extent that the death benefits are not to be paid to a charity, consider having payment divided among as many recipients as possible if 10-year averaging is not elected. The death benefits will be taxed as income in respect of a decedent (see §2.50). Therefore, by having the payments go to as many taxpayers as possible, the income tax bracket may be lowered. Moreover, if any one of the employee's beneficiaries is in a low income tax bracket, it may be advisable to have the entire death benefit paid to such person, and the nonincome with respect to decedent items paid to higher bracket recipients.

4.   Do not require that a death benefit, which is otherwise excludable from the employee's gross estate, be used to pay the employee's debts, taxes or expenses. If a death benefit is required to be used for such a purpose, it will be taxable in the employee's estate. (See §13.17.)

5.   Consider whether to make the death benefit payable to the employee's spouse. Such a designation should be avoided from an estate tax point of view because there is no need to have it paid to the spouse to escape

estate tax on the employee's death. Unless 10-year averaging or capital gain treatment is elected, it is already excluded from the gross estate (see §13.17). Payment to the spouse will, however, increase the spouse's estate. Nevertheless, there are two possible reasons for designating the spouse as the beneficiary.

Where a lump sum payment is made to a surviving spouse, the spouse may elect to "roll over" the distribution into an individual retirement account and thereby entirely exclude the payment from income in the year of receipt. See §13.16. When the surviving spouse dies, the proceeds payable from the individual retirement account will be included, however, in the spouse's taxable estate. Reg. §20.2039-4(c). On the other hand, where a bypass trust (see Chapter 5) is named as the beneficiary, the proceeds will not be included in the estate of the surviving spouse. It is difficult to predict in advance whether the income tax benefit of the "rollover" or the estate tax exclusion on the surviving spouse's death would be preferable. It may be possible, however, to word the beneficiary designation so that this decision can be deferred. The surviving spouse can be named as the beneficiary with the proviso that if such spouse disclaims the proceeds, they will pass into the bypass trust (see §5.2). See Letter Rul. 8012129. In that way the decision can be made later by the surviving spouse who, having access to more current facts, will be better equipped to make a wiser choice.

Additionally, if 10-year averaging or capital gain treatment is elected for income tax purposes, the death benefit will be taxable for estate tax purposes. In those instances, estate taxability can be avoided only if the benefit is payable to the spouse or to a marital deduction trust. Again, the best plan may be to make the death benefit payable to the spouse, but to leave open the opportunity of making a disclaimer.

When the death benefit is community property and the surviving spouse does not need her one-half of the death benefit, she should consider permitting her one-half to be paid (along with the decedent's one-half) to a third-party beneficiary. As previously indicated, the consent of the surviving spouse to such designation will not constitute a taxable gift and the benefit will also escape estate taxation on the surviving spouse's death. (See §13.18)

6. Always consider instituting a qualified retirement plan where the estate owner-employee is a major stockholder and will be a major participant in the plan. The institution of the plan will tend to decrease the estate owner's taxable estate from what it would have been for the following reasons. First, if the contribution paid into the plan would otherwise have been paid to the owner in the form of additional compensation, such compensation, after the payment of the income tax thereon, would have increased the owner's estate. Second, to the extent the contribution would not have been paid to the owner in the form of additional compensation, but would have been retained by the corporation, it would have increased the value of the corporation and, thereby, the estate tax due

on the owner's death. Third, the retirement plan, by enabling the stockholder to have sufficient funds for his retirement, will facilitate his making gifts of an interest in his business or of other assets during his lifetime. These gifts, if properly made, will be helpful in reducing estate taxes. Despite the unification of estate and gift taxes mandated by the Tax Reform Act of 1976, the estate may still be reduced by the $10,000 annual exclusion portion of each gift (see §8.3), the future appreciation on the gifted asset (see §8.4) and the amount of the gift tax paid on the gift. (See §8.5.) If not for the qualified retirement plan, the estate owner would have to be more concerned about his retirement and may not wish to make gifts.

§13.22 VI. $5,000 Death Benefit Exclusion

The Internal Revenue Code permits the first $5,000 paid by an employer to an employee's beneficiary or his estate by reason of his death to be excluded from gross income. I.R.C. §101(b). However, except for lump sum distributions under qualified retirement plans, this exclusion is generally not available where the employee had, immediately before his death, a nonforfeitable right to receive the amounts while living. I.R.C. §101(b)(2)(B). Hence where the employee has a deferred compensation contract providing for payments during his lifetime, and any remaining balance to be paid on or after his death, the $5,000 exclusion will not be allowed. However, if there were no lifetime payments required under the contract, the exclusion would be available.

There is only one $5,000 exclusion available for each employee, regardless of the number of payments made, the number of employers or the number of beneficiaries. See Reg. §1.101-2(a)(3). Accordingly, if a total of $10,000 is paid to four beneficiaries, each beneficiary may exclude only $1,250 ($5,000 divided by 4).

The $5,000 death benefit is an income tax fringe benefit which an employee stockholder should not overlook. Unless the exclusion will be used in some other way, he should consider entering into a contract with his corporation requiring a $5,000 payment to his beneficiary upon his death. For a discussion of whether such payment will be included in his gross estate, see §12.47.

VII. Recommended Reading

Abdalla, "Income Tax Analysis of Death Benefit Distributions" 115 *Trusts and Estates* 152 (1976)

Baker and Rothman, "Corporate and Non-Corporate Qualified Plans: A Comparison after ERISA" 114 *Trusts and Estates* 462 (1975)

Bornstein, "Estate Planning with ESOPS" 3 *Estate Planning* 138 (1975)

Kopple and Veenhuis, "Taxation of Lump-Sum Distributions" 42 *Journal of Taxation* 2 (1975)

Kopple, "Tax Considerations in Pension and Profit Sharing Trust Investments" 111 *Trusts and Estates* 686 (1972)

Knight, "ESOPS Offer Employee Benefits, Corporation Financing and Control, Estate Planning" 43 *Journal of Taxation* 258 (1975)

Langstroot, "Medical Reimbursement Plans — Changes for the 1980's" 58 *Taxes* 276 (1980)

Neal, "An Analysis of Newly Established Vesting Requirements under Pension Reform" 41 *Journal of Taxation* 258 (1974)

Reish, "Avoid Taxation of Pension Plan Death Benefits" 119 No 2 *Trusts and Estates* 53 (1980)

Roth, "The Individual Retirement Account: Clarification of Proposed Regulations" 114 *Trusts and Estates* 380 (1975)

Savage, "What Estate Planners Should Know about Direct and Indirect Effects of New Pension Reform Act" 2 *Estate Planning* 9 (1974)

Slavitt, "Problems in Distributions from Qualified Plans" 111 *Trusts and Estates* 276 (1972)

Solomon, "Estate Taxes and the Employee Benefit Plan" 38 *NYU Inst on Fed Tax* 37-1 (1980)

Thies, "New Participation and Eligibility Tests Under the Pension Reform Legislation" 41 *Journal of Taxation* 268 (1974)

Wilf, "Limitations on Benefits and Contributions for Corporate Employees Under New Pension Law" 41 *Journal of Taxation* 280 (1974)

Winkelman and Callery, "Participation, Coverage and Vesting Under the Pension Reform Act" 114 *Trusts and Estates* 4 (1975)

Zelinsky, "Insurance, Pensions and the Internal Revenue Code" 33 *The Tax Lawyer* 427 (1980)

"How to Set up a Successful Medical Reimbursement Plan" *Tax Ideas* Par 27,506 (Prentice-Hall)

Making Gifts to Charity

14

§14.1   I.   Introduction

One may wish to make contributions to charity, either lifetime gifts or those which take effect upon death. It is also possible to make "split interest" charitable gifts so that not only the charity, but also the donor or other individuals, will receive a direct benefit from the contribution. (See §§14.22 to 14.35.)

In advising the estate owner, it is important first to ascertain his objectives toward charitable giving. His desire to make gifts to charity, apart from tax considerations, should be considered. Many persons are inclined to make contributions to charity as a way of fulfilling their obligations to society. If the estate owner has such a desire, the fact that the tax laws encourage such gifts should then be taken into account. To receive any tax benefit, the gift must be made to an organization which qualifies under the tax laws. See I.R.C. §§170(c), 2055(a) and 2522. The gift must be properly structured in order to maximize the tax advantages of charitable contributions.

The tax rules discussed in this chapter are technical and complex. They should, however, be understood by the estate planner in order to properly advise the estate owner.

§14.2 II. Income Tax Consequences of Outright Gifts

An outright gift to charity by the donor during his lifetime will normally result in an income tax deduction for the gift. The availability and the amount of such deduction will depend on various factors, such as the nature of the charity, the type of gift, the value and tax basis of the property given, the timing of the gift, and the amount contributed to charity by the donor in recent years.

A. Cash Gifts

§14.3 1. Maximum Income Tax Deduction—The Fifty Per Cent Rule

For cash gifts to "public" charities an individual may deduct up to 50 per cent of his contribution base, which is his adjusted gross income computed without regard to any net operating loss carryback. See I.R.C. §170(b)(1). Hence, if an individual has a contribution base of $100,000, he may give up to $50,000 to "public" charities and may deduct the full amount. If he gives more than $50,000, he may be entitled to a carryover into future years. (See §14.7.)

§14.4 a. Organizations That Qualify for the Fifty Per Cent Deduction

I.R.C. §§170(b)(1)(A)(i) through (viii) list the types of organizations which qualify for this maximum deduction. In general, the list includes public charities such as churches, hospitals, nonprofit schools and charities which receive substantial public support such as the Community Chest. Ordinarily contributions to private foundations are not eligible for the maximum deduction. (See §14.5.) However, several types of private foundations do qualify and, for the purpose of the maximum deduction, are treated as "public" charities. The major ones are private operating foundations and private distribution foundations.

A private operating foundation is a private foundation (see §14.5) which meets specific requirements. Basically, an operating foundation must be actively engaged in the activities which constitute its charitable purpose. See I.R.C. §4942(j)(3). Private foundations conducting research for charitable purposes, or operating a facility for public use, will generally qualify. Private foundations that only make grants to others do not qualify as operating foundations.

A private distributing foundation is a private foundation which distributes contributions it receives to "public" charities within two and one-half months after the close of the year in which the contributions were made. I.R.C. §170(b)(1)(D). Gifts to these foundations also qualify for the 50 per cent deduction. The rationale is that the private foundation is merely redistributing the gifts to one or more public charities or operating foundations by making these "qualifying distributions" for charitable purposes.

§14.5 b. Gifts to Private Foundations—The Twenty Per Cent Deduction Rule

All charitable organizations are private foundations unless they qualify as "public" charities under I.R.C. §170(b)(1)(A). (See §14.4.) Various statutory restrictions are imposed on private foundations, and tax advantages encourage gifts to public charities as opposed to private foundations. One such disincentive is that the ceiling on the deductibility of cash gifts to private foundations is only 20 per cent of the individual's contribution base. I.R.C. §170(b)(1)(B). See §14.3 for the definition of contribution base.

§14.6 c. Interplay of the Fifty Per Cent and Twenty Per Cent Rules

In applying the percentage limitations, an individual's total charitable deduction in any year, for gifts to both "public" charities and private foundations, may not exceed 50 per cent of his contribution base. Gifts made to "public" charities are applied first, and if these contributions reach the 50 per cent limit, no further deduction is allowed for contributions to private foundations. If gifts to "public" charities total less than 50 per cent of the taxpayer's contribution base, then contributions to private foundations (up to the 20 per cent limit) may be used to make up the 50 per cent maximum total deduction allowed. I.R.C. §170(b)(1)(B). For example, if A has a contribution base of $100,000 and makes cash gifts of $40,000 to "public" charities and $15,000 to a private foundation, he may deduct the $40,000 contribution to the "public" charities and $10,000 of the gift to the private foundation, or a total of $50,000.

§14.7 2. Carryover of Excess Contributions

In the case of "public" charities, cash contributions in excess of the maximum deductible amount of the contribution base (50 per cent) may be carried forward and deducted over the five years following the contribution. I.R.C. §170(d). However, the total of contributions made in each year and the contributions carried over may not exceed the 50 per cent maximum allowed in any one year. I.R.C. §170(d)(1)(A). By way of example, assume that a taxpayer has a contribution base of $60,000 and contributes $40,000 in cash to a "public" charity. The maximum amount deductible is $30,000, but he may carry over the $10,000 difference and deduct it over the succeeding five years. If, in the succeeding year, his contribution base remains the same and he contributes $25,000 in cash to a "public" charity, he may use $5,000 of the $10,000 carryover to reach his 50 per cent limit. He can carry the remaining $5,000 into the next succeeding year.

Contributions to private foundations which exceed 20 per cent of the taxpayer's contribution base may not be carried over. The charitable deduction is lost at the time these contributions exceed the maximum amount deductible.

§14.8 B. Gifts of Noncash Property

With one major exception, a contribution of assets other than cash is deductible to the extent of their fair market value on the date of the gift on the same basis as are cash gifts. (See §§14.4 to 14.7.) The major exception is a gift of appreciated assets, i.e., those which have a fair market value in excess of their income tax basis. Differing income tax rules apply, depending upon whether the appreciated asset is ordinary income property (see §14.9) or capital gain property (see §14.10).

§14.9 1. Ordinary Income Property

"Ordinary income property" is any property which if sold would produce ordinary income or short-term capital gain. If such assets are contributed to a charitable organization, the deduction is limited to the tax basis of the property. I.R.C. §170(e). Thus, by reducing the amount of the charitable contribution by the potential income the property would produce if sold, no deduction is allowed for the amount of the appreciation.

The above rule may be illustrated by an example. The taxpayer contributes real estate which he has held for four months. The property has an income tax basis of $15,000 and a fair market value of $20,000 on the date of contribution. The $20,000 contribution is reduced by the $5,000 short-term capital gain which would have been realized if the property had been sold. Thus, he may only deduct his tax basis, $15,000.

The percentage limitations and carryover rules for gifts of ordinary income property are the same as those for cash gifts. (See §§14.4 to 14.7.) In short, there is a 50 per cent ceiling for gifts to "public" charities with a five-year carryover for the excess, and a 20 per cent limit on gifts to private foundations with no carryover allowed.

§14.10 2. Capital Gain Property

"Capital gain property," for purposes of this discussion, is property which if sold would give rise to long-term capital gain. Long-term capital gain arises on the sale or exchange of a capital asset held for more than one year. The amount of the charitable deduction allowed will depend on the nature of the charitable organization and, with respect to tangible personal property, the anticipated use of the property.

§14.11   a.   Gifts to Private Foundations

If capital gain property is given to a private foundation (see §14.5), the amount deductible is equal to the fair market value of the property reduced by 40 per cent of the appreciation. For example, assume that a taxpayer contributes real estate he has held for more than one year to a private foundation. The property cost $10,000 and is worth $26,000 when given to charity. The amount deductible is $19,600.

The contribution base ceiling on such gifts of appreciated property is the same as for cash gifts to private foundations. That limit is the lesser of (1) 20 per cent of the contribution base, or (2) the excess up to 50 per cent of the contribution base over the amount of charitable contributions qualifying for the 50 per cent deduction limitation. (See §§14.5 and 14.6.)

§14.12   b.   Gifts to "Public" Charities

If capital gain property is gifted to a "public" charity, that is, one which qualifies for the 50 per cent maximum deduction (see §14.4), the general rule is that such contribution is deductible to the full extent of its fair market value on the date of the gift. See §14.14, however, for an exception relating to the gift of tangible personal property which is unrelated to the charity's functions. Where the full fair market value is deducted, however, the contribution to the "public" charity is subject to a reduced deduction ceiling of 30 per cent of adjusted gross income rather than the 50 per cent ceiling applicable to cash gifts to "public" charities. I.R.C. §170(b)(1)(D). However, a special election, discussed in §14.13, is available.

The general rule described in this section may be illustrated by an example. Assume A has $60,000 of adjusted gross income (i.e., his contribution base). He contributes to a "public" charity capital gain securities worth $30,000 with an income tax basis of $10,000. The amount of the deduction will be $18,000 (30 per cent of $60,000), with a carryover of $12,000 ($30,000 minus $18,000) into the next succeeding five years. (See §14.7.)

§14.13   i.   Special Election Available

A special election is available for gifts to "public" charities of capital gain property (except tangible personal property not related to the purpose of the exemption). (See §14.14.) If the taxpayer makes the election, the amount deductible is computed as though the gift were to a private foundation (i.e., the fair market value of the property reduced by 40 per cent of the appreciation, see §14.11), but the maximum annual deduction is increased from 30 per cent to 50 per cent of the contribution base. I.R.C. §170(b)(1)(D)(iii). In effect, the election increases the amount of the current deduction, but decreases the amount which may eventually be deducted. An example is as follows: A taxpayer has an adjusted gross income of $60,000 and wishes to contribute capital gain property to a "public" charity. The property cost $20,000 and is now worth $50,000. Without the election, the deductions will total $50,000 (i.e., the fair market value), of which $18,000 (30 per cent of $60,000) will be deductible in the current year, and $32,000 as a carryover into the succeeding five years. (See §14.7.) If he makes the election, he can deduct a total of $38,000 ($50,000 minus 40 per cent of $30,000) of which $30,000 (50 per cent of $60,000) is deductible in the current year, with a carryover of $8,000.

§14.14   ii.   Gifts of Tangible Personal Property Unrelated to the Charity's Functions

If the "public" charity does not, and cannot reasonably be expected to, use a gift of tangible personal property in a manner related to its functions and activities, the deduction is reduced by 40 per cent of the capital gain which would have arisen if the property had been sold. I.R.C. §170(e)(1)(B)(i). Thus, the taxpayer may only deduct the fair market value of the property reduced by 40 per cent of the appreciation. The percentage limits on deducting such gifts are the same as those for cash gifts to "public" charities, namely 50 per cent of the donor's contribution base. (See §14.3.) As an example, a taxpayer contributes a capital gain painting to a hospital. The painting cost $1,000 and is worth $2,000 when donated. The hospital sells the painting and uses the proceeds to purchase medical supplies. The amount deductible is $1,600 ($2,-000 minus 40 per cent of $1,000).

On the other hand, if the actual or anticipated use of the property by the charity is related to its tax-exempt functions, the general rules governing the deductibility of all other appreciated property, that is, real estate and intangible personal property, apply.

Therefore, if we assume the same facts as in the above example, except that the donee organization is an art museum rather than a hospital, the donor may deduct $2,000, the full value of the painting.

§14.15   3.   Carryover of Excess Contributions of Appreciated Assets

As with cash gifts to private foundations, gifts of appreciated property to private foundations in excess of the maximum amount deductible may not be carried over into succeeding years. (See §14.7.)

Any excess capital gain property contributed to a "public" charity may be carried over as a contribution into the next five years. (See §14.7.) However, the carryover will be subject to the 30 per cent ceiling in each of the succeeding five years (see §14.12) unless the special election is made. Under this election the taxpayer may apply the 50 per cent ceiling, but his total deduction will be reduced by 40 per cent of the appreciation on the property, thereby decreasing the amount left to be carried over. (See §14.13.)

§14.16 4. Tax Advantage of Gifts of Appreciated Capital Gain Property

Contributions of appreciated long-term capital gain property may result in substantial tax savings when compared to gifts of cash or other assets. With the exception of "unrelated use" tangible personal property (discussed in §14.14), the donor may deduct the full market value of the property (up to the maximum limits of adjusted gross income) given to a "public" charity and yet pay no capital gain tax on the appreciation. A gift of the appreciated property, as is illustrated in the following example, may therefore be made at a lower cost than if the property were sold and the cash proceeds contributed. Assume that A is in a 50 per cent tax bracket. He owns capital gain securities which cost $1,000 and now have a value of $10,000. A contribution of the securities to a "public" charity will result in a $10,000 deduction for income tax purposes (subject to the special election discussed in §14.13) and, hence, a tax savings of $5,000, or a net after-tax cost of $5,000 ($10,000 [value of securities] minus $5,000 [tax savings]). On the other hand, if A desires to contribute cash and thereby sells the securities to raise such cash or to replenish cash which he otherwise uses, his net after-tax cost of the charitable contribution will be greater. If he sells the securities for $10,000, he will have to pay a capital gains tax of $1,800 so that his net after-tax cost will be $6,800 ($10,000 [value of securities] plus $1,800 [capital gains tax] minus $5,000 [tax savings]).

§14.17 5. Bargain Sales of Appreciated Capital Gain Property to Charity

The estate owner may wish to consider selling an appreciated capital gain asset to a "public" charity at less than its fair market value as an alternative to an outright gift of the asset. This will enable him to recoup a portion of the asset's value and at the same time deduct the excess of the fair market value over the selling price as a charitable contribution. Such a sale should ordinarily not be made to a private foundation because it may be a disqualifying transaction which will result in the imposition of a penalty on the donor. See I.R.C. §4941.

Before proceeding with a sale of an appreciated capital gain asset to charity, consideration should be given to the amount of gain that will be taxable. In computing such gain, the basis of the property must be proportionately allocated between the portion of the property sold and the portion given away in order to determine the gain on the sale. I.R.C. §1011(b). The result could be a realization of gain even though the selling price does not exceed the total basis of the assets. This may be illustrated by an example. A taxpayer owns a capital gain asset with a basis of $10,000, which is now worth $40,000. He wishes to contribute to a "public" charity, but would like to recover his initial investment in the asset, so he sells it to the charity for his cost of $10,000. Twenty-five per cent ($10,000/$40,000) of his $10,000 basis must be allocated to the portion sold, and the remaining 75 per cent allocated to the portion which is given away. Thus, he has a $7,500 ($10,000 minus $2,500) capital gain on the sale. In addition, he has a $30,000 charitable deduction.

Sometimes an apparent contribution of an asset results in a taxable sale. This result arises where the contributed property is encumbered. The amount of the liability is taxed as if it were the proceeds of a sale. Reg. §1.1011-2(b)(3); *Crane v Commr* 331 US 1, 67 SCt 1047, 91 LE 1301 (1947). This rule applies to a gift of encumbered property regardless of whether or not the charity assumes the liability. (Reg. §1.1011-2(b)(3) and whether or not the liability is with or without recourse. *Guest v Commr* 77 TC 9 (1981). As in the example set forth in the preceding paragraph, only a proportionate part of the basis of the property may be subtracted from such "sales proceeds" in computing the amount of gain. See Rev. Rul. 81-163, 1981-1 C.B. 433.

§14.18   C.   Gifts of Life Insurance

A charitable income tax deduction is frequently available for the contribution of a life insurance policy to charity. Normally, the value of the policy at the date of the gift constitutes the amount of the deduction. However, when the value of the policy exceeds the premiums and other amounts paid therefor, the policy may constitute ordinary income property (see §14.9) or capital gain property (see §14.10), and the amount of the deduction will be limited subject to the rules governing the contribution of such assets.

For a discussion of the principles used in valuing a life insurance policy while the insured is alive, see §10.18. Where the donor continues to pay the premiums after the gift is made, the amount of the premium payments will also constitute charitable deductions.

III.   Estate and Gift Tax Consequences of Outright Gifts

A.   Estate Tax

§14.19   1.   Deductibility of Outright Gifts to Charity

Outright bequests to those charitable organizations which are exempt under the estate tax law are deductible from the gross estate in computing the net estate. I.R.C. §2055(a). Not only are bequests made by the testator deductible, but also transfers to the charity resulting from an irrevocable disclaimer on the part of the otherwise named beneficiary I.R.C. §2055(a). If the estate owner wants to have a family member decide after the estate owner's death whether a bequest should go to charity, he can provide for a gift to the family member with the stipulation that if that person disclaims the gift it will go to the charity.

The amount of the estate tax deduction to be taken is the fair market value of the property transferred to the charity and available for its use. This is less restrictive than the income tax rule applicable to lifetime gifts, since there is no percentage ceiling on the allowable deduction. However, the charitable deduction is limited to the value of the transferred property which is includable in the donor's gross estate. I.R.C. §2055(d).

§14.20 2. Lifetime Charitable Gifts Compared to Bequests

It is much more advantageous from a tax point of view for the estate owner to make a charitable gift during his lifetime rather than upon his death. Lifetime gifts to charity provide an income tax deduction and the amount given is not taxed as part of his estate. The income tax deduction is lost, however, if the contribution takes place on death. The estate owner, however, for many nontax reasons, may not be willing to part with cash or other assets to make the contribution during his lifetime.

§14.21 B. Gift Tax

There is an unlimited deduction for gifts made to exempt charities. I.R.C. §2522. In effect, there is no gift tax on charitable transfers, but if the charitable gift exceeds the annual gift tax exclusion, a gift tax return is required to be filed. I.R.C. §6019.

IV. Gifts of Split Interests in Trust

§14.22 A. Introduction

A split interest trust is one that includes both charitable and noncharitable beneficial interests. It is an excellent estate planning tool for the estate owner who wishes to retain an interest in the trust assets for himself or his family, but desires a tax deduction for the value of the charitable interest. For a full discussion of the planning advantages, see §14.33

If the charitable interest is the remainder interest, the trust is called a "charitable remainder trust," which is discussed in §§14.23 to 14.33. If the charitable interest is the income interest, the trust is called a "charitable income trust." (See §14.34.) In most instances, the charitable deduction for split interests will not be allowed unless the gift is to a trust which qualifies as an annuity trust, a unitrust or a pooled income fund. See Cohan, Brown, Carr, Cornfeld, Hemmerling and Weinstock, "Accumulation Trusts and Charitable Remainder Trusts" 23 *Univ of So Cal Tax Inst* 501, 548-559 (1971).[1] See, however, §14.31

---

[1] Portions of the material in §§14.23 to 14.36 are taken from the cited article (of which the author of this book is a co-author) with the permission of Matthew Bender & Company, Inc., the copyright holder.

for a discussion of the estate and gift tax consequences if the *spouse* receives the income for life with the remainder to charity and the trust does not qualify as an annuity or unitrust. Moreover, the remainder interest in a personal residence or a farm, in which the grantor retains a legal life estate, may be transferred to a charity. A charitable deduction will be allowed for a transfer of these assets without the transfer qualifying as an annuity trust, unitrust or pooled income fund. I.R.C. §170(f)(3)(B).

B. Charitable Remainder Trusts

§14.23 1. Annuity Trust and Unitrust

In order for the charitable remainder trust to qualify as an annuity trust or a unitrust, the requirements of I.R.C. §664 and the detailed regulations thereunder must be strictly complied with. Sample provisions that meet these requirements and can be included in the trust instrument are contained in Revenue Ruling 72-395, 1972-2 C.B. 340. See also Rev. Rul. 80-123, 1980-1 C.B. 205. The most important of these requirements are discussed in §§14.24 to 14.29.

If the trust qualifies as an annuity trust or a unitrust, the income tax charitable deduction will be equal to the fair market value of the remainder interest in the assets at the time of their transfer to the trust, assuming the transfer is made during the donor's lifetime. See I.R.C. §170(f)(2)(A). It will give rise to an estate tax charitable deduction, if the transfer is made upon the donor's death (I.R.C. §2055(e)(2)(A)). See §§14.24 and 14.25 for the method to be used in valuing the remainder interest. If the donor, as a result of a lifetime transfer, names anyone other than himself or his spouse as an income beneficiary, the value of such income interest will be subject to gift tax, but the remainder interest will not.

§14.24 a. Annuity Trust

An annuity trust is one which specifies that a fixed dollar annuity is to be paid at least annually to the income beneficiary. The fixed sum must be an amount equal to at least 5 per cent of the initial net fair market value of all property placed in the trust. I.R.C. §664(d)(1)(A). These requirements may be illustrated by an example. The estate owner creates a trust to which he transfers an asset worth $100,000. The trust provides that he is to receive $5,000 per year during his lifetime. Upon the estate owner's death the remainder is to go to an exempt charity.

The fair market value of the remainder interest is determined actuarially by reference to the annuity tables set forth in §20.2031-10 of the Regulations. See Appendix, Table VIII. Assume that in the above example the estate owner is a male, age 50. The annuity factor at his age is 11.3329. The present value of the yearly payout is $56,665 ($5,000 times 11.3329). The remainder interest is therefore worth $43,335 ($100,000 minus $56,665), which amount is deductible for tax purposes. If the estate owner wishes to receive a greater payout than 5 per cent, the value of the remainder interest and, therefore, the charitable deduction, will be less than the amount based on a 5 per cent payout.

If the initial net fair market value is underestimated in good faith, the trust will nevertheless be considered to meet the minimum payout requirement, provided the grantor or his representative consents to accept an amount equal to 20 times the annuity as the fair market value for purposes of the appropriate charitable contribution deduction. Reg. §1.664(a)(2).

The Regulations also provide that the stated dollar amount payable by the annuity trust may be expressed alternatively as a percentage of the initial net fair market value of the property as finally determined for federal tax purposes. However, this alternate may be used only if the governing instrument specifically provides that in case the initial net fair market value is incorrectly determined in good faith, appropriate additional payments to the beneficiary or repayments to the trustee will be made when the correct value is determined. Reg. §1.664-2(a)(1)(iii). If the beneficiary is required to repay because of an overvaluation, he may either deduct the payment to the extent it was previously included in his income or treat it as a claim of right adjustment under I.R.C. §1341. Reg. §1.664-1(d)(4)(ii).

§14.25   b.   Unitrust

The basic form of unitrust is one where the "income" beneficiary is entitled to an annual payment based upon a fixed percentage of the fair market value of the trust assets, valued annually. The fixed percentage must be a minimum of 5 per cent. I.R.C. §664(d)(2). These requirements may be illustrated by an example. Assume the estate owner creates a trust to which he contributes $100,000. The trust provides that he is to receive an amount each year equal to 5 per cent of the net fair market value of the assets, valued annually on the last day of each year, at which time the payment is to be made. Upon the estate owner's death the remainder is to go to an exempt charity.

There is also an alternate type of unitrust permitted by the tax law. Under this type the trustee is required to distribute to the income beneficiary only the actual income received if this amount is less than 5 per cent of the net fair market value of the assets, valued annually. I.R.C. §664(d)(3). The trust may, but is not required to, provide that deficiencies in income, where the trust income is less than the stated amount payable to the income beneficiary, may be made up in later years to the extent the trust income exceeds the amount otherwise payable to the income beneficiary for that year. Rev. Rul. 72-395, 1972-2 C.B. 340 (§7.01). The determination of which items are trust income shall be determined under the terms of the governing instrument and applicable state law. See I.R.C. §643(b).

Under both types of unitrust, the trust is required to provide that, if the net fair market value is incorrectly determined, a deficiency in the unitrust payment resulting from an undervaluation should be paid to the beneficiary and an overpayment resulting from an overvaluation should be repaid to the trustee. Reg. §1.664-3(a)(1)(iii).

The rules for calculating the fair market value of the remainder interest in a unitrust for charitable deduction purposes are set forth in §1.664-4 of the Regulations. If in the above example the estate owner is a male, age 50, the value of the remainder interest for tax deduction purposes under either type of unitrust is $35,929.

Despite the fact that the charitable deduction, at least under the above example, is less than it would be where an annuity trust is used (see §14.24), it may nevertheless be more advantageous to use a unitrust rather than an annuity trust. In times of inflation the fair market value and thereby the payout to the noncharitable beneficiary will correspondingly increase. However, if an annuity trust is used the payout will never increase since it is a percentage of the initial fair market value of the trust assets.

§14.26   c.   Rights to Distributions

Under either an annuity trust or a unitrust the trustee must not be given any power whatsoever to make distributions in excess of the stated annuity or unitrust amounts. I.R.C. §§664(d)(1)(B) and 664(d)(2)(B). This absolute prohibition prevents a charitable remainder trust from providing for an increase in the stated amounts in the event of the life income beneficiary's emergency or other needs.

Upon the termination of the life interest under either an annuity trust or a unitrust, the entire charitable remainder must go to an exempt charitable organization. I.R.C. §§664(d)(1)(C) and 664(d)(2)(C). Accordingly, if the trust provides, for example, that the remainder is to be divided equally between the grantor's son and a charitable organization, no charitable deduction will be allowed because the entire remainder does not go to charity. If the donor's intention is to leave a portion of the remainder interest to a family member or other individual, he should create two separate trusts, with the remainder interest in one going exclusively to charity.

In order to ensure that the remainder interest, in fact, goes to a charity which is exempt, not only at the time the trust is created, but also at the time of the distribution to it, a necessary drafting precaution should be taken. The trust should provide that if, at the time the amounts are paid to the charity, it is not an organization exempt under I.R.C. §170(c), then such amount shall be transferred to an organization selected by the trustee which is exempt under such section. I.R.C. §§664(d)(1)(C) and 664(d)(2)(C).

§14.27   d.   Term of the Income Interest

The income interest of a charitable remainder trust may last for a period not to exceed 20 years, or for the life or lives of the income beneficiaries. Where the income interest is for the lives of several beneficiaries, all such beneficiaries must be living on the date of the creation of the trust. I.R.C. §§664(d)(1)(A) and 664(d)(2)(A). While members of a named class of persons may qualify as life beneficiaries, all of the persons in the class must be alive at the time that the trust is created in order to avoid the participation of unborn beneficiaries. Reg. §§1.664-2(a)(3) and 1.664-3(a)(3). Hence, in the case of a lifetime transfer to a charitable remainder trust, the trust should not provide that the annuity payments be made, for example, to the donor's children, without specifically naming them. He may have afterborn children. However, in the case of a trust taking effect on the donor's death, the trust may provide that an amount be paid to his children living at his death because all of such children will be living at that time.

§14.28   e.   Additional Contributions

In the case of an annuity trust, the trust instrument must specifically provide that after the initial transfer, no future contributions may be made to it. Reg. §1.664-2(b). Consequently, each time the estate owner wishes to make another contribution, he should create an additional trust. Additional contributions to a unitrust can only be permitted if the governing instrument contains certain specific provisions prescribing the time at which the additional property shall be valued and the manner for adjusting the percentage payout to take the additional contributions into account. Reg. §1.664-3(b).

§14.29   f.   Valuation of Assets

The determination of the initial net fair market value of assets transferred to an annuity trust and the annual valuation of the assets in a unitrust may present planning problems. The Regulations, as previously indicated (§§14.24 and 14.25), deal with the problem by requiring adjustments in the event of an incorrect valuation. The possibility of such adjustments can cause planning uncertainties. Therefore, a wise course of action is to select assets to contribute to a charitable remainder trust which can be easily and objectively valued, such as cash or marketable securities.

In satisfying the unitrust requirement that the assets be valued annually, consideration should be given to the selection of a valuation date. Valuation may be determined either on one specific date during the taxable year, or by taking the average valuations made on several dates during such year, as long as the same valuation date or dates and methods are consistently used each year. Reg. §1.664-3(a)(1)(iv). For ease of administration, it is usually advisable to set the valuation date or dates as close to the beginning of the taxable year as possible so that the required payments to be made during the course of the year will be definitely determined at the outset. Where the valuation date precedes the first payment date, the payout rate must first be adjusted under Table F of §1.664-4(b)(5) of the Regulations in order to arrive at the fair market value of the remainder interest for purposes of the charitable deduction. This table is constructed in such a way that the longer the time by which the valuation date precedes the payout date, the larger the amount of the charitable deduction.

§14.30   g.   Taxation of Charitable Remainder Trust Income

Neither an annuity trust nor a unitrust is subject to income tax unless such trust has unrelated business taxable income. I.R.C. §664(c). Because of its tax-exempt status, a charitable remainder trust is a valuable tool to achieve an increase in current income for the income beneficiary by the sale of appreciated assets without taxable gain. See §14.33 for a discussion of this point.

Insofar as the income beneficiary of a charitable remainder trust is concerned, the annuity or unitrust payments received by him shall be treated as having the following characteristics in his hands:

1. First, as distributions of ordinary income up to the amount of the trust's ordinary income for the year and undistributed income for prior years;
2. Second, as short-term capital gain to the extent of the sum of the trust's net short-term capital gain for the taxable year and its undistributed net short-term capital gains for prior years;
3. Third, as long-term capital gain to the extent of the sum of the trust's net long-term capital gain for the taxable year and its undistributed net long-term capital gains for prior years;
4. Fourth, as other income (e.g., tax-exempt income) to the extent of the trust's other income for those years;
5. Lastly, as nontaxable distributions of corpus. Reg. §1.664-1(d)(1)(i).

The above character of income rules may be illustrated by an example. Under an annuity trust the income beneficiary is to receive an annuity of $5,000 per year. The trust was created last year, at which time it had $500 of undistributed ordinary income and $1,000 of undistributed net long-term capital gain. In the current year the trust earned $2,000 of ordinary income, $1,000 of net long-term capital gain and $1,000 of tax-exempt income and paid $5,000 to the beneficiary. The beneficiary will have to report $2,500 of ordinary income and $2,000 of capital gain; $500 will be tax-free to him.

§14.31   h.   Estate and Gift Taxes Where Surviving Spouse Has Income Interest

If the estate owner creates a qualified annuity trust or unitrust and his spouse is the noncharitable beneficiary, there will be no estate or gift taxes to the estate owner. The income interest will qualify for the marital deduction (I.R.C. §§2056(b)(8) and 2523(g)) and the remainder interest will qualify for the charitable deduction.

Even if the trust does not qualify as an annuity trust or a unitrust, as would be the case if the spouse's income were not limited to the annuity or unitrust amount, but included *all* the income for her life, there will nonetheless be no adverse estate or gift tax consequences. The trust would qualify as a "QTIP" trust (see §§2.22 and 2.42), so if the grantor or his executor so elected, the entire value of the trust would qualify for the marital deduction. On the surviving spouse's death, the trust assets would be included in such spouse's estate, but they would also be deductible from her estate as an outright charitable bequest.

§14.32 2. Pooled Income Fund

In addition to the annuity trust and unitrust, a charitable deduction will be allowed for a transfer to a pooled income fund. I.R.C. §170(f)(2)(A). In this case, the grantor transfers assets to a charitable organization under an agreement where the charity will pay to him for the rest of his life and, perhaps, for the life of another, the same rate of return on his contribution that the organization earns on the fund as a whole. Upon the death of the life income beneficiary or beneficiaries, the remainder will belong to the charity. To illustrate, the estate owner contributes $100,000 to ABC Charity pooled income fund, and he receives the income for his life. Upon his death the remainder is to go to the ABC Charity.

In order for the value of the remainder interest to be deductible as a charitable contribution, the fund must have the following characteristics:

1. Various donors must transfer property to the fund, which property is commingled;
2. The fund may not invest in tax-exempt securities;
3. The fund must be maintained by the organization which is the remainder beneficiary, and no donor nor income beneficiary may be a trustee;
4. All contributions to the fund must meet the pooled income requirements. I.R.C. §642(c)(5).

The amount of the charitable remainder deduction is determined by computing the value of the income interest on the basis of the highest rate of return earned by the fund for any of the three immediately preceding taxable years. If the fund has not been in existence during the three preceding years, the rate of return will be prescribed by the Treasury Department. I R.C. §642(c)(5).

Once the rate of return has been determined, the present value of the remainder interest, for deduction purposes, is computed in accordance with the tables appearing in §1.642(c)-6(d)(3) of the Regulations. In the above example, if the estate owner is a male, age 50, and the applicable rate of return is 5 per cent, the value of the charitable remainder is $37,502. The lower the applicable rate of return, the greater will be the amount of the charitable deduction.

§14.33   3.   Estate Planning Advantages of Charitable Remainder Trusts

A charitable remainder trust may be used to excellent advantage. The estate owner can fulfill his charitable desires and often at the same time benefit himself or his family, often by increasing the income which would otherwise be available from the contributed assets.

Assume a wealthy estate owner in a very high income tax bracket wishes to retire next year and his spendable income will substantially decrease. He has securities, with a very low basis, which pay very low dividends. If he sold these securities, he would have to pay an immediate capital gains tax so that the net proceeds available for reinvestment in higher yield assets would be significantly reduced. By giving such assets to a charitable remainder trust, he will obtain an immediate income tax deduction which will put more money in his pocket this year. In addition, the charity could sell the securities and reinvest the proceeds in higher yield assets to enable it to make the required payout. Since the charity does not incur an immediate capital gains tax, the principal and thereby the income are not reduced by such tax as they would have been if the estate owner had made the sale.

As a further example, assume the estate owner also wants his wife to have sufficient income after his death. He can utilize the trust in the above example and provide that the payout continue for her life as well as his. This provision will, however, reduce the value of the charitable remainder interest and thereby the income tax deduction. See Reg. §§1.664-2(c) and 1.664-4; IRS Publication 723, "Valuation of Last Survivor Charitable Remainders." If an income tax deduction is not of major importance, there is another alternative which the estate owner can utilize. He may arrange that on his death a portion of his estate will be transferred to a charitable remainder trust where his wife will receive the required payout during her life. This trust will qualify for both the marital and charitable deductions so no part of the value of its assets will be subject to estate tax on the husband's death. See §14.31. Such deductions will increase the amount of assets otherwise available to produce income for the wife. Moreover, on the wife's subsequent death the trust assets will not be taxed in her estate.

§14.34   V.   Gifts of Charitable Income Interest

It is possible for the estate owner to make a charitable contribution of current income and obtain an immediate income tax deduction, while retaining the reversionary interest for himself or his family. This is achieved through a split interest trust known as a "charitable income trust" or "charitable lead trust," in which the charitable beneficial interest is the income interest.

§14.35   A.   Income Tax Consequences of Charitable Lead Trusts

The income tax charitable deduction will be allowed as long as two requirements are met. First, the trust must be set up so that the donor is taxable on the income from the trust under the grantor trust rules of I.R.C. §§671 through 677. This would be the case if, for example, the income interest was to last for a period of less than 10 years with the remainder reverting to the donor. See I.R.C. §673(a). Second, the trust must qualify as an annuity trust or a unitrust; that is, the charity income beneficiary must receive a guaranteed annuity or a payment based on a fixed percentage of the net fair market value of the trust. I.R.C. §170(f)(2)(B). There is no requirement that the annual payment to charity be at least 5 per cent.

If the charitable lead trust satisfies these requirements, the donor will have a current income tax deduction for the fair market value of the income interest on the date of contribution. Since the estate owner must pay income tax on the income earned by the trust, a charitable lead trust is seldom created by the estate owner during lifetime.

§14.36   B.   Estate and Gift Tax Consequences of Charitable Lead Trusts

In order to obtain the gift tax and estate tax deductions for lifetime transfers to a charitable lead trust, it is not required that the donor be taxable on the income. It is only necessary that the trust be an annuity trust or unitrust. For a discussion of the income tax disadvantage of creating a charitable lead trust during the donor's lifetime, see §14.35.

When created on the estate owner's death, the charitable lead trust has become a widely used technique in reducing estate taxes. Its recent popularity is attributable in large part to the fact that the amount of the estate tax deduction for the charitable interest is computed, in the case of an annuity trust, by using the valuation tables set forth in Reg. §20.2031-10 (see Appendix VIII, Table B), and in the case of a unitrust, by using the tables in the regulations under I.R.C §664. Both of these tables are predicated on a 6 per cent rate of interest. By providing for a gift on death to a charitable lead trust whereby the charity is to receive an annuity greater than 6 per cent for a designated period of time, the testator can, in effect, enable such gift to pass thereafter to his family, free of estate tax. If current high yields continue, the trustee can easily purchase long-term bonds with a rate of return equal to the annuity payment, leaving the entire principal intact. Should yields drop substantially or the Treasury Department valuation tables change during the testator's lifetime, his will can be changed to eliminate or modify the bequest.

To illustrate, assume a large estate owner provides by will or by revocable living trust that on his death $500,000 is to be distributed to a charitable lead trust. The trust provides that 12 per cent of the value of the bequest (i.e., $60,000) is to be paid each year to a designated charity for a period of 13 years.

At the expiration of the trust term, the remaining trust assets are to be distributed to the estate owner's children or other relatives. The estate tax deduction will be the full value of the bequest to the trust, namely $500,000. See Appendix VIII, Table B. ($60,000 times 8.8527 equals an amount in excess of $500,000, but only $500,000 is deductible.) See Reg. §20.2055-2(f)(2) Ex (1). At the expiration of 13 years, the estate owner's children or other relatives will receive the trust assets without depletion for estate taxes.

§14.37   VI.   Charitable Annuities

Many established charitable organizations offer charitable annuity programs under which the estate owner transfers assets to the charity in exchange for the charity's agreement to pay him and/or other designated individuals a lifetime annuity. To the extent that the fair market value of the transferred assets exceeds the value of the annuity contract, there is a charitable deduction for tax purposes. Revenue Ruling 72-438, 1972-2 C.B. 38 sets forth the annuity rate tables for computing the value of the charitable annuity contract.

To the extent that the value of the annuity contract received exceeds the income tax basis of the assets transferred to the charity, there will be a taxable gain to the estate owner. If he wishes to avoid this taxable gain, he should consider using a charitable remainder trust rather than purchasing a charitable annuity. (See §14.33.)

As each annuity payment is received, a portion is taxable income and a portion is excluded. For a full discussion of the income taxation of annuities, see §11.8.

VII.   Recommended Reading

Ashby, "Charitable Income Interests in Estate Planning" 115 *Trusts and Estates* 12 (1976)

Ashby, "Charitable Remainder Trusts: The New Look" 111 *Trusts and Estates* 530 (1972)

Moore, "Split-Interest Charitable Trusts" 7 *Univ of Miami Inst on Estate Planning* 1200 (1973)

Muskin, Lubelcheck and Grass, "Charitable Lead Trusts Can Provide Substantial Estate Planning Benefits" 49 *Journal of Taxation* 2 (1978)

Paul, "The 1969 Act and the Charitable Taxpayer: Individual Limitations, Including Type of Donee Instructions: 30 *NYU Inst on Fed Tax* 21 (1972)

"Model Charitable Remainder Unitrust," Report of Committee on Charitable Giving, Trusts and Foundations, 10 *Real Prop, Prob and Tr J* 535 (1975)

Sanders, "Traps for the Unwary Concerning Gifts of Appreciated Property to Charity; New Section 170(e)," 24 *Univ of So Cal Tax Inst* 719 (1975)

Sorlien and Olsen, "Analyzing the New Charitable Contributions Rules: Planning, Pitfalls, Problems" 32 *Journal of Taxation* 218 (1970)

Teitell, "Federal Tax Implications of Charitable Gift Annuities" 113 *Trusts and Estates* 642 (1974)

Tidd, "When to Make Charitable Contributions of Closely-held Stock" 118 No 6 *Trusts and Estates* 42 (1979)

Whitaker, "Dealing with Outright Gifts to Charity in Kind" 30 *NYU Inst on Fed Tax* 45 (1972)

Tax Planning the Estate After the Owner's Death

15

§15.1   I.   Introduction

Most tax and estate planning should take place before the estate owner dies. However, after the owner's death, it is not too late to supplement or remedy certain deficiencies in the before-death estate plan. This chapter details the manner in which this may be accomplished through the effective exercise of tax elections by the executor, the timing of income distributions from the decedent's estate, and the renunciation of certain unwanted bequests and powers by one or more of the beneficiaries. It should be kept in mind that, through planning, the fiduciary should attempt to reduce the tax obligation not only of the decedent and the decedent's estate, but also of the beneficiaries of the estate.

II. Tax Return Requirements

§15.2 A. Federal Tax Returns

The executor is required to file the following federal tax returns and information within the time limits indicated:

1. The decedent's final federal income tax return (Form 1040): This return is due three and one-half months after the close of the decedent's taxable year, without regard to his death. With the exception of a taxpayer using a fiscal year, the due date will therefore be April 15 of the year subsequent to his death. The return must be filed if the gross income for the taxable year, depending on the decedent's age and marital status, is in excess of:

Single person	$3,300
Single person, 65 or older	$4,300
Married couple, joint return	$5,400
Married couple, joint return, one spouse 65 or older	$6,400
Married couple, joint return, both 65 or older	$7,400
Surviving spouse	$4,400

2. The estate fiduciary income tax return (Form 1041): This is due three and one-half months following the end of each fiscal year of the estate. See §§15.12 to 15.14 for a discussion regarding selecting the estate's fiscal year. The return is required for any taxable period during which the estate's gross income is $600 or more.

3. The federal estate tax return (Form 706): This return is due nine months after the estate owner's death. It must be filed if the value of the gross estate exceeds the following amounts:

Year of Decedent's Death	Amount of Gross Estate
1982	$225,000
1983	$275,000
1984	$325,000
1985	$400,000
1986	$500,000
1987 and thereafter	$600,000

§15.3   B.   State Tax Returns

The state where the decedent was a resident, as well as the state where he earned income or leaves real property, may require income and death tax returns. The return due dates are generally similar to the federal deadlines, but should be ascertained for the particular state in question.

§15.4   III.   Making an Analysis of the Estate

An analysis of the estate should be made as soon as possible after the estate owner's death. For a relatively uncomplicated estate the fiduciary or tax planner should do the following:

1.   Estimate the cash requirements for expenses, taxes and debts.
2.   Project the estate income with specific emphasis on the following items:
    a.   The amount of income anticipated.
    b.   The types of income (i.e., ordinary, capital gain, exempt income).
    c.   The portion, if any, of the income that will be community property since one-half will be taxed to the surviving spouse rather than to the estate.
    d.   When the income will be received, by month if possible.
3.   Estimate the estate tax and income tax brackets of the estate.
4.   Determine how long the administration of the estate will last.
5.   Ascertain the income tax brackets of the beneficiaries.
6.   Determine the needs of the beneficiaries for income and principal distributions during the administration period.

Once this analysis is completed, the tax planner will be in a position to make intelligent tax-savings decisions.

IV.   Elections Available to the Executor

§15.5   A.   Decedent's Final Income Tax Return
(Form 1040)

The decedent's final income tax return includes only that portion of the income for the year earned up to the date of death. The balance is taxed to the estate when received. Only one-half of the community property income earned up to the date of death is included in the decedent's final income tax return. The other one-half is included in the surviving spouse's taxable income for the year. Certain significant elections may be made with regard to the decedent's final return. These are discussed in §§15.6 to 15.11, inclusive.

§15.6   1.   Should the Estate File a Joint Return with the Surviving Spouse?

The executor and the decedent's surviving spouse may elect to file a joint income tax return for the year when the decedent died. I.R.C. §6013(a)(2). However, a joint return is allowed only if the taxable years of the spouses began on the same day and the surviving spouse does not remarry before the close of his or her tax year. The joint return includes the income earned by the decedent up to the date of death and the income of the surviving spouse up to the end of the year.

§15.7   a.   Advantages of Joint Return

A joint return may provide a more favorable tax rate since the income and deductions are, in effect, split equally between two taxpayers. This is particularly advantageous where one spouse earns substantially more than the other. Furthermore, one spouse's deductions may provide greater tax benefits when applied against the joint income. For example, the estate will not be allowed a deduction for the decedent's net operating loss or capital loss. Therefore, it will be advantageous for the executor to file a joint income tax return so that he may use any available gains of the surviving spouse to offset these losses which are allowable on the final return.

§15.8   i.   Planning to Take Advantage of Joint Return

If the surviving spouse has little income in the year of the decedent's death, it may be wise for the executor to distribute estate income to him or her during that same tax year. When the surviving spouse files a joint return, this income may be taxed at a lower effective rate than if it had remained in the estate and had been taxed accordingly, or if it had been distributed in a later year when the surviving spouse could not take advantage of joint return rates. See I.R.C. §§2(a) and (b).

§15.9   b.   Disadvantage of Joint Return

A potential disadvantage of filing a joint return is that the estate will be jointly and severally liable for any tax, interest and civil penalties. I.R.C. §6013(d)(3). I.R.C. §6013(e) may protect the estate from these liabilities in the event that income of the surviving spouse is omitted from the return without the fiduciary's knowledge, and the omitted income exceeds 25 per cent of the gross income reported in the return. Despite this joint liability, only the decedent's portion of the income tax liability is deductible for estate tax purposes. Reg. §20.2053-6(f).

§15.10   2.   Medical Deduction Election

The fiduciary may elect to take a deduction for the decedent's unpaid medical expenses, which are paid out of his estate within one year after death, on either the decedent's final income tax return or on the federal estate tax return. I.R C. §213(d). Since a double deduction is not allowed, the fiduciary must file a waiver of right to claim an estate tax deduction if he wishes to deduct the medical expenses on the final income tax return. I.R.C. §213(d)(2). In making the election, the fiduciary should not only compare the effective income and death tax rates, but also take other factors into account.

The income tax deduction is limited to medical expenses in excess of 3 per cent of adjusted gross income. I.R.C. §213(a)(1). The portion not allowed as a deduction for income tax purposes is not deductible on the estate tax return as a claim against the estate under I.R.C. §2053(a)(3). Rev. Rul. 77-357, 1977-2 C.B. 328.

In determining whether to claim the medical expense deduction on the decedent's final income tax return as opposed to the estate tax return, the fiduciary should consider the effect on the decedent's final income tax liability as an estate tax deduction. By deducting such expenses on the income tax return, the decedent's income tax liability will be reduced and thereby the estate tax deduction for such liability. Reg. §20.2053-6(f). Conversely, if the medical expenses are deducted on the estate tax return, there will be a greater income tax liability deduction.

When the decedent leaves an optimum or maximum marital deduction bequest (see §4.8) to the surviving spouse, the medical expense deduction should ordinarily be taken on the decedent's income tax return. The deduction will be wasted if taken on the estate tax return, because even without such deduction there will be no estate tax payable. However, where an optimum marital deduction formula clause is used, taking the deduction on the decedent's final income tax return could also have a negative effect. The amount of this deduction would reduce the equivalent exemption amount (see §2.25) passing to the bypass trust or to beneficiaries other than the spouse. See §4.8. Thus, the amount would not be sheltered from estate tax on the surviving spouse's death. If the surviving spouse's maximum estate tax bracket is likely to be substantially higher than the decedent's top income tax bracket, and particularly if the surviving spouse appears to have a short life expectancy, consideration should be given to taking the medical expense deduction on the estate tax return.

For the factors to be considered when the decedent leaves a formula marital deduction bequest that was not amended subsequent to September 11, 1981, see §15.22.

§15.11   3.   U.S. Treasury Series E Bonds — Should Accrued Interest Be Reported?

Under I.R.C. §454(a), a cash basis taxpayer may defer reporting the interest income on Series E bonds until they are redeemed. However, in any one year, the taxpayer may elect to report all of the accrued interest to date as income for that year. The fiduciary also has the right to make this election for a decedent bondholder. It is wise to elect to recognize this previously untaxed income in a year when the taxpayer's income is abnormally low, which may very well be the year of the taxpayer's death, particularly if his death occurred early in the tax year. Any income tax liability incurred as a result of making this election on the decedent's final return will be deductible on the estate tax return.

If the fiduciary does not elect to report the accrued interest on the bonds, such interest will be taxable as "income in respect of a decedent" to the recipient when collected. I.R.C. §691(a)(1). Such recipient will be entitled to an offsetting deduction for the estate tax attributable to such accrued interest. I.R.C. §691(c). For a discussion of "income in respect of a decedent," see §2.50.

§15.12   B.   Selection of the Estate's Taxable Year

All income earned by the decedent's estate during the period of administration is for federal purposes reportable on Form 1041. The executor may initially elect to report this income on a fiscal year rather than a calendar year basis. If he does so, he must make his election within three and one-half months after the close of the fiscal year selected, and he is required to maintain "books." I.R.C. §441. If no timely election is made, the estate must report income on a calendar year basis.

Unless a fiscal year is elected, the first taxable year of the estate will end on December 31 of the year in which the decedent died. On the other hand, in electing a fiscal year, the executor has the opportunity to select the ending date of such year, provided it ends on the last day of a month and is not more than 12 months from the decedent's death. For example, if the decedent died on May 15, the executor could elect a fiscal year ending on the last day of any month from the May 31 following the death to the April 30 of the following year. I.R.C. §441(e). This permits the selection of a short first taxable year. All subsequent years, with the exception of the year in which the estate closes, must consist of a full 12 months. The final year will terminate on the date of final distribution of the estate even if it is less than 12 months. I.R.C. §443(a)(2).

1.   Planning Advantages in Selecting the Taxable Year

§15.13   a.   Reduce Tax Liability

Through an intelligent selection of a taxable year, it is possible to reduce the overall income tax liability of the estate. By selecting an ending date which results in a short initial year, the total income taxable years during the period of administration may be increased, causing the estate income to be stretched out over at least one more taxable period. Because the income tax rates are progressive and, in addition, because the estate is entitled to a $600 exemption for each taxable year (I.R.C. §642(b)), the total taxes may well be lowered. Moreover, the ability to select the cutoff date of the first year gives the executor an opportunity to allocate major receipts or expenses to a more advantageous tax year. For example, if a major receipt is due two months after the decedent's death, and a major deduction will be incurred in the third month, the executor can plan to have the deduction offset the income by electing a year ending no earlier than the end of the third month.

§15.14   b.   Delay Taxation

A beneficiary will report taxable distributions in his individual income tax return for his taxable year within which the estate's taxable year ends. Thus, if the estate selects a fiscal year ending January 31, 1983, and the individual beneficiary reports on a calendar year, taxable distributions will not be reportable by the beneficiary until the 1984 tax return is due (i.e., April 15, 1985), which is fourteen and one-half months later. If the beneficiary is a fiscal year individual or trust, recognition of income may be postponed even longer. (See §15.37.)

C.   Deduction Election for Administration Expenses and Losses

§15.15   1.   Disallowance of Double Deductions

Expenses of administration and casualty losses during administration may be deducted on either the estate income tax return (Form 1041) or the estate tax return (Form 706). With few exceptions, a double deduction for these items is not allowed. A waiver of the estate tax deductions allowed under I.R.C. §§2053 and 2054 must be filed pursuant to I.R.C. §642(g) in order to claim the deduction for income tax purposes. The executor must, therefore, after weighing all of the factors, decide on which return to take the deductions.

The prohibition against the double deduction does not apply to interest, taxes, business expenses and other I.R.C. §691(b) "deductions in respect of a decedent" accrued and unpaid at death. See I.R.C. §642(g). However, brokerage commissions and other selling expenses may not be deducted on both the estate tax return as administration expenses under I.R.C. §2053 and also as an offset against the selling price in computing the taxable gain on the estate income tax return. I.R.C. §642(g).

Interest paid on deferred federal estate taxes (see §§12.51 to 12.57), as compared to the other interest payments, is a proper expense of administration (see *Estate of Bahr v Commr* 68 TC 74 (1977); Rev. Rul. 79-252, 1979-2 C.B. 333), and accordingly the double deduction rule applies. See also Rev. Rul. 80-250, 1980-2 C.B. 278, which states that only the interest accrued up to the date of the filing of the federal estate return may be deducted as an expense of administration on the estate tax return when filed. Interest accrued after that date may be the subject of a claim for refund, but the estate will not receive a refund until the entire deferred tax liability has been paid.

§15.16   2.   Manner of Making the Election

The waiver required by I.R.C. §642(g) may be filed with the income tax return when it is filed, or the executor may wait to file the waiver anytime up to the close of the statutory period of limitations for that tax year, which is normally three years from the due date of the return. Reg. §1.642(g)-1. Prior to the expiration of such period, the executor may tentatively claim the deductions on the estate tax return without giving up the right to claim them later on the income tax return. However, once the waiver is filed, the option to use the deductions for estate tax purposes is lost. Thus, it is best to delay filing the waiver with the income tax return so that the decision may be reviewed and changed if subsequent events so warrant.

§15.17   3.   Considerations in Making the Election

In deciding on which return the deductions for administration expenses and losses should be taken, the factors discussed in §§15.18 to 15.25 should be considered.

§15.18   a.   Splitting the Deductions

It is not required that the total deductions, or even the total amount of any one item, be treated in the same way. One or more deductions, or a portion of one or more items, may be deducted for income tax purposes while the remaining items or portions may be taken as estate tax deductions. Reg. §1.642(g)-2. Since partial allocation is allowed, the executor should determine whether splitting the deductions is advantageous.

§15.19   b.   Maximizing the Income Tax Deductions

To the extent that the deductions will be taken on the federal estate tax return, it is not necessary that the underlying expenses be paid during any particular taxable period of the estate. However, if all or part of the deductions will be taken on the estate income tax return, consideration should be given to when such items are paid or incurred. For example, if the estate is on the cash basis, the expense items may be deducted only in the taxable period in which they are paid. Hence, the items, if possible, should be paid in a period that would enable the deductions to be used to offset high income. See §§15.20 and 15.36 for a discussion of excess deductions in the year of termination of the estate.

§15.20   c.   Comparison of Tax Rates

In making the election, the fiduciary should compare the respective income and estate tax rate brackets. In most situations, he should take the deduction on the return with the higher brackets. However, see §§15.21 and 15.22 for possible exceptions.

The projected income tax brackets of the beneficiaries should also be considered. If the beneficiaries are in a higher bracket than the estate is for both income and estate tax purposes, it may be more beneficial to pay the administrative expenses in the last taxable year of the estate and elect to take the deductions on the estate income tax return. As a result, upon distribution the deductions will either reduce the income reportable by the beneficiaries or, if there are excess deductions, the loss may be used by the beneficiaries to offset high income on their individual tax returns. (See §15.36.)

§15.21   d.   Effect on Marital Deduction Planning

In reaching a decision as to whether to deduct the administration expenses and losses on the estate tax return or on the income tax return, one should take into account the effect on the marital deduction. If the decedent leaves his spouse an unlimited or optimum marital deduction bequest (see §4.8), deducting the administration expenses and losses on the federal estate tax return, at least at first blush, will not save any estate taxes. Even without such deduction, usually no federal estate tax will be payable. However, if the administration expenses and losses exceed the amount of the equivalent exemption (see §2.25), there could be a federal estate tax payable if these items are deductible on the income tax return. For example, assume the gross estate has a value of $5,000,000, the administration expenses and losses are $800,000 and the decedent's will leaves the entire estate to the spouse. If the $800,000 is deducted on the income tax return, the maximum marital deduction will be $4,200,000 (i.e., the amount passing to the surviving spouse), resulting in a taxable estate of $800,000, which, after the application of the unified credit, will still result in an estate tax payable. On the other hand, if, in this instance, that portion of the administration expenses and losses which exceeded the equivalent exemption were deducted on the estate tax return, there would be no estate tax payable. Using the above example, and assuming the equivalent exemption in the year of the decedent's death is $600,000, $200,000 of the administration expenses and losses would be deducted on the estate tax return. This deduction, when added to the marital deduction of $4,200,000, totals $4,400,000, and leaves a taxable estate of $600,000, which amount will result in no estate tax.

Even where the administration expenses and losses are less than the amount of the equivalent exemption, it still may be worthwhile to deduct these items on the estate tax return. Such a situation arises where the decedent leaves under a formula clause in his will an optimum marital deduction bequest to his spouse and the equivalent exemption portion of the estate to other beneficiaries or to a bypass trust (see §4.8). Taking the administration expenses and losses on the income tax return will increase the amount of the marital deduction and correspondingly decrease the equivalent exemption amount. This will thereby increase the size of the surviving spouse's estate and cause a greater estate tax on such spouse's death. For example, assume a gross estate of $2,000,000 and administration expenses and losses of $100,000. Thus, the net disposable estate is $1,900,000. If the $100,000 of administration expenses and losses is deducted on the income tax return, the optimum marital deduction necessary to eliminate the estate tax on the decedent's death will be $1,400,000 and the equivalent exemption bequest will be reduced to $500,-000. Conversely, if the administration expenses and losses were deducted on the estate tax return, only $1,300,000 would be needed to satisfy the optimum marital deduction and the equivalent exemption would be $600,000. The executor must, therefore, decide whether the income tax reduction on the decedent's death is worth the estate tax increase on the surviving spouse's death. (See §15.10.)

§15.22   i.   Effect on Pre-September 12, 1981 Formula Marital Deduction Bequests

Where the decedent leaves a formula maximum marital deduction bequest under a will or trust dated prior to September 12, 1981, which was not subsequently amended, the marital deduction is limited to one-half of the adjusted gross estate. See §§4.4 to 4.7. Since not all decedents will have amended their marital deduction clauses, one should consider the effect the administration expense and loss election will have on the marital deduction in these estates.

To the extent that the deductions are taken on the estate tax return, the adjusted gross estate will be decreased. Therefore, the maximum marital deduction, if based on a formula pecuniary clause, will in turn be decreased. Hence, the net effect of the expense deductions is that only 50 per cent of the expenses are "deductible." On the other hand, if the expenses are deducted on the income tax return, the full benefit of the deduction will be utilized.

For example, assume a gross estate of $1,500,000 with administration expenses of $50,000. The will provides a formula pecuniary maximum marital deduction bequest. If the expenses are deducted on the estate tax return, the marital deduction will be only $725,000 (one-half of $1,450,000), as compared to a marital deduction of $750,000 if the expenses are deducted on the income tax return.

If a fractional share of the residue marital deduction clause is used, it will make no difference on which of the returns the expenses are deducted. The reason is that the maximum marital deduction can never exceed the net value of the interest that passes to the surviving spouse. The administration expenses will reduce the value of such interest regardless of where they are deducted. See Rev. Rul. 55-225, 1955-1 C.B. 460.

§15.23   e.   Effect on Community Property

If any portion of the administration expenses or losses is attributable to the surviving spouse's one-half of the community property, this portion may be deducted on such spouse's individual income tax return (Form 1040), but not on any tax return of the estate, regardless of whether or not decedent's one-half of such expenses or losses is taken on Form 1041 or Form 706.

§15.24   f.   Tax-Exempt Income

Expenses attributable to the production of tax-exempt income are not deductible for income tax purposes. They may, however, be deducted on the estate tax return even though a waiver has been filed. Rev. Rul. 59-32, 1959-1 C.B. 245.

§15.25   g.   Allocation of Tax Savings Among Beneficiaries

If the election is made to deduct administration expenses or losses on the estate income tax return, a portion of the resultant income tax savings must be allocated to the remainder beneficiaries to compensate for the increased estate tax burden. *Estate of Bixby v Commr* 140 CaAp2d 326, 295 P2d 68 (1956); see, also, *Estate of Warms v Commr* 140 NYS2d 169 (1955). In the *Bixby* case, the executor had discretion whether or not to make the election since the will was silent on the point. He elected to take the deduction on the estate income tax return, thereby benefiting the income beneficiaries at the expense of the remainder beneficiary. Since the deduction would have been available for estate tax purposes if not for the election, the court held that the income beneficiaries had to pay the residuary legatee an amount equal to the increase in the estate tax resulting from the loss of the deduction. The income beneficiaries were allowed to retain the tax savings in excess of the amount necessary to offset the depletion in the residue of the estate.

Application of this rule may be avoided by including a specific provision in the will giving the executor complete discretion in allocating the deductions and waiving any requirement of compensatory adjustments.

§15.26 D. "QTIP" Election

For decedents dying after 1981, a bequest to a qualified terminable interest property ("QTIP") trust will qualify for the marital deduction, if the requirements specified in §4.21 are satisfied and the executor elects to take the marital deduction. For a full discussion of "QTIP" trusts, see §§4.20 to 4.24. The advantage of electing to take the marital deduction is that it will ordinarily reduce the federal estate tax on the decedent's death. However, where the election is made, the value of the assets in the "QTIP" trust will be included in the surviving spouse's estate. I.R.C. §2044. For a full discussion of whether the maximum or optimum marital deduction should be taken on the first death or whether less than the maximum or optimum marital deduction should be taken in order to decrease the estate tax on the survivor's death, see §4.8. It is not clear whether the executor must elect to deduct the entire amount of the "QTIP" trust or whether he may elect only as to a portion of the amount. It is hoped that this matter will be clarified by forthcoming Treasury Department Regulations.

§15.27 E. Election of Alternate Valuation Date

The value of the gross estate is generally determined as of the date of death. However, for federal estate tax purposes, the fiduciary may elect to value the assets of the estate as of six months after the date of death. I.R.C. §2032. The election is irrevocable and, if made, all assets are valued as of the alternate date. However, any assets sold, distributed or otherwise disposed of within the six-month period are valued as of the date of such disposition.

In deciding whether or not to elect alternate valuation, the executor should take into account the effect of the valuation date used for federal estate tax purposes on the income tax basis of the assets. The income tax basis of the assets of a decedent is equal to the federal estate tax value of such assets. The executor must therefore decide whether to pay a larger or smaller estate tax at the expense of a higher or lower income tax basis.

It will usually be worthwhile to elect the federal estate tax valuation date which results in the smaller estate tax. The reason for this is that the lowest estate tax bracket (after considering the application of the unified credit) is 32 per cent (in 1982) and will be 37 per cent by 1986, while the maximum capital gain rate is 20 per cent. See I.R.C. §1202. However, where the assets consist of depreciable property, it may be preferable to elect a higher valuation date, because the income tax benefit provided by the increased depreciation deduction may exceed the additional estate tax.

Where the executor elects that valuation date which provides a higher income tax basis for the estate assets, but also a larger estate tax than would otherwise have resulted, the *Bixby* rule (see §15.25) should be followed in apportioning the burden of the increased estate tax among those beneficiaries who received an income tax saving.

If a decedent leaves a spouse, it may be preferable in many instances to elect the higher valuation date. When a maximum or optimum marital deduction bequest has been used (see §4.8), there will ordinarily be no federal estate tax on the decedent's death regardless of the value of the estate assets. By using the higher value, the income tax basis of the assets will be increased at no estate tax cost. Even when less than a maximum or optimum marital deduction is taken, the income tax basis will be increased while only the portion of the estate not qualifying for the marital deduction will be subjected to estate tax. For example, if the decedent leaves one-half of his estate to his spouse and the other one-half to his children, only one-half of the estate is, in effect, subject to estate tax, but both halves of the estate will receive a new basis equal to the estate tax value. Hence, the executor should, in effect, reduce the projected estate tax rate by one-half when comparing it with the income tax rate when deciding whether or not to elect alternate valuation. Assume an asset has increased in value by $10,000 between the date of death and the alternate valuation date. Assume further that this asset will be sold in the near future, and that the maximum income tax capital gains rate for the particular seller is 20 per cent. In this case, even if the estate tax bracket were as high as 37 per cent, it might be worthwhile to elect alternate valuation. The estate tax will be increased by $1,850 (37 per cent of $5,000), but the income tax saving would be $2,000 (20 per cent times $10,000). If there is no plan to sell the asset in the near future, it may be preferable not to elect the higher alternate valuation. The present saving in estate tax would outweigh a larger, but long delayed, income tax saving.

To deter an executor from deliberately overvaluing an estate to obtain a higher income tax basis, I.R.C. §6659 provides a tax penalty.

§15.28   F.   Special Valuation Election for Real Estate Used in Farming or by Other Closely Held Businesses

If certain conditions are met, the executor may elect to value real property used for farming or other closely held business use on the basis of such property's value rather than on the basis of its highest and best use. I.R.C. §2032A. This special valuation may not be used to decrease the value of the decedent's gross estate by more than $700,000 in 1982 and $750,000 in 1983, and thereafter.

In general, the tax benefits derived from electing the special valuation are recaptured if the property is disposed of to nonfamily members or ceases to be used for farming or closely held business purposes within 10 years after the decedent's death. See §12.4

The election, if it is made, must be made on the federal estate tax return.

See I.R.C. §2032A(d). The election is valid even if the return is not timely filed. I.R.C. §2032A(d)(1).

§15.29   G.   Election to Defer Paying the Estate Tax

Where an interest in a closely held business constitutes more than a designated percentage of the estate and certain other requirements are met, the executor may elect to pay a portion of the estate tax in deferred installments. For a full discussion, see §§12.51 to 12.55.

§15.30   H.   Election to Waive Executor's Fees

Executor's fees may be taken as a deduction against either estate income tax or estate tax. However, the executor must report his fees as ordinary income. I.R.C. §61(a)(1). When the executor is also the residuary legatee, he may wish to waive his fees, depending on his personal income tax bracket as compared to the estate's bracket. For example, assume the executor, who is the residuary legatee, is entitled to a fee of $20,000 and is in a 50 per cent income tax bracket. The maximum tax bracket of the estate is 41 per cent. If he takes his fee, his net benefit will be $10,000 ($20,000 less the $10,000 income tax payable on his individual tax return). If the executor waives his fee, the residuary estate will be increased by $11,800 ($20,000 less the $8,200 tax paid by the estate), which will be distributed to him as an income tax-free inheritance. I.R.C. §102(a).

If the waiver is not made properly, the executor may be taxable on income constructively received, and then be deemed to have made a taxable gift to the other beneficiaries. However, under Revenue Ruling 66-167, 1966-1 C.B. 20, the waiver will be effective if made within a reasonable time after the executor commences service, and if his actions are consistent with the intention to render gratuitous service. When possible, he should furnish a formal written waiver to the principal beneficiaries within six months of his appointment. Even without formal notice, it is possible to establish an effective waiver through consistent actions.

V.   Distribution Planning

§15.31   A.   Introduction

In general, income collected by the estate is taxable to the estate and not to the heirs or legatees. I.R.C. §641. The estate, however, is allowed a deduction equal to the total of the income required to be distributed currently plus any other amounts paid or credited during the taxable year, but not to exceed the estate's distributable income. I.R.C. §661. These distributions will be taxable income to the beneficiary under §662. Distributions of bequests are treated as distributions of income, unless the bequest is one of a specific sum of money or specific property, that is not payable out of current or prior estate income, and the bequest is paid in not more than three installments. I.R.C. §663(a)(1).

Hence, if the estate during the taxable year earns $20,000 of net income and distributes the decedent's residence to a residuary legatee, the estate will have a deduction of $20,000 and the residuary legatee will have taxable income of $20,000. If, however, the home is distributed to a specific devisee, the $20,000 will not be treated as an income distribution nor be deductible by the estate.

B.   Objectives of Distribution Planning

§15.32   1.   Equalize Tax Rates

A primary objective in planning distributions is to equalize the effective income tax rates of the estate and the beneficiaries. If the beneficiaries are in a lower bracket than the estate, distributions should be made to take advantage of the lower rates. Where the beneficiaries are in different brackets, the fiduciary should attempt to distribute income-producing assets to the beneficiaries having lower personal income tax rates. Also, capital gain property may be distributed to a beneficiary who sustained a capital loss, or other estate income to a beneficiary who could use it to offset a net operating loss carryover. These and other possibilities for tailoring the distributions to the individual needs of the beneficiaries should not be overlooked.

On the other hand, if the estate has a lower effective income tax rate than the beneficiaries, the fiduciary should delay closing the estate as long as possible to take advantage of the lower bracket. In this way the estate can accumulate income, pay the tax and then in a subsequent taxable year pass on the estate property to the beneficiaries who will have no additional tax liability. However, the period of administration cannot be "unduly prolonged" or it will be treated as having closed for tax purposes. Reg. §1.641(b)(3). The estate is not unduly prolonged if there is a bona fide business purpose for holding it open (*Carson v US* 317 F2d 370 (Ct Cl 1963)), or if outstanding contested claims are pending (*Edwin M Peterson v Commr* 35 TC 962 (1961)). The throwback rule (discussed in §8.45) is not a problem since it applies only to trusts, not to estates.

§15.33   a.   Family Allowance

A court may order a family allowance under local law for the support of the widow or other dependents during the administration of the estate. Such an award is deemed to be an income item, even if paid out of principal. Reg. §1.661(a)-2(e). Therefore, if the surviving spouse is in a lower income tax bracket than the estate, the fiduciary should attempt to pay a family allowance so that the estate will be entitled to the deduction and the distribution will be taxable to the recipient.

2. Maximize Deductions

§15.34 a. Personal Exemption

An estate is entitled to a personal annual exemption of $600 during administration. I.R.C. §642(b). Creating an extra personal exemption through use of a short initial tax year was discussed in §15.13. Furthermore, the estate should retain sufficient taxable income, after taking into account any available expense deductions, to take advantage of the full exemption amount.

§15.35 b. Loss Carryovers

Unused net operating loss carryovers or capital loss carryovers of the estate may be deducted by the beneficiary in the year the estate terminates. These losses may also be carried over by the beneficiary into future years. The last year of the estate and the first tax year of the succeeding beneficiary each constitute a tax year for determining the remaining number of years in which the deduction will be available. Reg. §1.642(h)-1(b). Since the beneficiaries may only carry the loss forward and not backward, the fiduciary should consider an early termination if the beneficiary is in a high bracket and will be able to use the carryovers more effectively.

§15.36 c. Excess Deductions

In the year of termination, deductions in excess of the estate's income are available to the succeeding beneficiaries. I.R.C. §642(h). If the beneficiaries are in higher income tax brackets than the estate, the fiduciary should consider paying administration and other expenses in the year of termination, which may be a short tax year, elect to take the deduction on the estate income tax return and pass the loss through to the beneficiaries as excess deductions on their own income tax returns to offset their high income.

§15.37 3. Create Additional Taxpayers by Use of Trusts

In addition to the flexibility that trusts can provide, many income tax advantages may be obtained through proper planning of the distributions from the estate to trusts which are estate beneficiaries. A trust is taxed for income tax purposes in a similar manner to estates, except the throwback rule applies. (See §§15.31 and 8.44 and 8.45). The beneficiary trusts should often be funded by estate distributions as early as possible to create additional tax entities. In this way, the income will be taxed to the trusts which accumulate income at lower rates than would have been the case if all of the income were taxed to the estate.

Careful selection of fiscal years for the trusts can lower tax brackets and defer taxation of income. If, for example, the estate's taxable year ends February 28, the trust's taxable year January 31, and the income beneficiary's taxable year December 31, a distribution of income from the estate to the trust and then to the beneficiary will not be taxed for a considerable period of time after the income was earned. The reason is that each distribution is income to the distributee in the taxable year in which the distributee's taxable year ends. I.R.C. §§652(c) and 662(c).

VI. Disclaimers

§15.38 A. Introduction

A disclaimer is the refusal to accept benefits conferred by will or by operation of law. If a beneficiary does not want his share of the estate because his income, estate, or both will be increased, he should consider disclaiming his interest. For example, assume A's will leaves his estate to B, but provides that if B does not survive A, then A's estate is to go to B's children. B already has a very substantial estate. From a tax point of view, it would have been better planning for A to have left his estate directly to B's children. If A dies, B should consider disclaiming his inheritance from A. In the absence of a contrary provision in the estate owner's will or other dispositive instrument, the disclaimed assets will go to those persons who would have received the inheritance if the disclaiming party had predeceased the estate owner. Hence, as a result of B's disclaimer, A's estate will go to B's children.

In order to prevent the disclaimed inherited asset from increasing B's estate, the disclaimer must not be deemed to constitute a taxable gift from B to his children. Otherwise, under the unified estate and gift tax, the value of the inheritance on the date of the disclaimer will be added back to B's taxable estate. See §§2.2 and 2.3. Moreover, if the disclaimer is deemed to be a gift from B, and as a result of the disclaimer the assets go into a trust from which B receives the income, the disclaimed assets, valued as of the date of B's death, will be included in his gross estate. I.R.C. §2036(a).

Prior to the enactment of the Tax Reform Act of 1976, the disclaimer may or may not have constituted a gift to the disclaiming party depending upon whether there was an unqualified refusal to accept ownership and such refusal was effective under state law. The Internal Revenue Code now provides definitive rules for purposes of federal gift, estate and generation-skipping transfer taxes. See I.R.C. §2518. If the requirements provided in the statute are met, a refusal to accept assets, followed by a disclaimer, will not be considered as a taxable transfer for the above-described federal taxes.

In brief, a disclaimer is not deemed to be a transfer if there is an irrevocable and unqualified refusal to accept an interest in property that satisfies four conditions. First, the refusal must be in writing. Second, it must be made within nine months of the time that the interest is transferred, which, for example, in the event of an inheritance would be nine months from the date of the decedent's death. Third, the disclaiming party must not have accepted the interest or any of its benefits before making the disclaimer. Fourth, the interest must pass to a person other than the disclaiming party without any direction on the part of the disclaiming party. The statute also provides that an undivided interest may be disclaimed and that an interest includes a power of appointment.

Where the disclaiming person is the surviving spouse of the decedent, such spouse may disclaim an interest in property, even if, as a result, the property passes to a trust in which the spouse has an interest. I.R.C. §2518(b)(4). See §5.2 for a discussion of a planning technique permitting the surviving spouse to disclaim an outright interest in the decedent spouse's estate in favor of an "A-B" trust. The spouse, however, may not disclaim an interest which passes into a trust where the spouse has the power to direct to whom the interest will go. For example, if the spouse has a limited power to appoint the trust assets to third parties (see §5.8), the spouse will be deemed to have the power of direction and the disclaimer will not be a qualified one. See proposed Reg. §25.2518-2(e)(2) Ex (5).

Except in the case of a bank account, it is doubtful whether a surviving joint tenant may disclaim his interest because he had previously accepted the benefits of such interest before the death of the decedent joint tenant. See Letter Ruls. 7829008 and 8124118. The Internal Revenue Service also takes the position that a disclaimer of a partial interest is not effective, unless the interest disclaimed is severable. Letter Rule. 8015014. For example, in the view of the Service, a one-half interest in the residue of an estate may be disclaimed; but the gift of a specific asset in a trust (without disclaiming the entire trust interest) may not be disclaimed. See also proposed Reg. §25.2518-3, which states that a general power of appointment over principal may not be effectively disclaimed unless all interests in the principal are disclaimed.

B. Additional Factors to be Considered

§15.39 1. Effect on Marital Deduction

A surviving spouse may wish to disclaim that portion of a bequest in excess of the optimum marital deduction, since such excess will increase the survivor's estate without reducing the tax in the estate of the first spouse to die. See §4.8 for the definition of the "optimum" marital deduction. For example, if the husband leaves all of his $2,000,000 estate outright to his wife, she could disclaim the amount of the equivalent exemption, without causing any estate tax to be paid in the husband's estate, and, at the same time, prevent the disclaimed assets from being taxed in her estate. If the husband's estate plan provides a bypass trust for the wife's benefit (see Chapter 5), which will receive all assets disclaimed by the wife, her disclaimer will accomplish the above result and also allow her to receive the lifetime benefits from the disclaimed assets. See §§5.2 and 15.38. The wife may also disclaim an even greater portion of the marital deduction than would be necessary to reduce it to the optimum amount. This will cause some estate tax to be paid on the husband's death, but will achieve an even greater saving on the wife's death. For a full discussion, see §4.8.

On the other hand, if the decedent's estate plan did not take advantage of the maximum marital deduction, a third person receiving an interest could disclaim such interest. If, by reason of the disclaimer, the interest goes to the surviving spouse, there will be an increase in the marital deduction in the decedent spouse's estate. I.R.C. §2045. For example, assume that a husband leaves $100,000 to his son. The husband's will provides that if the son does not survive the husband or disclaims his bequest, such bequest shall go to the husband's spouse. The son may disclaim the bequest and thereby increase the marital deduction in the husband's estate by the $100,000.

§15.40   2.   Powers of Appointment

A beneficiary may disclaim a power of appointment without the disclaimer being treated as a taxable transfer. He may wish to do so to avoid having the property subject to the general power of appointment includable in his estate under I.R.C. §2041. For example, if a husband leaves the nonmarital deduction portion of his estate to a trust where the wife is given all the income and a general testamentary power of appointment, the wife could disclaim the testamentary power of appointment so that the trust assets will not be includable in her estate. I.R.C. §§2045 and 2518(c)(2). However, see proposed Reg. §25.2518-3, which states that a general power of appointment over principal may not be effectively disclaimed unless all interests in the principal are disclaimed.

§15.41   3.   Gifts to Charity

Just as a bequest may be disclaimed to increase the amount of the marital deduction (see §15.39), so may a bequest be disclaimed to increase the charitable deduction. The estate owner's will, however, should make it clear that in the event of a disclaimer the bequest is to go to a named charity.

One might think that although the disclaimer will reduce the estate tax liability in the decedent's estate, the beneficiary could achieve an even greater income tax saving if he accepted the bequest and then donated the property to charity. However, because, after 1982, the lowest estate tax bracket is 34 per cent and the highest income tax bracket is 50 per cent, there will always be a greater tax saving if the disclaimer is made. For example, assume that A leaves $50,000 to B with the proviso that, if B disclaims, the bequest goes to XYZ Charity. If B disclaims, A's estate will receive a charitable deduction in the amount of $50,000. If the top bracket in A's estate is 34 per cent, the estate tax saving in A's estate will be $17,000. However, even if B is in a 50 per cent income tax bracket, the income tax savings to him by taking the bequest and then donating it to the XYZ Charity will be only $16,500 (50 per cent $\times$ [$50,000 minus $17,000]). Hence, B should disclaim the bequest.

VII.   Recommended Reading

Berall, "Using Disclaimers Effectively: An Analysis of a Useful Post-Mortem Tax Planning Tool" 34 *Journal of Taxation* 92 (1971)

Buttrey, "Post-Mortem Planning: A Guide to the Elections Available to Estates" 40 *Journal of Taxation* 148 (1974)

Clapp, "Post-Mortem Planning" 1 *The Probate Lawyer* 1 (1974)

Darling, "Estate Elections" 33 *NYU Inst on Fed Tax* 390 (1975)

Ferguson, Freeland and Stephens, *Federal Income Taxation of Estates and Beneficiaries* (Little, Brown and Co 1974)

Ledwith, "Opportunities for Tax Savings Through Post-Death Actions Increased by Repeal of Carryover Basis" 7 *Estate Planning* 130 (1980)

Lyons, "Income Tax Planning by Executors" 114 *Trusts and Estates* 598 (1975)

Saunders and Jackson, "Use of Disclaimers in Estate Planning Clarified" 6 *Estate Planning* 24 (1979)

Weigel and Trost, "Tax Elections: When and How to Make Compensatory Adjustments" 6 *Estate Planning* 130 (1979)

Wright, "Post-Mortem Planning and Management of Estate to Minimize Tax Burden" 1 *Estate Planning* 130 (1974)

"Recent Developments in Estate and Gift Taxes: Disclaimer—The Proposed Regulations" 15 *Real Prop, Prob and Tr J* 743 (1980)

TABLE I   345

Appendixes

I.   TABLE I.   FEDERAL INDIVIDUAL INCOME TAX RATES

1. Joint Return Rates

Taxable Income	1982 % on Tax + Excess		1983 % on Tax + Excess		1984 % on Tax + Excess	
0— $3,400	-0-	-0-	-0-	-0-	-0-	-0-
$3,400— 5,500	-0-	12	-0-	11	-0-	11
5,500— 7,600	$252	14	$231	13	$231	12
7,600— 11,900	546	16	504	15	483	14
11,900— 16,000	1,234	19	1,149	17	1,085	16
16,000— 20,200	2,013	22	1,846	19	1,741	18
20,200— 24,600	2,937	25	2,644	23	2,497	22
24,600— 29,900	4,037	29	3,656	26	3,465	25
29,900— 35,200	5,574	33	5,034	30	4,790	28
35,200— 45,800	7,323	39	6,624	35	6,274	33
45,800— 60,000	11,457	44	10,334	40	9,772	38
60,000— 85,600	17,705	49	16,014	44	15,168	42
85,600—109,400	30,249	50	27,278	48	25,920	45
109,400—162,400	42,149	50	38,702	50	36,630	49
162,400—215,400	68,649	50	65,202	50	62,600	50
215,400—.	95,149	50	91,702	50	89,100	50

2. Head of Household Rates

Taxable Income	1982 % on Tax + Excess		1983 % on Tax + Excess		1984 % on Tax + Excess	
0— $2,300	-0-	-0-	-0-	-0-	-0-	-0-
$2,300— 4,400	-0-	12	-0-	11	-0-	11
4,400— 6,500	$252	14	$231	13	$231	12
6,500— 8,700	546	16	504	15	483	14
8,700— 11,800	898	20	834	18	791	17
11,800— 15,000	1,518	22	1,392	19	1,318	18
15,000— 18,200	2,222	23	2,000	21	1,894	20
18,200— 23,500	2,958	28	2,672	25	2,534	24
23,500— 28,800	4,442	32	3,997	29	3,806	28
28,800— 34,100	6,138	38	5,534	34	5,290	32
34,100— 44,700	8,152	41	7,336	37	6,986	35
44,700— 60,600	12,498	49	11,258	44	10,696	42
60,600— 81,800	20,289	50	18,254	48	17,374	45
81,800—108,300	30,889	50	28,430	50	26,914	48
108,300—161,300	44,139	50	41,680	50	39,634	50
161,300—.	70,639	50	68,180	50	66,134	50

3. Unmarried Individuals (other than surviving spouses and heads of households) Rates

Taxable Income	1982 Tax	% on Excess	1983 Tax	% on Excess	1984 Tax	% on Excess
0— $2,300	-0-	-0-	-0-	-0-	-0-	-0-
$2,300— 3,400	-0-	12	-0-	11	-0-	11
3,400— 4,400	$132	14	$121	13	$121	12
4,400— 6,500	272	16	251	15	241	14
6,500— 8,500	608	17	566	15	535	15
8,500— 10,800	948	19	866	17	835	16
10,800— 12,900	1,385	22	1,257	19	1,203	18
12,900— 15,000	1,847	23	1,656	21	1,581	20
15,000— 18,200	2,330	27	2,097	24	2,001	23
18,200— 23,500	3,194	31	2,865	28	2,737	26
23,500— 28,800	4,837	35	4,349	32	4,115	30
28,800— 34,100	6,692	40	6,045	36	5,705	34
34,100— 41,500	8,812	44	7,953	40	7,507	38
41,500— 55,300	12,068	50	10,913	45	10,319	42
55,300— 81,800	18,968	50	17,123	50	16,115	48
81,800—108,300	32,218	50	30,373	50	28,835	50
108,300—......	45,468	50	43,623	50	42,085	50

4. Married Individuals Filing Separate Returns Rates

Taxable Income	1982 Tax	% on Excess	1983 Tax	% on Excess	1984 Tax	% on Excess
0— $1,700	-0-	-0-	-0-	-0-	-0-	-0-
$1,700— 2,750	-0-	12	-0-	11	-0-	11
2,750— 3,800	$126	14	$115	13	$115	12
3,800— 5,950	273	16	252	15	241	14
5,950— 8,000	617	19	574	17	542	16
8,000— 10,100	1,006	22	923	19	870	18
10,100— 12,300	1,468	25	1,322	23	1,248	22
12,300— 14,950	2,018	29	1,828	26	1,732	25
14,950— 17,600	2,787	33	2,517	30	2,395	28
17,600— 22,900	3,661	39	3,312	35	3,137	33
22,900— 30,000	5,728	44	5,167	40	4,886	38
30,000— 42,800	8,852	49	8,007	44	7,584	42
42,800— 54,700	15,124	50	13,639	48	12,960	45
54,700— 81,200	21,074	50	19,351	50	18,315	49
81,200—107,700	34,324	50	32,601	50	31,300	50
107,700—......	47,574	50	45,851	50	44,550	50

TABLE I 347

5. Estates and Trusts Rates

Taxable Income	1982 Tax +	% on Excess	1983 Tax +	% on Excess	1984 Tax +	% on Excess
0— $1,050	-0-	12	-0-	11	-0-	11
$1,050— 2,100	$126	14	$115	13	$115	12
2,100— 4,250	273	16	252	15	241	14
4,250— 6,300	617	19	574	17	542	16
6,300— 8,400	1,060	22	923	19	870	18
8,400— 10,600	1,468	25	1,322	23	1,248	22
10,600— 13,250	2,018	29	1,828	26	1,732	25
13,250— 15,900	2,787	33	2,517	30	2,395	28
15,900— 21,200	3,661	39	3,312	35	3,137	33
21,200— 28,300	5,728	44	5,167	40	4,886	38
28,300— 41,100	8,852	49	8,007	44	7,584	42
41,100— 53,000	15,124	50	13,639	48	12,960	45
53,000— 79,500	21,074	50	19,351	50	18,315	49
79,500—106,000	34,324	50	32,601	50	31,300	50
106,000—.	47,574	50	456,851	50	44,550	50

II.   TABLE II: FEDERAL UNIFIED TRANSFER TAX RATES

A.   1982

| If the amount is: | | Tentative tax is: | | |
Over	But not over	Tax	+ %	On Excess Over
0	$ 10,000	0	18	0
$ 10,000	20,000	$ 1,800	20	$ 10,000
20,000	40,000	3,800	22	20,000
40,000	60,000	8,200	24	40,000
60,000	80,000	13,000	26	60,000
80,000	100,000	18,200	28	80,000
100,000	150,000	23,800	30	100,000
150,000	250,000	38,800	32	150,000
250,000	500,000	70,800	34	250,000
500,000	750,000	155,800	37	500,000
750,000	1,000,000	248,300	39	750,000
1,000,000	1,250,000	345,800	41	1,000,000
1,250,000	1,500,000	448,300	43	1,250,000
1,500,000	2,000,000	555,800	45	1,500,000
2,000,000	2,500,000	780,800	49	2,000,000
2,500,000	3,000,000	1,025,800	53	2,500,000
3,000,000	3,500,000	1,290,800	57	3,000,000
3,500,000	4,000,000	1,575,800	61	3,500,000
4,000,000	. . . . . .	1,880,800	65	4,000,000

TABLE II   349

B.   1983

If the amount is:		Tentative tax is:			
Over	But not over	Tax	+	%	On Excess Over
0	$ 10,000	0	18		0
$ 10,000	20,000	$ 1,800	20	$ 10,000
20,000	40,000	3,800	22	20,000
40,000	60,000	8,200	24	40,000
60,000	80,000	13,000	26	60,000
80,000	100,000	18,200	28	80,000
100,000	150,000	23,800	30	100,000
150,000	250,000	38,800	32	150,000
250,000	500,000	70,800	34	250,000
500,000	750,000	155,800	37	500,000
750,000	1,000,000	248,300	39	750,000
1,000,000	1,250,000	345,800	41	1,000,000
1,250,000	1,500,000	448,300	43	1,250,000
1,500,000	2,000,000	555,800	45	1,500,000
2,000,000	2,500,000	780,800	49	2,000,000
2,500,000	3,000,000	1,025,800	53	2,500,000
3,000,000	3,500,000	1,290,800	57	3,000,000
3,500,000	. . . . . .	1,575,800	60	3,500,000

C.   1984

If the amount is:		Tentative tax is:			
Over	But not over	Tax	+	%	On Excess Over
0	$ 10,000	0	18		0
$ 10,000	20,000	$ 1,800	20		$ 10,000
20,000	40,000	3,800	22		20,000
40,000	60,000	8,200	24		40,000
60,000	80,000	13,000	26		60,000
80,000	100,000	18,200	28		80,000
100,000	150,000	23,800	30		100,000
150,000	250,000	38,800	32		150,000
250,000	500,000	70,800	34		250,000
500,000	750,000	155,800	37		500,000
750,000	1,000,000	248,300	39		750,000
1,000,000	1,250,000	345,800	41		1,000,000
1,250,000	1,500,000	448,300	43		1,250,000
1,500,000	2,000,000	555,800	45		1,500,000
2,000,000	2,500,000	780,800	49		2,000,000
2,500,000	3,000,000	1,025,800	53		2,500,000
3,000,000	. . . . . .	1,290,800	55		3,000,000

TABLE II   351

D.   1985 and thereafter

| If the amount is: | | Tentative tax is: | | |
Over	But not over	Tax	+	%	On Excess Over
0	$ 10,000	0	18	0
$ 10,000	20,000	$ 1,800	20	$ 10,000
20,000	40,000	3,800	22	20,000
40,000	60,000	8,200	24	40,000
60,000	80,000	13,000	26	60,000
80,000	100,000	18,200	28	80,000
100,000	150,000	23,800	30	100,000
150,000	250,000	38,800	32	150,000
250,000	500,000	70,800	34	250,000
500,000	750,000	155,800	37	500,000
750,000	1,000,000	248,300	39	750,000
1,000,000	1,250,000	345,800	41	1,000,000
1,250,000	1,500,000	448,300	43	1,250,000
1,500,000	2,000,000	555,800	45	1,500,000
2,000,000	2,500,000	780,800	49	2,000,000
2,500,000	. . . . . .	1,025,800	50	2,500,000

III.   TABLE III: MAXIMUM CREDIT AGAINST FEDERAL ESTATE TAX FOR STATE DEATH TAXES

Adjusted Taxable Estate[1]	Amount of Credit	Rate on Excess
$ 40,000	$ -0-	0.8%
90,000	400	1.6
140,000	1,200	2.4
240,000	3,600	3.2
440,000	10,000	4.0
640,000	18,000	4.8
840,000	27,600	5.6
1,040,000	38,800	6.4
1,540,000	70,800	7.2
2,040,000	106,800	8.0
2,540,000	146,800	8.8
3,040,000	190,800	9.6
3,540,000	238,800	10.4
4,040,000	290,800	11.2
5,040,000	402,800	12.0
6,040,000	522,800	12.8
7,040,000	650,800	13.6
8,040,000	786,800	14.4
9,040,000	930,800	15.2
10,040,000	1,082,800	16.0

1. Adjusted Taxable Estate is the Taxable estate minus $60,000.

TABLE IV   353

IV.   TABLE IV: UNIFIED CREDIT

Year		Amount of Credit	Amount of Exemption Equivalent
1977	. . . .	$ 30,000	$120,667
1978	. . . .	34,000	134,000
1979	. . . .	38,000	147,333
1980	. . . .	42,500	161,563
1981	. . . .	47,000	175,625
1982	. . . .	62,800	225,000
1983	. . . .	79,300	275,000
1984	. . . .	96,300	325,000
1985	. . . .	121,800	400,000
1986	. . . .	155,800	500,000
1987	and thereafter	192,800	600,000

V.   TABLE V: CALIFORNIA INHERITANCE AND GIFT TAX RATES AND EXEMPTIONS

Class A

Total Amount of Beneficiaries' Interest Before Exemption		Surviving Spouse (All transfers except limited powers of appointment are exempt)		Minor Child (1st $40,000 Exempt)		Lineal Ancestor, Mutually Acknowledged Child or Lineal Issue of the Decedent (1st $20,000 Exempt)	
I Amount Equal to	II Amount Not in Excess of	Tax on Amount in Col. I	Rate on Excess Over Amount in Col. I (Percent)	Tax on Amount in Col. I	Rate on Excess Over Amount in Col. I (Percent)	Tax on Amount in Col. I	Rate on Excess Over Amount in Col. I (Percent)
$ 0	$ 20,000	. . . . .	3	. . . . .	. . . .	. . . . .	. . . .
20,000	25,000	$ 600	3	. . . . .	. . . .	. . . . .	3
25,000	40,000	750	4	. . . . .	. . . .	$ 150	4
40,000	50,000	1,350	4	. . . . .	4	750	4
50,000	100,000	1,750	6	$ 400	6	1,150	6
100,000	200,000	4,750	8	3,400	8	4,150	8
200,000	300,000	12,750	10	11,400	10	12,150	10
300,000	400,000	22,750	12	21,400	12	22,150	12
400,000	. . . . .	34,750	14	33,400	14	34,150	14

TABLE V   355

Total Amount of Beneficiaries' Interest Before Exemption		Class B Brother, Sister, Descendants of Brother or Sister, Wife or Widow of Son, Husband or Widower of Daughter (1st $10,000 Exempt)		Class C Any Person Not Mentioned Before; Includes Organizations, Stranger, Uncle, Aunt, or Descendant of Either (1st $3,000 Exempt)	
I Amount Equal to	II Amount Not in Excess of	Tax on Amount in Col. I	Rate on Excess Over Amount in Col. I (Percent)	Tax on Amount in Col. I	Rate on Excess Over Amount in Col. I (Percent)
$ 0	$ 3,000	. . . . .	. . . .	. . . . .	. . . .
3,000	10,000	. . . . .	. . . .	. . . . .	10
10,000	25,000	. . . . .	6	$ 700	10
25,000	50,000	$ 900	10	2,200	14
50,000	100,000	3,400	12	5,700	16
100,000	200,000	9,400	14	13,700	18
200,000	300,000	23,400	16	31,700	20
300,000	400,000	39,400	18	51,700	22
400,000	. . . . .	57,400	20	73,700	24

VI.   TABLE VI: NEW YORK STATE ESTATE TAX RATES

New York Taxable or Net estate (Before adding credits or deducting exemptions)		Tax =	+	%	Of Excess Over
From	To				
$ 0	$ 50,000	$ 0		2%	$ 0
50,000	150,000	1,000		3%	50,000
150,000	300,000	4,000		4%	150,000
300,000	500,000	10,000		5%	300,000
500,000	700,000	20,000		6%	500,000
700,000	900,000	32,000		7%	700,000
900,000	1,100,000	46,000		8%	900,000
1,100,000	1,600,000	62,000		9%	1,100,000
1,600,000	2,100,000	107,000		10%	1,600,000
2,100,000	2,600,000	157,000		11%	2,100,000
2,600,000	3,100,000	212,000		12%	2,600,000
3,100,000	3,600,000	272,000		13%	3,100,000
3,600,000	4,100,000	337,000		14%	3,600,000
4,100,000	5,100,000	407,000		15%	4,100,000
5,100,000	6,100,000	557,000		16%	5,100,000
6,100,000	7,100,000	717,000		17%	6,100,000
7,100,000	8,100,000	887,000		18%	7,100,000
8,100,000	9,100,000	1,067,000		19%	8,100,000
9,100,000	10,100,000	1,257,000		20%	9,100,000
10,100,000	. . . .	1,457,000		21%	10,100,000

TABLE VII   357

VII.   TABLE VII: NEW YORK STATE GIFT TAX RATES

New York Taxable Gifts

From		To	Tax =	+ %	Of Excess Over
$ 0	$	50,000	$ 0	1½%	$ 0
50,000		150,000	750	2¼%	50,000
150,000		300,000	3,000	3%	150,000
300,000		500,000	7,500	3¾%	300,000
500,000		700,000	15,000	4½%	500,000
700,000		900,000	24,000	5¼%	700,000
900,000		1,100,000	34,500	6%	900,000
1,100,000		1,600,000	46,500	6¾%	1,100,000
1,600,000		2,100,000	80,250	7½%	1,600,000
2,100,000		2,600,000	117,750	8¼%	2,100,000
2,600,000		3,100,000	159,000	9%	2,600,000
3,100,000		3,600,000	204,000	9¾%	3,100,000
3,600,000		4,100,000	252,750	10½%	3,600,000
4,100,000		5,100,000	305,250	11¼%	4,100,000
5,100,000		6,100,000	417,750	12%	5,100,000
6,100,000		7,100,000	537,750	12¾%	6,100,000
7,100,000		8,100,000	665,250	13½%	7,100,000
8,100,000		9,100,000	800,250	14¼%	8,100,000
9,100,000		10,100,000	942,750	15%	9,100,000
10,100,000		. . . .	1,092,750	15¾%	10,100,000

VIII.   TABLE VIII: VALUATION OF ANNUITIES; LIFE ESTATES AND REMAINDERS (Reg. §20.2031-10)

TABLE A (1)

Table, single life male, 6 per cent, showing the present worth of an annuity, of a life interest, and of a remainder interest

1 Age	2 Annuity	3 Life Estate	4 Remainder
0	15.6175	.93705	.06295
1	16.0362	.96217	.03783
2	16.0283	.96170	.03830
3	16.0089	.96053	.03947

1 Age	2 Annuity	3 Life Estate	4 Remainder
4	15.9841	.95905	.04095
5	15.9553	.95732	.04268
6	15.9233	.95540	.04460
7	15.8885	.95331	.04669
8	15.8508	.95105	.04895
9	15.8101	.94861	.05139
10	15.7663	.94598	.05402
11	15.7194	.94316	.05684
12	15.6698	.94019	.05981
13	15.6180	.93708	.06292
14	15.5651	.93391	.06609
15	15.5115	.93069	.06931
16	15.4576	.92746	.07254
17	15.4031	.92419	.07581
18	15.3481	.92089	.07911
19	15.2918	.91751	.08249
20	15.2339	.91403	.08597
21	15.1744	.91046	.08954
22	15.1130	.90678	.09322
23	15.0487	.90292	.09708
24	14.9807	.89884	.10116
25	14.9075	.89445	.10555
26	14.8287	.88972	.11028
27	14.7442	.88465	.11535
28	14.6542	.87925	.12075
29	14.5588	.87353	.12647
30	14.4584	.86750	.13250
31	14.3528	.86117	.13883
32	14.2418	.85451	.14549
33	14.1254	.84752	.15248
34	14.0034	.84020	.15980
35	13.8758	.83255	.16745
36	13.7425	.82455	.17545
37	13.6036	.81622	.18378
38	13.4591	.80755	.19245
39	13.3090	.79854	.20146
40	13.1538	.78923	.21077

TABLE VIII   359

1 Age	2 Annuity	3 Life Estate	4 Remainder
41	12.9934	.77960	.22040
42	12.8279	.76967	.23033
43	12.6574	.75944	.24056
44	12.4819	.74891	.25109
45	12.3013	.73808	.26192
46	12.1158	.72695	.27305
47	11.9253	.71552	.28448
48	11.7308	.70385	.29615
49	11.5330	.69198	.30802
50	11.3329	.67997	.32003
51	11.1308	.66785	.33215
52	10.9267	.65560	.34440
53	10.7200	.64320	.35680
54	10.5100	.63060	.36940
55	10.2960	.61776	.38224
56	10.0777	.60466	.39534
57	9.8552	.59131	.40869
58	9.6297	.57778	.42222
59	9.4028	.56417	.43583
60	9.1753	.55052	.44948
61	8.9478	.53687	.46313
62	8.7202	.52321	.47679
63	8.4924	.50954	.49046
64	8.2642	.49585	.50415
65	8.0353	.48212	.51788
66	7.8060	.46836	.53164
67	7.5763	.45458	.54542
68	7.3462	.44077	.55923
69	7.1149	.42689	.57311
70	6.8823	.41294	.58706
71	6.6481	.39889	.60111
72	6.4123	.38474	.61526
73	6.1752	.37051	.62949
74	5.9373	.35624	.64376
75	5.6990	.34194	.65806
76	5.4602	.32761	.67239
77	5.2211	.31327	.68673

1 Age	2 Annuity	3 Life Estate	4 Remainder
78	4.9825	.29895	.70105
79	4.7469	.28481	.71519
80	4.5164	.27098	.72902
81	4.2955	.25773	.74227
82	4.0879	.24527	.75473
83	3.8924	.23354	.76646
84	3.7029	.22217	.77783
85	3.5117	.21070	.78930
86	3.3529	.19955	.80045
87	3.1450	.18870	.81130
88	2.9703	.17822	.82178
89	2.8052	.16831	.83169
90	2.6536	.15922	.84078
91	2.5162	.15097	.84903
92	2.3917	.14350	.85650
93	2.2801	.13681	.86319
94	2.1802	.13081	.86919
95	2.0891	.12535	.87465
96	1.9997	.11998	.88002
97	1.9145	.11487	.88513
98	1.8331	.10999	.89001
99	1.7554	.10532	.89468
100	1.6812	.10087	.89913
101	1.6101	.09661	.90339
102	1.5416	.09250	.90750
103	1.4744	.08846	.91154
104	1.4065	.08439	.91561
105	1.3334	.08000	.92000
106	1.2452	.07471	.92529
107	1.1196	.06718	.93282
108	.9043	.05426	.94574
109	.4717	.02830	.97170

TABLE VIII   361

TABLE A (2)

Table, single life female, 6 per cent, showing the present worth of an annuity, of a life interest, and of a remainder interest

1 Age	2 Annuity	3 Life Estate	4 Remainder
0	15.8972	.95383	.04617
1	16.2284	.97370	.02630
2	16.2287	.97372	.02628
3	16.2180	.97308	.02692
4	16.2029	.97217	.02783
5	16.1850	.97110	.02890
6	16.1648	.96989	.03011
7	16.1421	.96853	.03147
8	16.1172	.96703	.03297
9	16.0901	.96541	.03459
10	16.0608	.96365	.03635
11	16.0293	.96176	.03824
12	15.9958	.95975	.04025
13	15.9607	.95764	.04236
14	15.9239	.95543	.04457
15	15.8856	.95314	.04686
16	15.8460	.95076	.04924
17	15.8048	.94829	.05171
18	15.7620	.94572	.05428
19	15.7172	.94303	.05697
20	15.6701	.94021	.05979
21	15.6207	.93724	.06276
22	15.5687	.93412	.06588
23	15.5141	.93085	.06915
24	15.4565	.92739	.07261
25	15.3959	.92375	.07625
26	15.3322	.91993	.08007
27	15.2652	.91591	.08409
28	15.1946	.91168	.08832
29	15.1208	.90725	.09275
30	15.0432	.90259	.09741
31	14.9622	.89773	.10227
32	14.8775	.89265	.10735
33	14.7888	.88733	.11267
34	14.6960	.88176	.11824
35	14.5989	.87593	.12407

1 Age	2 Annuity	3 Life Estate	4 Remainder
36	14.4975	.86985	.13015
37	14.3915	.86349	.13651
38	14.2811	.85687	.14313
39	14.1663	.84998	.15002
40	14.0468	.84281	.15719
41	13.9227	.83536	.16464
42	13.7940	.82764	.17236
43	13.6604	.81962	.18038
44	13.5219	.81131	.18869
45	13.3781	.80269	.19731
46	13.2290	.79374	.20626
47	13.0746	.78448	.21552
48	12.9147	.77488	.22512
49	12.7496	.76498	.23502
50	12.5793	.75476	.24524
51	12.4039	.74423	.25577
52	12.2232	.73339	.26661
53	12.0367	.72220	.27780
54	11.8436	.71062	.28938
55	11.6432	.69859	.30141
56	11.4353	.68612	.31388
57	11.2200	.67320	.32680
58	10.9980	.65988	.34012
59	10.7703	.64622	.35378
60	10.5376	.63226	.36774
61	10.3005	.61803	.38197
62	10.0587	.60352	.39648
63	9.8118	.58871	.41129
64	9.5592	.57355	.42645
65	9.3005	.55803	.44197
66	9.0352	.54211	.45789
67	8.7639	.52583	.47417
68	8.4874	.50924	.49076
69	8.2068	.49241	.50759
70	7.9234	.47540	.52460
71	7.6371	.45823	.54177
72	7.3480	.44088	.55912

TABLE VIII   363

1 Age	2 Annuity	3 Life Estate	4 Remainder
73	7.0568	.42341	.57659
74	6.7645	.40587	.59413
75	6.4721	.38833	.61167
76	6.1788	.37073	.62927
77	5.8845	.35307	.64693
78	5.5910	.33546	.66454
79	5.3018	.31811	.68189
80	5.0195	.30117	.69883
81	4.7482	.28489	.71511
82	4.4892	.26935	.73065
83	4.2398	.25439	.74561
84	3.9927	.23956	.76044
85	3.7401	.22441	.77559
86	3.5016	.21010	.78990
87	3.2790	.19674	.80326
88	3.0719	.18431	.81569
89	2.8808	.17285	.82715
90	2.7068	.16241	.83759
91	2.5502	.15301	.84699
92	2.4116	.14470	.85530
93	2.2901	.13741	.86259
94	2.1839	.13103	.86897
95	2.0891	.12535	.87465
96	1.9997	.11998	.88002
97	1.9145	.11487	.88513
98	1.8331	.10999	.89001
99	1.7554	.10532	.89468
100	1.6812	.10087	.89913
101	1.6101	.09661	.90339
102	1.5416	.09250	.90750
103	1.4744	.08846	.91154
104	1.4065	.08439	.91561
105	1.3334	.08000	.92000
106	1.2452	.07471	.92529
107	1.1196	.06718	.93282
108	.9043	.05426	.94574
109	.4717	.02830	.97170

TABLE B

Table showing the present worth at 6 per cent of an annuity for a term certain, of an income interest for a term certain, and of a remainder interest postponed for a term certain

1 Number of Years	2 Annuity	3 Term Certain	4 Remainder
1	0.9434	.056604	.943396
2	1.8334	.110004	.889996
3	2.6730	.160381	.839619
4	3.4651	.207906	.792094
5	4.2124	.252742	.747258
6	4.9173	.295039	.704961
7	5.5824	.334943	.665057
8	6.2098	.372588	.627412
9	6.8017	.408102	.591898
10	7.3601	.441605	.558395
11	7.8869	.473212	.526788
12	8.3838	.503031	.496969
13	8.8527	.531161	.468839
14	9.2950	.557699	.442301
15	9.7122	.582735	.417265
16	10.1059	.606354	.393646
17	10.4773	.628636	.371364
18	10.8276	.649656	.350344
19	11.1581	.669487	.330513
20	11.4699	.688195	.311805
21	11.7641	.705845	.294155
22	12.0416	.722495	.277505
23	12.3034	.738203	.261797
24	12.5504	.753021	.246979
25	12.7834	.767001	.232999
26	13.0032	.780190	.219810
27	13.2105	.792632	.207368
28	13.4062	.804370	.195630
29	13.5907	.815443	.184557
30	13.7648	.825890	.174110

TABLE VIII 365

1 Age	2 Annuity	3 Life Estate	4 Remainder
31	13.9291	.835745	.164255
32	14.0840	.845043	.154957
33	14.2302	.853814	.146186
34	14.3681	.862088	.137912
35	14.4982	.869895	.130105
36	14.6210	.877259	.122741
37	14.7368	.884207	.115793
38	14.8460	.890761	.109239
39	14.9491	.896944	.103056
40	15.0463	.902778	.097222
41	15.1380	.908281	.091719
42	15.2245	.913473	.086527
43	15.3062	.918370	.081630
44	15.3832	.922991	.077009
45	15.4558	.927350	.072650
46	15.5244	.931462	.068538
47	15.5890	.935342	.064653
48	15.6500	.939002	.060998
49	15.7076	.942454	.057546
50	15.7619	.945712	.054288
51	15.8131	.948785	.051215
52	15.8614	.951684	.048316
53	15.9070	.954418	.045582
54	15.9500	.956999	.043001
55	15.9905	.959433	.040567
56	16.0288	.961729	.038271
57	16.0649	.963895	.036105
58	16.0990	.965939	.034061
59	16.1311	.967867	.032133
60	16.1614	.969686	.030314

IX.   TABLE IX: ORDINARY LIFE ANNUITIES—ONE LIFE—EXPECTED RETURN MULTIPLES (Reg. §1.72-9)

Ordinary Life Annuities—One Life—Expected Return Multiples

| Ages | | Multiples | Ages | | Multiples | Ages | | Multiples |
Male	Female		Male	Female		Male	Female	
6	11	65.0	41	46	33.0	76	81	9.1
7	12	64.1	42	47	32.1	77	82	8.7
8	13	63.2	43	48	31.2	78	83	8.3
9	14	62.3	44	49	30.4	79	84	7.8
10	15	61.4	45	50	29.6	80	85	7.5
11	16	60.4	46	51	23.7	81	86	7.1
12	17	59.5	47	52	27.9	82	87	6.7
13	18	58.6	48	53	27.1	83	88	6.3
14	19	57.7	49	54	26.3	84	89	6.0
15	20	56.7	50	55	25.5	85	90	5.7
16	21	55.3	51	56	24.7	86	91	5.4
17	22	54.9	52	57	24.0	87	92	5.1
18	23	53.9	53	58	23.2	88	93	4.8
19	24	53.0	54	59	22.4	89	94	4.5
20	25	52.1	55	60	21.7	90	95	4.2
21	26	51.1	56	61	21.0	91	96	4.0
22	27	50.2	57	62	20.3	92	97	3.7
23	28	49.3	58	63	19.6	93	98	3.5
24	29	48.3	59	64	18.9	94	99	3.3
25	30	47.4	60	65	18.2	95	100	3.1
26	31	46.5	61	66	17.5	96	101	2.9
27	32	45.6	62	67	16.9	97	102	2.7
28	33	44.6	63	68	16.2	98	103	2.5
29	34	43.7	64	69	15.6	99	104	2.3
30	35	42.8	65	70	15.0	100	105	2.1
31	36	41.9	66	71	14.4	101	106	1.9
32	37	41.0	67	72	13.8	102	107	1.7
33	38	40.0	68	73	13.2	103	108	1.5
34	39	39.1	69	74	12.6	104	109	1.3
35	40	38.2	70	75	12.1	105	110	1.2

TABLE IX   367

Ages		Multiples	Ages		Multiples	Ages		Multiples
Male	Female		Male	Female		Male	Female	
36	41	37.3	71	76	11.6	106	111	1.0
37	42	36.5	72	77	11.0	107	112	.8
38	43	35.6	73	78	10.5	108	113	.7
39	44	34.7	74	79	10.1	109	114	.6
40	45	33.8	75	80	9.6	110	115	.3
						111	116	0

X.   TABLE X: P. S. NO. 58 RATES (Rev. Rul. 55-747, 1955-2 C.B. 228; Rev. Rul. 66-110, 1966-1 C.B. 12)
Uniform One Year Term Premiums for $1,000
Life Insurance Protection
(Based on Table 38, U.S. Life Tables and Actuarial Tables
(U.S. Government Printing Office, Washington, D.C.—1946),
and 2½% interest.)

Age	Premium	Age	Premium	Age	Premium
15	$1.27	37	$ 3.63	60	$ 20.73
16	1.38	38	3.87	61	22.53
17	1.48	39	4.14	62	24.50
18	1.52	40	4.42	63	26.63
19	1.56	41	4.73	64	28.98
20	1.61	42	5.07	65	31.51
21	1.67	43	5.44	66	34.28
22	1.73	44	5.85	67	37.31
23	1.79	45	6.30	68	40.59
24	1.86	46	6.78	69	44.17
25	1.93	47	7.32	70	48.06
26	2.02	48	7.89	71	52.29
27	2.11	49	8.53	72	56.89
28	2.20	50	9.22	73	61.89
29	2.31	51	9.97	74	67.33
30	2.43	52	10.79	75	73.23
31	2.57	53	11.69	76	79.63
32	2.70	54	12.67	77	86.57
33	2.86	55	13.74	78	94.09
34	3.02	56	14.91	79	102.23
35	3.21	57	16.18	80	111.04
36	3.41	58	17.56	81	120.57
		59	19.08		

Statutes (IRC)

Treasury Regulations

Revenue Rulings and Procedures

Rulings

53-189, 1953-2 CB 294 §**12.64**

55-119, 1955-1 CB 352 §**11.16**

55-225, 1955-1 CB 460 §**15.22**

55-747, 1955-2 CB 228 §§**10.57,
  10.58**

56-103, 1956-1 CB 159 §**12.33**

56-222, 1956-1 CB 155 §§**4.30, 7.32**

56-484, 1956-2 CB 23 §**8.29**

58-111, 1958-1 CB 173 §**12.33**

58-614, 1958-2 CB 920 §**10.53**

59-32, 1959-1 CB 245 §**15.24**

59-60, 1959-1 CB 237 §§**12.2, 12.9**

59-184, 1959-1 CB 65 §**10.53**

59-233, 1959-2 CB 106 §**12.33**

59-357, 1959-2 CB 212 §§**8.31,
  10.45**

60-18, 1960-1 CB 145 §**12.33**

60-84, 1960-1 CB 159 §**10.58**

60-331, 1960-2 CB 189 §**9.16**

64-328, 1964-2 CB 11 §**10.57**

65-284, 1965-2 CB 28 §**10.28**

65-289, 1965-2 CB 86 §**12.38**

66-161, 1966-1 CB 164 §**9.9**

66-167, 1966-1 CB 20 §**15.30**

66-262, 1966-2 CB 105 §**10.53**

66-283, 1966-2 CB 297 §**7.25**

67-74, 1967-1 CB 194 §**4.19**

67-383, 1967-2 CB 325 §**5.19**

68-99, 1968-1 CB 193 §**10.54**

68-453, 1968-2 CB 163 §**10.58**

68-609, 1968-2 CB 327 §**12.5**

68-670, 1968-2 CB 413 §**8.36**

69-54, 1969-1 CB 221 §**10.56**

69-74, 1969-1 CB 43 §**11.15**

69-187, 1969-1 CB 45 §**10.29**

69-344, 1969-1 CB 225 §§**8.34,
  10.20**

71-497, 1971-2 CB 329 §§**10.15,
  10.36**

72-25, 1972-1 CB 127 §**10.54**

72-81, 1972-1 CB 98 §**11.16**

72-395, 1972-2 CB 340 §§**14.23,
  14.25**

72-438, 1972-2 CB 38 §**14.37**

72-571, 1972-2 CB 533 §**9.9**

73-61, 1973-1 CB 408 §**9.21**

73-97, 1973-1 CB 404 §**7.30**

74-613, 1974-2 CB 153 §**7.18**

75-72, 1975-1 CB 310 §**8.1**

75-240, 1975-1 CB 315 §**13.18**

75-365, 1975-2 CB 471 §**12.54**

75-366, 1975-2 CB 472 §**12.54**

75-367, 1975-2 CB 472 §**12.54**

75-487, 1975-2 CB 488 §§**12.52,
  12.56**

76-274, 1976-2 CB 278 §**10.57**

76-304, 1976-2 CB 269 §**12.47**

Procedures

Letter Rulings

Cases

Index

W

Cisco Networking Academy Program: First-Year Companion Guide Supplement

Vito Amato, Series Editor
Wayne Lewis, Contributor

CISCO SYSTEMS

CISCO PRESS

Cisco Press
201 West 103rd Street
Indianapolis, IN 46290

Cisco Networking Academy Program: First-Year Companion Guide Supplement

Vito Amato, Series Editor

Copyright © 2000 by Cisco Systems, Inc.

FIRST EDITION, Revised Printing

International Standard Book Number: 1-58713-015-7

Library of Congress Catalog Card Number: 00-100255

02   01   00   3   2   1

Interpretation of the printing code: The rightmost double-digit number is the year of the book's printing; the rightmost single-digit, the number of the book's printing. For example, the printing code 00-1 shows that the first printing of the book occurred in 2000.

Printed in the United States of America

Trademark Acknowledgments

Warning and Disclaimer

Feedback Information

At Cisco Press, our goal is to create in-depth technical books of the highest quality and value. Each book is crafted with care and precision, undergoing rigorous development that involves the unique expertise of members from the professional technical community.

Readers' feedback is a natural continuation of this process. If you have any comments regarding how we could improve the quality of this book, or otherwise alter it to better suit your needs, you can contact us at ciscopress@mcp.com. Please make sure to include the book title and ISBN in your message.

We greatly appreciate your assistance.

Publisher	*John Wait*
Executive Editor	*Dave Dusthimer*
Managing Editor	*Patrick Kanouse*
Development Editor	*Kitty Wilson Jarrett*
Technical Reviewers	*Denise Hoyt*
	Mark McGregor
	Wayne Jarvimaki
Senior Editor	*Jennifer Chisholm*
Indexer	*Kevin Fulcher*
	Tim Wright
Acquisitions Coordinator	*Amy Lewis*
Associate Editor	*Shannon Gross*
Manufacturing Coordinator	*Chris Moos*
Cover Designer	*Louisa Klucznik*
Production	*Argosy*
	Gina Rexrode
	Steve Gifford

About the Series Editor and Contributor

Vito Amato is a senior technical writer at Cisco Systems for World Wide Education. Previously, he was the Information Technology Director at the Arizona Department of Education. Vito earned his Ph.D. at Arizona State University, specializing in curriculum and instruction with an emphasis on educational media and computers. In addition, Vito is currently teaching distance education theory and practice at ASU. During the last three years, Vito has been involved in the planning, writing, and implementation of the Cisco Networking Academy program. Lastly, his research, writing, and teaching focus is the integration of information technology into the teaching/learning environment.

Wayne Lewis is the Cisco Academy Training Center Coordinator for Honolulu Community College. He provides training to Cisco Academy Instructors in Japan, Taiwan, Indonesia, Hong Kong, and the U.S. Wayne received a Ph.D. in math from the University of Hawaii in 1992. He is a Cisco Certified Network Professional (CCNP), Cisco Certified Design Associate (CCDA), Cisco Certified Design Professional (CCDP), Cisco Certified Academy Instructor (CCAI), and Microsoft Certified Professional (MCP). In his free time, Wayne enjoys surfing the North Shore of Oahu.

About the Technical Reviewers

This book's reviewers contributed their considerable practical, hands-on expertise to the entire development process for *Cisco Networking Academy Program: First-Year Companion Guide*, Revised Printing. As the book was being written, these folks reviewed all the material for technical content, organization, and flow. Their feedback was critical to ensuring that *Cisco Networking Academy Program: First-Year Companion Guide*, Revised Printing, fits our readers' need for the highest-quality technical information.

Denise Hoyt has been a teacher for 16 years. She received her bachelor's degree from California State University, Chico, and her master's degree in administration from the University of Redlands. She received her Cisco Networking Academy Program Instructor certification in the summer of 1998. In the fall of 1998, she became the Cisco Systems Academy Regional Coordinator for San Bernardino County. Denise also serves as the county's technology coordinator and teaches the Cisco Networking Academy Program Curriculum at Yucaipa High School in Yucaipa, California.

Mark McGregor, CCNA, is a Cisco Networking Academy Program Instructor at Los Medanos College and Antioch Adult School in Northern California. He holds a bachelor's degree in English from the University of California, Davis, and has taught in public schools for five years with a focus on at-risk youth and alternative education.

Wayne Jarvimaki, CCNA, CCAI, is an Instructor and Program Director at North Seattle CATC. He has been training Regional and CATC instructors since 1989. As a Networking Instructor, he was responsible for developing the Certificate/Degree option for Cisco Specialist at North Seattle Community College. Wayne also serves on the Cisco Networking Academy Curriculum Review Team.

Acknowledgments

This book would have not been possible without the vision and commitment of George Ward, Kevin Warner, Alex Belous, and David Alexander to the Cisco Networking Academy Program Program. Their support for the book has been tremendous. I would like to acknowledge their support not only in making the book a reality, but also in making the Cisco Networking Academy Program Program come alive. I also would like to acknowledge Jai Gosine and Dennis Frezzo for sharing their subject matter expertise, which allowed me to organize the content of this book. Most importantly, I would to thank my wife, Bonnie, and my kids, Tori, Michael, Matthew, and Laura, for their patience and support.

This book is a synthesis and integration of many Cisco educational publications. I would like to thank the education marketing development team at Cisco for their contribution. Finally, I would like to thank the team at Cisco Press, Dave Dusthimer, Amy Lewis, and Kitty Jarrett, for guiding me through the publication of this book.

Overview

Preface

With the full implementation of the Cisco Networking Academy Program program over the past two years, Cisco has instituted an online learning systems approach that integrates the multimedia delivery of a networking curriculum with testing, performance-based skills assessment, evaluation, and reporting through a Web interface. The Cisco Networking Academy Program curriculum goes beyond traditional computer-based instruction by helping students develop practical networking knowledge and skills in a hands-on environment. In a lab setting that closely corresponds to a real networking environment, students work with the architecture and infrastructure pieces of networking technology. As a result, students learn the principles and practices of networking technology.

The Cisco Networking Academy Program provides in-depth and meaningful networking content, which is being used by regional and local academies to teach students around the world by utilizing the curriculum to integrate networking instruction into the classroom. The focus of the Cisco Networking Academy Program is the integration of a Web-based network curriculum into the learning environment. This element is addressed through intensive staff development for teachers and innovative classroom materials and approaches to instruction, which are provided by Cisco. The participating educators are provided with resources, the means of remote access to online support, and the knowledge base for the effective classroom integration of the Cisco Networking Academy Program curriculum into the classroom learning environment. As a result, the Cisco Networking Academy Program provides the means for dynamic exchange of information by providing a suite of services that redefine the way instructional resources are disseminated, resulting in a many-to-many interactive and collaborative network of teachers and students functioning to meet diverse educational needs.

What makes the Cisco Networking Academy Program curriculum exciting to educators and students is the fact that the courseware is interactive. Because of the growing use of interactive technologies, the curriculum is an exciting new way to convey instruction with new interactive technologies that allow instructors and trainers to mix a number of media, including audio, video, text, numerical data, and graphics. Consequently, students can select different media from the computer screen and custom design their instructional content to meet their instructional needs, and educators have the option of either designing their own environment for assessment or selecting from the applicable assessments.

Finally, by developing a curriculum that recognizes the changing classroom and workforce demographics, the globalization of the economy, changing workforce knowledge and skill requirements, and the role of technology in education, the Cisco Networking Academy Program program supports national educational goals for K–12 education. As support for the Cisco Networking Academy Program, Cisco Press has published this book, *Cisco Networking Academy Program: First-Year Companion Guide,* Revised Printing, as a companion guide for the curriculum used in the Cisco Networking Academy Program program.

Introduction

Cisco Networking Academy Program: First-Year Companion Guide, Revised Printing, is designed to act as a supplement to the student's classroom and laboratory experience with version 2.1 of the Cisco Networking Academy curriculum. Since the first version of this book was published in the spring of 1999, the online curriculum has gone through two revisions. This revised printing was developed to provide you with a companion text that includes all of the information added to the curriculum. Because the publication of a book is an expensive and time-consuming endeavor, we have added the material new to version 2.1 in five appendixes in the back of the book. We did not reorganize the entire book. Instead, we have included a detailed mapping guide in this introduction that will help students and teachers track the reading assignments from this book to the chapters in version 2.1 of the curriculum. We have also included tracking references for the *Cisco Networking Academy Program: Engineering Journal and Workbook*, Volume 1.

Semester 1 v2.1 is structured entirely around the OSI model, with a structured cabling project midway through the semester. With these changes in the mind, the book includes a "Computer Basics" appendix, which provides foundational material essential to the course. In addition, the "Electronics and Signals" and the "Signaling and Data Transmission" appendixes have been introduced to make the media and electronics section of the course more meaningful. The "Binary and Hexadecimal Conversion" appendix reflects the binary and hexadecimal math content in the curriculum, which is taught separately from IP addressing to allow students time to master the math before applying it. The book also includes a "Network Troubleshooting" appendix to support the curriculum.

Finally, this book aims not only to prepare you for your CCNA test and certification, but also to prepare you for the CompTIA Net + networking certification exam. The OSI model is absolutely essential for all networking students preparing for the CCNA exam. The sections on collisions and segmentation are also very important for the CCNA exam, along with Ethernet, which is important to understand the dominant LAN technology. The IP addressing chapters are perhaps the most conceptually difficult, yet are very important chapters, especially for the CCNA exam. Lastly, the skills in the structured cabling and electricity chapters are crucial if you are seeking network-cabling related employment.

This mapping guide will help you implement the Companion Guide and Engineering Journal/Workbook with version 2.1 of the curriculum.

Curriculum Mapping Guide

The online curriculum is the most dynamic part of the Networking Academy Program. We suggest that you begin your study of each chapter with the online material and then move to the print products. Use the mapping guide to ensure that you get the most from the various components of the program.

Online Curriculum		1st Year Companion Guide, Revised Printing		1st Year Engineering Journal/Workbook	
Ch.	Title	Ch.	Title	Ch.	Title
1	Basics of Computing	D	Computer Basics	1	Basics of Computing
2	The OSI Model	1	Networking and the OSI Reference Model	2	The OSI Model
3	Local Area Networks	1	Networking and the OSI Reference Model	3	LANs
		3	Networking Devices	17	LANs: Layers 1, 2, 3
		4	LANs and WANs		
4	Electronics and Signals	E	Electronics and Signals	4	Electronics and Signals
5	Media Connections and Collisions	2	The Physical and Data Link Layers	5	Layer 1: Networking Media
6	Layer 2 Concepts	2	The Physical and Data Link Layers	6	Layer 2: Data Link Layer
7	Layer 2 Technologies	4	LANs and WANs	7	Layer 2: Technologies
8	Design and Documentation	8	Structured Cabling and Electricity	8	Design and Documentation

Online Curriculum		1st Year Companion Guide, Revised Printing		1st Year Engineering Journal/Workbook	
Ch.	Title	Ch.	Title	Ch.	Title
9	Structured Cabling Project	8	Structured Cabling and Electricity	9	Structured Cabling
10	Layer 3: Routing and Addressing	5	IP Addressing	10	Layer 3: Routing and Addressing
		7	Topologies		
		11	The Network Layer and Routing		
		G	Binary and Hexadecimal Conversion		
11	Layer 3 Routing Protocols	6	ARP and RARP	11	Layer 3: Routing Protocols
12	Layer 4 Transport Layer	9	The Application, Presentation, Session, and Transport Layers	12	Layer 4: The Transport Layer
				18	Layers 4, 5, 6, and 7
		10	TCP/IP		
13	Layer 5 Session Layer	9	The Application, Presentation, Session, and Transport Layers	13	Layer 5: The Session Layer
				18	Layers 4, 5, 6, and 7

Online Curriculum		1st Year Companion Guide, Revised Printing		1st Year Engineering Journal/Workbook	
Ch.	Title	Ch.	Title	Ch.	Title
14	Layer 6: The Presentation Layer	9	The Application, Presentation, Session, and Transport Layers	14	Layer 6: The Presentation Layer
				18	Layers 4, 5, 6, and 7
15	Layer 7: The Application Layer	9	The Application, Presentation, Session, and Transport Layers	15	Layer 7: The Application Layer
				18	Layers 4, 5, 6, and 7
Semester Two					
1	Review	1	Networking and the OSI Reference Model	16	OSI Review
2	Routers	4	LANs and WANs	19	WANs
		13	Displaying Router Configuration Information	20	Routing
3	Using the Router	12	The Router User Interface and Modes	21	Using the Router
4	Router Componets	13	Displaying Router Configuration Information	22	Router Components

Online Curriculum		1st Year Companion Guide, Revised Printing		1st Year Engineering Journal/Workbook	
Ch.	Title	Ch.	Title	Ch.	Title
5	Router Startup and Setup	14	Router Startup and Setup Configuration	23	Router Startup and Setup
6	Router Configuration	15	Router Configuration	24	Router Configuration
7	IOS	16	Sources for Cisco IOS Software	25	IOS
8	Individual Router Config Practice				
9	TCP/IP	10	TCP/IP	26	TCP/IP
10	IP Addressing	17	Configuring Router Interfaces with IP Addresses	27	IP Addressing
11	Routing	11	The Network Layer and Routing	20	Routing
12	Routing Protocols	18	Router Configuration and Routing Protocols: RIP and IGRP	28	Routing Protocols

This Book's Features

Many of this book's features help facilitate a full understanding of the networking and routing covered in this book:

- *Chapter objectives*—At the beginning of each chapter is a list of objectives to be mastered by the end of the chapter. In addition, the list provides a reference to the concepts covered in the chapter, which can be used as an advanced organizer.

- *Figures, listings, and tables*—This book contains figures, listings, and tables that help explain theories, concepts, commands, and setup sequences; they reinforce concepts and help you visualize the content covered in the chapter. In addition, listings and tables provide such things as command summaries with descriptions, examples of screen outputs, and practical and theoretical information.

- *Chapter summaries*—At the end of each chapter is a summary of the concepts covered in the chapter; it provides a synopsis of the chapter and serves as a study aid.

- *Review questions*—After the summary of each chapter are 10 review questions that serve as an end-of-chapter assessment. In addition, the questions reinforce the concepts introduced in the chapter and help you test your understanding before you move on to new concepts.

Conventions Used in This Book

In this book, the following conventions are used:

- Important or new terms are *italicized*.

- All code examples appear in `monospace` type, and parts of code use the following conventions:
    — Commands and keywords are in **bold** type.
    — Arguments, which are placeholders for values the user inputs, appear in *italics*.
    — Square brackets ([ ]) indicate optional keywords or arguments.
    — Braces ({ }) indicate required choices.
    — Vertical bars (|) are used to separate required choices.

This Book's Organization

This book is divided into 19 chapters, 8 appendixes, and a glossary.

Chapter 1, "Networking and the OSI Reference Model," discusses networking terms and concepts, local-area networks (LANs), and wide-area networks (WANs). In addition, it covers the seven-layer Open System Interconnection (OSI) reference model and the communication process between the model's lower layers.

Chapter 2, "The Physical and Data Link Layers," presents the network functions that occur at the physical and data link layers of the OSI reference model and the different types of networking media that are used at the physical layer. In addition, it discusses the fact that access to the networking media occurs at the data link layer of the OSI model and how data is able to locate its intended destination on a network.

Chapter 3, "Networking Devices," describes networking devices, which can be used to filter traffic across a network and reduce large collision domains, which are areas where packets are likely to interfere with each other.

Chapter 4, "LANs and WANs," presents LAN and WAN technologies, standards, and networking devices that operate at the physical, data link, and network layers of the OSI model.

Chapter 5, "IP Addressing," describes IP addresses and the three classes of networks in IP addressing schemes, as well as the IP addresses that have been set aside by InterNIC and cannot be assigned to any network. Finally, it discusses subnetworks and subnet masks and describes their IP addressing schemes.

Chapter 6, "ARP and RARP," discusses devices on LANs that use Address Resolution Protocol (ARP) before forwarding data to a destination and what happens when a device on one network does not know the MAC address of a device on another network.

Chapter 7, "Topologies," describes the topologies that are used to build networks.

Chapter 8, "Structured Cabling and Electricity," presents structured cabling and electrical specifications used in LANs and wiring and electrical techniques used in building networks.

Chapter 9, "The Application, Presentation, Session, and Transport Layers," discusses the four upper layers of the OSI reference model. It describes in detail the processes used at the transport layer to provide reliable delivery of data as well as to provide effective control of traffic flow.

Chapter 10, "TCP/IP," describes Transmission Control Protocol/Internet Protocol (TCP/IP) and its operation to ensure communication across any set of interconnected networks.

Chapter 11, "The Network Layer and Routing," describes the router's use and operations in performing the key internetworking functions of the OSI reference model network layer.

Chapter 12, "The Router User Interface and Modes," discusses the network administrator's role in operating a router to ensure efficient and effective delivery of data on a network with routers.

Chapter 13, "Displaying Router Configuration Information," describes the correct procedures and commands to access a router, examine and maintain its components, and test its network connectivity.

Chapter 14, "Router Startup and Setup Configuration," explains how to start a router when it is used the first time by using the correct commands and startup sequence to do an initial router configuration.

Chapter 15, "Router Configuration," explains how to use router modes and configuration methods to update a router's configuration file with current and prior versions of Cisco IOS software.

Chapter 16, "Sources for Cisco IOS Software," explains how to use a variety of Cisco IOS software source options, execute commands to load Cisco IOS software onto the router, maintain backup files, and upgrade Cisco IOS software.

Chapter 17, "Configuring Router Interfaces with IP Addresses," describes the process of configuring IP addresses.

Chapter 18, "Router Configuration and Routing Protocols: RIP and IGRP," describes the initial configuration of a router to enable the IP routing protocols RIP and IGRP.

Chapter 19, "Network Management," discusses the basic fundamentals of managing a network by using techniques such as documenting, auditing, monitoring, and evaluating.

Appendix A, "QuickTime Movie Reference," contains cross-referenced information about each of the QuickTime movies on the CD-ROM.

Appendix B, "Command Summary," describes and defines the commands related to configuring and using Cisco routers utilized in this book. It is alphabetically arranged so you can easily find information on a given command.

Appendix C, "Answers to Review Questions," provides the answers to the review questions you'll find at the end of each chapter.

Appendix D, "Computer Basics," provides backup reading for the new online Chapter 1.

Appendix E, "Electronics and Signals," covers the additional electricity and electronics information added to the online curriculum version 2.1.

Appendix F, "Signaling and Data Transmission," covers the new signaling information added to the online curriculum version 2.1.

Appendix G, "Binary and Hexadecimal Conversion" includes text and practice problems to increase your understanding of this critically important topic.

Appendix H, "Network Troubleshooting," covers the new information added to the online curriculum dealing with troubleshooting.

The Glossary defines the terms and abbreviations related to networking utilized in this book.

Computer Basics

Introduction

This appendix looks at the components of a computer and at the role of computers in a network. This text takes a ground-up approach to networking, starting with the most basic component of a network, the computer. The more you know about computers, the easier it is to understand how networks are built.

To get an idea of the role of computers, it helps to think of the Internet. You can compare the Internet to a living organism: the computers play the role of the cells within that organism. Computers are sources of information and receivers of information, both giving to and taking from the Internet. Although cells often can live independently of the organism of which they are a part, the organism itself cannot live entirely without the cells that comprise it. Computers and the Internet depend on each other to some extent for survival. Computers can exist without the Internet, but as time goes on computers are becoming more and more dependent on the Internet.

The computer also plays a vital role in the work world. Companies use computers and computer software in different ways, but some uses are common to most companies. Servers are used to store important data and to manage employee accounts. Spreadsheet software is used to organize financial information. Word processor software is used to generate memos and text documents. Database software is used to maintain detailed records of customer. Web browsers are used to access company Web sites. Today, of course, computers are absolutely essential to the success of a company.

This appendix introduces you to the inner workings of a computer and gives you the foundation you need to begin the study of networking.

Computer Components

Because computers are important building blocks in a network, it is important to be able to recognize and name the major components of a personal computer (PC). Many networking devices are themselves special-purpose computers with many of the same parts as "normal" PCs. To use your computer as a reliable means of obtaining information, such as accessing Web-based curriculum, your computer must be in good working order, which means you might occasionally need to troubleshoot simple problems in your computer's hardware and software. You should be able to recognize, name, and state the purpose of the following PC components.

Small, Discrete Components

■ Transistor—A device that amplifies (enlarges) a signal or opens and closes a circuit.

■ Integrated circuit—An electronic device made out of semiconductor material (material that can control the amount of electricity it conducts).

■ Resistor—A device that offers resistance to the flow of an electric current.

■ Capacitor—An electronic component that stores energy in the form of an electrostatic field (an electric field that is not changing); it consists of two conducting metal plates separated by an insulating material.

FIGURE D-1
Capacitors.

■ Connector—The part of a cable that plugs into a port or an interface.

FIGURE D-2
Connectors.

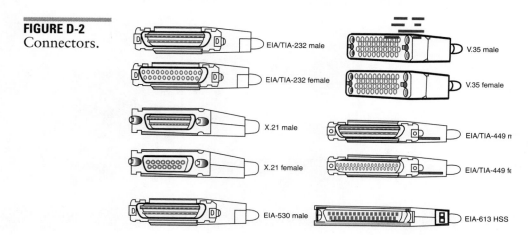

■ Light emitting diode (LED)—A device that lights up when electricity passes through it.

■ Solder—An easily melted alloy (mixture of metals) used for joining metals.

Personal Computer Subsystems

■ Printed circuit board (PCB)—A thin plate on which chips and other electronic components are placed.

■ CD-ROM drive—A compact disc read *only memory* drive, which is a device that can read information from a CD-ROM.

FIGURE D-3
CD-ROM
drive.

■ Central Processing Unit (CPU)—The central processing unit (CPU) is the brains of the computer where most calculations take place.

FIGURE D-4
Central processing units (CPUs).

■ *Floppy disk drive*—A disk drive that can read and write to floppy disks.

FIGURE D-5
Floppy disk drive.

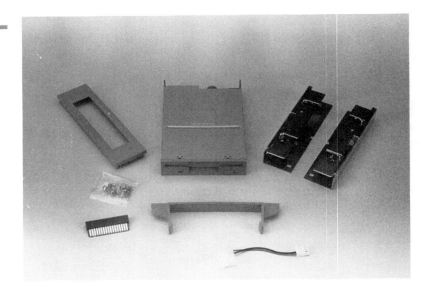

■ *Hard disk drive*—The device that reads and writes data on a hard disk.

Hard disk
drive.

■ *Microprocessor*—A silicon chip that contains a CPU. In the world of PCs, the terms *microprocessor* and *CPU* are interchangeable.

■ *Motherboard*—The main circuit board of a personal computer.

Mother-
board.

■ *Bus*—A collection of wires through which data is transmitted from one part of a computer to another. It connects all the internal computer components to the CPU.

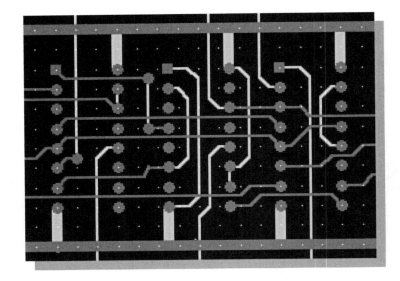

■ *Random access memory (RAM)*—A type of computer memory where any byte of memory can be accessed without touching the preceding bytes.

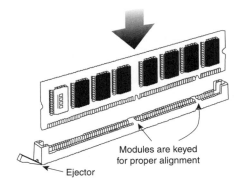

Modules are keyed for proper alignment

Ejector

- *Read-only memory (ROM)*—Computer memory on which data has been prerecorded; after data has been written onto a ROM chip, it cannot be removed and can only be read.

FIGURE D-10
Read-only
memory
(ROM).

FIGURE D-10
Read-only
memory
(ROM).

- *System unit*—The main part of a PC; the system unit includes the chassis, microprocessor, main memory, bus, and ports, but does not include the keyboard, monitor, or any external devices connected to the computer.
- *Expansion slot*—An opening in a computer where a circuit board can be inserted to add new capabilities to the computer.

FIGURE D-11
Expansion
slots

■ *Power supply*—The component that supplies power to a computer.

FIGURE D-12
Power sup-
ply.

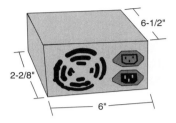

Backplane Components

Expansion card—A printed circuit board you can insert into a computer to give it added capabilities.

FIGURE D-13
Expansion
card.

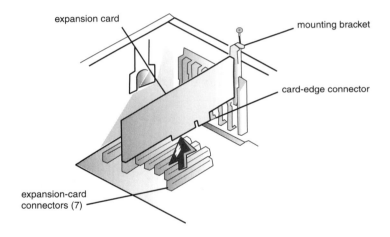

■ *Backplane*—The large circuit board that contains sockets for expansion cards. A backplane is distinguished from a motherboard by the fact that it might contain almost no logical circuitry for performing computing functions.

■ *Network card*—An expansion board inserted into a computer so the computer can be connected to a network.

■ *Modem*—The modem (modulator/demodulator) is a device that enables a computer to transmit data over telephone lines; there are internal (installed as expansion cards) and external (connected to ports) modems.

■ *Video card*—A board that plugs into a PC to give it display capabilities.

■ *Sound card*—An expansion board that enables a computer to manipulate and output sounds.

■ *Interface*—A piece of hardware, such as an electrical connector, that allows two devices to be connected together.

■ *Port*—An interface on a computer to which you can connect an electronic device.

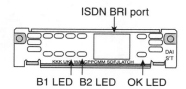

■ *Parallel port*—An interface capable of transferring more than one bit simultaneously. It is used to connect external devices such as printers.

Parallel port expansion card.

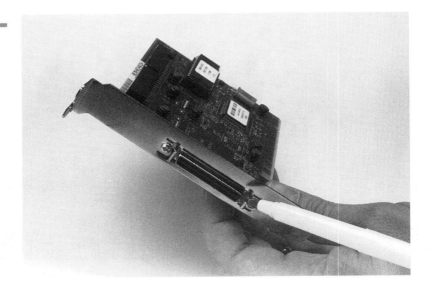

■ *Serial port*—An interface that can be used for serial communication (data communication in which only 1 bit is transmitted at a time).

Serial port expansion card.

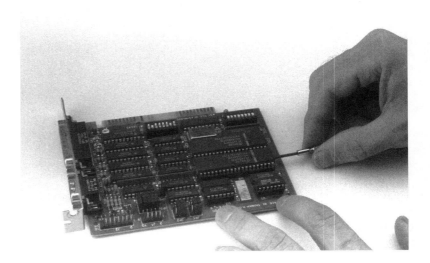

■ *Mouse port*—A port designed for connecting a mouse to a PC.

- *Power cord*—A cord used to connect an electrical device to an electrical outlet to provide power to the device.

Figure D-19 shows the basic components of an idealized computer. You can think of the internal components of a PC as a network of devices, all attached to the system bus. In a sense, a PC is a small computer network.

FIGURE D-19
The main components of a computer are the CPU, the memory, and the interfaces.

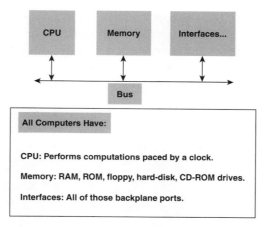

Information and electric power are constantly flowing in a PC. It helps to understand networking—designing, building, and maintaining networks—by thinking of the computer as a miniature network, with all the various devices within the system unit attached to, and communicating with, each other. The following are some of the important information flows (almost all of which occur via the bus):

- *Boot instructions*—Stored in ROM until they are sent out.
- *Software applications*—Stored in RAM after they have been loaded.
- *RAM and ROM*—Constantly talk to the CPU via the bus.
- *Application information*—Stored in RAM while applications are being used.
- *Saved information*—Flows from RAM to some form of storage device.
- *Exported information*—Flows from RAM and the CPU, via the bus and expansion slots, to the serial port, parallel port (usually for printers), video card, sound card, or network card.

Network Interface Cards

A network interface card (NIC) is a printed circuit board that provides network communication capabilities to and from a personal computer. Also called a *LAN adapter*, it plugs into a motherboard and provides a port for connecting to the network.

A *network card* communicates with the network through a serial connection (one bit transmitted at a time), and with the computer through a parallel connection (more than one bit transmitted at a time). Each card requires an IRQ, an I/O address, and an upper memory address for DOS and for Windows 95/98. IRQ, or interrupt request line, is a hardware line over which devices can send interrupts to the microprocessor. An interrupt is a signal informing a program that an event has occurred, such as running out of memory. An I/O address is a location in memory used to enter data or to retrieve data from a computer. In DOS-based systems, upper memory refers to the memory area between the first 640 kilobytes (KBs) and 1 megabyte (MB).

FIGURE D-20
A PCI bus is pictured on the right and an ISA bus on the left.

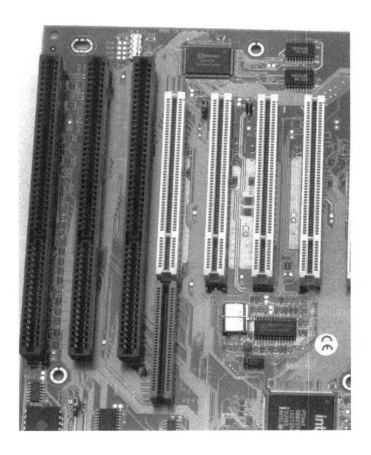

When you select a network card, consider the following three factors:

- Type of network (for example, Ethernet, Token Ring, or FDDI)
- Type of cable (for example, twisted-pair, coaxial, or fiber-optic)
- Type of system bus (for example, PCI or ISA)

The NIC allows networks to function and is, therefore, considered a key component. From time to time, you might need to install a NIC. Some possible situations that might require you to do so include the following:

- Adding a NIC to a PC that does not already have one.
- Replacing a bad or damaged NIC.
- Upgrading from a 10-Mbps (megabits, or millions of bits, per second) NIC to a 10/100-Mbps NIC.
- Altering settings on a NIC jumper. A *jumper* is a metal bridge that closes an electrical circuit; typically, a jumper consists of a plastic plug that fits over a pair of pins. The jumper is moved in order to change settings, such as the IRQ (especially on older NICs).

To perform the installation, you should have the following resources:

- Knowledge of how the network card is configured, including jumpers, plug-and-play software, and *erasable programmable read-only memory* (EPROM is a type of memory that retains its contents until it is exposed to ultraviolet light).
- Use of network card diagnostics, including the vendor-supplied diagnostics and a loopback test. (A test signal sent to a network destination that is returned as received to the originator; in the case of a network card, the test signal travels between the PC and network card, whether or not there is an external cable attached.)
- Capability to resolve hardware resource conflicts—these resources might include IRQ, I/O Base Address, or *direct memory address* (DMA is used to transfer data from RAM to a device without going through the CPU).

Laptop Components

Laptop computers and notebook computers are becoming increasingly popular, as are palm top computers, personal digital assistants, and other small computing devices. The information described in the previous sections also pertains to laptops. The main difference is that components in a laptop are smaller. The expansion slots become Personal Computer Memory Card International Association (PCMCIA) slots, where network cards, modems, hard drives, and other useful devices, usually the size of a thick credit card, can be inserted into various places along the perimeter.

Software

Now that you have a good idea of what's involved with computer hardware, you need the second ingredient: computer software. The purpose of software is to allow you to interact with the computer or networking device, to get it to do what you want it to do.

So, after the PC hardware is set up, the software must be configured. For example, the following tasks need to be completed prior to viewing Web-based curriculum:

STEP 1. Select the NIC.

STEP 2. Input the correct TCP/IP settings, including network address settings (TCP/IP is introduced in Chapter 10).

STEP 3. Adjust the monitor (if necessary).

STEP 4. Install and set up the browser.

STEP 5. Perform a few other tasks (if necessary).

Browsers

A Web server is a software application used to locate and display Web pages. A Web browser interfaces with a user by sequentially contacting a Web server, requesting information, receiving information, and then displaying the results onscreen. A browser is software that interprets hypertext markup language (HTML), the language used to create Web page content. HTML can display graphics and play sound, movies, and other multimedia files. Hyperlinks, elements in an electronic document that link to another place in the same document or to an entirely different document, allow the user to connect to other Web pages and to files that can be downloaded.

The two most popular browsers are Netscape Communicator and Internet Explorer (IE). Here are some of the similarities and differences between these two browsers:

Netscape

- First popular browser
- Takes less disk space
- Considered by many to be simple
- Displays HTML files
- Does e-mail, file transfers, and other functions

Internet Explorer (IE)

- Powerfully connected to other Microsoft products
- Takes more disk space
- Considered more difficult to use
- Displays HTML files
- Does e-mail, file transfers, and other functions

Plug-ins

There are also many proprietary (privately owned and controlled) file types that standard Web browsers are not able to display. To view these files, you must configure your browser to use plug-in applications. These applications work in conjunction with the browser to launch the program required to view the special files.

- Shockwave—Plays multimedia (integrated text, graphics, video, animation, and/or sound) files; created by Macromedia Authorware, Director, and Flash programs.
- QuickTime—Plays movies and sounds that have been saved in the Apple QuickTime file format.
- RealAudio—Plays audio files that have been saved in RealAudio format.
- RealPlayer G2—Plays movie files with high resolution that have been saved in RealPlayer format.

Office Applications

Beyond configuring your computer to view Web-based curriculum, you use your computer to perform many other useful tasks. In business, employees regularly use a set of applications that come in the form of an office suite, such as Microsoft Office. The office applications typically include spreadsheet software, word processing software, database management software, presentation software, and a personal information manager that includes an e-mail program. Spreadsheet software contains tables consisting of columns and rows and is often used with formulas to process and analyze data. Word processing software is an application used to create and edit text documents; modern word processor programs allow the user to create sophisticated documents that include graphics and richly formatted text. Database software is used to store, maintain, organize, sort, and filter records (a record is a collection of information identified by a common theme, such as a customer's name).

Presentation software is used to design and develop presentations to deliver at meetings, classes, or sales presentations. Personal information managers include such things as e-mail, contact lists, a calendar, and a to do list. Office applications are now as much a part of everyday work as typewriters were before the advent of the PC.

Networks

A network is an intricately connected system of objects or people. Networks are all around you, even inside you. Your own nervous system and cardiovascular system are networks. The cluster diagram, shown in Figure D-21, shows several types of networks; you might think of others. Notice the groupings:

FIGURE D-21
The term network is used in many different ways, but the meaning is similar in each case to that of a computer network.

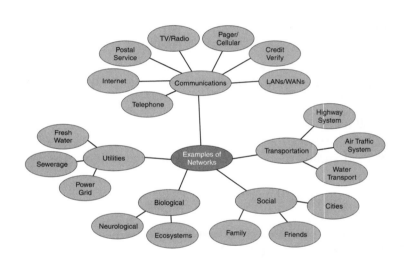

- Communications
- Transportation
- Social
- Biological
- Utilities

Data communication networks are designed to make it possible for two computers that are located anywhere in the world to be able to communicate with each other. They also make it possible for different types of computers to communicate, regardless of whether they are Macintosh, PC, or mainframe computers. The only major concern is that all computers and devices understand the other languages, or protocols.

Protocol means a formal description of a set of rules that govern how devices on a network exchange information. Most data networks are classified as local-area networks (LANs), metropolitan-area networks (MANs), or wide-area networks (WANs). LANs usually are located in single buildings or campuses, and handle interoffice communications. MANs are data networks designed for a town or city. WANs cover a large geographical area, and interconnect cities and countries. Internetworking is the practice of connecting LANs, MANs, and WANs together.

Early computers were standalone devices. Each one operated on its own, independent from any other computer. As time progressed, it became apparent that this was not an efficient or cost effective manner in which to operate businesses. What was needed was a solution that would successfully address the following two questions:

1. How to avoid duplication of equipment and resources (such as requiring a separate printer for every pair of PCs)?

2. How to share and exchange information efficiently?

One early solution to these problems was the creation of local-area networks (LANs). Because they could connect all of the workstations, peripherals (external devices attached to a computer), terminals, and other devices in a single building, LANs made it possible for businesses using computer technology to efficiently share such things as files and printers.

As computer use in businesses grew, it soon became apparent that even LANs were not sufficient. In a LAN system, each department or business was a kind of electronic island.

What was needed was a way for information to move efficiently and quickly from one business to another. The solution, then, was the creation of metropolitan-area networks (MANs) and wide-area networks (WANs). Because WANs could connect user networks over a large geographic area, they made it possible for businesses to communicate with each other across great distances.

Early development of LANs, MANs, and WANs was chaotic in many ways. The early 1980s saw a tremendous growth in networking. Companies recognized how much money they could save and how much productivity they could gain by using networking technology. For example, memos could be distributed instantaneously over the network to all employees without requiring someone to print out the document, make sufficient copies, and physically distribute them to all the employees. Companies began to add networks and to expand existing networks almost as rapidly as new network technologies and products were introduced.

By the mid-1980s, growing pains were felt. Many of the network technologies that had emerged had been built by using hardware and software implementations from a number of different manufacturers and developers. Consequently, many of the new network technologies were incompatible. It became increasingly difficult for networks using different specifications, such as Ethernet and Token Ring, to communicate with each other. Not surprisingly, much of the work since the mid-1980s has involved creating and implementing networking technologies and standards that allow different vendors' networking devices or technologies to work together on the same network. For example, there are now *bridges* (devices that connect two LANs or two segments of the same LAN) that allow for Ethernet and Token Ring networks to communicate.

As with all other technological implementations, there is a need to somehow measure the capabilities of LANs and WANs to determine their usefulness to companies and end users. The primary way this is done is by using the measure of *bandwidth* to describe the capabilities of the networks. This term can be difficult to understand, but it is an essential concept in networking. This is the topic of the next section.

Bandwidth

Bandwidth is the measure of how much information can flow from one place to another in a given amount of time. There are two common uses of the word bandwidth: one deals with analog signals, and the other with digital signals (these signals are explored in Appendix F, "Signaling and Data Transmission"). You will work with digital bandwidth, simply called bandwidth, for the remainder of the text.

You have already learned that the most basic unit used to describe the flow of digital information, from one place to another, is the bit. The next term you need to know is the one used to describe the basic unit of time. It is the second. Now you see where term bits per second (bps) comes from.

Bits per second is a unit of bandwidth. Of course, if communication happened at this rate, 1 bit per 1 second, it would be very slow. The American Standard Code for Information Interchange (ASCII, pronounced ask-ee) is a code for representing English characters as numbers, with each letter assigned a number from 0 to 127. Now, imagine trying to send the ASCII code for your name and address at 1 bit per second—it would take minutes! Fortunately, much faster communication is now possible. Table D-1 summarizes the various units of bandwidth.

TABLE D-1   Units of Bandwidth

Unit of Bandwidth	Abbreviation	Equivalence
Bits per second	Bps	1 bps = fundamental unit of bandwidth
Kilobits per second	Kbps	1 kbps = 1000 = 10^3 bps
Megabits per second	Mbps	1 Mbps = 1,000,000 bps + 10^6 bps
Gigabits per second	Gbps	1 Gbps = 1,000,000,000 bps = 10^9 bps

Bandwidth is a very important element of networking, yet it can be rather abstract and difficult to understand. The following are three analogies that might help you picture what bandwidth is:

1. Bandwidth is like the width of a pipe (see Figure D-22). Think of the network of pipes that brings water to your home and carries sewage away from it. Those pipes have different widths: the city's main water pipe might be 2 meters wide, whereas the kitchen faucet might be 2 centimeters wide. The width of the pipe measures the water-carrying capacity of the pipe. In this analogy, the water is like information and the width of the pipe is like bandwidth. In fact, many networking experts will talk in terms of "putting in bigger pipes," meaning more bandwidth; that is, more information-carrying capacity.

FIGURE D-22
The wider the pipe, the greater the rate of fluid that can flow through it.

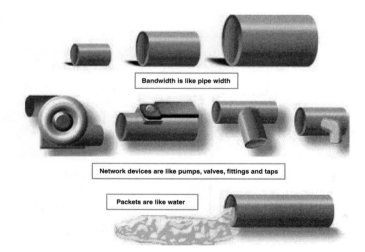

Bandwidth is like pipe width

Network devices are like pumps, valves, fittings and taps

Packets are like water

2. Bandwidth is like the number of lanes on a highway (see Figure D-23). Think about a network of roads that serves your city or town. There might be eight-lane highways, with exits onto two- and three-lane roads, which might then lead to two-lane undivided streets, and eventually to your driveway. In this analogy, the number of lanes is like bandwidth, and the number of cars is like the amount of information that can be carried.

FIGURE D-23
The more lanes in a highway, the greater the capacity for traffic flow..

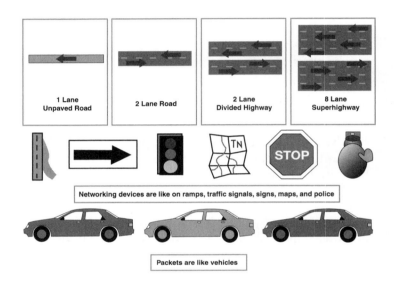

3. Bandwidth is like the quality of sound in an audio system. The sound is the information, and the quality of the sound you hear is the bandwidth; that is, the sound is the data and the measure of the frequency of the sound is the bandwidth. If you were to rank your preferences on how you would rather hear your favorite song—over the telephone, on an AM radio, on an FM radio, or on a CD-ROM—you would probably make the CD your first preference, then FM radio, then AM radio, and finally the telephone. The actual analog bandwidths for these are, respectively, 20 kHz, 15 kHz, 5 kHz, and 3 kHz.

Keep in mind that the true, actual meaning of bandwidth, in this context, is the maximum number of bits that can, in theory, pass through a given area of space in a specified amount of time under the given conditions. The analogies used here are to make it easier to understand the concept of bandwidth.

Bandwidth is a very useful concept. It does, however, have its limitations. No matter how you send your messages, no matter what kind of cable you use, bandwidth is limited. This is due both to the laws of physics and to the current technological advances.

Table D-2 illustrates the maximum digital bandwidth possible, including length limitations, for some common types of cable. Always remember that limits are both physical and technological (technology drives the quality of the manufacturing of the cable, which in turn determines bandwidth limitations).

TABLE D-2   Maximum Bandwidths and Length Limitations.

Typical Media	Maximum Theoretical Bandwidth	Maximum Physical Distance
50-Ohm Coaxial Cable (Ethernet 10Base2, ThinNet)	10-1000 Mbps	200 m
75-Ohm Coaxial Cable (Ethernet 10Base 5, Thicknet)	10-100 Mbps	500 m
Category 5 Unshielded Twisted Pair (UTP) (Ethernet 100Base-TX) (Fast Ethernet)	100 Mbps	100 m
Multimode (62.5/125um) Optical Fiber 100Base-FX	100 Mbps	200 m
Singlemode (10um core) Optical Fiber 1000Base-LX	1000 Mbps (1.000 Gbps)	3000 m
Other technologies being researched	2400 Mbps (2.400 Gbps)	40 km = 40,000 m
Wireless	2.0 Mbps	100 m

Bandwidth is also limited by the capacity of the specific technology, such as ISDN (integrated services digital network), subscribed from the service provider.

Table D-3 summarizes different WAN services and the bandwidth associated with each service. Which service do you use at home? At school?

TABLE D-3   WAN Services and Bandwidths.

Type of WAN Service	Typical User	Bandwidth
Modern	Individuals	33 kbps = 0.033 Mbps
Frame Relay	Small institutions (schools); reliable WANs	56 kbps = 0.056 Mbps

continues

TABLE D-3   **WAN Services and Bandwidths. (Continued)**

Type of WAN Service	Typical User	Bandwidth
ISDN	Telecommuters, small businesses	128 kbps = 0.128 Mbps
T1	Larger entities	1.544 Mbps
T3	Larger entities	44.736 Mbps
STS-1 (OC-1)	Phone companies; DataComm company backbones	51.840 Mbps
STS-3 (OC-3)	Phone companies; DataComm company backbones	155.251 Mbps
STS-48 (OC-48)	Phone companies; DataComm company backbones	2.488320 Gbps

Imagine that you are lucky enough to have a brand new cable modem (a modem designed to operate over cable TV lines), or your local store just installed an ISDN (integrated services digital network) line, or your school just received a 10-MB Ethernet LAN. Imagine the movie you want to view, or the Web page or software you want to download takes forever to receive. You probably believed you were getting all the bandwidth that was advertised. There is another important concept you should have considered; it's called throughput.

Throughput refers to actual, measured bandwidth, at a specific time of day, using specific Internet routes (paths that data will follow on the Internet), while downloading a specific file. Unfortunately, for many reasons, the throughput is often far less then the maximum possible digital bandwidth of the medium that is being used. Some of the factors that determine throughput and bandwidth include the following:

- Internetworking devices (such as routers and switches)
- Type of data being transferred
- Topology (the shape of a network, such as *ring* or *star*)
- Number of users
- User's computer
- Server computer

■ Power and weather-induced outages

When you design a network, it is important to consider the theoretical bandwidth (recall that this is the maximum number of bits that can, in theory, pass through a given area of space in a specified amount of time). Your network will be no faster than your media will allow. When you actually work on networks, you will want to measure throughput and decide if the throughput is adequate for the user (see Figure D-24).

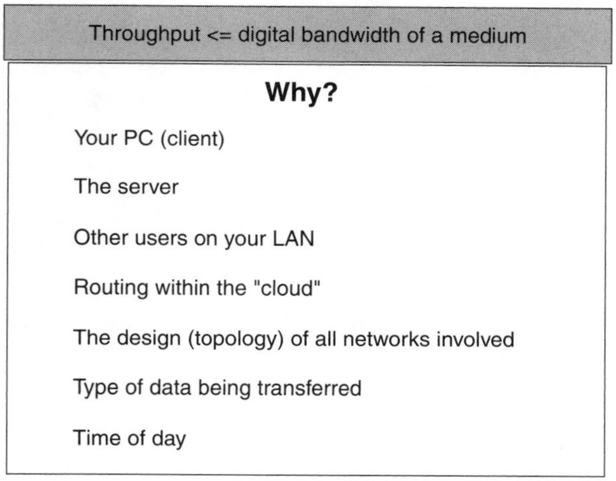

FIGURE D-24
Throughput is the actual amount of data passing through a given area of space in a specific amount of time.

Throughput <= digital bandwidth of a medium
Why?
Your PC (client)
The server
Other users on your LAN
Routing within the "cloud"
The design (topology) of all networks involved
Type of data being transferred
Time of day

An important part of networking involves making decisions about which medium to use. This often leads to questions regarding the bandwidth required by the user's applications. The graphic summarizes a simple formula that will help you with such decisions. The formula is Estimated Time = Size of File / Bandwidth (see Figure D-25). The resulting answer represents the fastest that data could be transferred. It does not take into account any of the previously discussed issues that affect bandwidth, but does give you a rough estimate of the time it will take to send information using that specific medium/application.

FIGURE D-25
Here's a formula for computing the time it takes to download a file.

BW = Maximum theoretical bandwidth of the "slowest" link between the source host and the destination host.

P = Actual throughput at the moment of transfer.

T = Time for file transfer to occur.

S = File size in bits.

$$\text{Best Download} \quad T = \frac{S}{BW}$$

$$\text{Typical Download} \quad T = \frac{S}{P}$$

Now that you are familiar with the units for digital bandwidth, try the following sample problem:

Problem:
GB stands for gigabyte and one gigabyte is one billion bytes. Similarly, 1 Gbps is one billion bits per second. SONET stands for *synchronous optical network* and is a standard for connecting fiber-optic transmission systems. OC-48 stands for a 2.488 Gbps *optical carrier* network conforming to the SONET standard. With these definitions out of the way, which would be faster: sending a floppy disk full of data over an ISDN line, or sending a 10 GB hard drive full of data over an OC-48 line?

Why Is Bandwidth Important?

1. First, bandwidth is finite (not infinite). Regardless of the media, the laws of physics limit bandwidth. For example, the bandwidth limitation (due to the physical properties of the twisted-pair phone wires that come into many homes) is what limits the throughput of standard phone modems to about 56 Kbps (1 Kbps is 1 kilobit per second or 1000 bits per second). The bandwidth of the electromagnetic spectrum (the full range of wavelengths for electromagnetic waves) is finite. There are only so many frequencies in the radio wave, microwave, and infrared spectrum. Consequently, the FCC (Federal Communications Commission) has a whole division to control bandwidth and who uses it. Fiber-optic cable permits such a large capacity for bandwidth that, in practice, it can

appear to be limitless. However, the technology used to make extremely high bandwidth networks, which fully utilize the potential of optical fiber, are just now being developed and implemented.

2. Knowing how bandwidth works, and that it is finite, can save you a lot of money. For example, the cost of various connection options from Internet service providers depends in part on how much bandwidth, on average and at peak usage (maximum attainable), you require.

3. As a networking professional, you will be expected to know about bandwidth and throughput. They are major factors in analyzing network performance. In addition, as a network designer of new networks, bandwidth will always be a major design issue.

4. It is not uncommon that once a person or an institution starts using a network, they eventually want more and more bandwidth. New multimedia software programs require much more bandwidth than those used in the mid-1990s. Creative programmers and users are busily designing networks that are capable of performing more complex tasks, thus requiring greater bandwidth.

Summary

- Computers are vital components of every network. The more you know about computers, the easier it is to understand networks.

- It is important to be familiar with the components of a computer and to be able to install a NIC. Also, troubleshooting PCs is a necessary skill for someone who works on networks.

- Software is the piece of the puzzle that allows the user to interface (connect with and make use of) the hardware. In networking, Web browsers and e-mail are commonly used software programs. In general, office applications, browsers, and e-mail programs are used to conduct business.

- The two main types of networks are LANs and WANs. WANs connect LANs together. LANs and WANs use protocols as languages to allow for computers and networking devices to communicate with each other.

- Bandwidth and throughput are measures of the speed or capacity of a network.

Electronics and Signals

Introduction

The function of the physical layer is to transmit data by defining the electrical specifications between the source and the destination. After it reaches a building, electricity is carried to workstations, servers, and network devices via wires concealed in walls, floors, and ceilings. Data, which can consist of such things as text, pictures, audio, or video, travels through the wires and is represented by the presence of either electrical pulses on copper conducting wires or light pulses in optical fibers.

In this appendix, you will learn about the basic theory of electricity, which provides a foundation for understanding networking at the physical layer of the OSI model. The concepts you learn here will help you understand how data is transmitted through physical media, such as cables and connectors, and the factors that affect data transmission (discussed in Chapter 2, " The Physical and Data Link Layers").

Basics of Electricity

All matter is composed of atoms. *The Periodic Table of Elements* (see Figure E-1) lists all known types of atoms and their properties.

FIGURE E-1
The Periodic Table of Elements

Periodic Table of Elements

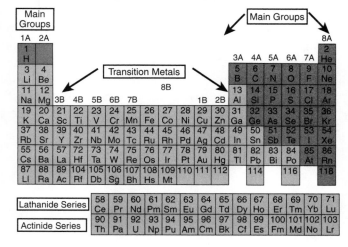

The names of the parts of the atom are

- *Nucleus*—The center part of the atom, formed by protons and neutrons.
- *Protons*—Particles with a positive charge that, along with neutrons, form the nucleus.
- *Neutrons*—Particles with no charge (neutral) that, along with protons, form the nucleus.
- *Electrons*—Particles with a negative charge that orbit the nucleus.

To help you understand the electrical properties of elements/materials, locate helium on the periodic chart. It has an *atomic number* of 2, which means that it has two protons and two electrons. It has an *atomic weight* of 4. By subtracting the atomic number (2) from the atomic weight (4), you learn that helium also has two neutrons.

Example:
Atomic number of helium = 2

$$\begin{array}{r} 2 \text{ protons} \\ + \ 2 \text{ electrons} \\ \hline 4 \text{ atomic weight} \\ - \ 2 \text{ atomic number} \\ \hline 2 \text{ neutrons} \end{array}$$

The Danish physicist, Niels Bohr, developed a simplified model to illustrate atoms. Figure E-2 shows the model for a helium atom. Notice the scale of the parts. If the protons and neutrons of this atom were the size of a soccer ball in the middle of a soccer field, then the electrons would be the size of cherries and would be orbiting near the outermost seats of the stadium. The space inside the atom would be the size of the soccer field.

This model provides a setting useful for discussing the concepts of force within an atom. Coulomb's (Electric Force) Law states that *opposite charges* react to each other with a force that causes them to be attracted to each other, and *like charges* react to each other with a force that causes them to repel each other. A force is a pushing or pulling motion—in the case of opposite and like charges, the force increases as the charges move closer to each other.

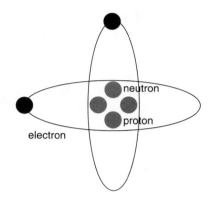

FIGURE E-2
The helium atom has two protons, two electrons, and two neutrons.

Refer to Bohr's model of the helium atom in Figure E-2. If Coulomb's Law is true, and if Bohr's model describes helium atoms as stable, then there must be other laws of nature at work. How can these two concepts be consistent?

Question 1: Why don't the electrons fly in towards the protons?

1. Coulomb's Law—Like charges repel.

2. Bohr's model—Protons are positive charges. There is more than one proton in the nucleus.

Question 2: Why don't the protons fly away from each other?

The answer to these questions is that there are other laws of nature that must be considered. Following are the answers to each of the preceding questions.

Answer 1: The electrons stay in orbit, even though they are attracted by the protons, because they have just enough velocity to keep orbiting and to not let themselves be pulled into the nucleus.

Answer 2: The protons do not fly apart from each other because of a nuclear force that is associated with neutrons. The nuclear force is an incredibly strong force that acts as a kind of glue to hold the protons together.

The protons and neutrons are bound together by a very powerful force; however, the force that binds electrons to their orbit around the nucleus is weaker. Figure E-3 illustrates these forces. It is as a result of this "weaker" force that electrons in certain types of atoms can be pulled free from their atoms and made to *flow*. This is electricity—a free flow of electrons.

FIGURE E-3
Forces within
an atom.

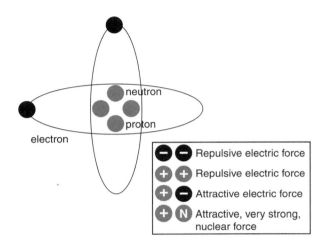

Types of Electrical Materials

Groups of atoms form *molecules*. In turn, *materials* are composed of molecules. Materials are classified as belonging to one of three groups, depending on how easily electricity (free electrons) flows through them. The three types are *electrical insulators*, *electrical conductors*, and *electrical semiconductors*.

Electrical Insulators

Electrical insulators, or *insulators,* are materials that allow electrons to flow through them with great difficulty, or not at all. Electrical insulators are not the same kind of thermal insulators, or insulation, that keep your house warm in winter. Examples of electrical insulators include plastic, glass, air, dry wood, paper, rubber, and certain atoms such as helium. These materials have very stable chemical structures, with orbiting electrons tightly bound within the atoms.

A good example of an electrical insulator is glass. Fiber-optic cable is made of glass, and it serves as a medium for carrying light pulses. Because it does not carry electrical signals, it is immune to induced electrical signals and impulses. And because glass is an electrical insulator, using fiber-optic links within a network avoids the problem of network ground loops.

Electrical Conductors

Electrical conductors, or *conductors*, are materials that allow electrons to flow through them with great ease. They flow easily because the outermost electrons are bound very loosely to the nucleus, and are easily freed. At room temperature, these materials have a large number of free electrons that can provide conduction. The introduction of voltage, (discussed in detail in the following "Voltage" section), causes the free electrons to move and a current to flow.

The periodic table categorizes some groups of atoms by listing them in columns. The atoms in each column belong to particular chemical families. Although they might have different numbers of protons, neutrons, and electrons, their outermost electrons have similar orbits and behave similarly when interacting with other atoms and molecules. The best conductors are metals, such as copper (Cu), silver (Ag), and gold (Au). All of these metals are located in one column of the periodic chart, and have electrons that are easily freed, making them excellent materials for carrying a *current*.

Other conductors include solder (a mixture of lead (Pb) and tin (Sn)) and water. Water is a conductor because of the presence of *ions*. An ion is an atom that has more electrons, or fewer electrons, than a neutral atom. The human body is made of approximately 70% (ionic) water, which means that our bodies are also conductors.

Of course, conductors are pervasive in the world of networking. Conductors allow electrical signals to transmit through a computer and over a network.

Electrical Semiconductors

Semiconductors are materials that can control the amount of electricity they conduct. These materials are listed together in one column of the periodic chart. Examples include carbon (C), germanium (Ge), and the alloy gallium arsenide (GaAs). The most important semiconductor, however, and the one that makes the best microscopic-sized electronic circuits, is silicon (Si).

Silicon is very common and can be found in sand, glass, and many types of rocks. The region around San Jose, California is known as Silicon Valley because the computer industry, which depends on silicon microchips, started in that area. The *switches, or gates,* inside a microprocessor are made up of semiconductors.

TABLE E-1   A Summary of the Three Main Types of Electrical Materials

Insulators	Electrons flow poorly	Plastic Paper Rubber Dry Wood Air Glass
Conductors	Electrons flow well	Copper (Cu) Silver (Ag) Gold (Au) Solder Water with Ions Humans
Semiconductors	Electron flow can be precisely controlled	Carbon (C) Germontum (Ge) Gallium Arsenide (GaAs) Silicon (Si)

Whether materials are classified as insulators, conductors, or semiconductors, it is the knowledge of how each one controls the flow of electrons, and how they work together in various combinations, that is the basis for all electronic devices.

Measuring Electricity

As with any other physical process or concept, we need to be able to measure electricity in order to make use of it. There are numerous ways of measuring electricity—we'll focus on *voltage, current, resistance,* and *impedance.*

Voltage

Voltage, sometimes referred to as *electromotive force (EMF),* is an electrical force, or pressure, that occurs when electrons and protons are separated. The force that is created pushes toward the opposite charge and away from the like charge. This process occurs in a battery, where chemical action causes electrons to be freed from the battery's negative terminal, and to travel to the opposite, or positive, terminal. The separation of charges results in voltage. Voltage also can be created by friction (static electricity), by magnetism (electric generator), or by light (solar cell).

Voltage is represented by the letter "V," and sometimes by the letter "E," for electromotive force. The unit of measurement for voltage is volt (V), and is defined as the amount of work per unit charge needed to separate the charges.

Current

Electrical current, or *current*, is the flow of charges that is created when electrons move. In electrical circuits, current is caused by a flow of free electrons. When voltage is applied, and there is a path for the current, electrons move from the negative terminal (which repels them) along the path to the positive terminal (which attracts them).

Current is represented by the letter "I." The unit of measurement for current is ampere (amp), and is defined as the number of charges per second that pass by a point along a path.

There are two ways in which electrical current flows: *alternating current* and *direct current*.

Alternating Current

Alternating current (AC) varies with time by changing *polarity,* or direction, about 60 times per second. AC flows in one direction, and then reverses its direction and repeats the process. AC voltage is positive at one terminal and negative at the other; then it reverses its polarity, so that the positive terminal becomes negative and the negative terminal becomes positive. This process repeats itself continuously.

Alternating current is the type of electricity that we use most often in daily life. Electricity is brought to your home, school, and office by power lines and these power lines carry electricity in the form of alternating current. AC power is suitable for many types of devices, but is totally unsuitable for use within low-voltage devices, such as computers.

Direct Current

Direct current (DC) always flows in the same direction, and DC voltages always have the same polarity. One terminal is always positive, and the other is always negative. They do not change or reverse.

Direct current can be found in flashlight batteries, car batteries, and as power for the microchips on the motherboard of a computer. The power supply in your system converts AC line power into DC, which is what the computer requires for operation. Many external peripherals (such as printers, external modems, and external storage drives) come with an *AC adapter* that looks like a little, heavy black box that plugs into the wall. That little black box is also a power converter, changing the AC power from the wall into DC power that the computer uses. Usually, the input and output electrical specifications are printed right on it.

It is important to understand the difference between DC and AC and when each is applied.

We can quantify a material's capability to allow current to flow. This is made possible by the concepts of *resistance* and *impedance*.

Resistance

Materials through which current flows offer varying amounts of opposition, or *resistance,* to the movement of electrons. Materials that offer very little or no resistance are called *conductors*. Those that do not allow the current to flow, or severely restrict its flow, are called *insulators*. The amount of resistance depends on the chemical composition of the materials.

Resistance is represented by the letter "R." The unit of measurement for resistance is the ohm (Ω). This symbol is pronounced "omega" and is a capital letter in the Greek alphabet. Greek letters are used extensively in math and physics.

For AC and DC electrical systems, the flow of electrons is always from a negatively charged source to a positively charged source. However, for the controlled flow of electrons to occur, a complete circuit is required. Generally speaking, electrical current follows the path of least resistance. Because metals such as copper provide little resistance, they are frequently used as conductors for electrical current. Conversely, materials such as glass, rubber, and plastic provide more resistance. Therefore, they do not make good electrical conductors. Instead, these materials are frequently used as insulators. They are used on conductors to prevent shock, fires, and short circuits.

Impedance

Impedance is the total opposition to current flow (due to AC and DC voltages). The term *resistance* is generally used when referring to DC voltages. Impedance is the general term, and is the measure of how the flow of electrons is resisted, or impeded.

Impedance is represented by the letter "Z." Its unit of measurement, like that for resistance, is the ohm (Ω). You often hear engineers or technicians speak of *matching* impedances; this just means that you have to use the right equipment with each type of medium utilized in a network. For example, UTP cable has a characteristic impedance of 100 ohms and STP has a characteristic impedance of 150 ohms, so the NIC's must accommodate these respective impedances to prevent reflection (resulting in corrupted signals).

The concepts of voltage, current, and resistance are related. Currents only flow in closed loops, called *circuits*. These circuits must be composed of conducting materials, and must have sources of voltage. Voltage causes current to flow, while resistance and impedance oppose it.

The formulas $P=I^2R$ and $V=IR$ relate power (P), resistance (R), and voltage (V). For example, with a fixed resistance, as in unshielded twisted-pair cable, increasing the voltage by a factor of 5 results in decreasing power by a factor of 25 (the square of the factor 5)!

Water flow (see Figure E-4) helps to explain the concepts of voltage, current, and resistance. The higher the water (and the greater the pressure), the more the water flows. The water current depends on how open the tap is. Similarly, the higher the voltage (the greater the electrical pressure), the more current produced. The electric current then encounters resistance that, like the water tap, reduces flow. If it is on an AC circuit, the amount of current depends on how much impedance is present. The pump is like a battery: it provides pressure to keep the flow moving.

FIGURE E-4
Useful parallels can be made between water flow and electricity.

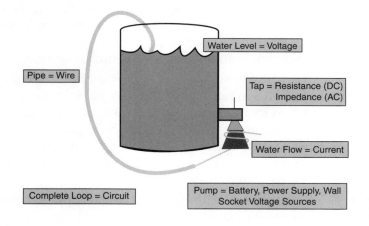

The following list summarizes the electrical concepts encountered thus far. These concepts are the basis upon which signaling and data transmissions are described in Appendix F, "Signaling and Data Transmission." Understanding these electrical concepts makes it relatively easy to understand the processes occurring at the physical layer of the OSI model.

- Electrons flow in closed loops call circuits
- Definitions
    - *Voltage*—Electrical pressure due to the separation of electrical charge (+ and -)
    - *Current (I)*—Flow of charged particles, usually electrons
    - *Resistance*—Property of a material that opposes and can control electrical flow
    - *Impedance*—Equivalent to resistance but for AC and pulsed circuits
    - *Short Circuit*—Conducting path
    - *Open Circuit*—Discontinuity in conducting path
- Voltage causes currents; resistance and impedance limit currents

Electrical Grounds

Another electrical concept that comes up frequently in networking is that of an electrical *ground*. Understanding the term *ground* can be difficult because people use the term for many different purposes:

- Ground can refer to the place on the earth that touches your house (probably by way of the buried water pipes), eventually making an indirect connection to your electric outlets. When you use an electric appliance that has a plug with three prongs, the third prong is the ground. It gives the electrons an extra conducting path to flow to the earth, rather than through your body.
- Ground can also mean the reference point, or the 0 volts level, when making electrical measurements. Voltage is created by the separation of charges, which means that voltage measurements must be made between two points. A *multimeter* (which measures voltage, current, and resistance) has two wires for that reason. The black wire is referred to as the ground, or reference ground. A negative terminal on a battery is also referred to as 0 volts, or the reference ground.

Figure E-5 shows a familiar object: electricity as supplied through wall outlets. The top two connectors supply power. The round connector on the bottom protects people and equipment from shocks and short circuits. This connector is called the safety ground connection. In electrical equipment where a safety ground is used, the safety ground wire is connected to any exposed metal part of the equipment. The motherboards and computing circuits in computing equipment are electrically connected to the chassis of the computer. This also connects them to the safety grounding wire, which is used to dissipate static electricity.

FIGURE E-5
The familiar neutral, hot, and safety ground wires in a wall outlet.

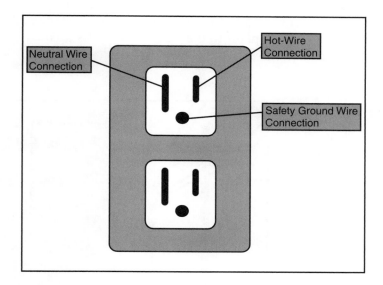

Neutral Wire Connection

Hot-Wire Connection

Safety Ground Wire Connection

The purpose of connecting the safety ground to exposed metal parts of the computing equipment is to prevent such metal parts from becoming energized with a hazardous voltage resulting from a wiring fault inside the device.

An accidental connection between the hot wire and the chassis is an example of a wiring fault that could occur in a network device. If such a fault were to occur, the safety ground wire connected to the device would serve as a low resistance path to the earth ground. The safety ground connection provides a lower resistance path than your body.

When properly installed, the low resistance path, provided by the safety ground wire offers sufficiently low resistance and current carrying capacity to prevent the build up of hazardously high voltages. The circuit links directly to the hot connection to the earth.

Whenever an electrical current is passed via this path into the ground, it causes protective devices such as circuit breakers and Ground Fault Circuit Interrupters (GFCIs) to activate. By interrupting the circuit, circuit breakers and GFCIs stop the flow of electrons and reduce the hazard of electrical shock. The circuit breakers protect you and your house wiring, but further protection, often in the form of surge suppressors and Uninterrupted Power Supplies (UPSs), is required to protect computing and networking equipment.

The power that is consumed by computers and networking equipment is supplied from a pole-mounted transformer (see Figure E-6). The transformer, which is also connected to the earth ground, reduces the high voltages originating from a power plant to the 120 or 240 volts used by typical consumer electrical appliances.

FIGURE E-6
Surge suppressors, uninterruptible power supplies, and wall outlets all connect to a transformer and to the earth ground.

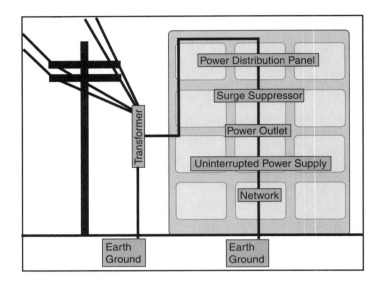

Now we see how electricity makes it to our homes, our schools, and our work places from the power plant. All the electrical considerations we've seen thus far play a role in the fundamental building block of electronic devices—the *circuits* that compose the ever present electronic equipment we use.

A Simple Circuit

Electrons flow only in circuits that are closed, or complete, loops. The diagram in Figure E-7 shows a simple circuit, typical of a lantern-style flashlight. The chemical processes in the battery cause charges to be separated, which provides a voltage, or electrical pressure, enabling electrons to flow through various devices. The lines represent a conductor, usually copper wire.

You can think of a switch as two ends of a single wire that can be opened (or broken) and then closed (also known as fixed or shorted) to prevent or to allow electrons to flow. The bulb provides resistance to the flow of electrons, causing the electrons to release energy in the form of light. The circuits involved in networking use the same concepts as in this very simple circuit, but are much more complex.

Circuits are the bottom line in networking equipment, including computers. All electronic devices are ultimately composed of circuits and switches. The simple example in Figure E-7 is replicated millions of times in the electronic devices we use. Typically, a microchip contains three to five million of these switches within one quarter-inch square.

FIGURE E-7
A simple circuit used in a 6-volt flashlight.

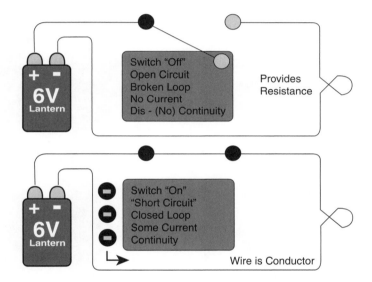

Summary

- Electricity is based on the capability of electrons of certain types of atoms to separate, or flow, from the confines of these atoms.
- Opposite charges attract and like charges repel. Electricity flows from negative to positive within electrical circuits.
- Materials can be classified as either insulators, conductors, or semiconductors, depending on their capability to allow electrons to flow.
- The concepts of voltage, current, resistance, and impedance provide a means of measuring electricity, which is required to be able to design and manufacture electronic devices.

- Alternating current and direct current are the two types of current. AC is used to provide power to our homes, schools, and work places. DC is used with electrical devices that depend on a battery to function.

- Electrical grounds provide a baseline from which to measure voltage. They also are used as a safety mechanism to prevent hazardous shocks.

- All electronic equipment is composed of electrical circuits that regulate the flow of electricity via switches.

Signaling and Data Transmission

Introduction

Appendix E, "Electronics and Signals," establishes the underlying physical principles governing computer networking. The physical layer of the OSI model is the setting in which the requisite physical phenomena is harnessed for the purposes of signaling. *Signaling* is the means by which data transmission is made possible. *Data transmission* is the means by which networking devices can operate within the remaining layers of the OSI model.

It is interesting to see the bottom-up approach that makes the world of networking possible. All of what we learn and do in computer networking is ultimately dependent on the underlying physics of electricity. Just as it is easier to learn about IP addressing and subnetting if we have a solid understanding of binary numbers and associated base conversions, it is much easier to understand networking at the physical and data link layers if we have a solid understanding of the physics of electricity.

In this appendix, you will study in detail the various concepts related to signaling and data transmission. This appendix culminates in a discussion of the formation of frames from bits at the physical layer, which completes your study of the physical layer.

Signals and Noise in Communication Systems

The term *signal* refers to a desired electrical voltage, light pattern, or modulated electromagnetic wave. Each of these entities can carry networking data. The two main types of signaling are *analog* and *digital*. Let's take a look at the specific attributes of each of these types of signals.

Comparing Analog and Digital Signals

One type of signal is analog. An analog signal has the following characteristics:

- It is wavy.
- It has a continuously varying voltage-versus-time graph.
- It is typical of things in nature.
- It has been widely used in telecommunications for more than 100 years.

Figure F-1 shows a *sine wave*. The two important characteristics of a sine wave are its *amplitude (A)*, its height and depth, and its *period (T)*, the length of one complete cycle (in our case, this is a time measurement). You can calculate the *frequency (f)* of the wave, measured in cycles per second, with the formula f = 1/T.

FIGURE F-1
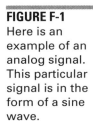
Here is an example of an analog signal. This particular signal is in the form of a sine wave.

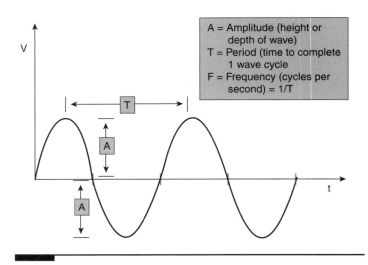

A = Amplitude (height or depth of wave)
T = Period (time to complete 1 wave cycle
F = Frequency (cycles per second) = 1/T

• Continuous voltage
• Can have any voltage
• "Wavy" voltage as time progresses
• Many encodings possible

Another type of signal is digital. A digital signal has the following characteristics:

■ It has discrete, or jumpy, voltage-versus-time graphs.

■ It is typical of technology (man-made), rather than nature.

Figure F-2 shows a digital networking signal. A digital signal has a fixed amplitude, but its amplitude, period, and frequency can be altered. Digital signals can be approximated by square waves (see Figure F-3), which have instantaneous transitions from low to high voltage states. Although this is an approximation, it is a reasonable one, and is used frequently herein.

FIGURE F-2
Here is an example of a digital signal.

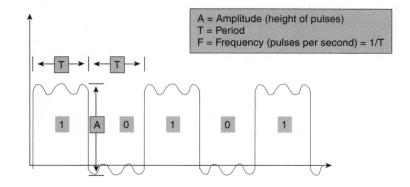

A = Amplitude (height of pulses)
T = Period
F = Frequency (pulses per second) = 1/T

- Not continuous (discreet) pulses
- Can only have one of two voltage levels
- Voltage jumps between levels
- Made up of many particular sine waves

FIGURE F-3
Here's a square wave. These waves can be approximated by a series of sine waves.

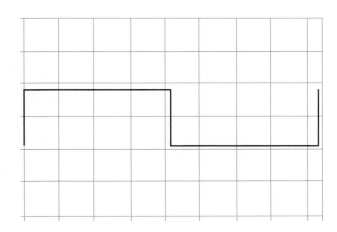

Using Digital Signals To Build Analog Signals

Jean Baptiste Fourier (1768-1830), a French mathematician, is responsible for proving mathematically that a special sum of sine waves with harmonically related frequencies, all multiples of some basic frequency, can be added together to create any wave pattern. The fundamental principle here is that complex waves can be built out of simple waves. This is how voice recognition devices and heart pacemakers work.

A square wave, or a square pulse, can be built by using the right combination of sine waves. Figure F-4 shows how the square wave (digital signal) can be built with sine waves (analog signals). This is important to remember as you examine what happens to a digital pulse as it travels along networking media. The infinite sum of sine waves that "adds up to" a square wave is called a *Fourier series* (this topic is studied in advanced engineering mathematics).

FIGURE F-4
Here's a square wave being approximated by a series of sine waves.

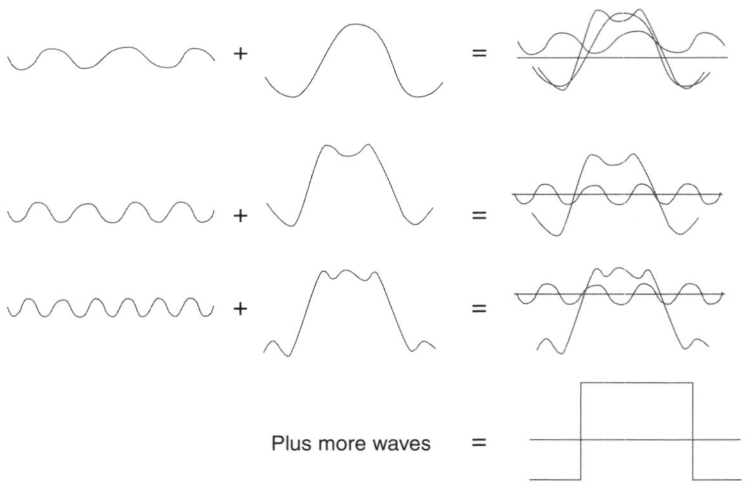

Now you know that digital waves can be approximated by sums of sine waves. Therefore, digital signals can be constructed from analog signals. Next, you'll see how electrical signals represent a bit.

Representing One Bit on a Physical Medium

Data networks have become increasingly dependent on digital (binary, two-state) systems. The basic building block of information is a binary digit, known as a bit or pulse. One bit, on an electrical medium, is the electrical signal corresponding to binary 0 or binary 1. This can be as simple as 0 volts for binary 0 and +5 volts for binary 1, or a more complex encoding. The signal reference ground is an important concept relating to all networking media that uses voltages to carry messages.

To function correctly, a signal reference ground must be physically close to a computer's digital circuits. Engineers have accomplished this by designing circuit boards to contain ground planes. The computer cabinets are used as the common point of connection for the circuit board ground planes to establish the signal reference ground. Signal reference ground establishes the 0 volts line in diagrams, such as Figure F-5.

With optical signals, binary 0 would be encoded as low light, or no light, intensity (darkness). Binary 1 would be encoded as a higher-light intensity (brightness), or other more complex patterns.

With wireless signals, binary 0 might be a short burst of waves; binary 1 might be a longer burst of waves, or another more complex pattern. The 0 bit is commonly represented by a horizontal line appearing on the t-axis (it's black in Figure F-5). It's also common to use +5 volts to indicate the 1 bit (the upper horizontal black line in the voltage versus time graph on the left).

FIGURE F-5
The signal reference ground is used to set a baseline.

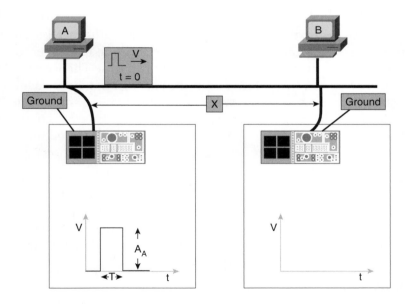

The following six things can affect a single bit:

- Propagation
- Attenuation

- Reflection
- Noise
- Timing problems
- Collisions

Propagation

Propagation means to travel through a medium. When a NIC puts out a voltage or light pulse onto a physical medium, that square pulse made up of waves travels along the medium (propagates). Propagation means that a lump of energy, representing 1 bit, travels from one place to another. The speed at which it propagates depends on the actual material used in the medium, the geometry (structure) of the medium, and the frequency of the pulses. The time it takes the bit to travel from one end of the medium and back is referred to as the *round trip time* (*RTT*). Assuming no other delays, the time it takes the bit to travel down the medium to the far end is RTT/2 (see Figure F-6).

The fact that the bit travels does not cause a problem for the network. The signaling occurs so quickly that to humans it sometimes appears to be instantaneous. In any case, it is important to account for the various timings involved with signaling in a network.

There are two extreme situations to consider. Either the bit takes "0" time to travel, meaning it travels instantaneously, or it takes forever to travel. The first case is wrong according to Albert Einstein, whose Theory of Relativity says no information can travel faster than the speed of light in a vacuum. This means that the bit takes at least a small amount of time to travel. The second case is also wrong, because with the right equipment, you can actually time the pulse. Lack of knowledge of propagation time is a problem, because you might assume the bit arrives at some destination either too soon or too late.

This problem can be resolved. Again, propagation time (see Figure F-6) is not inherently a problem; it's simply a fact that you should be aware of. If the propagation time is too long, you should reevaluate how the rest of the network deals with this delay. If the propagation delay is too short, you might have to slow down the bits, or save them temporarily (known as *buffering*), so the rest of the networking equipment can catch up with the bit.

Attenuation

Attenuation is the loss of signal strength as a signal traverses a physical medium, particularly in the case that the maximum recommended length for a cable is exceeded. This means that a 1-bit voltage signal loses amplitude as energy passes from the intrinsic signal to the cable (see Figure F-7). Although choosing materials carefully (such as using copper instead of carbon) and taking geometry (the shape and positioning of the wires) into account can reduce electrical attenuation, some loss is unavoidable due to electrical resistance. Attenuation also occurs with optical signals; the optical fiber absorbs and scatters some of the light energy as the light pulse, 1 bit, travels down the fiber. This can be minimized by the wavelength, or color, of the light that you choose. This can also be minimized by whether or not you use single mode or multimode fiber, and by the actual glass that is used for the fiber. Even with these choices, some signal loss is unavoidable.

FIGURE F-6
The familiar formula Distance = Rate x Time comes in handy sometimes in networking. Here is one application of the D=RT formula: computing the propagation delay (half the round-trip time) for a bit traveling from host A to host B.

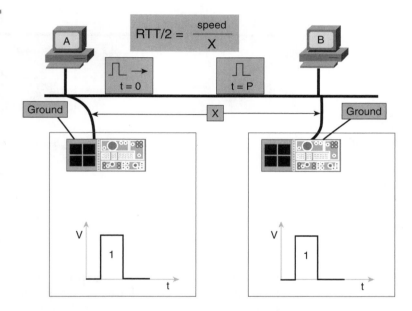

Attenuation also takes place with radio waves and microwaves, as they are absorbed and scattered by molecules in the atmosphere.

Attenuation can affect a network because it limits the length of network cabling over which you can send a message. If the cable is too long, 1 bit sent from the source can look like a 0 bit by the time it gets to the destination.

You can resolve this problem by choosing the appropriate networking media for a given design scenario. Another way to fix the problem is to use a repeater after a certain distance limitation is met. There are repeaters for electrical, optical, and wireless bits.

Reflection

To understand reflection, imagine having a slinky or a jump rope stretched out with a friend holding the other end. Now, imagine sending your friend a pulse or a 1-bit message. If you watch carefully, you can see that a small wave (pulse) returns (reflects) to you..

FIGURE F-7
Attenuation is the loss of signal energy as the distance traveled by a bit on the cable increases. You can see this indicated by the reduced height and protracted base of the square wave pictured on the right relative to its original condition on the left.

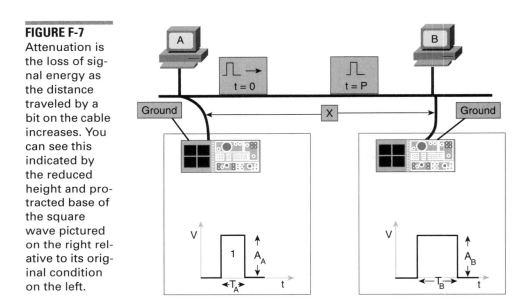

Reflection occurs in electrical signals. When voltage pulses, or bits, encounter a discontinuity, some energy can be reflected. This can occur wherever there is a change in a material's connection to another, or even the same, material. If not carefully controlled, this energy can confuse other bits. Remember, although you are focused on only 1 bit at a time right now, in real networks you send millions or billions of bits every second, thus requiring you to keep track of this reflected pulse energy. Depending on the cabling and connections that the network uses, reflections might or might not be a problem. A complex electrical characteristic involving resistance (the opposition to the flow of electrons) and reactance (the opposition to changes in voltage and current) is known as impedance.

Reflection also occurs with optical signals. Optical signals reflect whenever they encounter a discontinuity in the glass fiber, such as when a connector is plugged into a device. You can see this effect at night if you look out a window. You can see your reflection in the window even though the window is not a mirror. Some of the light that is reflected off your body reflects in the window. This also happens with radio waves and microwaves as they encounter different layers in the atmosphere.

This can cause problems on your network (see Figure F-8). For optimal network performance, it is important that the network media have a specific impedance in order to match the electrical components in the NICs. Unless the network media have the correct impedance, the signal suffers some reflection and interference is created. Then, multiple reflecting pulses can occur. Whether the system is electrical, optical, or wireless, impedance mismatches cause reflections. If enough energy is reflected, the binary, two-state system can become confused by all the extra energy bouncing around. You can resolve this by ensuring that all networking components are carefully impedance matched. You can avoid discontinuities in impedance through a variety of technologies.

FIGURE F-8

Reflection is caused by discontinuities in the medium. This could be a result of kinks in a cable or poorly terminated cables.

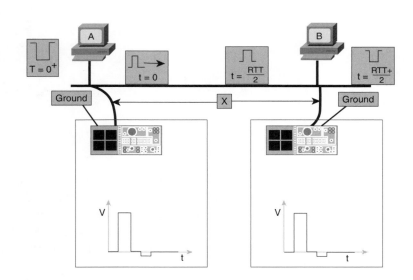

Noise

Noise in data communications is the unwanted addition of electrical signals to voltage, optical, or electromagnetic signals. In other words, each bit gets additional unwanted signals from various sources. Too much noise can corrupt a binary 1, changing it to a binary 0, and thus destroying the 1-bit message. Or, a 0-bit message can be mistaken for a 1 bit due to noise. No electrical signal is without noise; however, you must keep the signal-to-noise (S/N) ratio as high as possible. Figure F-9 shows five sources of noise that can affect a bit on a wire.

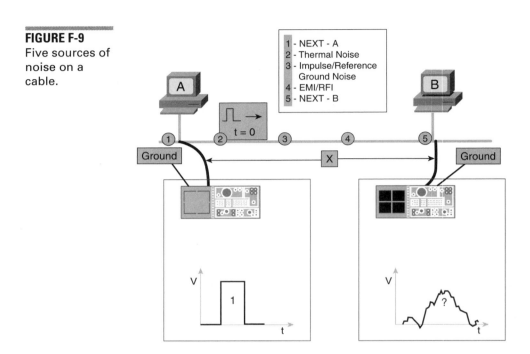

FIGURE F-9
Five sources of noise on a cable.

NEXT

When electrical noise on the cable originates from signals on other wires in the cable, this is known as *crosstalk*. NEXT stands for *near-end crosstalk*. When two wires are near each other and untwisted, energy from one wire can wind up in an adjacent wire and vice versa. This can cause noise at both ends of a terminated cable. Actually, many forms of crosstalk exist that must be considered when building networks.

NEXT can be addressed by termination technology, strict adherence to standard termination procedures, and use of quality twisted-pair cables.

Thermal Noise

Thermal noise is the random motion of electrons caused by temperature fluctuations of the media, and usually has a relatively small impact on signals. Nothing can be done about thermal noise other than to give the signals large enough amplitudes so the thermal noise influence is inconsequential.

AC Power/Reference Ground Noise

AC power and reference ground noises are serious problems in networking. AC line noise creates problems in homes, schools, and offices. Electricity is carried to appliances and machines by wires concealed in walls, floors, and ceilings. Consequently, inside these buildings, AC power line noise is all around. If not properly dealt with, power line noise can cause problems for a network.

Ideally, the signal reference ground should be completely isolated from the electrical ground. Isolation keeps AC power leakage and voltage spikes off the signal reference ground. The problem is that the chassis (case) of a computing device serves as the signal reference ground and as the AC power line ground. Because there is a link between the signal reference ground and the power ground, problems with the power ground can lead to interference with the data system. Such interference can be difficult to detect and trace. Usually, the problem occurs because electrical contractors and installers are not concerned about the length of the neutral and ground wires that lead to each electrical outlet. Unfortunately, when these wires are long, they can act as antennas for electrical noise. This noise interferes with the digital signals (bits) that computers must be able to recognize and process.

AC line noise coming from a nearby video monitor or hard disk drive can be enough to create errors in a computer system. It does this by interfering (changing the shape and voltage level) with the desired signals, preventing a computer from detecting the leading and trailing edges of the square waves. This problem can be compounded further when a computer has a poor ground connection.

To avoid the problem of AC/reference ground noise as described above, it is important to work closely with the electrical contractor and the power company. This enables you to get the best and shortest electrical ground. One way to do this is to investigate the cost of getting a single power transformer dedicated to your LAN installation area. If you can afford this option, you can control the attachment of other devices to your power circuit. Restricting how and where devices, such as motors or high-current electrical heaters, attach can eliminate much of the electrical noise generated by them.

When working with your electrical contractor, you should ask that separate power distribution panels, known as breaker boxes, be installed for each office area. Because the neutral wires and ground wires from each outlet come together in the breaker box, taking this step increases your chances of shortening the length of the signal ground. Although installing individual power distribution panels for every cluster of computers increases the up-front cost of power wiring, it reduces the length of the ground wires and limits several kinds of signal-burying electrical noise.

EMI/RFI

External sources of electrical impulses that can attack the quality of electrical signals on the cable include lighting, electrical motors, and radio systems. These types of interference are referred to as *electromagnetic interference (EMI)* and *radio frequency interference (RFI)*. Each wire in a cable can act like an antenna. When this happens, the wire actually absorbs electrical signals from other wires in the cable and from electrical sources outside the cable. If the resulting electrical noise reaches a high enough level, it can become difficult for NICs to discriminate the noise from the data signal. This is particularly a problem because most LANs use frequencies in the 1 to 100 megahertz (MHz) range, which happens to be where FM radio signals, TV signals, and many appliances have their operating frequencies as well.

To understand how electrical noise, regardless of the source, impacts digital signals, imagine that you want to send data, represented by the binary number 1011001001101, over the network. Your computer converts the binary number to a digital signal. Figure F-10 shows what the digital signal for 1011001001101 looks like. The digital signal travels through the networking media to the destination. The destination happens to be near an electrical outlet that is fed by both long neutral and long ground wires. These wires act as possible antennas for electrical noise. Figure F-10 shows what electrical noise looks like. Because the destination computer's chassis is used for both the earth ground and the signal reference ground, the noise generated interferes with the digital signal that the computer receives. Figure F-10 shows what happens to the signal when it is combined with this electrical noise. Instead of reading the signal as 1011001001101, the computer reads the signal as 1011000101101, making the data unreliable (corrupted).

There are many ways to limit EMI and RFI. One way is to increase the size of the conductors. Another way is to improve the type of insulating material used. However, such changes increase the size and cost of the cable faster than they improve its quality. Therefore, it is more typical for network designers to specify a cable of good quality and to provide specifications for the maximum recommended cable length between nodes.

Two techniques that cable designers have used successfully in dealing with EMI and RFI are *shielding* and *cancellation*. In cable that employs shielding, a metal braid or foil surrounds each wire pair or group of wire pairs. This shielding acts as a barrier to any interfering signals. However, as with increasing the size of the conductors, using braid or foil covering increases the diameter of the cable and the cost. Therefore, cancellation is the more commonly used technique to protect the wire from undesirable interference.

FIGURE F-10
The first graph is a digital signal, the second graph represents electrical noise, and the third graph shows the combined result. Note the red 0 and 1 are permuted relative to the original.

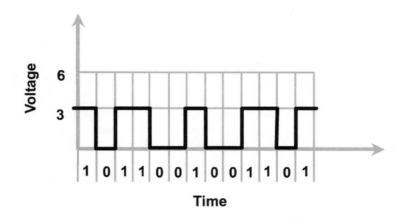

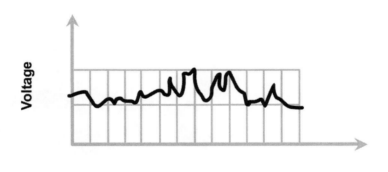

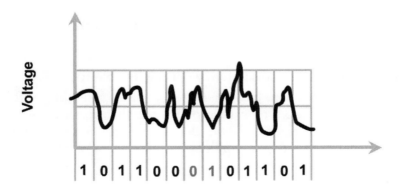

When electrical current flows through a wire, it creates a small, circular magnetic field around the wire (see Figure F-11). The direction of these magnetic lines of force is determined by the direction in which the current flows along the wire. If two wires are part of the same electrical circuit, electrons flow from the negative voltage source to the destination along one wire. Then, the electrons flow from the destination to the positive voltage source along the other wire. When two wires in an electrical circuit are placed close together, their magnetic fields are the exact opposite of each other. Thus, the two magnetic fields cancel each other out. Moreover, they cancel out some outside magnetic fields as well. Twisting the wires can enhance this cancellation effect. By using cancellation in combination with twisted wires, cable designers can provide an effective method of providing self-shielding for wire pairs within the network media.

FIGURE F-11
Electrical current in a wire induces a magnetic field around the wire.

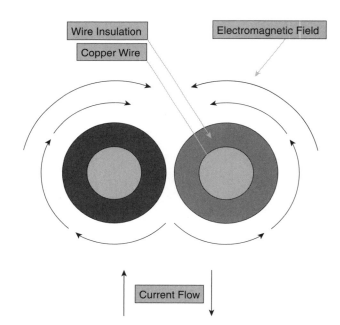

Wire Insulation

Copper Wire

Electromagnetic Field

Current Flow

Dispersion, Jitter, and Latency (Timing Problems)

Although dispersion, jitter, and latency are actually three different things that can happen to a bit, they are grouped together because they each affect the same thing: the timing of a bit. Because you are trying to understand what problems might occur as millions and billions of bits travel on a medium in one second, timing matters a lot.

Dispersion is when the signal broadens in time (see Figure F-12). The degree of dispersion depends on the type of media involved. If serious enough, one bit can start to interfere with the next bit, resulting in confusion as to which bit is which. Because you want to send millions or billions of bits per second, you must be careful not to allow the signals to spread out. You can minimize dispersion by designing cable properly, by limiting cable lengths, and by finding the proper impedance. In optical fibers, you can control dispersion by using laser light of a very specific wavelength. For wireless communications, you can minimize dispersion by the frequencies used to transmit.

FIGURE F-12
Dispersion elongates digital signals sometimes to the point where networking devices cannot distinguish where one bit ends and another begins.

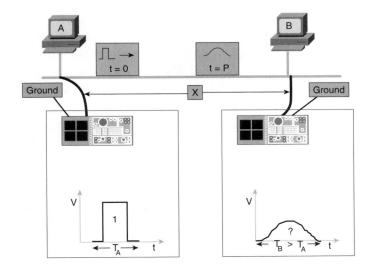

All digital systems are clocked, meaning that clock pulses govern electronic activity. Clock pulses cause a CPU to calculate, data to store in memory, and the NIC to send bits. If the clock on the source host is not synchronized with the destination, which is quite likely, you get timing *jitter*. This means that bits arrive a little earlier or later than expected. You can fix jitter by using a series of complicated clock synchronizations, including hardware, software, or protocol synchronizations.

Latency, also known as *delay*, has two main causes. First, Einstein's Theory of Relativity states that nothing can travel faster than the speed of light in a vacuum (3.0 x 10^8 m/s). Wireless networking signals travel slightly less fast than the speed of light (2.9 x 10^8 m/s). Signals on copper cables travel 2.3 x10^8 m/s, and in optical fiber they travel 2.0 x 10^8 m/s. So to travel a distance, a bit takes at least a small amount of time to get to its destination. Second, if the bit goes through any devices, the transistors and electronics introduce more latency. Some solutions to the latency issue are careful use of internetworking devices, utilizing various encoding strategies, and implementing appropriate layer protocols.

Modern networks typically work at speeds from 1 Mbps to 155 Mbps or greater. Soon, they will work at 1 Gbps or 1 billion bits per second. If bits are broadened by dispersion, then 1s can be mistaken for 0s, and 0s for 1s. If groups of bits get routed differently and there is no attention paid to timing, the jitter can cause errors as the receiving computer tries to reassemble packets into a message. If groups of bits are late, the intermediate networking devices and the destination computers might get hopelessly overwhelmed by a billion bits per second.

Collisions

A *collision* occurs when two bits from two different communicating computers simultaneously propagate on a shared medium. In the case of shared media, the voltages of the two binary signals are added and cause a third voltage level. This voltage variation is not allowed in a binary system, which only understands two voltage levels. The bits are destroyed. Figure F-13 illustrates a collision.

FIGURE F-13
Collisions are a common phenomenon on Ethernet networks.

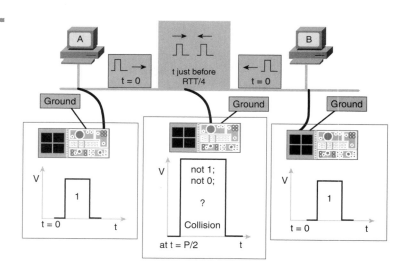

Some technologies, such as Ethernet, function by negotiating whose turn it is to transmit on the shared media when hosts are attempting to communicate. In some instances, collisions are a natural part of the functioning of a network. However, excessive collisions can slow the network down or bring it to a halt. Therefore, a lot of network design goes into minimizing and localizing collisions.

There are many ways to deal with collisions. One way is to detect them and simply have a set of rules for dealing with them when they occur, as in Ethernet. Another way is to try to prevent collisions by allowing only one computer at a time to transmit on a shared media environment. This requires that a computer have a special bit pattern, called a token, to transmit. This is the technology used with Token Ring and FDDI.

Messages in Terms of Bits

You now know that within a medium, a bit can experience attenuation, reflection, noise, dispersion, or collisions. Of course, you'll transmit far more than 1 bit. In fact, you'll transmit billions of bits in one second. All of the effects described so far can occur to one bit apply indirectly to the various protocol data units (PDUs) of the OSI model: 8 bits equals 1 byte, multiple bytes comprise one frame (see Figure F-14), frames contain packets, and packets contain segments. Segments carry the message you want to communicate. This brings us full circle, back to the layers of the OSI model serviced by the physical layer: the data link, network, transport, session, presentation, and application layers.

FIGURE F-14
Bits string together to form bytes, and bytes link together to form frames.

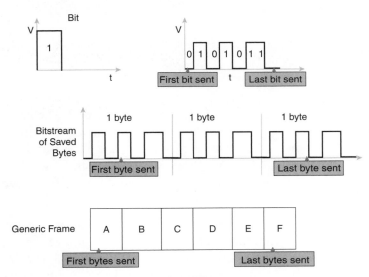

A, B, C, D, E, F multiple, often many, bytes

Encoding Networking Signals

When you want to send a message over a long distance, there are two problems you must solve: how to express the message (*encoding* or *modulation*), and which method to use to transport the message (*carrier*).

Throughout history there have been a variety of ways in which the problem of carrying a long distance communication has been solved: runners, riders, horses, optical telescopes, carrier pigeons, and smoke signals (see Figure F-15). Each method of delivery required a form of encoding. For example, smoke signals announcing that good hunting had just been found might be three short puffs of smoke, carrier pigeon messages relaying that someone had reached a destination safely might be a picture of a smiling face.

FIGURE F-15
Historical versions of transmitting signals with encoding.

☐ Smoke Signals

☐ Telegraph/Morse Code

☐ Telephone

☐ TV/Radio

☐ Pony Express

☐ Carrier Pigeon

In more modern times, the creation of Morse code revolutionized communications. Two symbols, the dot and the dash, encode the alphabet. For example, ●●● - - - ●●● means SOS (see Figure F-16), the universal distress signal. Modern telephones, FAX, AM, FM, short wave radio, and TV all encode their signals electronically, typically using the modulation of different waves from different parts of the electromagnetic spectrum.

Encoding is the process of converting binary data into a form that can travel on a physical communications link. *Modulation* means using the binary data to manipulate a wave. Computers use three particular technologies, all of which have their counterparts in history. These technologies are: encoding messages as voltages on various forms of copper wire; encoding messages as pulses of guided light on optical fibers; and encoding messages as modulated, radiated electromagnetic waves.

FIGURE F-16
Historical versions of transmitting signals with encoding.

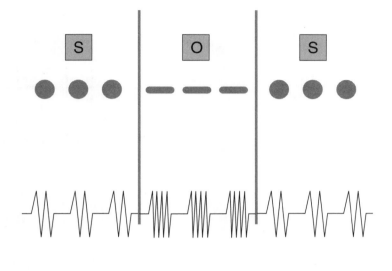

Morse code was the first widespread use of voltages to encode messages.

Encoding and Modulation

Encoding converts 1s and 0s into something real and physical, such as:

- An electrical pulse on a wire
- A light pulse on an optical fiber
- A pulse of electromagnetic waves in space

Two methods of accomplishing this are *NRZ encoding* and *Manchester encoding*. Figure F-17 illustrate these methods.

NRZ (non-return to 0) encoding is the simplest. It is characterized by a high signal and a low signal (often +5 or +3.3 V for binary 1 and 0 V for binary 0). In optical fibers, binary 1 might be a bright LED or laser light, and binary 0 might be darkness or no light. In wireless networks, binary 1 might mean a carrier wave is present, and binary 0 might mean that no carrier is present.

Manchester encoding is more complex, but is more immune to noise and is better at remaining synchronized. In Manchester encoding, the voltage on copper wire, the brightness of LED or laser light in optical fiber, or the power of an electromagnetic wave has the bits encoded as transitions. Specifically, in

Manchester encoding, upward transitions in the signal mean binary 1 and downward transitions mean binary 0.

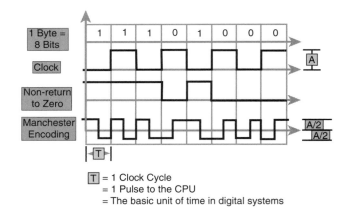

FIGURE F-17
NRZ encoding and Manchester encoding are the primary methods of encoding.

Closely related to encoding is modulation, which takes a wave and changes (modulates) it so that it carries information. To give you an idea of what modulation is, examine the following three forms of modifying, or modulating, a carrier wave to encode bits:

- *AM (amplitude modulation)*—The amplitude of a carrier sine wave is varied to carry the message.
- *FM (frequency modulation)*—The frequency of the carrier wave is varied to carry the message.
- *PM (phase modulation)*—The phase (beginning and ending points of a cycle) of the carrier wave is varied to carry the message.

Other more complex forms of modulation also exist. Figure F-18 shows three ways binary data can be encoded onto a carrier wave by the process of modulation. Binary 11 (note: read as "one one", not "eleven"!) can be communicated on a wave by either AM (wave on/wave off), FM (wave wiggles a lot for 1s, a little for 0s), or PM (one type of phase change for 0s, another for 1s).

FIGURE F-18
hree ways for
encoding
binary data
into a carrier
wave.

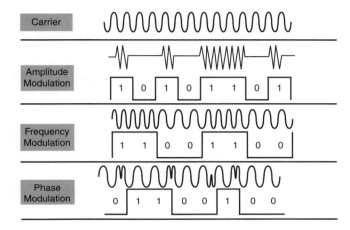

Messages can be encoded in a variety of ways:

- As voltages on copper; Manchester and NRZ encodings are popular on copper-based networks.
- As guided light; Manchester and 4B/5B encodings are popular on fiber-based networks.
- As radiated EM waves; a variety of encoding schemes (variations on AM, FM, and PM) are used on wireless networks.

Summary

- The computer converts the binary number to a digital signal.
- When a computer attached to a network receives data in the form of digital signals, it recognizes the data by measuring and comparing the voltage signals it receives to a reference point called the signal reference ground.
- Ideally, the signal reference ground should be completely isolated from the electrical ground. Isolation would keep AC power leakage and voltage spikes off the signal reference ground.
- If not properly addressed, power line noise can present serious problems for a network.
- The five types of noise are NEXT, thermal noise, AC power/reference, ground noise, and EMI/RFI.

- Timing problems include dispersion, jitter, and latency.
- Collisions occur when two bits from two different communicating computers simultaneously propagate on a shared medium.
- The two primary methods of encoding bits are NRZ encoding and Manchester encoding.
- The three main types of modulation for carrier waves are frequency modulation, amplitude modulation, and phase modulation.

Binary and Hexadecimal Conversion

Introduction

Computers are electronic devices made up of electronic switches. At the lowest levels of computation, computers depend on these electronic switches to make decisions. As such, computers react only to electrical impulses. These impulses are understood by the computer as either "on" or "off" states, or as 1s or 0s. Because the computer can't speak your language, you need to learn to speak the computer's language. That is the language of *binary arithmetic*.

The *binary number system*, or *Base 2*, is made up entirely of 0s and 1s. Computers use Base 2 in expressing IP addresses. One of the goals of this appendix is to provide a better understanding of the process of converting between binary numbers (used with IP addresses) and their equivalent decimal values.

At higher levels of computation, computers sometimes process information using the *hexadecimal number system*, or *Base 16*. Base 16 is a number system that uses 16 characters: 0, 1, 2, 3, 4, 5, 6, 7, 8, 9, A, B, C, D, E, and F. Computer scientists use Base 16 because it makes expressing bytes more manageable. This is because 16 is a power of 2: 16=2×2×2×2. Only two hexadecimal digits are needed to represent one 8-bit byte. Of course, Base 15 or Base 20 would not work as well because neither 15 nor 20 are powers of 2.

Computers don't think in the *decimal number system*, or *Base 10*, as humans do. Electronic devices are structured in such a way that binary and hexadecimal numbering is natural: computers have to *translate* in order to use decimal numbering. It's like a person who speaks two languages, one is their first language and the other is their second language: it is faster and more accurate to communicate in the first language.

In this appendix, you will learn how to think in binary and hexadecimal numbering systems so you can make the necessary translations when performing certain networking tasks, such as designing an IP addressing scheme for a network (binary) or working with memory addresses or MAC addresses on a router (hexadecimal).

As you know, it takes time and practice to learn new concepts in math. You won't master binary and hexadecimal numbers the first time you read about them. So, if you are learning about the binary and hexadecimal numbering systems for the first time, remember that it is a step-by-step process.

Preliminaries

How Do You Know What Base Someone Is Referring To?

The binary numbering system uses two characters, 0 and 1. Any decimal number you can imagine can be expressed in binary. The characters used in the decimal number system are 0, 1, 2, 3, 4, 5, 6, 7, 8, and 9. Because both number systems use the characters 0 and 1, there is a potential for confusion. For example, what does 10110 mean? Well, it depends on whether you're referring to 10110 in Base 10 or 10110 in Base 2. Because of the potential for confusion, sometimes mathematicians write 10110_{10} to mean 10110 in Base 10 and 10110_2 to mean 10110 in Base 2. However, writing down these subscripts every time you write a number quickly becomes very tedious, so what you usually do is make it clear from the context what base is being referred to without explicitly writing down the base. So, first make sure that it is clear in your mind when you look at a *string* of characters, such as 10110, that you know what base the person who wrote 10110 was thinking of when he wrote it. If you are unsure, then the person who wrote it did a poor job of making it clear or did not intend to refer to a particular base (this is what a computer scientist calls a *string*, an abstract list of characters strung together).

Some Miscellaneous Facts

There is one important *convention* (agreed upon rule) that should be made clear and that almost goes without saying. It is taken for granted after years of working with decimal numbers: The convention is to read, write, and pronounce strings, such as 10110, from left to right. For example, you read 10110 as "one, zero, one, one, zero".

If you come across a string like 10110, it usually is coming from some kind of computer output. There are specific notations that certain programs, such as protocol analyzers, use to differentiate between binary, decimal, and hexadecimal notation. For example, the % sign precedes a binary string; thus, %10110 means 10110 in Base 2. In addition, the 0x sign precedes a hexadecimal string, so 0x10110 means 10110 in Base 16.

One practical consideration to keep in mind when using different bases is that the bigger the base, the less characters used to express the number. For example, the decimal number 16 in Base 2 is 10000 and the decimal number 16 in Base 16 is 10. In addition, although we focus only on Base 2 and Base 16, there is no numerical limit to the base you can use. Although it is not practical for computer-related work, you could work in Base 23,037 or Base 1,002,395. To illustrate, the decimal number 15 is represented by the letter F in Base 16, the decimal number 20 is represented by the letter K in Base 21, and the decimal number 29 is represented by the letter T in Base 30. What character in Base 36 represents the decimal number 35 (assuming you use the English alphabet)?

Another important fact to keep in mind is that each base you work in has a fixed set of characters. For example, Base 2 has 2 characters, Base 10 has 10 characters, and Base 16 has 16 characters. Note that no character 2 exists in Base 2 (just 0 and 1—you know you can't be working in binary if there's a number with a 2 in it!). No character 3 exists in Base 3 (just 0, 1, and 2). No character 9 exists in Base 9 (just 0, 1, 2, 3, 4, 5, 6, 7, and 8). No character A exists in Base 10 (just 0, 1, 2, 3, 4, 5, 6, 7, 8, and 9). No character G exists in Base 16 (just 0, 1, 2, 3, 4, 5, 6, 7, 8, 9, A, B, C, D, E, and F). You get the idea. Also, note that the number of characters in a base is equal to the decimal value of the base. Here are a couple silly examples: 0 is the only character in Base 1 (so you can't express any number greater than 0 in Base 1!) and there are no characters in Base 0.

Whether you're working in Base 2, 10, 16, or whatever, numbers are expressed as strings of characters, such as 101011 in Base 2, 14932 in Base 10, or A2E7 in Base 16. This is actually a convenience. Did you know that writing the decimal number 124 is actually a shortcut? It is short for $1\times100+2\times10+4\times1$, which would be tedious to write out. Imagine if every time you wrote down a decimal number you had to express it this way! Each number in a string of characters represents a value that depends on its *place* in the string. For example, the character 7 in the Base 10 number 23761 represents 7×100, or 700. You also can use tables with columns to emphasize the importance of place value when converting between bases. Among other things, the tables help illustrate that when you read strings of characters from left to right, the characters represent decreasing place values. For example, in the decimal number 234, 2 represents 2 hundreds, 3 represents 3 tens, and 4 represents 4 ones. In summary, two things are essential to understand with each string of characters: the characters in the string and their place value in the string.

Base Conventions

You use the words *ten, eleven, twelve, thirteen, ..., twenty, twenty-one,* and so on only when working in decimal. These *are* decimal (Base 10) numbers. When you say "thirty," it is just a short way of saying "three tens." When you talk about the string 23 in Base 5, you don't say "twenty-three in Base 5," you say "two three in Base 5." Saying "twenty-three" would mean "two tens and three"—you are talking in Base 10 when you say "twenty-three." You pronounce numbers differently when working in bases *other than ten*. As another example, 101 in Base 2 is spoken "one zero one in Base 2," or just "one zero one" if it's clear that you're referring to Base 2. You wouldn't say "one hundred one in Base 2" or "one hundred one." The reason for this is you don't want to confuse people by verbalizing a string of characters in Base 10 when the string represents a Base 2 number.

Note that the string "21" in "3A2 in Base 21" is pronounced "twenty-one" and it means exactly that, 21 in decimal. To emphasize this, sometimes people just write "3A2 in Base twenty-one." Another example: the string "16" in "Base 16" is "sixteen;" that is, it is assumed that 16 is a decimal number (as opposed to 16 in another base). As a last example, "847 in Base 20" is spoken "eight four seven in Base twenty." The convention is to think, read, write, and speak in decimal when referring to the string appearing after the word "Base."

One other thing to keep in mind is the role of the character 0. Every base uses the character 0. *Whenever the character 0 appears on the left side of a string of characters, it can be removed without changing the value of the string of characters.* For example, in Base 10, 02947 equals 2947. In Base 2, 0001001101 equals 1001101. Sometimes people include 0s on the left side of a number to emphasize places that would otherwise not be represented. Because the 8-bit byte is sometimes thought of as a unit, binary strings are often *padded out* to be eight characters long. For example, when *subnetting*, the decimal number 6 is most conveniently expressed as 00000110 in binary. It's very common when working with IP addresses to express binary numbers with 0s in the front because, with IP addresses, you work with *octets* (strings of eight characters at a time). For example, it's not unusual to express the binary number 10000 as 00010000.

Working with Exponents

Last, you need to work with *powers* of numbers, called *exponents*, when dealing with different number systems. Recall from mathematics that powers are used to represent repeated multiplication of the same number. The following example illustrates how exponents work with the number 2—the rules hold for other numbers as well. First, $2^0=1$, which is spoken "two to the zero equals one" (2 is called the *base* and 0 is called the *exponent*). This fact is not derived from previous knowledge, it is part of the definition of 2^n, where n is an *integer*. Second, $2^1=2$ ("two to the one equals two") according to mathematical definition. Third, $2^2=2\times2=4$: "two to the two equals two times two equals four." Continuing, $2^3=2\times2\times2=8$: "two to the three equals two times two times two equals eight." This provides a pattern that can be used for any power of 2. A common mistake is to confuse taking powers with multiplying, so be careful: $2^4\neq2\times4=8$, $2^4=2\times2\times2\times2=16$.

Exponents are very convenient when working with binary numbers. For example, the number of objects that n bits can represent is calculated by using the formula s^n. If there are 8 bits set aside for describing or naming an object, then there are $2^8=256$ possible variations for assigning a binary number to that object. This fact is very important to understand: if there are 8 bits available, that means there are eight *slots* or places for a binary number—there are 256 different binary numbers that can be expressed with 8 bits and there are 256 different strings consisting of 0s and 1s that can be formed with 8 slots or places.

You have seen many concepts up to this point regarding different bases and how to work with them. You should now have a better understanding of the fundamentals necessary to be able to work in different numbering systems.

Binary Numbers

First, you will learn how to use tables to represent numbers in a particular base. Then, you will learn about the two main concepts of interest: converting binary numbers to decimal numbers, and converting decimal numbers to binary numbers. After that, you will learn how to *count* in binary, which is useful when determining *subnetwork addresses*.

In Base 10, you work with powers of ten. For example, 23,605 in Base 10 means $2\times10,000+3\times1000+6\times100+0\times10+5\times1$. Note that $10^0=1$, $10^1=10$, $10^2=100$, $10^3=1000$, and $10^4=10,000$. In addition, even though $0\times10=0$, you don't leave out the 0 in 23,605 because, if you did, you would have $2365=2\times1000+3\times100+6\times10+5\times1$, which is not what you meant to express by 23,605: the 0 acts as a *placeholder*. On the other hand, if for some reason you wanted to focus on the one hundred thousand place and the one million place, you would express 23,605 as 0,023,605.

As the previous paragraph demonstrates, if you want to literally express the meaning of a decimal number, you can use powers of 10 (10^0, 10^1, 10^2, and so on). You use the expanded form of the powers (1, 10, 100, and so on) when you focus on the actual value of a decimal number. It helps to use tables to keep track of all this. Table G-1 has three rows: the first row lists *powers of 10*; the second row expresses the *expanded* (multiplied out) *powers of 10*; and the third row is where you place numbers to communicate how many (between 0 and 9) of that power of 10 you want.

TABLE G-1

10^7	10^6	10^5	10^4	10^3	10^2	10^1	10^0
10,000,000	1,000,000	100,000	10,000	1000	100	10	1

For example, Table G-2 shows how to express 23,605 in a Base 10 table.

TABLE G-2

10^4	10^3	10^3	10^1	10^0
10,000	1000	100	10	1
2	3	6	0	5

The pattern for expressing binary numbers is very similar to what you just read about decimal numbers. Binary numbers use the principle of place value just as decimal numbers do. The difference is that you use powers of 2 instead of powers of 10, and you use only the characters 0 and 1 (there's no 2, 3, 4, 5, 6, 7, 8, or 9). So, the binary table (comparable to Table G-1) has three rows: the first row lists *powers of 2*; the second row expresses the *expanded* (multiplied out) *powers of 2*; and the third row is where you place numbers to communicate how many (between 0 and 1) of that power of 2 you want (see Table G-3). *Notice that the second row has numbers written in Base 10!*

TABLE G-3

2^7	2^6	2^5	2^4	2^3	2^2	2^1	2^0
128	64	32	16	8	4	2	1

As an example, you can *break down* the binary number 1101 by placing the digits in a binary table (see Table G-4). After making the table, you can use it to convert the binary number to its Base 10 equivalent.

TABLE G-4

2^3	2^2	2^1	2^0
8	4	2	1
1	1	0	1

You can use Table G-4 to *convert* the binary number 1101 to Base 10:

1101=1×8+1×4+0×2+1×1=8+4+0+1=13.

As another example, you can examine the binary number 10010001 by placing the digits in a binary table (see Table G-5). After making the table, you can use it to convert the binary number to its Base 10 equivalent.

TABLE G-5

2^7	2^6	2^5	2^4	2^3	2^2	2^1	2^0
128	64	32	16	8	4	2	1
1	0	0	1	0	0	0	1

You can use Table G-5 to convert the binary number 10010001 to Base 10:

10010001=1×128+0×64+0×32+1×16+0×8+0×4+0×2+1×1=128+16+1=145.

The binary number 11111111 occurs as often as any other in networking (see Table G-6).

TABLE G-6

2^7	2^6	2^5	2^4	2^3	2^2	2^1	2^0
128	64	32	16	8	4	2	1
1	1	1	1	1	1	1	1

You can use Table G-6 to convert the binary number 11111111 to Base 10:

11111111=1×128+1×64+1×32+1×16+1×8+1×4+1×2+1×1=255.

Most of the work you do with binary numbers in networking involves working with one byte, or one octet, at a time; that is, working with 8-bit binary numbers.

An IP address is expressed as a dotted-decimal number, W.X.Y.Z, where W, X, Y, and Z are decimal numbers whose binary representations each consist of 8 bits. The smallest decimal value that can be represented by one byte

(00000000 in binary) is 0. The largest decimal value that can be represented by one byte (11111111 in binary) is 255, as calculated in Table G-6. It follows that the range of decimal numbers that can be represented by a byte is 0 to 255, a total of 256 possible values. Therefore, in an IP address, the decimal numbers (W, X, Y, and Z) are between 0 and 255. Some examples of IP addresses are 140.57.255.0, 204.65.103.243, and 5.6.7.8.

Now you know how to convert a binary number to a decimal number. As an exercise, use a table to show that the binary number 11111001 is equal to the decimal number 249. After doing several problems like this, you can develop your own shortcuts that might not include using a table at all.

Converting a Decimal Number into a Binary Number

Converting a decimal number into a binary number is one of the most common procedures performed while working with IP addresses. As with most problems in math, there are several ways to solve the problem. This section introduces one method, but feel free to use another method if you find it easier.

To convert a decimal number to binary, you first find the largest power of 2 that fits into the decimal number. Consider the decimal number 35. If you refer to Table G-3, what's the largest power of 2 that is less than or equal to 35? Well, 64 is too large, but 32 just fits, so you know that there is be a 1 in the 2^5 column. Now, how much is left over? You find this by subtracting 32 from 35: 35–32=3. Next, you look at each remaining powers of 2, one column at a time. Because the next smaller power of 2 is 2^4, you determine if 2^4, or 16, is less than or equal to 3. Because it is not, you put a 0 in the 2^4 column. The next power is 2^3, so you decide if 2^3, or 8, is less than or equal to 3; it is not, so you put a 0 in the 2^3 column as well. Next, is 2^2, or 4, less than or equal to 3? It is not, so place a 0 in the 2^2 column. Next, is 2^1, or 2, less than or equal to 3? It is, so place a 1 in the 2^1 column. Now, how much is left over? Subtract: 3–2=1. Finally, you ask if 2^0, or 1, is less than or equal to the remainder 1? Because it is, you put a 1 in the 2^0 column. Therefore, the decimal number 35 is equal to the binary number 00100011 or 100011. That's it. Table G-7 summarizes this process.

TABLE G-7

2^7	2^6	2^5	2^4	2^3	2^2	2^1	2^0
128	64	32	16	8	4	2	1
0	0	1	0	0	0	1	1

As a second example of converting a decimal number to binary, consider the decimal number 239. Notice that we're taking the byte-oriented approach here; that is, we're working with numbers between 0 and 255, which are the decimal numbers that can be expressed with one byte. If you refer to Table G-3, what's the largest power of 2 that is less than or equal to 239? You can see that 128 meets the criteria, so you put a 1 in the 2^7 column. Now, how much is left over? You find this by subtracting 128 from 239: 239–128=111. Because the next smaller power of 2 is 2^6, you determine if 2^6, or 64, is less than or equal to 111. Because it is, you put a 1 in the 2^6 column. How much is left over? You find this by subtracting 64 from 111: 111–64=47. The next power is 2^5, so you decide if 2^5, or 32, is less than or equal to the remainder 47; it is, so you put a 1 in the 2^5 column as well. How much is left over? Find this by subtracting 32 from 47: 47–32=15. Next, is 2^4, or 16, less than or equal to 15? It is not, so place a 0 in the 2^4 column. Next, is 2^3, or 8, less than or equal to 15? It is, so place a 1 in the 2^3 column. How much is left over? Subtract: 15–8=7. Next, is 2^2, or 4, less than or equal to the remainder 7? It is, so place a 1 in the 2^2 column. How much is left over? Subtract: 7–4=3. Next, is 2^1, or 2, less than or equal to 3? It is, so you put a 1 in the 2^1 column. How much is left over? Subtract: 3–2=1. Finally, you ask if 2^0, or 1, is less than or equal to the remainder 1? Because it is, you put a 1 in the 2^0 column. Therefore, the decimal number 239 is equal to the binary number 11101111. Table G-8 summarizes the result.

TABLE G-8

2^7	2^6	2^5	2^4	2^3	2^2	2^1	2^0
128	64	32	16	8	4	2	1
1	1	1	0	1	1	1	1

This procedure works for any decimal number. Consider the decimal number 1,000,000 (one million). What's the largest power of 2 less than or equal to 1,000,000? With a little patience, you can find that 2^{19}=524,288 and 2^{20}=1,048,576, so 2^{19} is the largest power of 2 that fits into 1,000,000. If you continue with the procedure previously described, you determine that the decimal number one million is equal to the binary number 11110100001001000000.

You see that binary numbers take up a lot more space than decimal numbers. This is partly why humans don't think in binary. Probably the main reason humans use Base 10, though, is because we have 10 fingers. If we had 12 fingers, we would probably think in Base 12.

Counting in Binary

You can divide a network into *subnetworks* (*subnets* for short) by "borrowing bits" from the leftmost portion of the host field of the network IP address. The borrowed bits allow you to differentiate the subnets by the binary strings that define them. For example, if you borrow 2 bits from the fourth octet of the Class C network 200.10.20.0, you form four subnets. The four possible combinations obtainable from 2 bits are the binary strings 00, 01, 10, and 11. You normally discard the first and the last subnets (associated with all 0s and all 1s). Note that 00, 01, 10, and 11 is how you count from 0 to 3 in binary.

So, when determining the subnet addresses for a given IP network, it is useful to be able to count in binary. Counting in binary allows you to explicitly list the binary representations of the subnet IP addresses obtained by borrowing bits.

With 4 bits, you can express 2^{14}=16 possible combinations of 0s and 1s. For your reference, here's a list of the first 16 binary numbers in order (counting from 0 to 15 in binary):

`0, 1, 10, 11, 100, 101, 110, 111, 1000, 1001, 1010, 1011, 1100, 1101, 1110, 1111.`

Even and Odd

Sometimes it's useful to recognize how the concepts of *even* and *odd* translate into binary numbers. An even decimal number is one that is a multiple of 2 (such as 0, 2, 4, 6, 8, 10, 12, and so on). Notice in the second row of Table G-9 that all the numbers are multiples of 2 except the one on the right: 1.

TABLE G-9

2^7	2^6	2^5	2^4	2^3	2^2	2^1	2^0
128	64	32	16	8	4	2	1

If you think about it, this means that *a binary number is a multiple of 2 if and only if the rightmost digit is a 0*. Therefore, **a binary number is even if and only if the rightmost digit is 0.** An odd number is one that is not even (such as the decimal numbers 1, 3, 5, 7, 9, 11, and so on). Hence, **a binary number is odd if and only if the rightmost digit is 1.**

Here are some examples: the binary number 10011 is odd (19 in decimal) and the binary number 1010100010 is even (674 in decimal).

Hexadecimal Numbers

In Base 16, or *hexadecimal*, you work with powers of sixteen. You use hexadecimal notation with data link layer addressing (such as MAC addresses) and when referring to memory addresses in electronic devices. The 16 hexadecimal characters are 0, 1, 2, 3, 4, 5, 6, 7, 8, 9, A, B, C, D, E, and F. The A corresponds to the decimal number 10; B to 11; C to 12; D to 13; E to 14; and F to 15. Some examples of hexadecimal numbers are 2A384C5D9E7F, A001, and 237. Again, you have to be careful that it is clear from the context as to what base you're referring; otherwise, the previous example of 237 might be mistaken for a decimal number.

There are two special notations used with hexadecimal numbers. Sometimes, you see notation like 0x1A3B or 1A3Bh. These mean the same thing: 1A3B in hexadecimal. To reiterate, if you see a string preceded by "0x" or followed by "h", you know to interpret the string as a hexadecimal number. In particular, you see these notations when you work with memory registers.

Another fact that is important to understand is that one hexadecimal character can represent any decimal number between 0 and 15. In binary, 15 is 1111 and A is 1010. It follows that *4 bits are required to represent a single hexadecimal character in binary.* A MAC address is 48 bits long (6 bytes), which translates to 48÷4=12 hexadecimal characters required to express a MAC address. You can check this by typing **winipcfg** in Windows 95/98 or **ipconfig /all** in Windows NT4/2000 at the command prompt.

Table G-10 is a hexadecimal table (comparable to Table G-1) that has three rows. The first row lists *powers of 16*; the second row expresses the *expanded* (multiplied out) *powers of 16*; and the third row is where you place numbers to communicate how many (between 0 and F) of that power of 16 you want. *Notice that the second row has numbers written in Base 10!* This table uses only four columns because the powers of 16 become very large as the exponent increases; also, it is common to express hexadecimal characters in groups of two or four.

TABLE G-10

16^3	16^2	16^1	16^0
4096	256	16	1

Consider the hexadecimal number 3A. You can determine the value of 3A in decimal by using a hexadecimal table (see Table G-11).

TABLE G-11

16^1	16^0
16	1
3	A

You can use Table G-11 to convert the hexadecimal number 3A to Base 10:

3A=3×16+A×1=3×16+10×1=48+10=58.

Now, consider the hexadecimal number 23CF. Table G-12 helps put it in perspective.

TABLE G-12

16^3	16^2	16^1	16^0
4096	256	16	1
2	3	C	F

You can use Table G-12 to convert the hexadecimal number 23CF to Base 10:

23CF=2×4096+3×256+C×16+F×1=2×4096+3×256+12×16+15×1
.=8192+768+192+15=9167.

The smallest decimal value that can be represented by four hexadecimal characters, 0000, is 0. The largest decimal value that can be represented by four hexadecimal characters, FFFF, is 65,535. It follows that the range of decimal numbers that can be represented by four hexadecimal characters is 0 to 65,535, a total of 65,536 or 2^{16} possible values.

Now you know how to convert a hexadecimal number to a decimal number. As an exercise, use a table to show that the hexadecimal number 8D2B3 converts to the decimal number 578,227. As with binary to decimal conversion, after repeating this procedure several times, you'll probably develop your own shortcuts that might include not using a table at all.

Converting a Decimal Number into a Hexadecimal Number

Again, there's more than one way to proceed, so stick with your favorite method. The following process demonstrates one way to go about this conversion. If you are already comfortable with a particular method, you might want to skip the rest of this section.

To convert a decimal number into a hexadecimal number, the idea is to first find the largest power of 16 that is less than or equal to the decimal number, and then to determine how many times it fits into the decimal number. Now that you've been through a similar process with decimal to binary conversion, you can just get right to it. One difference to note is that the highest power of 16 to fit into a decimal number sometimes fits multiple times.

Consider the decimal number 15,211. Looking at Table G-10, what's the largest power of 16 that is less than or equal to 15,211? Well, 4096 meets the criteria. How many times does it fit in 15,211? Checking, you see that 4096 fits three times and no more (4096×3=12,288), so you know there will be a 3 in the 4096 (or 16^3) column. Now, how much is left over? You find this by subtraction: 15,211–12,288=2923. Next, you see that 256 fits 11 times (and no more) into 2923 (256×11=2816), so you know there is a B (not 11!) in the 256 (or 16^2) place. Subtracting, you get 2923–2816=107. Because 16 fits six times (and no more) into 107 (16×6=96), you know there is a 6 in the 16 (or 16^1) column. Subtracting, you get 107-96=11, so the last digit is a B. The hexadecimal value for the decimal number 15,211 is 3B6B. Table G-13 summarizes this process.

TABLE G-13

16^3	16^2	16^1	16^0
4096	256	16	1
3	B	6	B

Converting a Hexadecimal Number into a Binary Number

It's relatively easy to convert a hexadecimal number into a binary number. You can do it one hexadecimal character at a time. Note that this method does not work in general for converting between various bases; the method only works here because 16 is a power of 2: $16=2^4$.

As an example, the hexadecimal number A3 is equal to the binary number 10100011 because A converts to 1010 and 3 converts to 0011. *Be especially careful to include four binary digits for each hexadecimal character for this method to work.* (If you forgot to do this in the last example, your result would be 101011, which you can check is incorrect.) The hexadecimal number F0F0 converts to 1111000011110000 because F converts to 1111 in binary and 0 converts to 0000 in binary. Last, the broadcast MAC address FF-FF-FF-FF-FF-FF converts to the binary equivalent of 11111111-11111111-11111111-11111111-11111111-11111111. You see that hexadecimal representations take up much less space than their binary counterparts.

This concludes the discussion of binary and hexadecimal numbers. Remember that these concepts take some time to get used to, but you can do it. Stick with it and, after getting a lot of practice over time, you'll be explaining it to others!

Exercises

1. Convert the binary number 1010 to Base 10.
2. Convert the Base 2 number 11110000 to decimal notation.
3. Convert the binary number 10101111 to a decimal number.
4. Convert the decimal number 1111 to binary notation.
5. Convert the decimal number 249 to Base 2.
6. Convert the decimal number 128 to Base 2.
7. Convert the decimal number 65 to a binary number.
8. Convert the Base 10 number 63 to binary notation.
9. Convert the Base 10 number 31 to a binary number.
10. Convert the decimal number 198 to binary notation.
11. Is the binary number 11100011 even or odd?
12. Convert 0xAB to Base 10.
13. Convert ABCDh to Base 10.
14. Convert 0xFF to decimal notation.
15. Convert the decimal number 249 to Base 16.
16. Convert the decimal number 65,000 to hexadecimal notation.
17. Convert 0x2B to Base 2.
18. Convert 0x10F8 to Base 2.
19. Change the MAC address 00-A0-CC-3C-4A-39 to binary notation.
20. Change both the IP address 166.122.23.130 and the subnet mask 255.255.255.128 to dotted-hexadecimal form.

Network Troubleshooting

Introduction

By performing router labs, you become more familiar with the troubleshooting process. In this appendix, you explore troubleshooting in more detail. To some extent, troubleshooting is an individualized process. However, some principles are common to any troubleshooting methodology. In the following pages, we use the language of the OSI model to put troubleshooting in perspective as it relates to Semester 2 router labs. Then, we present a general problem-solving approach for networking.

Troubleshooting Semester 2 Labs

You gained quite a bit of skill in troubleshooting during the time you spent configuring routers in Semester 2 (see Figure H-1). You learned to work upward from layer 1 of the OSI model, progressing from the physical layer to the data link layer to the network layer and beyond. A review of some of the common layer 1, layer 2, and layer 3 issues you learned to resolve follows.

Layer 1 errors can include

- Broken cables
- Disconnected cables
- Cables connected to the wrong ports
- Intermittent cable connections
- Cables incorrectly terminated
- Wrong cables used for the tasks at hand (must use cross-connects, rollovers, and straight-through cables correctly)
- Transceiver problems
- DCE cable problems
- DTE cable problems
- Devices powered off

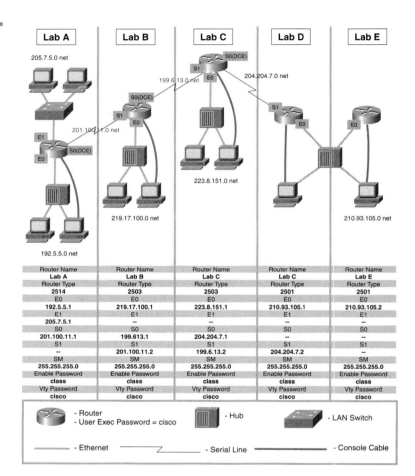

FIGURE H-1
Here is the Semester 2 lab configuration with all the usual settings.

Router Name	Router Name	Router Name	Router Name	Router Name
Lab A	**Lab B**	**Lab C**	**Lab C**	**Lab E**
Router Type	Router Type	Router Type	Router Type	Router Type
2514	**2503**	**2503**	**2501**	**2501**
E0	E0	E0	E0	E0
192.5.5.1	**219.17.100.1**	**223.8.151.1**	**210.93.105.1**	**210.93.105.2**
E1	E1	E1	E1	E1
205.7.5.1	--	--	--	--
S0	S0	S0	S0	S0
201.100.11.1	**199.613.1**	**204.204.7.1**	--	--
S1	S1	S1	S1	S1
--	**201.100.11.2**	**199.6.13.2**	**204.204.7.2**	--
SM	SM	SM	SM	SM
255.255.255.0	**255.255.255.0**	**255.255.255.0**	**255.255.255.0**	**255.255.255.0**
Enable Password	Enable Password	Enable Password	Enable Password	Enable Password
class	**class**	**class**	**class**	**class**
Vty Password	Vty Password	Vty Password	Vty Password	Vty Password
cisco	**cisco**	**cisco**	**cisco**	**cisco**

FIGURE H-2
Always start troubleshooting by analyzing layer 1 issues.

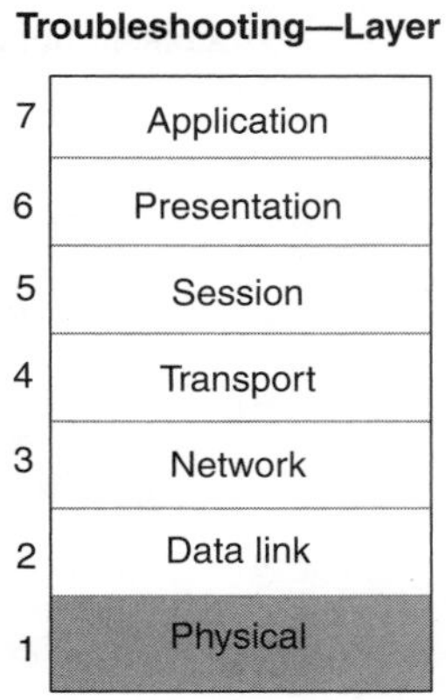

Troubleshooting—Layer 1

7	Application
6	Presentation
5	Session
4	Transport
3	Network
2	Data link
1	Physical

FIGURE H-3
The second OSI layer you should troubleshoot is layer 2.

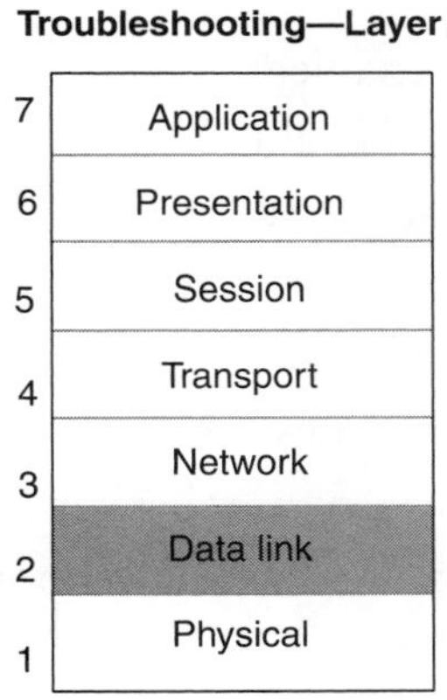

Troubleshooting—Layer 2

7	Application
6	Presentation
5	Session
4	Transport
3	Network
2	Data link
1	Physical

Layer 2 errors can include

- Improperly configured serial interfaces
- Improperly configured Ethernet interfaces
- Incorrect clock rate settings on serial interfaces
- Improper encapsulation set on serial interfaces (HDLC is default)
- Faulty NIC

FIGURE H-4
Normally, you
complete your
troubleshoot-
ing with layer 3
of the OSI
model.

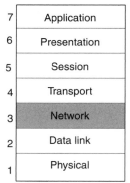

Troubleshooting—Layer 3

7	Application
6	Presentation
5	Session
4	Transport
3	Network
2	Data link
1	Physical

Layer 3 errors can include

- Routing protocol not enabled
- Wrong routing protocol enabled
- Incorrect network/IP addresses
- Incorrect subnet masks
- Incorrect interface addresses
- Incorrect DNS to IP bindings (host table entries)
- Wrong autonomous system number for IGRP

It's important to be familiar with troubleshooting the layer 1, layer 2, and
layer 3 errors previously listed. That's not the end of the story, however,
because you also need to know where to look for help if you can't immediately
determine why a network is not working as desired. Figure H-5 lists some of
these resources. One resource that networking professionals use frequently is
the documentation website at CCO (Cisco Connection Online:
www.cisco.com)

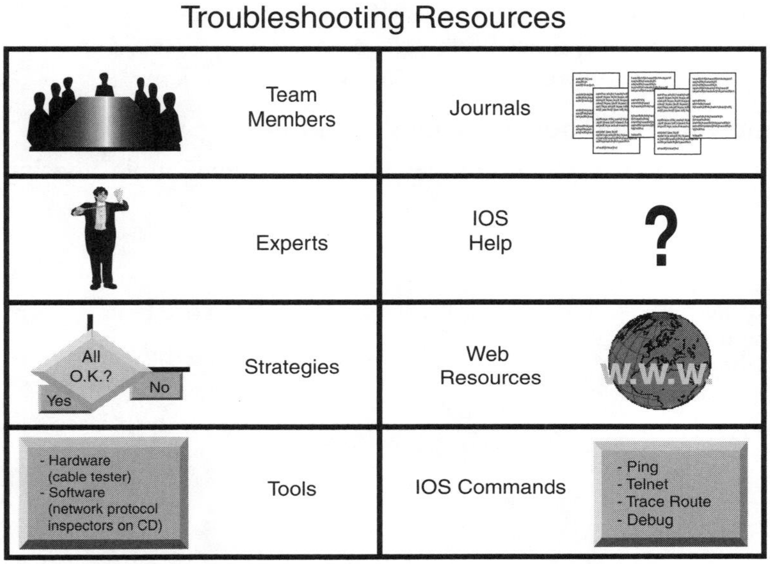

FIGURE H-5
FIGURE H-5
Here is a list of troubleshooting resources, in case the usual troubleshooting techniques don't work

Troubleshooting Resources

Team Members | Journals
Experts | IOS Help
Strategies | Web Resources
Tools | IOS Commands

A General Model for Troubleshooting

It's useful to have a general method to refer to when troubleshooting computer networks. This section outlines one such method, which is used by many networking professionals.

The steps are as follows:

STEP 1. *Define the problem*. What are the symptoms and the potential causes?

STEP 2. *Gather the facts*. Isolate the possible causes.

STEP 3. *Consider the possibilities*. Based on the facts gathered, narrow the focus to those areas relevant to the specific problem. This is the step where you set the boundaries for the problem.

STEP 4. *Create an action plan*. Devise a plan in which you manipulate only *one* variable at a time.

STEP 5. *Implement the action plan*. Perform each step carefully while testing to see if the symptom disappears.

STEP 6. *Observe the results.* Determine whether you resolved the problem. If so, the process is complete.

STEP 7. *Repeat the process.* If you did not resolve the problem, move to the next, most likely cause on your list. Return to step 4, and repeat the process until you solve the problem.

Applying the Model for Troubleshooting

Here is an example of how you can apply the troubleshooting model in a router lab.

FIGURE H-6
The familiar Semester 2 router lab diagram

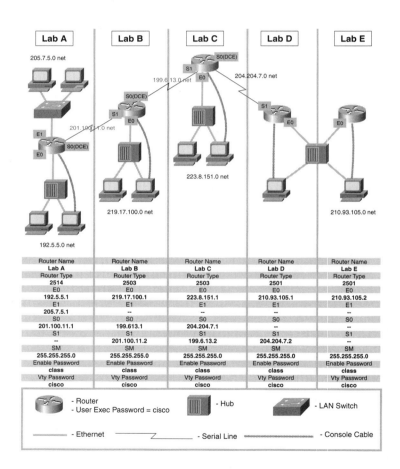

Router Name	Router Name	Router Name	Router Name	Router Name
Lab A	**Lab B**	**Lab C**	**Lab D**	**Lab E**
Router Type	Router Type	Router Type	Router Type	Router Type
2514	**2503**	**2503**	**2501**	**2501**
E0	E0	E0	E0	E0
192.5.5.1	**219.17.100.1**	**223.8.151.1**	**210.93.105.1**	**210.93.105.2**
E1	E1	E1	E1	E1
205.7.5.1	**--**	**--**	**--**	**--**
S0	S0	S0	S0	S0
201.100.11.1	**199.613.1**	**204.204.7.1**	**--**	**--**
S1	S1	S1	S1	S1
--	**201.100.11.2**	**199.6.13.2**	**204.204.7.2**	**--**
SM	SM	SM	SM	SM
255.255.255.0	**255.255.255.0**	**255.255.255.0**	**255.255.255.0**	**255.255.255.0**
Enable Password	Enable Password	Enable Password	Enable Password	Enable Password
class	**class**	**class**	**class**	**class**
Vty Password	Vty Password	Vty Password	Vty Password	Vty Password
cisco	**cisco**	**cisco**	**cisco**	**cisco**

- Router
- User Exec Password = cisco
- Hub
- LAN Switch
- Ethernet
- Serial Line
- Console Cable

When trying to ping Lab-E from Lab-A, you receive a series of time out messages.

```
lab-a#ping lab-e

Type escape sequence to abort.
Sending 5, 100-byte ICMP Echos to 210.93.105.2, timeout is 2 seconds:
.....
Success rate is 0 percent (0/5)
```

You now begin step 1 of the troubleshooting model:

STEP 1. *Define the problem.* What are the symptoms and the potential causes?

Begin by listing the symptoms:

— Unable to ping Lab-E from Lab-A.

Then, list the potential causes by layer:

a. Layer 1

— Bad cable
— Cable not connected
— Power loss on hub

b. Layer 2

— Interface shut down
— Improper encapsulation set (HDLC is the default on serial interfaces)
— Incorrect clock rate settings on serial interfaces

c. Layer 3

— Wrong interface address
— Wrong subnet mask
— Wrong routing information

STEP 2. *Gather the facts.* Isolate the possible causes.

You can do this by using the router's show commands to isolate the problem. Begin by testing the whole network. Because this network is under the control of one management, the routing table of each router contains all the networks in the WAN.

Type **show ip route** at the privileged EXEC prompt on Lab-A. This shows the routing table for Lab-A. All eight networks should be displayed. In the following, only seven of the eight networks appear in the routing table:

```
lab-a#show ip route
Codes: C - connected, S -  static, I - IGRP, R - RIP, M - mobile, B - BGP
    D - EIGRP, EX - EIGRP external, O - OSPF, IA - OSPF inter area
    N1 - OSPF NSSA external type 1, N2 - OSPF NSSA external type 2
    E1 - OSPF external type 1, E2 - OSPF external type 2, E - EGP
    i - IS-IS, L1 - IS-IS level-1, L2 - IS-IS level-2, * - candidate default
    U - per-user static route, o - ODR

Gateway of last resort is not set

C  205.7.5.0/24 is directly connected, Ethernet1
R  219.17.100.0/24 [120/1] via 201.100.11.2, 00:00:24, Serial0
R  199.6.13.0/24 [120/1] via 201.100.11.2, 00:00:24, Serial0
R  204.204.7.0/24 [120/2] via 201.100.11.2, 00:00:24, Serial0
C  192.5.5.0/24 is directly connected, Ethernet0
R  223.8.151.0/24 [120/2] via 201.100.11.2, 00:00:24, Serial0
C  201.100.11.0/24 is directly connected, Serial0
```

STEP 3. *Consider the possibilities.* Based on the facts gathered, narrow the focus to those areas relevant to the specific problem. Set the boundaries of the problem. To do this, you must simplify the search area; move from the big picture to a more focused and detailed look of where the problem could be.

The information from the routing table shows that network 204.204.7.0 is two hops away, which is displayed as [120/**2**] in the line R 204.204.7.0/24 [120/**2**] via 201.100.11.2, 00:00:24, Serial0. Two hops from Lab-A is Lab-C, which is the last router that shared its RIP information. You should begin troubleshooting at the last router from which you received information. Now, gather information on a smaller scale. Focus on a single router. Telnet to the router Lab-C. At Lab-C, type **show run** to see the router's running configuration. Be sure to log the configuration file (write the configuration in your journal or copy and paste the configuration into a Notepad file).

```
lab-a#lab-c                          interface Ethernet0
Trying lab-c (199.6.13.2)... Open      ip address 223.8.151.1 255.255.255.0
                                     !
                                     interface Serial0
User Access Verification               ip address 204.204.7.1 255.255.255.0
                                       no ip mroute-cache
Password:                              clockrate 56000
lab-c>ena                             !
Password:                            interface Serial1
lab-c#show run                         ip address 199.6.13.2.255.255.0
```

```
Building configuration...                      !
                                               interface BRI0
                                                no ip address
Current configuration:                          shutdown
!                                              !
version 11.3                                    router rip
service timestamps debug uptime                 network 199.6.13.0
service timestamps log uptime                   network 204.204.7.0
no service password-encryption                  network 223.8.151.0
!                                              !
hostname lab-c                                  ip host lab-a 192.5.5.1 205.7.5.1
!                                               ip host lab-b 201.100.11.2.219.17.100.1
enable password class                           <more>
<more>
```

Gather information on the interface connected to the last
displayed network from the **show ip route** command. At the
prompt, type **show int s0**; this displays all the current
information about the interface. Log this information.

```
lab-c#sho int s0
Serial0 is up, line protocol is up
 Hardware is HD64570
 Internet address is 204.204.7.1/24
 MTU 1500 bytes, BW 1544 Kbit, DLY 20000 usec,,
  reliability 255/255, txload 1/255, rxload 1/255
 Encapsulation HDLC, loopback not set, keepalive set (10 sec)
 Last input 00:00:01, output 00:00:00, output hang never
 Last clearing of "show interface" counters never
 Input queue: 0/75/0 (size/max/drops); Total output drops: 0
 Queueing strategy: weighted fair
 Output queue: 0/1000/64/0 (size/max total/threshold/drops)
  Conversations 0/1/256 (active/max active/max total)
  Reserved Conversations 0/0 (allocated/max allocated)
5 minute input rate 0 bits/sec, 0 packets/sec
5 minute output rate 0 bits/sec, 0 packets/sec
 185 packets input, 12570 bytes, 0 no buffer
 Received 185 broadcasts, 0 runts, 0 giants, 0 throttles
 0 input errors, 0 CRC, 0 frame, 0 overrun, 0 ignored, 0 abort
 241 packets output, 20487 bytes, 0 underruns
 0 output errors, 0 collisions, 21 interface resets
 0 output buffer failures, 0 output buffers swapped out
 10 carrier transitions
DCD=up DSR=up DTR=up RTS=up CTS=up
```

STEP 4. *Create an action plan.* Devise a plan in which you manipulate only
one variable at a time.

From the information about Lab-C's running configuration,
you see that everything is correctly configured. Looking then
at the information from the **show int s0** report, you see that
the interface is up and the line protocol is up. This tells you
that the cable is connected to a device on the other end and
that the data link layer is functional. If the cable is not
connected properly, the line protocol will be down. From

these two show commands, you know that this router is correctly configured and functioning. The problem must be at the next router, Lab-D. This is an example of the process of elimination, or of simplifying the problem. A good action plan would start by attempting to telnet to router Lab-D, and then moving to Lab-D's terminal to check the running configuration for errors. If you do not find errors in the configuration, you might need to examine the S1 interface.

STEP 5. *Implement the action plan.* Perform each step carefully while testing to see if the symptom disappears.

You tried to telnet to router Lab-D and failed. You must now go to the terminal connected to Lab-D. Enter privileged EXEC mode and type **show run**. From this report, you notice that the routing protocol on Lab-D is IGRP instead of RIP (which router Lab-C uses). To correct this error, you need to enter global configuration mode, type **no router igrp 111**, and enter the command **router rip**. Now enter the network commands **network 210.93.105.0** and **network 204.204.7.0** (these are the networks directly connected to Lab-D). Then, type **Ctrl-Z** and issue the **copy run start** command.

STEP 6. *Observe the results.* Determine whether you resolved the problem. If so, the process is complete.

Now, test connectivity by pinging Lab-A and Lab-E.

```
lab-d#ping lab-a

Type escape sequence to abort.
Sending 5, 100-byte ICMP Echos to 192.5.5.1, timeout is 2 seconds:
!!!!
Success rates is 100 percent (5/5), round-trip min/avg/max = 96/100/108 ms

lab-d#ping lab-e

Type escape sequence to abort.
Sending 5, 100-byte ICMP Echos to 210.93.105.2, timeout is 2 seconds:
!!!!
Success rate is 100 percent (5/5), round-trip min/avg/max =  1/3/4 ms
```

STEP 7. Repeat the process. If you did not resolve the problem, move to the next, most likely cause on your list. Return to step 4, and repeat the process until you solve the problem.

Although you found an error in the configuration file of the router and corrected it, this might not successfully restore connectivity. Some problems have compound, or multiple, causes. If this fails to fix the problem, return to step 4 and develop a new action plan. Just as most network problems are caused by user error, your action plan might also contain errors. Most errors in an action plan are omissions, simply overlooked causes. The process of troubleshooting can be frustrating. Remember, don't panic. If you reach a point at which you need help, don't be afraid to ask.

To put all this in perspective, Figure H-7 shows a flowchart for the troubleshooting model.

FIGURE H-7
Each person develops his own troubleshooting methods. It helps to have a general method to refer to should all else fail.

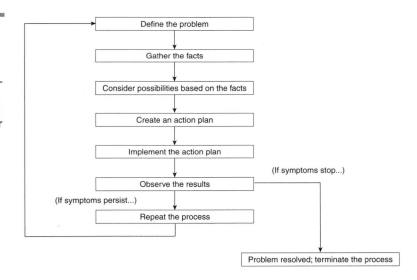

With this guide, you can resolve most network failures that confront you. As a networking professional, troubleshooting plays a vital role in day-to-day work, so it is critical that you get a lot of hands-on experience to improve your troubleshooting skills. For many, troubleshooting is the most enjoyable and rewarding part of networking. With a little time and patience, the process of troubleshooting will become second nature.

Notes

Notes

Notes

Notes

Notes

Notes